Global Trends in Land Tenure Reform

This book explores the gendered dimensions of recent land governance transformations across the globe in the wake of unprecedented pressures on land and natural resources. These complex contemporary forces are reconfiguring livelihoods and impacting women's positions, their tenure security and well-being, and that of their families.

Bringing together fourteen empirical community case studies from around the world, the book examines governance transformations of land and land-based resources resulting from four major processes of tenure change: commercial land-based investments; the formalization of customary tenure; the privatization of communal lands; and post-conflict resettlement and redistribution reforms. Each contribution carefully analyses the gendered dimensions of these transformations, exploring both the gender impact of the land tenure reforms and the social and political economy within which these reforms materialize. The cases provide important insights for decision-makers to better promote and design an effective gender lens into land tenure reforms and natural resource management policies.

This book will be of great interest to researchers engaging with land and natural resource management issues from a wide variety of disciplines, including anthropology, sociology, development studies, and political science, as well as policy-makers, practitioners, and activists concerned with environment, development, and social equity.

Caroline S. Archambault is an anthropologist and researcher in the International Development Studies Group at Utrecht University, the Netherlands.

Annelies Zoomers is a human geographer and Professor of International Development Studies at Utrecht University, the Netherlands.

Routledge Studies in Gender and Development

Global Trends in Land Tenure Reform
Gender Impacts
Edited by Caroline S. Archambault and Annelies Zoomers

"This carefully researched book is a welcome new contribution to our understanding of the implications of major ongoing changes on the land front, which are taking place all around the world, especially in developing countries. The case studies – which span a range from Argentina to Zimbabwe – deepen our understanding of the risks as well as potential benefits for women and men, for productivity and growth as well as equity. The book provides relevant and important lessons and insights for anyone interested in development."

Jeni Klugman, Harvard University, USA

"Powerful changes in land tenure regimes are taking place globally, yet all too often a gender lens is missing. Through 14 case studies, this volume documents the gender impacts of land grabs, the formalization of customary tenure, the privatization of communal lands, and post-conflict resettlement reforms and makes a strong case for the urgency of improving women's tenure security. This is a must-read for all those concerned with processes of agrarian change."

Carmen Diana Deere, University of Florida, USA

"Gender is so frequently and scandalously overlooked in discussions of land tenure reform that one can only welcome this exciting new collection, which ranges across the continents and provides compelling examples of women's struggles to assert the rights which are so frequently denied them."

Robin Palmer, Mokoro, UK

"This volume provides much-needed empirical evidence on the gender impacts of a range of transformations of land rights. The case studies provide nuance to our understanding of how many planned land tenure reforms as well as new economic opportunities have affected women's security of tenure. Alas, despite growing evidence of the importance of women's land rights, few of the reforms have strengthened women's control over land, but there are many lessons in this volume on what can be done (or not done) to improve this in the future."

Ruth Meinzen-Dick, International Food Policy Research Institute, USA

Global Trends in Land Tenure Reform

Reform
Gender impacts

Edited by Caroline S. Archambault
and Annelies Zoomers

LONDON AND NEW YORK

First published 2015
by Routledge

2 Park Square, Milton Park, Abingdon, Oxfordshire OX14 4RN
711 Third Avenue, New York, NY 10017

Routledge is an imprint of the Taylor & Francis Group, an informa business

First issued in paperback 2017

British Library Cataloguing-in-Publication Data
A catalogue record for this book is available from the British Library

Library of Congress Cataloging-in-Publication Data
Global trends in land tenure reform : gender impacts / edited by Caroline
S. Archambault and Annelies Zoomers.
pages cm. -- (Routledge studies in gender and development)
1. Land tenure--Developing countries. 2. Land reform--Developing
countries. 3. Women in agriculture--Developing countries. I.
Archambault, Caroline S. II. Zoomers, E. B.
HD1131.G56 2015
333.3'1--dc23
2014031767

ISBN: 978-1-138-78794-0 (hbk)
ISBN: 978-0-8153-9406-8 (pbk)

Typeset in Goudy by Saxon Graphics Ltd, Derby

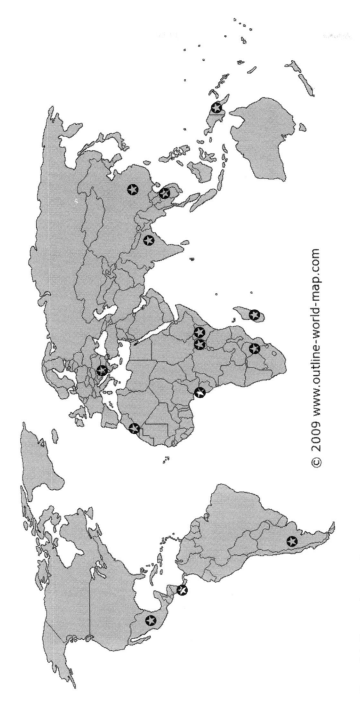

© 2009 www.outline-world-map.com

Figure 0.1 Case study countries.

Contents

Figures

Tables

Abbreviations

Numbers in parentheses indicate chapter number.

ANR	Agriculture and natural resources (1)
BANRURAL	Banc Nacional de Crédito Rural (9)
CCO	Certificate of Customary Ownership (14)
CEDAW	Convention on Discrimination Against Women (6)
CGNs	Collection group networks (4)
CMCA	Community mine continuation agreements (2)
DLC	District Land Committee (12)
DLIC	District Land Identification Committees (12)
ESAP	Economic Structural Adjustment Programme (12)
EULEX	European Rule of Law Mission (13)
FAO	Food and Agriculture Organization (1)(6)
FTLRP	Fast Track Land Reform Program (12)
FYR	Former Yugoslav Republic of Macedonia (13)
GDP	Gross domestic product (2)(8)(9)(13)
GIC	Groupe d'initiative commune (4)
FDI	Foreign direct investment (1)
IDPs	Internally displaced persons (14)
INMECAFE	Instituto Mexicano Cafe (9)
LBC	Lao Banana Company (1)
LLO	Local Land Offices (6)
LPDR	Lao People's Democratic Republic (1)
LRRP	Land Reform and Resettlement Program (12)
LRA	Lord's Resistance Army (14)
LTL	Lao Tobacco Limited (1)
MCA	Millennium Challenge Account Madagascar (6)
MCC	Millennium Challenge Corporation (6)
MDC	Movement for Democratic Change (12)
MIS	Market information system (4)
MLE	Mine life extension (2)
MoA	Memorandum of agreement (2)
MoU	Memorandum of understanding (1)

NAFTA	North American Free Trade Agreement (9)
NCFO	Network of Community Forest Organizations (4)
NGNB	Nijo Griha Nijo Bhumi (7)
NGO	Non-governmental organization (4)
NORMA	Women Lawyers Association of Kosovo (13)
NPFE	Non-Permanent Forest Estate (4)
NTFPs	Non-Timber Forest Products (1)(4)
OECD	Organisation for Economic Co-operation and Development (6)
OTDF	Ok Tedi Fly River Development Foundation (2)
OTFRDP	Ok Tedi Fly River Development Program (2)
OTML	Ok Tedi Mining Limited (2)
PFE	Permanent Forest Estate (4)
PISG	Provisional Institutions of Self-Government (13)
PLC	Provincial Lands Committee (12)
PLOF	Plan local d'occupation foncière (6)
PNF	National Land Program (6)
PNG	Papua New Guinea (2)
PNGSDP	Papua New Guinea Sustainable Development Program (2)
PRC	People's Republic of China (10)
PROCEDE	Programa de Certificación de Derechos Ejidales (9)
PROMUSAG	Programa de la Mujer en el Sector Agrario (9)
REFACOF	African Women's Network for Community Management of Forests (4)
RMB	Renminbi (10)
SC	Scheduled Castes (7)
SCFSE	State Commerce-Foodstuff Enterprise (1)
SNV	Netherlands Development Organization (4)
SOE	State-owned enterprise (1)
ST	Scheduled Tribes (7)
UFAs	Unités forestières d'aménagement (4)
UN	United Nations (6)(13)
UNMIK	United Nations Interim Administration Mission in Kosovo (13)
UPDF	Ugandan People's Defence Forces
ZANU	Zimbabwe African National Union (12)
ZAPU	Zimbabwe African People's Union (12)
ZANU–PF	Zimbabwe African National Union–Patriotic Front (12)
ZNLWA	Zimbabwe National Liberation War Veterans Association (12)

Contributors

Caroline S. Archambault is an anthropologist and researcher in the International Development Studies Group at Utrecht University in the Netherlands. Her research focuses broadly on the areas of human rights, development, and demography in sub-Saharan Africa. Topics of focus include land tenure reform, education, gender, pastoralism, and childhood. Her current NWO VENI research program explores tenure transformations and women's well-being among the Maasai of Southern Kenya.

Nicholas Barber is a doctoral candidate in cultural anthropology at McGill University, Canada, where he is a member of the Centre for Society for Technology and Development (STANDD) and the Project on Indigenous Rights and Identity (PIRI). His areas of interest include indigenous and community media, indigenous identity, and visual anthropology. He has recently completed 16 months of ethnographic research examining the impact of participatory videomaking on rights and identity in Baka indigenous communities in southeast Cameroon.

Marguerite Belobo Belibi is a Value Chain Development Adviser with the SNV Netherlands Development Organisation in Cameroon. Her work focuses on building capacity in governance and social inclusion in the context of value chains. Her expertise includes development of non-timber forest product value chains and community forestry. She currently works on the Cameroon Cocoa-Eco Project on cooperative development, market linkage, and youth integration in cocoa production.

Lisa Bossenbroek is a social scientist. She is currently a PhD candidate at the Water Resources Management group at the University of Wageningen, the Netherlands. Her research focuses on the mutually interactive changes of agrarian change and agricultural modernization and gender relations in the rural society of the region of the Sais in Morocco. In her research Lisa focuses on changing gender subjectivities and how these interact with agrarian and rural transformations. Other research interests include the role of youngsters in irrigated agriculture in the Maghreb countries and changing agricultural labour relations and their gendered implications.

Manase Kudzai Chiweshe is a senior lecturer in the Centre for Development Studies at the Chinhoyi University of Technology in Zimbabwe. He is a widely published author focusing on the sociology of everyday life in African spaces. His research work concentrates on agrarian studies, rural sociology, and sustainable livelihoods. Currently his work focuses on livelihood options and life aspirations of rural female youths in Zimbabwe.

Elizabeth Daley is a Principal Consultant of Mokoro Ltd. She has worked with governments, civil society, the private sector, and international development partners in Laos, Mozambique, Nigeria, Rwanda, South Sudan, Tanzania, and Uganda. Elizabeth has published on land tenure and social change in Tanzania, women's land rights in Eastern Africa, and women and land deals in Africa and Asia. Core long-standing research interests include land tenure security, land registration and policy-reform processes, and women's land rights. Her most recent work has a strong focus on 'land grabbing', gender and governance of tenure, pastoral women's land rights, and gender issues within family farming.

Judith van Eijnatten is a social scientist and international development professional with SNV Netherlands Development Organisation in Cameroon. Her work focuses on capacity building, organizational development, and social inclusion in contexts of natural resource management, sustainable agriculture and rural development. She is currently Project Manager for the Cameroon Cocoa-Eco Project which seeks to integrate REDD+ in cocoa production while building capacities in good agricultural, business, organizational, and social practices.

Diana Fletschner is the Senior Director of Research, Monitoring and Evaluation at Landesa. Diana has over 20 years of experience teaching, conducting research, designing programs and tools, and monitoring and evaluating interventions with a special focus on rural women. Diana's recent work includes leading quantitative research and field-informed desk research; assessing rural women's access and rights to land; assessing the effectiveness of innovative approaches to secure women's and girls' rights to land; developing land and property rights tools that pay attention to women's preferences and constraints; training government representatives; and directing the Women's Land Rights Visiting Professionals Program.

Renee Giovarelli, senior attorney and adviser to the Landesa Center for Women's Land Rights, has 19 years' experience in intra-household and gender issues associated with land tenure and customary and legal property rights. Giovarelli has designed and conducted fieldwork on women's access and rights to land in Azerbaijan, Bulgaria, Burkina Faso, China, Ethiopia, Ghana, India, Kyrgyz Republic, Madagascar, Russia, Tajikistan, Uganda, and Uzbekistan. Her policy-oriented research and writing has focused on the issue of gender in relation to land tenure reform, pasture management, and rural development.

Leslie Hannay is an attorney and land tenure specialist at the Landesa Center for Women's Land Rights, where she designs and implements projects seeking to address the gap between formal law and customary practice around women's rights to land. She has worked on issues of community rights and land and natural resources in Ghana, Liberia, Democratic Republic of Congo, Rwanda, and Uganda and has contributed to research and analysis on women's land tenure security in the context of large-scale land-based investments in developing countries.

Georgia Harley is a justice reform specialist for Eastern Europe and Central Asia at the World Bank. She's currently leading a review of justice system performance in Serbia. Prior to joining the Bank, Ms Harley was Executive Legal Adviser to the Australian Department of Foreign Affairs and Trade and Senior Legal Adviser to the Australian Attorney-General's Office of International Law. Ms Harley earned a Bachelors of Arts and Laws (Honours) from the University of Queensland, a Masters of Laws from the Australian National University and a Masters in Economic Development Policy from Duke University.

Matthias vom Hau is an assistant professor in comparative politics at the Institut Barcelona d'Estudis Internacionals (IBEI). A sociologist by training, his research is centrally concerned with the relationship between identity politics, institutions, and development, with a regional focus on Latin America. His most recent line of work brings together ethnic politics and resource governance. Based on case studies from Argentina, Chile, South Africa, and Namibia, the project examines the impact of indigenous movements on land tenure transformations and water provision.

Sandra F. Joireman is the Weinstein Chair of International Studies and Professor of Political Science at the University of Richmond in Richmond, Virginia, USA. Joireman specializes in comparative political economy with a focus on property rights and customary law. The geographic focus of her research has been sub-Saharan Africa and the Western Balkans. She is currently engaged in a cross-national research project related to post-conflict property rights.

Nicholas Menzies is a senior counsel, justice reform, at the World Bank. His work involves reform of institutions of the justice sector as well as mainstreaming justice and conflict across development, including in extractives and health. He focuses on countries in sub-Saharan Africa and the South-West Pacific, as well as working on global initiatives. He has a current learning and technical assistance program on the use of community development agreements to address conflict, governance and development issues between mining companies and host communities in Sierra Leone.

Femke van Noorloos is an assistant professor at the International Development Studies group at Utrecht University in the Netherlands. She is a social science researcher with a broad interest in international development, including land governance, climate change, sustainability, tourism, migration, and urban development. She has conducted research in Latin America and Africa and is currently working on various projects related to climate change adaptation and land governance.

Clara Mi Young Park is a PhD candidate with the Political Economy of Resources, Environment and Population research group at the International Institute of Social Studies in The Hague, and Gender Officer with the Regional Office for Asia and the Pacific of the Food and Agriculture Organization of the United Nations (FAO). Her research has focused on agricultural and land policy, tenure and property rights, land grabbing, gender and social inequalities in Africa and Asia. Her current research explores the intersection of land grabbing, climate change mitigation strategies, conflicts, and gender in Cambodia and Myanmar.

Florence Santos is a senior research, monitoring and evaluation specialist at Landesa. She has more than eight years of experience conducting policy research and impact evaluation using quantitative and qualitative techniques, with a particular focus on gender, agriculture, rural land tenure, and natural resource conservation. Florence is currently leading the monitoring and impact evaluation of a project in Rwanda that aims to test a model that would strengthen women's land rights and mitigate future land conflict.

Vivien Savath is a research and evaluation specialist at Landesa. She has designed and implemented several studies on land rights programs, including a multi-year intervention for adolescent girls' land rights and the Landesa Visiting Professionals Program, using a mix of qualitative and quantitative methods. Vivien holds a BA in Economics from Dartmouth College and an MPA from the Evans School of Public Affairs at the University of Washington, USA.

Elisa Scalise is an attorney and director of the Landesa Center for Women's Land Rights, where her technical experience includes analysis and reform on property rights to land for women and men, including formal and customary land tenure regimes, land administration, land tenure regularization, land institutions, dispute resolution mechanisms, forestland tenure, and communal property. She has also assessed the links between secure land tenure for women and economic empowerment, agricultural productivity, natural resources management, conflict management and resolution, and social inclusion. She has worked on projects in Afghanistan, Burundi, Burkina Faso, China, India, Kenya, Kyrgyzstan, Liberia, Rwanda, Uganda, Tanzania, and Vietnam.

Verónica Vázquez-García is a sociologist and Full Professor in the Colegio de Postgraduados, Texcoco, Mexico. Her research focuses broadly on gender, the environment, and sustainability in rural Mexico. Topics of focus include water, land and forest governance with a gender approach. Her current research program explores gender and water management in three different regions of Mexico.

Xiaobei Wang is a gender and land-tenure specialist at Landesa. With a background in law and sociology, she conducts quantitative and qualitative research on customary law, conflict resolution, mediation, and the legal aid system in rural China. She also has substantial experience in empirical studies and legislative advocacy on women's issues in China, including rural women's land tenure, domestic violence, sexual harassment, and women's retirement age. She is now focused on land access and tenure security issues in China, with a particular emphasis on gender issues and women's access and secure rights to land.

Marit Widman is a PhD candidate in the Department of Economics at the Swedish University of Agricultural Sciences in Uppsala, Sweden. Her research area is gender, development, and environmental and natural resource economics. Topics of interest include land-tenure reform, intra-household decision-making and resource allocation, and environmental policy. Her PhD research focuses on women's land rights in Madagascar. Marit is also a lecturer in environmental economics and sustainable development.

Annelies Zoomers is a human geographer and Professor of International Development Studies at Utrecht University in the Netherlands. She directs various research programs, and has published extensively on the global land grab hype, international migration, and livelihood change in Africa, Asia, and Latin America. She is chair of the Land Academy, which aims to promote "land governance for sustainable and equitable land development" (www.landgovernance.org).

Margreet Zwarteveen is an irrigation engineer and social scientist. She currently works as professor of water governance at UNESCO-IHE in Delft and the University of Amsterdam in the Netherlands. Margreet studies water allocation policies and practices, focusing on questions of equity and justice. Her research includes the investigation of different modalities of regulating water flows (technologies, institutions) and of ways to understand (knowledges) or legitimize these. She uses an interdisciplinary approach, seeing water allocation as the outcome of interactions between nature, technologies, and society. The relation between power and water is central in her work, and has an explicit attention to gender.

Introduction

The pressing need to secure women's property rights under unprecedented land pressure and tenure reform

Caroline S. Archambault and Annelies Zoomers

Introduction

Around half the world's countries are engaging in some form of land tenure reform in the wake of unprecedented pressures on land and natural resources (Wily, 2012). Human population growth, economic growth and large-scale investments in mining, food and biofuels, as well as rapid urbanization, climatic instability and space needed for post-conflict reconstruction and community mobilization, are just some of the powerful forces spurring the competition for land and catalyzing tenure reforms across the world. Among the latter are new comprehensive land policies and land laws, including customary codifications in some countries; guidelines and codes of conduct for new commercial land-based investments; new systems of registration and land administration; new programs for land titling, and post-conflict resettlement and redistribution efforts.

These transformations in land governance are having widespread gendered impacts as they reconfigure men's and women's rights and access to land and other productive resources. Yet many of these radical changes do not carefully apply a gender lens in their designs, and thereby perpetuate the issues regarding secondary ownership and access rights that often exist for women, in some cases making *de facto* secondary rights *de jure* secondary rights, or even turning *de facto* primary rights into *de jure* secondary ones.

At an elementary level, this lack of a gender lens is surprising as getting such aspects 'right' has obvious instrumental value. After all, in many areas, women comprise the majority of rural populations and are the primary food producers on the land; land-tenure reforms that distribute rights and access to land and productive resources can boost the productivity of women alongside that of men, with resultant macro benefits for nations' food production and economic activity while also securing livelihoods at a micro level.

The lack of a focus on gender in many tenure reforms points to a number of potential barriers: it could be that the benefits have not been fully understood, or even if they have been, there could be concern that incorporating a gender lens may prove difficult in practice. Alternatively, there could be a gender bias among those in positions of political authority, who seek to direct the benefits of tenure reforms toward men.

Against this background, and using fourteen in-depth case studies from different parts of the world written by academics and practitioners, the goal of this volume is therefore to better understand both the gender impact of different kinds of land tenure reforms and the political economy within which these reforms materialize, and to provide insights from these experiences that can help decision-makers better promote and design an effective gender lens into land-tenure reforms.

The first part of the book traces the gendered consequences of the penetration of corporate capital through land-based investments, including agricultural schemes, mining, and real estate development for tourism, through case studies from Lao PDR, Papua New Guinea, and Costa Rica. Part II explores the gender impacts of recent attempts to codify customary tenure practices in the forests of Cameroon, among indigenous communities in Argentina, for the landless in India and as part of comprehensive land reform in Madagascar. Part III demonstrates the far-reaching gendered effects of initiatives aimed at privatizing communal or collective pastoral, agricultural, and forest lands, with contributions from Mexico, Kenya, Morocco, and China. Finally, Part IV investigates the gender dynamics of post-conflict land-reform efforts aimed at resettling populations and reconstructing society, with contributions from Zimbabwe, Kosovo, and Uganda.

Pressures for land reform

Human population growth continues to spur competition for land in many countries. Over the past ten years, world population has grown at an average annual rate of 1.2%—from 6.3 billion people in 2003 to 7 billion in 2012—and is projected to reach 9.6 billion by 2050 (World Bank, 2014a, 2014b; UN, 2013: xv). By 2050, food production will need to increase by 70% globally and up to 100% in developing countries (FAO, 2011a). There are 3 billion hectares of land suitable for crop production globally, and by 2008 half was already being cultivated (Smith *et al.*, 2010). While expansion of agriculture is still possible in parts of sub-Saharan Africa, Latin America, and the Caribbean, regions such as South and East Asia, the Near East, and North Africa have almost no land available to fall back on. Up to "one quarter of the world's 1.1 billion poor people are landless (including 200 million living in rural areas)" (UN Habitat, 2008), and many of the countries with the most rapidly growing demand for food are also those with the greatest land scarcity.

Fast economic growth over the past decade in many low- and middle-income countries is going hand-in-hand with a rapid increase of commercial land-based investments, including agri-business, extractive industrial development, and property development. Over 40 countries had GDP per capita growth rates of over 200% between 2003 and 2012, meaning that these countries had effectively doubled their economies in less than five years (Word Bank, 2014c). The top 20 countries projected by the IMF to have the highest compounded annual growth rates from 2013 through 2017 are all from sub-Saharan Africa (10), Asia (8), and the Middle East/North Africa (2) (*Business Insider*, 2014).

Furthermore, in many countries climate change is exacerbating land pressures, as weather patterns are increasingly more unpredictable, variable, and extreme, leading to more frequent and longer periods of drought and flooding in different regions (IPCC, 2014). This causes the displacement of farmers as well as new migration patterns, major disruptions in production, and unpredictable harvests, and also leads to volatile food prices and heightened food insecurity. In the period since 2000, food prices have been more unstable than in the preceding two decades, and the period since 2006 has been particularly volatile (Interagency Report, 2011). The global food crisis of 2007–08, when the prices of basic food commodities such as wheat and rice more than doubled, illustrates how these divergent pressures can converge to fuel even more competition for land. The crisis ushered in a rush for the acquisition of land as a means of securing food production for growing populations under these adverse conditions, including large-scale deals backed by foreign investment (Zoomers, 2010; Kaag and Zoomers, 2014). What has now come to be known as the "global land rush" continues to be driven by increasing demands for food but also for biofuels, carbon markets, and speculation.

Other countries torn apart by conflict have entered (often fragile) post-conflict transitions in the past decade, enacting new laws and creating legal systems as they resettle and reconstruct communities. In the process, improved communication technology and mass media, in addition to the expansion of education, has enabled different civil society groups—including those representing the landless, the most poor and those with indigenous rights—to become increasingly politically active and influential, to exercise demands for land reform, and to secure property rights for their constituents. Moreover, donors and other important international players are advocates for tenure reform, as secure property rights are viewed by many as the foundation for economic growth, freedom, and well-being.

Gender inequities in land ownership and control

Men and women are linked to land and property in different ways. In most contexts they maintain different resource rights, endowments, roles, and opportunities. These relationships to land are also importantly mediated by other aspects of identity, such as socio-economic status, class, ethnicity, and age among others. In general, women are often primary producers on land and caretakers of property, especially on more marginal lands in more isolated areas. The feminization of farming has been propelled by an increase in the number of men migrating to urban centers in search of waged work, but also by rural-to-rural and international migration (Deere, 2005; Lastarria-Cornhiel, 2006). Wives remain in rural households and take up the primary responsibility for managing family farms. According to The Food and Agriculture Organization of the United Nations (FAO, 2011b), women account for nearly half (43%) of the world's farmers and grow or raise much of the world's food. In some countries women's contributions to the agricultural labor force exceed 60%. For example, among countries represented in this volume, more than 65% of the rural labor force in China are women (Wang *et al.*, this volume). And in Uganda, 90% of all rural women work in agriculture, compared to only 53% of rural men (Hannay and Scalise, this volume).

Despite women's predominant role in many rural areas, particularly in food production but also in food preparation, provision, and marketing, women often have significantly fewer rights and access to productive resources, including land, than men (World Bank, 2014). Doss *et al.* (2014) rightfully warn of the methodological and conceptual limitations of single, overly simplified statistics on women and land ownership. A lack of disaggregated and comparable data gives rise to inaccuracies as does the fact that in many regions of the world, most notably sub-Saharan Africa, the majority of land is not under private title but rather is held under customary tenure or some form of collective or communal holding. Nevertheless, there appears to be consensus that globally there exist large gender inequities in land ownership and control (FAO 2010; 2014). It appears that the majority of women in many contexts have only secondary rights, where they must rely on others to gain access to land and productive resources, most commonly on men—husbands, other male kin, or (often male) traditional authorities and governing assemblies of elders.

Many women with secondary rights to land are vulnerable in other ways too, as is the case for widows, divorcees, those in informal unions, and those who have never married. Other factors also give rise to overlapping disadvantages for women to access and own land (World Bank, 2014). In some contexts ethnicity adds another layer of deprivation. For example, the Baka of Cameroon, traditionally hunter-gatherers, and the indigenous Diaguita Calchaquí of Argentina have faced a long history of economic, social, and political marginalization in their respective countries (Belibi *et al.*, this volume; vom Hau, this volume). In Lao PDR, although the majority of ethnic groups maintain matrilineal descent systems, some practice patrilineality and patrifocality, customary systems that tend to disadvantage women in land ownership (Park and Daley, this volume). In Mexico, old age can be a significant additional deprivation in a context where there is a lack of young labor and social services to assist the elderly (Vásquez-García, this volume). And in Northern Uganda, among Acholi women, victims of war and "soldier brides" face especially difficult circumstances and are unable to access secure land rights (Hannay and Scalise, this volume). Such overlapping deprivations make women particularly vulnerable to tenure changes. Secure access and control over productive resources can make important differences to women's well-being by reducing or eliminating interconnected deprivations. But, by the same token, implementing tenure changes without considering the gendered effects may exacerbate inequalities and women's vulnerabilities.

There is often considerable ambiguity as to which tenure regime would be best for improving women's well-being. This is not only because women do not constitute a uniform social group but also because each tenure regime is complex and carries its own advantages and disadvantages. As the privatization processes in Morocco and Kenya and the land investment projects in Papua New Guinea, Lao PDR, and Costa Rica clearly demonstrate, changes in tenure and consequent changes in land use may provide significant opportunities for improving the lives of women and their families if carefully implemented and with gender concerns at the forefront of the reform. All too often, however, this is rarely the case.

Reasons to secure women's land rights

In addition to the intrinsic properties of promoting gender equality and human rights, strengthening women's property rights can have many obvious instrumental properties. While there is an unfortunate lack of gender-disaggregated data and impact evaluations that would allow for the rigorous testing of the impacts of enhancing property rights for women on various dimensions of well-being, much recent research supports commonsense links.

Women may gain many personal benefits from tenure security. Having well-recognized property rights may increase their confidence and social status (Datta, 2006). It may help to solidify and recognize the identities of women from ethnic minorities or indigenous groups, and establish for them a sense of belonging. Having direct and secure access to land may also provide women with important psychological security and the autonomy from husbands and other male relatives to pursue the livelihoods they value (Friedemann-Sánchez, 2006; Garikipati, 2009). It may lead to significant improvements in household bargaining power and decision-making authority (see Savath *et al.*, this volume, also Allendorf, 2007; Doss, 2013). As such, some research suggests that women with strong land rights are not only more actively involved in important household decisions, but are also more effectively positioned to avoid abusive partnerships, domestic violence, and exploitative household labor arrangements, and can better control sexual relations (Agarwal and Panda, 2007; Grabe, 2010; Bhattacharyya *et al.*, 2011).

However, property rights for women can be equally important for men, children, and the elderly, not to mention, on a broader canvas, the future of individual countries. Secure land rights and productive inputs for women can translate into significantly more efficient production on the land; the FAO (2011b) argues that if women had the same access as men to land, inputs, and productive services, they could produce 20–30% more food, enough to take 100–150 million people out of hunger (4). Given land scarcity and the inability to expand agriculture in many regions, addressing gender inequalities in agriculture appears to be a key strategy for meeting the growing food demands of the decade and for ensuring household food security, family nutrition, and family health (Richards *et al.*, 2013, Swaminathan *et al.*, 2012; Menon *et al.*, 2014).

Property rights for women also open up new economic opportunities. Beyond subsistence cultivation, women can engage more productively as emerging farmers, playing more prominent roles as agro-entrepreneurs and in agricultural marketing. The new possibilities of loan services and micro-credit options provide important support for female entrepreneurship and increasing household incomes (Song and Vernooy, 2014; Fletschner and Kenney, 2014). Increasing control over revenues and decision-making around household consumption, could result in increasing household investments in such things as children's education or food, or maintaining biodiversity, which may be more of a spending priority for women than men (Deininger *et al.*, 2013; Menon *et al.*, 2014).

The cross-cutting nature of these rights infuses them with powerful transformative effects. In securing women's property rights, there is a substantial opportunity to make important advances in eradicating poverty while enhancing economic growth, promoting sustainable land use, and achieving social goals (including gender equity). Unfortunately, while we are in a time of unprecedented tenure change in so many different countries and regions across the world, attention to the gendered impacts of tenure reform and explicit efforts at addressing women's tenure security are often insufficient or meeting with limited success.

Worrisome trends: The masculinization of rural space

A worrying trend has appeared in the wake of recent tenure transformations, whether commercial land investments, formalizing customary tenure, privatizing collective and communal lands, or post-conflict reconstruction efforts: namely, a re-masculinization of rural space and increasing rural stratification, as several contributions to this book illustrate. As noted above, in many contexts, women are the dominant producers in rural livelihoods and male outmigration is still an important (and even increasing) phenomenon, but many tenure reforms appear to be quite persistently entrenching and solidifying men's disproportionate control of, and access to, land and natural resources.

By means of tenure changes that give rise to new agricultural land investments (such as in Lao PDR and Morocco, this volume), extractive industry concessions (as in PNG and Cameroon, this volume), and housing development for tourism (as in Costa Rica, this volume), (young) men often reap the greatest benefits, the most employment, better salaries, higher positions, and better conditions, while women's access to important resources diminishes and their workloads and responsibilities increase. Although a few cases demonstrate important gains for some women, these new "modern", intensive commercial opportunities have a strong tendency to further stratify rural society, often along gender, age, and ethnic lines. Several of the cases in this volume (such as those drawing on cases from Morocco, Mexico, and Cameroon) demonstrate the risks of such tenure transformations in producing a growing division between a young male rural professional class and a (new)-home bound traditionalism for poor and older women.

Efforts to codify the customary often overlook the ways in which customary systems are unequal. Women tend to occupy very few positions in customary governance institutions around land and natural resources (see for example Cameroon, Kenya, Argentina, and Mexico, this volume). As such the formalization of customary systems often reproduces men's privileged positions of authority and leadership in local governance structures.

In a similar vein, efforts to privatize collective and communal lands appear to vest ownership of land in men and not in women, since men are often the registered and recognized members of collective and communal lands (see, for example, the cases from China, Kenya, Mexico, and Morocco, this volume). Furthermore, the process of privatization is facilitating the disarticulation of land from family, kinship, and community. Women appear to be importantly impacted by residential, demographic, and social changes that reduce sociality as well as labor pooling and social assistance and women's land base is thus rendered vulnerable to land sales, land leasing, and a loss of inheritance rights.

Even in post-conflict situations when countries and communities have an opportunity to promote gender equity through land reforms, male privileges become implanted on newly resettled lands and continued inequality can be perpetuated through the process of nation-building (see the cases from Zimbabwe and Kosovo, this volume).

Conclusion: The road ahead

Continue to address legal barriers to women's land rights

Globally significant progress has been made in legislating women's legal rights to property. A recent study tracing the evolution of legal rights for women and girls has found that over half of the legal constraints that were present in 1960 (including lack of property rights and constitutional protections of equality and non-discrimination) had been removed by 2010 (Hallward-Driemeier *et al.*, 2013).

Unfortunately, the impact of protective laws and constitutional provisions is sometimes limited without the reinforcing effect of other laws such as laws governing marital property regimes and inheritance. Default marital regimes with no joint titling of property acquired before or during marriage can leave spouses, women in particular, especially vulnerable to dispossession upon divorce or separation. And some inheritance laws allocate less property to female heirs than to male heirs.

Poorly formulated laws and regulations can also pose a significant barrier to women's property rights. In some countries certain property laws pertain only to formally and legally married women, yet in many parts of the world, especially in poor rural contexts, customary marriages prevail. The costs and complexity of registering marriages is prohibitive for many couples and this can leave a significant population legally unprotected. In addition, some laws, regulations, and policies around land ownership and use are too complex, too bureaucratic, and too costly for people to navigate, especially so in light of what are often plural and parallel legal systems (see Argentina and Cameroon, this volume). And some formulations of laws and policies represent weaker alternatives to more effective protections, such as limited consent clauses instead of co-ownership provisions (see Uganda, this volume; ILC, 2011).

Furthermore, even if general laws and constitutional provisions promote gender equity, exemptions for customary and religious laws may limit the impact that these provisions have on securing equal land rights. For example, some customary laws discriminate against women's property ownership via patrilineal decent systems and patrilocal marital arrangements. Between 70–80 percent of countries in sub-Saharan Africa, Middle East and North Africa, and South Asia recognize customary or religious law under their constitutions, while for countries in Latin America and the Caribbean, and East Asia and the Pacific, it is 25% and 35% respectively. In Europe and Central Asia, no countries recognize customary or religious law (Amin *et al.*, 2013). In several countries, constitutions do not stipulate that customary law is bound by constitutional protections of non-discrimination, leaving open the possibility for indirect discrimination through biases in customary law. In fact, according to Hallward-Driemeier *et al.* (2013), more countries today in sub-Saharan Africa, Middle East, North Africa, and South Asia exempt customary and religious law from equality and non-discrimination provisions and laws than back in 1960 (15).

Where applicable, the case studies in this book advocate legal reforms and better drafted legislation with the overall aim of improving gender equity.

To better implement and enforce equitable land rights

While continuing to address legal barriers to gender equity is essential, the fourteen case studies in this book highlight that the most important impediment to ensuring women's tenure security in practice is arguably the poor implementation and enforcement of the rights for women that now exist in many countries; even among the most egalitarian legal systems with well-formulated laws and regulations, effective implementation is a major challenge (see Kosovo, this volume). Perhaps the most prevalent of these barriers is a lack of genuine commitment to gender-informed and equitable land reforms among politicians and those in charge of implementing reforms. For example, opportunities to address gender inequities in property rights were not embraced by administrators in Kosovo, when gender sensitive legislation was passed only to meet EU standards, nor were they in Madagascar, where the initiative for joint titling was completely donor-driven. As the authors of Chapter 1 argue, in Lao DPR, while voluntary guidelines help raise awareness about gender issues in commercial land investment, in order to effect real change there will need to be "politically powerful agents" with voice and commitment.

Feeble commitment also translates into very practical implementation barriers. In some contexts, administrative institutions lack the necessary infrastructure, equipment, technology, capacity training, and proper working conditions for staff (see Madagascar, this volume). Men, who may not consider these policies a priority or even in their best interest, also tend to disproportionately staff these institutions. Similarly, employees (male and female) may carry their own prejudices and persistent social norms (see China, in this volume). Kosovo's implementing institutions are not only overstretched but also tend to be staffed by people who, in the spirit of nationalism, favor a customary system of patrilineal decent (Kosovo, this volume).

On the other hand, several case studies highlight instances where leadership did commit to integrating gender equity into land reforms. The success in joint-titling in India's West Bengal NGNB program, which allocated land to impoverished landless families, is partially attributed to the political commitment of the Chief Minister, who gave it attention, weight, and resources. And the groundbreaking company–community negotiations that secured women in the Ok Tedi region in Papua New Guinea with much greater benefits than are typical from mining activities were, in major part, attributable to a genuine commitment and understanding by the mining company that efforts to involve and benefit women were key to producing positive development outcomes and reducing company–community conflict, and thus sustaining the future presence of the mine.

Furthermore, commitment problems are not only an issue among politicians, civil servants, and customary authorities. The case studies highlight that local community members must work together to integrate gender equity into land reforms, thereby bolstering the pledges of those in leadership positions. Effective grassroots activism is particularly stymied by poorly informed rural populations, and women in particular often know little about their rights under new reforms. When this commitment from below is lacking, poor or ineffective implementation often results (see, for example, Madagascar and China, this volume).

To address the lack of commitment both at the top and at the bottom of the reform process, these case studies underscore the importance of efforts to inform policy-makers and local community members that gendered land reforms are not a competing priority but a solution to many of the challenges that land reforms are designed to address. Better gender disaggregated data and more (impact) evaluation findings are needed to make the case. Creative awareness-raising efforts are also vital for reaching local populations, and India serves again as an example: part of the success of the joint-titling initiative was attributed to the high level of civic engagement and the creative use of public ceremonies to raise awareness, increase acceptability, and change social norms.

In short, rural tenure reforms need to be designed and implemented in accordance to rural (gender) realities if these reforms are to give a solution to problems such as land scarcity and environmental pressures, climatic instability, food shortages, poverty, conflict, displacement, landlessness etc. In many rural contexts women are the main residents and the principle producers. In customary settings and collective holdings, women should not only be brought in as fully-fledged members, but should also take up positions of leadership and authority in governance structures. In commercial ventures and land acquisitions, women should not merely be consulted, they should be prominent decision-makers and leading recipients of land-based investment benefits. Women should play a much greater role in land administration institutions, in policy and program design, in reform decisions and planning, and the monitoring of implementation. Secure property rights for women can be both an outcome and a catalyst for increasing rural women's capacity. In several cases (see for example Papua New Guinea and Argentina) the fight for property rights is providing women with a foothold or initiation into politics and civic engagement.

Achieving this requires that women are recognized for the leading and often growing roles they play in many countries in rural (food) production and securing family livelihoods. The case studies highlight the need to mobilize local communities and actors in positions of leadership around this recognition to ensure commensurate participation by women in the governance of land and natural resources. Bestowing secure property rights to women has important impacts on the welfare of women, their families, and the future of nations.

References

Allendorf, K. (2007) "Do Women's Land Rights Promote Empowerment and Child Health in Nepal?," *World Development*, vol. 35, no. 11, pp. 1975–1988.

Amin, M., Bin-Humam, Y., & Iqbal, S. (2013) "Mapping the Legal Gender Gap in Accessing Business Environment Institutions," *Women, Business and the Law Note*, Washington, D.C.: The World Bank.

Bhattacharyya, M., Bedi, A., & Chhachhi, A. (2011) "Marital Violence and Women's Employment and Property Status: Evidence from North Indian Villages," *World Development*, vol. 39, no. 9, pp. 1676–1689.

Business Insider (2014) Available: www.businessinsider.com/worlds-fastest-economies-2012-10?op=1 Access Date: June 16, 2014

Datta, N. (2006) "Joint Titling—A Win-win Policy? Gender and Property Rights in Urban Informal Settlements in Chandigarh, India," *Feminist Economics*, vol. 12, no. 1–2, pp. 271–298.

Deere, D. (2005) "The Feminization of Agriculture? Economic Restructuring in Rural Latin America," *United Nations Research Institute for Social Development Occasional Paper*.

Deininger, K., Goyal, A., & Nagarajan, H. (2013) "Women's Inheritance Rights and Intergenerational Transmission of Resources in India," *Journal of Human Resources*, vol. 48, no. 1, pp. 114–141.

Doss, C. (2013) "Intrahousehold Bargaining and Resource Allocation in Developing Countries," *World Bank Research Observer*, vol. 28, no. 1, pp. 52–78.

Doss, C., Kovarik, C., Peterman, A., Quisumbing, A. R., and van den Bold, M. (2013) *Gender Inequalities in Ownership and Control of Land in Africa: Myth versus Reality*, IFPRI Discussion Paper 01308.

FAO (2010) *Gender and Land Rights: Understanding Complexities: Adjusting Policies*. Policy Brief 8, Economic and Social Perspectives. FAO: Rome.

FAO (2011a) *The State of the World's Land and Water Resources for Food and Agriculture: Managing Systems at Risk*.

FAO (2011b) *FAO At Work 2010–2011: Women–Key to Food Security*.

FAO (2014) *Female Land Ownership. Gender and Land Rights Database*

Fletschner, D. & Kenney, L. (2014) "Rural Women's Access to Financial Services: Credit, Savings, and Insurance," in Quisumbing, A. R., Meinzen- Dick, R., Raney, T.L., Croppenstedt, A., Behrman, J. A., & Peterman, A. (eds) *Gender in Agriculture Closing the Knowledge Gap*, Food and Agriculture Organization of the United Nations and Springer Science + Business Media B.V.

Friedemann-Sánchez, G. (2006) "Assets in Intra-Household Bargaining among Women Workers in Colombia's Cut-Flower Industry," *Feminist Economics*, vol. 12, no.1-2, pp. 247–270.

Grabe, S. (2010) "Promoting Gender Equality: The Role of Ideology, Power, and Control in the Link Between Land Ownership and Violence in Nicaragua," *Analyses of Social Issues and Public Policy*, vol. 10, no. 1, pp. 146–170.

Garikipati, S. (2009) "Landless but Not Assetless: Female Agricultural Labour on the Road to Better Status, Evidence from India," *The Journal of Peasant Studies*, vol. 36, no. 3, pp. 517–545.

Hallward-Driemeier, M, Hasan T, Bogdana Rusu A., (2013) *Women's Legal Rights over 50 Years: Progress, Stagnation or Regression?*, The World Bank Policy Research Working Paper 6616.

ILC (2011) *Assessing the Implementation of the Spousal Consent Clause of the Land Act 1998, and Upscaling Advocacy for Women's Rights to Access and Control of Land, A Case for Kayunga District, Uganda.*

Interagency Report (2011) *Price Volatility in Food and Agricultural Market: Policy Responses.*

IPCC (2014) *Climate Change Report: Impact, Adaptation and Vulnerability*, Chapter 22.

Kaag, M. & Zoomers, A. (eds) (2014) *The Global Land Grab. Beyond the Hype*. London: Zed Books, p. 288.

Lastarria-Cornhiel, S. (2006) *Feminization of Agriculture: Trends and Driving Forces.* Background paper for the World Development Report 2008.

Menon, N., van der Meulen Rodgers, Y.., & Nguyen, H. (2014) "Women's Land Rights and Children's Human Capital in Vietnam," *World Development*, vol. 54, pp. 18–31.

Agarwal, B & Panda, P. (2007) "Toward Freedom from Domestic Violence: The Neglected Obvious." Journal of Human Development 8(3):359-388.

Richards, E., Theobald, S., George, A., Kim, J. C., Rudert, C., Jehan, K., & Tolhurst, R. (2013) "Going Beyond the Surface: Gendered Intra-household Bargaining as a Social determinant of Child Health and Nutrition in Low- and Middle-income Countries," *Social Science & Medicine*, vol. 95, pp. 24–33.

Smith, P., Gregory, P. J., van Vuurun, D., Obersteiner, M., Havlik, P., Rounsevell, M., Woods, J., Stehfest, E., & Bellarby, J. (2010) "Review: Competition for Land." *Philosophical Transactions of the Royal Society B: Biological Sciences* vol. 365, pp. 2941–2957.

Song, Y. & Vernooy, R. (2014) "Seeds of Empowerment: Action Research in the Context of the Feminization of Agriculture in Southwest China," *Gender, Technology and Development*, vol. 14, no. 1, pp. 25–44.

Swaminathan, H., Lahoti, R., & Suchitra, J. Y. (2012) *Women's Property, Mobility, and Decisionmaking: Evidence from Rural Karnataka, India*, IFPRI Discussion Paper 01188.

UN (2013) *World Population Prospects, The 2012 Revision.*

UN Habitat (2008) *Secure Land Rights for All.*

The World Bank (2014) *Voice and Agency; Empowering Women and Girls for Shared Prosperity.* Washington, D.C.: World Bank.

The World Bank (2014a) *Data: Population Growth (annual %)*, [Online], Available: http://data.worldbank.org/indicator/SP.POP.GROW [16 June 2014].

The World Bank (2014b). Data: *Population (Total)*, [Online], Available: http://data.worldbank.org/indicator/SP.POP.TOTL [16 June 2014].

The World Bank (2014c) *Data: GDP per Capita Growth Rates*, [Online], Available: [16 June 2014] http://data.worldbank.org/indicator/NY.GDP.PCAP.KD.ZG

Wily, L. A. (2012) "Land Reform in Africa: A Reappraisal: Rights to Resources in Crisis: Reviewing the Fate of Customary Tenure in Africa," –Brief #3 of 5.

Zoomers, A. (2010) "Globalisation and the Foreignisation of Space: Seven Processes Driving the Current Global Land Grab," *Journal of Peasant Studies*, vol. 37, no. 2, pp. 429–47.

Part I

From small farms to firms

A bad deal for women?

Caroline S. Archambault and Annelies Zoomers

Many low- and middle-income countries around the world are currently experiencing a period of large-scale transformation of rural space as foreign corporations and domestic elites are investing in land on a huge scale, particularly for mining and the cultivation of food and biofuel crops (Borras and Franco, 2010; McMichael and Scoones, 2010; Cotula *et al.*, 2009; von Braun and Meinzen-Dick, 2009; Kaag and Zoomers, 2014). While numbers are hotly debated and comparative data difficult to obtain (Anseeuw *et al.*, 2013; Oya, 2013; Edelman, 2013; Cotula and Oya, 2014), Arezki *et al.* (2011) state that in 2009 cross-border land acquisitions deals (complete or under negotiation) claimed 56.6 million hectares of land globally, with the large majority in Africa. The amount of land transacted by foreign entities in Africa alone (39.7 million hectares) is equivalent to the total cultivated lands of Belgium, Denmark, France, Germany, the Netherlands, and Switzerland. According to Oxfam Novib, in 2011 the total number of land deals is even larger, covering more than 227 million hectares (Oxfam Novib, 2011), but the "real" area of affected land is of course very much dependent on how one defines large-scale land acquisition.

These investments are market-driven, pushed by concerns for "global" food and energy crises; and supported by recipient governments (especially in Africa) looking for new opportunities to realize "modernization" (which often goes hand in hand with mono-cultivation) and economic growth. Investments are focused on remaining areas of frontier land; while these are sometimes fertile terrain with good road access, they are often large tracts of "empty" ground in off-road areas, or open commons, which are given away by governments.

Such large-scale land acquisitions often further squeeze small farms that occupy less than a quarter of the world's farmland but which still comprise the majority of farms globally (GRAIN, 2014). Rangelands are also being fragmented as commercial ranching and cultivation, conservation, tourism, and hunting concessions take out large chunks of grasslands, disrupting livestock mobility and access to critical resources (Shete and Rutten, 2013; Archambault *et al.*, 2014). In many places the rapid expansion of monocrops is followed by deforestation, which in turn leads to a loss in biodiversity. In addition, in places where forests are given away to the timber industry and commercial concessions, or nature conservation (including REDD+), local people are put under increasing pressure to use 'their' common pool resources. Finally, also in the urban sphere, local land markets are also under mounting stress: large investments are made in real-estate development, urban expansion, and modern infrastructure; land prices are rapidly increasing, and are commonly followed by processes of gentrification.

Much ongoing research explores the consequences of large-scale land investments, including assessing attendant changes in terms of "hectares affected" or the number of people impacted by such moves. It is clear, however, that in most cases and for most people directly affected, the benefits (in terms of potential employment and investments in infrastructure and services) do not outweigh the costs: people lose access to land and natural resources and in most cases are insufficiently compensated (Behrman *et al.*, 2012; Kaag and Zoomers, 2014). It appears to be increasingly acknowledged that these acquisitions have many negative effects: local people—who are displaced or enclosed—are hindered in their access to, and use of, natural resources; the projected benefits (employment, technology transfer, etc.) are often not realized, or simply bypass local communities entirely. Some governments and international organizations are implementing policies to prevent land "grabbing" or to stop incursions into ecologically vulnerable areas. These include recognizing customary rights and establishing "modern systems of land administration" so that local people are more informed and consulted, and better capable of defending their rights (FPICC); and developing "codes of conducts" as a way of encouraging businesses to act more responsibly and share benefits (Deininger *et al.*, 2011; von Braun and Meinzen-Dick, 2009; Zoomers, 2013).

The consequences of large-scale investments in farming, extractive industries, and housing developments are usually described in gender-neutral terms such as "affected communities" or "numbers of displaced people"; proposed solutions are framed in terms of "need for community consultations" and the "importance of respecting human rights." To the extent that attention is given to the gendered impact of large-scale land investments (Doss *et al.*, 2014; Behrman *et al.*, 2012; Wonani, 2013; and Kachingwe, 2012), it is often stressed that local women benefit less than men, and that women play a crucial role in compensating for the costs. Greater detailed understanding is needed of the different extents to which such processes impact men and women and of how gender relations and inequalities are reconfigured.

Drawing on case studies from Lao PDR, Costa Rica, and Papua New Guinea, the first part of this book does just this. These chapters trace the gender implications of the penetration of foreign and domestic corporate capital through different types of commercial land-based investments.

In Lao PDR, four different large land-based agricultural investments have had varying impacts on rural livelihoods. While some men and women clearly benefit from the opportunities generated by these investments, women appear to bear a disproportionate burden, with increased labor demands and a reduction in access to non-timber forest products.

In Costa Rica, the fast development of residential tourism is having myriad gender effects on local populations. Women and men have had different experiences regarding their social exposure to new foreign migrant lifestyles, employment and economic opportunities, political activism and mobilization, displacement, and gentrification.

The case study from Papua New Guinea offers an insight into how an innovative company–community mining agreement gave rise to a negotiating process wherein women held a prominent place at the negotiating table. This resulted in important, legally enforceable economic and political entitlements for women that were integral to the company's licence to operate. However, challenges persist in effective implementation to harness these benefits.

References

Anseeuw, W., Lay, J., Messerli, P., Giger, M., & Taylor, M. (2013) "Creating a Public Tool to Assess and Promote Transparency in Global Land Deals: The Experience of the Land Matrix," *Journal of Peasant Studies*, vol. 40, no. 3, pp. 521–530.

Archambault, C., Matter, S., Ole Riamit, S. K., & Galaty, J. (2014) "Maasai Livelihood Pathways in Kenya: Macro-level Factors in Diversifying Diversification," in Sick, D. (ed.), *Rural Livelihoods, Regional Economies and Processes of Change*, New York: Routledge.

Arezki, R., Deininger, K., & Selod, H. (2011) *What Drives the Global Land Rush?* IMF Working Papers 11/251, Washington, D.C.: International Monetary Fund.

Behrman, J., Meinzen-Dick, R., and Quisumbing, A. (2012) "The Gender Implications of Large-scale Land Deals," *Journal of Peasant Studies*, vol. 39, no. 1, pp. 49–79.

Borras, S., Jr. & Franco, J. C. (2010) "From Threat to Opportunity? Problems with the Idea of a 'Code of Conduct' for Land-grabbing," *Yale Human Rights and Development Law Journal*, vol. 13, no. 2, pp. 507–523.

Chu, J. (2011) "Gender and 'Land Grabbing' in sub-Saharan Africa: Women's Land Rights and Customary Tenure," *Development*, vol. 54, no. 1, pp. 5–39.

Cotula, L. & Oya, C. (2014) "Testing Claims about Large Land Deals in Africa: Findings from a Multi-Country Study," *Journal of Development Studies*, vol. 50, no. 7, pp. 903–925.

Cotula, L., Vermeulen, S., Leonard, R., & Keeley, J. (2009) *Land Grab or Development Opportunity? Agricultural Investments and International Land Deals in Africa*, London: IIED.

Deininger, K., Byerlee, D., Lindsay, J., Norton, A., Selod H., & Sticker, M. (2011) *Rising Global Interest in Farmland: Can It Yield Sustainable and Equitable Benefits?*, Washington, D.C.: World Bank.

Doss, C., Summerfield, G., & Tsikata, D. (2014) "Land, Gender, and Food Security: Feminist Economics'," *The Journal of Feminist Economics* vol. 20, no. 1, pp. 1–23.

Edelman, M. (2013) "Messy Hectares: Questions about the Epistemology of Land Grabbing Data," *Journal of Peasant Studies*, vol. 40, no. 3, pp. 485–501.

GRAIN (2014) *Hungry for Land: Small Farmers Feed the World with Less than a Quarter of all Farmland*. (www.grain.org/article/entries/4952-media-release-hungry-for-land) Access Date: June 10, 2014.

Kaag, M. & Zoomers, A. (eds) (2014) *The Global Land Grab. Beyond the Hype*, London: Zed Books, p. 288.

Kachingwe, N. (2012) *From under Their Feet: A Think Piece on the Gender Dimensions of Land Grabs in Africa*, London: ActionAid International.

McMichael, P. & Scoones, I. (2010) "The Politics of Biofuels, Land and Agrarian Change," *Journal of Peasant Studies*, vol. 37, no. 4.

Oxfam Novib (2011) *Land and Power*, Oxford: Oxfam International, Available: www.oxfamnovib.nl/Redactie/Downloads/Rapporten/bp151-land-power-rights-acquisitions-220911-en%5B1%5D.pdf Access Date: June 11, 2014.

Oya, C. (2013) "Methodological Reflections on 'Land Grab' Databases and the 'Land Grab' Literature Rush," *Journal of Peasant Studies*, vol. 40, no. 3, pp. 503–520.

Shete, M. & Rutten, M. (2013) *Impact of Large-scale Agricultural Investment on Income and Food Security in Oromiya Region, Ethiopia*, Research paper for the annual World Bank conference on land and poverty, Available: www.commercialpressuresonland.org/research-papers/impact-large-scale-agricultural-investment-income-and-food-security-oromiya-region Access Date: June 10, 2014.

von Braun, J. & Meinzen-Dick, R. (2009) "'Land Grabbing' by Foreign Investors in Developing Countries: Risks and Opportunities," Washington, D.C.: IFPRI. IFPRI Policy Brief [20 January 2011].

Wonani (2013) *The Gender and Equity Implications of Land-Related Investments on Land Access, Labour and Income-Generating Opportunities*, A Case Study of Selected Agricultural Investments in Zambia, Available: www.fao.org/docrep/018/aq536e/aq536e.pdf Access Date: June 10, 2014.

Zoomers, A. (2013) "A Critical Review of the Policy Debate on Large-scale Land Acquisitions: Fighting the Symptoms or Killing the Heart?," in Evers, J.T.M., Seagle, C., & Krijtenburg, F. (eds) *Africa for Sale? Positioning the State, Land and Society in Foreign Large-scale Land Acquisitions in Africa*, Leiden and Boston: Brill, pp. 55–78.

1 Gender, land and agricultural investments in Lao PDR

Clara Mi Young Park and Elizabeth Daley

Introduction

Since 2008, following initial attention from civil society and the media, large-scale land acquisitions and agricultural investments have been increasingly on the research agenda of academics, land rights activists and global development organizations (Anseeuw *et al.*, 2012; Edelman *et al.*, 2013; Oya, 2013). Various aspects of this 'global land grab' phenomenon have been analyzed but, with some notable exceptions, gender has received relatively less attention (see Daley, 2011; Behrman *et al.*, 2012; Julia & White, 2012; Daley & Pallas, 2014; Doss *et al.*, 2014).

Those most affected by land grabs – 'rural communities' and 'local people' – are not homogeneous groups (Borras, 2010; Vermeulen & Cotula, 2010). They are linked to land and natural resources in different ways and have access to different resource rights and endowments according to their status, class, gender, age, ethnicity, etc. This, in turn, defines their position vis-à-vis agribusinesses (Fairhead *et al.*, 2012), including potential opportunities for them to engage profitably in income generation or conversely the likelihood of marginalization and dispossession. Moreover, women and men will be differentially affected by land grabs because of their different social roles, rights and opportunities (Behrman *et al.*, 2012), and women are also more likely to be adversely affected than men because of systemic gender discrimination (Daley, 2011).

Although data on the scale of the global land grab varies significantly, the phenomenon seems to be gathering pace (Cotula, 2012; Edelman *et al.*, 2013). Large-scale land acquisitions and agricultural investments have the potential for:

> radically restructuring agrarian economies, transforming livelihoods and rural social relations and, with this, changing the power dynamics in the countryside across the global South, with major implications for national, and indeed regional and international, politics.
>
> (White *et al.*, 2012: 624)

Existing gender and social inequalities may be exacerbated as a result of these processes. Together with the recognition that a gender perspective can enhance understanding of how different people are affected by agrarian transformations, this highlights the importance of assessing gender in respect of large-scale land acquisitions and agricultural investments for both analytical and policy purposes.

The present chapter takes an agrarian political economy perspective, incorporating a gender lens, to explore some of the changes unfolding in Lao PDR as corporate capital penetrates rural areas (cf. Bernstein, 2010). We build on a Food and Agriculture Organization (FAO) study of the gender and social equity implications of land-based agricultural investments in Laos, for which fieldwork was conducted in late 2011 (Daley *et al.*, 2013). The fieldwork took place in rural areas of three of Lao PDR's 17 provinces – Borikhamxai (Borikhan, Pakkading and Pakksan districts), Vientiane (Vangvieng district) and Vientiane Capital (Thourakhon and Xaithani districts) – with primary data supported by a desk-based review of background literature and supporting documents collected in the field. Over 68 key informants were interviewed from 37 national government ministries and organizations, provincial and district government offices, and development partner and civil society organizations, as well as from eight companies investing in agriculture. In addition, over 114 farmers and agricultural workers (51 women and 63 men) involved with six different agricultural investments were consulted in 17 focus group discussions across ten villages.[1]

The four cases discussed in the present chapter were foreign-financed and private sector-led to differing degrees and each operated through a different business model. One was a state-owned enterprise (SOE) with foreign marketing contracts (cassava), another was a joint venture between a foreign firm and the Lao government (tobacco), while the remaining two were 100% private foreign direct investment (FDI) (bananas and jatropha). Two were fully operational in the fieldwork areas at the time of the study (tobacco and bananas), one was a new investment (cassava) and the fourth had ceased operations (jatropha). See Table 1.1.

The FAO study examined the different implications that land-based agricultural investments in Laos had for women and men in terms of their access, use and management of land and their labour and income-generating opportunities (Daley *et al.*, 2013). It offered a broad perspective on the modus operandi of corporate capital in Laos, whereby, in a situation of ongoing agrarian change, characterized by governance problems across the board, contract farming schemes appeared as a way in which control over land use was taken away from farmers. This chapter builds on the FAO study by looking more deeply at the gender dimensions of our four selected cases. However, the chapter is not intended to provide a fully comprehensive discussion of the gendered effects of agricultural investments and large-scale land acquisitions in Laos. Instead, it attempts to contribute gendered insights to the global debate on land grabbing more broadly, as research moves into "the post-'making sense period,'" by addressing the significant "silences" on gender (Edelman *et al.*, 2013: 1526–1527).

Table 1.1 Basic data on case-study investments

Investment name	Dates	Ownership structure	Crop	Business model	Number of participating farming families
KoLao Farm & Bio-Energy Co. Ltd. (a division of a larger conglomerate)	2006–11 (still functioning as a company at the time of fieldwork but no longer operational in fieldwork area)	100% private FDI (Korean)	Jatropha	1+4 contract farming*	No data on number of contract farming families or workers who had been under 1+4 in fieldwork area, but 30,000 contract farming families under 2+3 nation-wide, plus around 20 factory workers
State Commerce-Food Stuff Enterprise	1996–2011 (fully operational but new to fieldwork area)	100% Lao government (an SOE)	Cassava	2+3 contract farming*	827 contract farming families under 2+3 nationwide, no data on exact number in fieldwork area
Lao Tobacco Limited	2001–11 (fully operational)	Foreign-led joint venture: 47% Lao government, 53% private FDI (British)	Tobacco	Conventional contract farming	3,200 contract farming families organized into 88 farmer groups, plus 700 factory employees (of whom at least 350 were women)
Lao Banana Company Ltd.	2008–11 (operational but not exporting at the time of fieldwork)	100% private FDI (British)	Bananas	Conventional plantation	60–70 agricultural workers (of whom majority were women), comprising 54 employees and some casual labourers

Source: Adapted from Table 3 in Daley et al. 2013: 30.
* Lao PDR's 1+4 and 2+3 contract farming models are described below.

Land tenure and women's land rights in Lao PDR

The legal and policy framework regulating land and property rights in Laos is well established (Sihavong, 2007). Private property rights, including use, disposal and inheritance rights, are constitutionally protected. However, the 1997 *Land Law* (No. 01/97/NA, amended as *Law on Land*, 21 October 2003, No. 04/NA) confirms state ownership and overall control of land, including through land allocation and land management (Government of Lao PDR, 1997; 2003a; Mann & Luangkhot, 2008). Furthermore, although local people's rights to use forest land and products in accordance with customary practices have been legally protected since 1992, these were heavily watered down under the 2007 *Forestry Law* (No. 6/NA), which allows customary usage only if it is "practiced in accordance with a designed plan and with village regulations and laws and regulations on forests" (Government of Lao PDR, 2007, Article 42; Mann & Luangkhot, 2008; Sipaseuth & Hunt, n.d.).

Although all land is property of the state, individual households are allowed to register ownership rights over the land they hold privately for farming, grazing, housing, vegetable gardening, fish ponds and so on. This was facilitated by the government through a systematic titling program in most urban areas under two donor-funded land-titling projects (1997–2002 and 2003–2009) and a land-policy development project (2008–2011) (Sihavong, 2007; World Bank 2009). Data from the National Land Management Authority in 2011 indicated that some 600,000 parcels of land in urban and peri-urban areas had been titled – with a Land Title including rights to use, inherit, lease, sell, mortgage and exclude others (Schoenweger & Üllenberg, 2009).

As several of our informants emphasized, the majority of people in rural areas do not have formal documents for all or any of their land. In some instances, even when they could get documents, they prefer not to in order to avoid paying the taxes that registering their land would incur. Most rural people who have formal documents register for a Temporary Land Use Certificate at the district level. This is legally valid for three years and obliges holders to pay taxes, but it does not include the rights to sell, mortgage or claim compensation on expropriation (Wehrmann *et al.*, 2007; Schoenweger & Üllenberg, 2009).

Women and men in Laos have equal rights under its 1991 Constitution, strengthened by amendments made in 2003 to protect women's rights and promote their development (Government of Lao PDR, 2003b). In 2004 the government enacted the *Law on Development and Protection of Women* and in 2006 formulated a *National Strategy for the Advancement of Women* (Government of Lao PDR, 2004; 2006). Laos has also ratified the international *Convention on the Elimination of all Forms of Discrimination against Women*. However, there are problems around lack of coordination between the various institutional mechanisms for promoting gender equality in Laos, and knowledge about women's rights is generally inadequate, particularly among rural women and especially elderly and disabled women and those from Lao Soung ethnic minorities.

Over 50% of Lao women live in areas with strong matrifocal and matrilocal traditions, particularly among the majority Lao Loum ethnic groups. Female land inheritance within areas practicing matrilineal land tenure is both legally recognized and commonplace, and any property acquired within marriage in Laos is legally considered as the joint property of husband and wife (Mann & Luangkhot, 2008; FAO, 2012). However, women's inheritance is often transferred as 'bride price' and is thus dependent on marriage: "women are consistently disadvantaged with respect to land and property rights on divorce, widowhood, and remaining unmarried" and the situation is worse in ethnic groups where patrilineal land tenure is practiced (Mann & Luangkhot, 2008: 24, 49). Management of village and communal land is also male-dominated, through (usually male) village elders and socio-cultural practices related to customary tenure and spiritual beliefs linked to this type of land (ibid: 25–26).

Because joint ownership of property is recognized within marriage, the names of both husband and wife have usually been recorded in documents in urban areas where systematic land titling has taken place. However the situation is very different in rural areas, where, according to traditional practices, women, especially from ethnic minorities, may refuse to have their name on a land document because of fears of social ostracism or simply because it is considered normal that the title should be in the husband's name. As elaborated by one of our informants from the national government:

> Women never think about what would happen in the case of divorce…In the case of the parents' death, the daughter sometimes does not accept her share of the property because of the traditional belief that a man will take care of her as a wife…Among the Hmong and hills ethnicities [Lao Soung and Lao Theung], most of the land and property will be given to sons only. Girls do not really dare to ask for it, even though they are supposed to have their share by law…Once I tried to speak to a young Hmong woman about this [putting her name on a land document], but she said 'no I could not do so and our village leader would not agree with that. This is our tradition.'
>
> (as first cited in Daley *et al.*, 2013: 16)

Gender relations and gendered divisions of labour in Laos

Women farmers are responsible for over half of the agricultural activities carried out in Laos and they make up 54% of the total agricultural labour force (ADB, 2011a). Women traditionally do most of the farm work, including more than half of the planting, weeding, harvesting, threshing and post-harvest operations; they also tend livestock and spend long hours performing off-farm and household chores like collecting firewood, preparing meals and caring for children (FAO & MAF, 2010). Women's role in farming increased in some areas due to shortages of male labour during the years of the Indo-China wars (when lots of men were fighting), and within rice farming women are now increasingly involved in formerly male-dominated tasks such as ploughing, land preparation, irrigation, and preparing bunds and seedbeds (FAO, 2012). Participants in our focus group discussions explained that while women do more of the work in farming and housework, men instead may leave their villages to undertake construction work in towns, or to go fishing or collecting aquatic products or non-timber forest products (NTFPs). As one woman explained:

> Men do some heavy work such as land preparation, spraying, building the dykes of the paddy fields, and cutting grass on the dykes…Women are in charge of looking after children, cooking, house cleaning, vegetable growing and poultry husbandry…[Men] go fishing early morning and at lunchtime. The hooks and the fishing nets are usually prepared in the evening and sometimes all day long and this work is done by the men. After fishing in the morning, the men bring the fish back home for the wives to cook. After eating, they go to the paddy field together.
>
> (as first cited in Daley *et al.*, 2013: 11)

Women in rural Laos are traditionally responsible for family finances and for their family's food and nutrition, in addition to being responsible for marketing agricultural produce in local markets (ADB, 2011b). As one male focus group participant said: "They breastfeed the children but also their husbands! Wives manage the household economy." Yet despite their visibly strong economic role at the household level, women are circumscribed by land-related economic dependence on men – and particularly by the socio-cultural conventions and land inheritance practices (as above) that promote the 'household' and tend to prohibit single women living alone (Mann & Luangkhot, 2008).

Some ethnic groups are more open in terms of gender relations, particularly among the Lao Loum, but others are more repressive for women, with domestic violence a serious issue throughout the country. Relatively low rates of female literacy and education in Laos reflect cultural preferences for the schooling of boys and the customary practice for girls to assist their mothers at home (FAO, 2012). One of our key informants summed up the overall situation well: "It is true that decision-making is shared within Lao households, but beyond the rhetoric, when it comes to real power, the reality is different and only men participate. Extension services are male dominated and there is a low level of participation of women in government" (as first cited in Daley *et al.*, 2013: 11–12).

Land and agricultural investments in Laos

Despite the global economic crisis and a sharp decline in global FDI of −18%, South-East Asia saw a 2% rise in FDI inflows in 2012 to US$ 111 billion (UNCTAD, 2013). FDI inflows to Lao PDR declined from US$ 324 million in 2007 to US$ 294 million in 2012, but the overall trend indicates Laos as "having the potential to attract further FDI" (ibid, 2013: 79). Intra-regional investments dominate in South-East Asia, with China playing a major role alongside the increasingly powerful middle-income countries of Thailand, Vietnam, Malaysia and Indonesia. Within Laos, domestic private and government investors are also key players in large-scale land acquisitions and agricultural investments.

Historically, FDI in agriculture in South-East Asia has been driven by export-linked 'crop booms,' including strong current demand for biofuels, timber and the products of industrial tree crops, as well as by concerns about their own food supplies on the part of some investing countries (Schoenweger & Üllenberg, 2009; Hall, 2011; Montemayor, 2011). In Laos over the past ten years or so the impact, scale and speed of FDI inflows into its agriculture and natural resources (ANR) sector, especially in the lowlands along the Mekong plains, has been far greater than was anticipated (Fraser, 2009). According to data from the Ministry of Agriculture and Forestry, there were some 600 foreign companies from over 30 countries investing in agriculture, livestock, fisheries and forestry in Laos by late 2011 – almost all with land concessions. The biggest sub-sector within ANR was industrial tree crops, especially rubber, but 163 foreign companies were investing directly in food crop production. However, there is a serious lack of accurate data about the true scale of the phenomenon, with one estimate putting some 2–3 million hectares (ha) as having been granted to both foreign and domestic investors in land concessions across all sectors, or up to 13% of Lao PDR's total land area; specific concerns have also been raised about the process of granting land concessions, for example over the transparency and fairness of site selection and compensation for lost farms (Fraser, 2009; Schoenweger & Üllenberg, 2009).

A number of investors have established 1+4 and 2+3 contract farming arrangements with local farmers on land for which the individual farming families hold private ownership and/or use rights. These are two types of contract farming that the Lao government has promoted as an alternative to conventional plantations. Under 1+4, farmers lend their land to the investor, while the investor is responsible for planting and maintenance with hired labour. The investor retains a 70% share of the profits, while the farmers retain their private ownership rights to the land and often a minority share of the crop harvest in addition to the wages received by some of them for working directly for the investor. Under 2+3, farmers provide and use their own land and labour in return for a 70% share of the profits, while the investor provides capital (seedlings, fertilizers and equipment), technical know-how and marketing. The cost of the capital is deducted from the income before profits are shared, with contracts sometimes signed for as long as 30 or 35 years (Schoenweger & Üllenberg, 2009). Both business models raise questions related to farmers' ability to retain and exercise control over their land.

Village and communal land, i.e. that which is not claimed by individual households as privately owned, has been especially vulnerable to land pressures from increasing investment in agriculture. In some cases, investors wanting land concessions for conventional plantations and 1+4 contract farming, especially for industrial tree crops such as rubber, teak, eucalyptus and acacia, have deliberately sought out forested areas with insecure tenure in order to gain access to the right to clear existing forest and, allegedly, carry out straightforward logging operations disguised as plantations (Hall, 2011; Sipaseuth & Hunt, n.d.). When such land concessions are awarded in areas of "political forest" – those classified as forest but which local people consider as village or communal land and use regularly for farming, collecting NTFPs and sometimes for housing – the effects are especially detrimental (Hall, 2011: 844, 848, citing Peluso & Vandergeest, 2001). As one of our informants indicated, where it is no longer possible for men to hunt and women to collect NTFPs, this can then "cause food shortages and stress in families and villages, which can lead to problems of violence and drinking" (as first cited in Daley et al., 2013: 23). Conflicts also arise when companies acquire a land concession but do not use it all, and therefore do not create the jobs anticipated locally, or when they try to plant on a larger area than they have been allocated and encroach onto areas still used for collecting NTFPs and other livelihood activities.

Gender dimensions of investments: evidence from the field

The implications from our four cases of agricultural investment in Laos with respect to people's access to land, their labour, cash incomes and family food situation, all tended to centre on the changes in land use that were brought about by the investment and the consequent changes in labour requirements and income-generating possibilities within participating farming families.

Case 1: Jatropha (1+4 contract farming)

KoLao Farm and Bio-Energy Co. Ltd was established in 2006 for the production of biodiesel and was part of the Korean-owned KoLao Group that had been operating in Laos since 1996. In 2007 KoLao started a demonstration jatropha farm/project in our fieldwork area. The following year, the company signed a memorandum of understanding (MoU) with the Ministry of Planning and Investment. It surveyed 10,000 ha of land that it wanted to operate through 1+4 contract farming, planted on some of the land and hired employees and casual wage labourers to farm it. However, by the time of our fieldwork the company had been unable to obtain a formal land concession agreement for this land and had instead switched to 2+3 contract farming on other land elsewhere in Laos, involving 30,000 families and 20,000 ha across six provinces by 2009; it had also built a processing factory by the end of 2010. Our focus group participants in this case were all from the area where KoLao had originally sought to acquire its 10,000 ha and start 1+4 contract farming, and thus had engaged with the company as casual labourers rather than as 2+3 contract farmers or factory employees.

Women and men in one of the affected villages had been using the KoLao area largely to collect NTFPs since the government had allocated it to the village as communal land in 1998. Before that it had been used for farming upland rice, but that was then banned and the land was designated as government forest. When the KoLao jatropha plantations started, many kinds of NTFPs declined and consequently the scale of collection diminished. Although both women and men received some cash income from working as casual labourers for KoLao, they were no longer able to practise (illicit) shifting cultivation on the land nor use it for livestock grazing, and their income from NTFPs reduced. This latter affected the women in particular because they had relied heavily on these items to supplement their family food supply. At the time of our fieldwork the jatropha plantation had fallen into neglect and only about 30% of the jatropha seedlings that were planted had actually developed into bushes. The women had therefore gone back to using some small trees for fuel wood and fence-making, and carrying out small-scale collection of bamboo shoots, mushrooms, rattan and edible wildlife such as rats.

Some of our informants suggested that the jatropha plantation had been abandoned because KoLao could not attract enough workers, as the wages were considered low for the work. Local farming families embarking as 1+4 contract farmers received an annual lump sum payment to maintain a specific area over a whole season, while casual labourers received only 20,000 kip (US$ 2.5) per day to clear land and plant jatropha. This was much less than the 30,000 kip (US$ 3.75) per day wages for casual labour in rice farming in the same village and 35,000 kip (US$ 4.38) per day in other nearby villages.[2] Nevertheless, both women and men who had worked for KoLao as casual labourers reported that they appreciated the opportunity to work on the jatropha plantations because they had limited access to other local sources of cash income. Yet at the same time, they claimed to have been worse off in terms of their food situation because of lack of time to farm and collect NTFPs while working for KoLao.

Women who had worked as casual labourers for KoLao said that although their workloads doubled – because the casual labour came in addition to their usual rice farming and household work – they got more cash income which they used on clothes, food, medicine and, in one case, a motorbike. Before KoLao came to the area, their main source of cash income was working as casual labourers on other people's rice farms, as well as some selling of fish and NTFPs and, for a minority of men, looking for work as casual labourers on construction sites in towns. Since the jatropha plantations had fallen into neglect, the women had resumed these previous income-generating activities but overall they felt worse off now because the new work opportunities in the village that were created by KoLao had been lost.

Case 2: Cassava (2+3 contract farming)

State Commerce-Food Stuff Enterprise (SCFSE) was established in 1996 as an SOE. It operated shipping and restaurant/hotel services, imported consumer goods and exported timber and agricultural products. In 2002 it started an agricultural division that mainly focused on cassava and maize and promoted a 2+3 contract farming model of cassava growing to farmers who had their own land. At the time of our fieldwork, SCFSE had contracts with 739 farming families in 45 villages across five districts, plus 88 families of individual government officers and soldiers who had signed contracts to grow cassava directly.

SCFSE provided cassava seeds, technical assistance, fertilizers, and land-clearing and preparation services while farmers provided the land. Contracts were signed for three to five years, with the company providing the initial investment of 5 million kip per ha (US$ 625) to open and clear land in the first year and 3.5 million kip (US$ 437) to re-clear before re-planting in the second year – all of which was deducted from the post-harvest base price of 400kip/kg (US$ 0.05) of cassava roots before the farmers received any money. Other costs to farmers were 1.5 million kip (US$ 187.5) on cassava seeds and 250,000 kip (US$ 31.25) on roots stimulator/fertilizer. The farmers had to undertake all labour from planting onwards but the company organized the land clearance and preparation itself.

SCFSE was relatively new to our fieldwork area – it was the company's first year of operations there and farmers were yet to harvest. Women in our focus group discussions expressed real concern that they would be in debt to the company if the harvest was not good enough to repay the initial land-clearing costs. The land used for cassava farming was owned by the farming families and had previously been used for growing upland rice for household consumption under shifting cultivation. However, the two crops were not directly substituted (at least in this first year) because, under the fallowing required with shifting cultivation, upland rice was not grown on the land every year. They were thus growing cassava on fallow rice land.

Women cassava farmers said that NTFPs like bamboo, mushrooms and wild vegetables were all still available in their village but to a more limited extent than in the past because land previously used for collecting NTFPs on the way back from their farms had been cleared for cassava planting. They were also worried that in the coming harvesting season, they would not have enough time to collect wild foods from the local forests because they would now be too busy harvesting cassava. Furthermore, the women explained that the bamboo shoots would not be ready for collection at the time of cassava harvesting, when they would be going to and from their farms. Instead, they had started growing vegetables in their own gardens and continued to fish, as they felt they could no longer rely on NTFPs for food, but this was not felt to be adequate compensation for the loss of those items.

Some women cassava farmers pointed out that since they had started growing cassava their workload had increased because they had to do it in addition to their rice farming. In contrast, male farmers welcomed cassava farming as they found it less labour-intensive than rice farming; one man put the total labour input for cassava as 70% of that for rice. However, one woman clarified that the family's tasks overall, and the total workload of both husband and wife, had increased "because everyone has also planted rice." It was too early to know how much more cash income the cassava farming might bring in, and thus to know whether the extra labour requirements would be felt to be worthwhile.

This case also affected demand for casual labourers in our fieldwork area. In one village, around 60 households out of a total of 146 had members who worked as casual labourers for other households because of being land-poor – they had less land to farm (even though some were renting land from other households) and therefore also more time available to earn the money they needed to purchase food. Casual labourers were paid a standard rate of 35,000 kip (US$ 4.38) per day for any kind of work on any crop in this village, and around 70% of them were women. Men cassava farmers reported that 77 households in this village were under contract with SCFSE and nearly all of them hired casual labourers for both their rice and their cassava. Since cassava farming had started, overall demand for casual labour had thus gone up and some of the labourers now came from neighbouring villages to meet that increased demand.

Case 3: Tobacco (conventional contract farming)

Lao Tobacco Limited (LTL) is a 25-year joint venture between the UK's Imperial Tobacco and the Government of Lao PDR, and was established in 2001 to revive the failing state-owned Lao Tobacco Company. LTL was seen as a good business model by provincial and district authorities in our fieldwork area, positively contributing to poverty reduction in leaf-growing areas. One of our informants from Pakkading district explained how the company was increasing farmers' incomes: "Many people have very small houses but after five years of farming tobacco they now have big houses."

By the time of our fieldwork, LTL had around 3,200 conventional contract farmers, mostly growing flue-cured tobacco along the Mekong River, plus around 700 employees in a processing and packaging factory. Around half the factory employees were women, and there were a handful of female technicians working in the leaf production side of the business. However, they were few in number because of security and cultural issues LTL had encountered for women working in the villages, especially those who were married.

The tobacco contract farmers were organized in groups in villages, with the heads of the groups responsible for enforcing adherence to the contract with each of their members. In 2011 there were 88 farmer groups in total. LTL established its tobacco-growing policy at the start of each season in consultation with its farmers, local governments and the Ministry of Agriculture and Forestry, with the aim of helping farmers improve their quality of production so as to generate higher yields and thus more cash income.

At the time of our fieldwork, all heads of farmers' groups were men, as were most of the farmers who had signed up with the company. However, according to LTL, and confirmed by both women and men participants in our focus groups, even if the man signed the contract, he could not start tobacco farming without his wife, and the wives had the power "to say yes or no." Company representatives said that sometimes a wife would sign the contract, and payment was always made to the person who signed, but the work was done by the whole family. Because of the amount of work involved in tobacco farming – building barns for flue-curing, for example – farmers needed cash upfront and most got a bank loan to start growing tobacco.

The labour implications of this investment were particularly gendered. Tobacco farming was presented as a household operation (as above), but the actual work seemed to be largely managed by women who perceived their workloads to have increased. Tasks included preparing seedbeds, planting, weeding, harvesting, grading and curing the leaf. Women made the seedbeds and did most of the weeding, harvesting and post-harvesting work. In addition, they were responsible for managing, looking after and feeding the casual labourers required for production. In most families these were two male labourers hired for six months to perform tasks that included building and maintaining barns and collecting fuel wood for the flue-curing process. Because the casual labourers were almost all men, as the work was very heavy, the benefits in terms of new labour and income-generating opportunities from tobacco farming therefore tended to be biased towards men.

Nothing had been done specifically by LTL to promote contract farming to women, and households headed by women seemed unlikely to have either the labour or capital resources to benefit much from tobacco farming in their own right. Among the women in tobacco farming families we spoke with, some felt their family's food situation had improved from the extra cash income the investment had generated as they could buy more meat, while others said it had not changed because they continued to rely on fish for protein from the Mekong River. Men tobacco farmers, however, all felt better off.

Case 4: Bananas (conventional plantation)

Lao Banana Company (LBC) is 100% owned by the UK-based Pacific Farming Company, which has run banana plantations in Latin America for the past 30 years. LBC started operating in Laos in 2008 with a 30-year land concession of 100 ha, and in 2009 it obtained a 100 ha land concession in another village for a second plantation. It took nine months to obtain its first land concession and start operations, including carrying out site surveys six times, "because each time we tried to survey the concession area someone else in the village said that part of the communal land was their land" (as first cited in Daley et al., 2013: 25). The plot ended up in a different shape than initially envisaged, and LBC's second concession comprised three separate and non-contiguous pieces of land.

On each plantation, 150 casual labourers were initially hired from the village where it was based to clear all the land and plant banana trees. Once this preparatory work had been completed, labour requirements dropped to a total of 54 permanent workers and another dozen or so casual labourers, but this was expected to reduce further to around 30–35 workers at rice-harvesting time, when some would want to go off to their own farms. Company representatives said they had not found it hard to persuade people to give up some of their land for the plantations as they wanted jobs and there was year-round work to be had in banana production; LBC was also supporting technical training in small-scale aquaculture and mushroom farming for those who did not get jobs on its plantations. However, the company found training its new workers difficult because there was no previous local culture or experience of formal employment.

Women comprised more than half of LBC's workforce, doing the picking, spraying and cutting in the fields. Most of the plantation workers at the time of our fieldwork were married but some were young people with little or no education who had not yet married. Some tasks were different each day and women generally packed up fewer bags of bananas than men, but LBC paid the same day rate to permanent employees and casual labourers of both sexes. After six months of working for the company, many workers, both employees and casual labourers, women and men, had bought motorbikes for transportation to work; this was a significant enough change for LBC to build a motorbike shelter for them.

LBC had also provided opportunities for its employees, including women, to gain promotion to supervisory work and accompanying pay rises. The female supervisors we spoke with did not report particular difficulties relating to their role and reported only occasional problems when supervising older male workers, saying that they had to be diplomatic when those workers were in the wrong.

Many of LBC's plantation workers were from the minority Lao Soung ethnic groups who had been relocated to the area under previous government policies; these workers had had less and worse quality land than their Lao Loum neighbours, which made the prospect of regular cash income from plantation work very attractive to them. All our focus group participants considered the banana plantations important to the local economy due to the labour and income-generating opportunities they provided women, especially young single women, and those from poorer households and minority ethnic groups. Most of the plantation workers we spoke with felt better off in terms of both cash income and their family's food situation, as they were using their earnings to buy more and better food. However, some women workers were saving their earnings instead. There were also still places available in their villages for collecting NTFPs, so no one had completely lost out on that source of food since the establishment of the banana plantations.

Gender, land, labour and capital

There was great diversity regarding means of access to land in our fieldwork areas. In most cases the families of focus group participants had acquired different plots of land in a mixture of ways, including through inheritance, purchase, government allocation, clearing uncultivated land and renting. Inheritance came through both husbands and wives, and from mothers and fathers, and it was more common among people who were native to the villages we were in. Government land allocation was more common in villages where there had been a lot of inwards migration and resettlement of people from different ethnic groups, while clearing uncultivated or 'empty' land was more common in the more remote villages we visited, where there were fewer population pressures. Purchase and renting seemed to be increasingly common everywhere. See Table 1.2.

Although not shown in the table, some participants in our focus groups, such as many of the female banana plantation workers, had no land either because of being newcomers to their village or because they were still young and living with their parents or alternatively newly-establishing themselves in separate households. Those renting land tended to be the land-poor in general, and they were often renting from others in their villages who were native to the area and had acquired more land, in particular through inheritance. For example, among cassava farmers we spoke with, some of the Lao Loum families were renting out

Table 1.2 Some examples of smallholder landholdings among focus group participants

Farming family	Areas	Crops	Comments on means of acquisition
Cassava 1	1.2 ha	Paddy rice	This family inherited their paddy fields from the husband's father. Some of the land used for cassava was also inherited this way, some was allocated by the government and some was purchased from other villagers.
	2 ha	Cassava	
	2 ha	Cassava	
Cassava 2	1 ha	Paddy rice	This family purchased all their paddy fields and acquired their land used for cassava via government allocation when they were resettled into the village.
	4 ha	Cassava	
	1 ha	Cassava	
Tobacco 1	2 ha	Paddy rice	This family purchased all their land. They had been renting it previously, and saved up their income from tobacco farming to purchase it.
	8 rai	Tobacco	
Tobacco 2	2 ha	Paddy rice	This family rents the land used for growing tobacco and acquired the paddy fields through purchase.
	8 rai	Tobacco	
Tobacco 3	2 ha	Paddy rice	This family rents the land used for growing tobacco and inherited 1 ha of paddy fields each from the husband's mother and the wife's mother.
	10 rai	Tobacco	

land to poorer households in their village as many of the women had inherited land from their parents and thus these families had larger plots which they did not need all of for their own farming.

In general, our focus group participants felt that those with access to one or more plots of land (and capital) could engage more readily with investors as contract farmers of high-value crops, whether they owned or rented the land. Among the tobacco contract farmers we spoke with, a few who were land-poor were renting in land to grow tobacco, while others who were wealthier were renting in additional land to expand their tobacco production. However, those who were landless or had relatively less land, such as young people, poor people and ethnic minorities, generally thought they could only work on plantations or as casual labourers for other farmers – and we found it was notably women who were more likely to work as casual labourers, and younger women from ethnic minorities who were more likely to work on plantations.

Women's access to and control over land was in most cases mediated by cultural norms and this also had implications for their possibilities to engage as individuals with the agricultural investments described in the four cases above. For example, even where a family's plot was the wife's, the husband had usually signed any contract in accordance with local traditions of the male household head (and not due to company requirements), as was the case among both cassava and tobacco farmers.

While none of our cases involved the physical dispossession of people from their farms, the banana and jatropha plantations on land that was previously communal village land and the cassava farming on farmers' fallow land had either been used for NTFP collection or for shifting cultivation of upland rice. Diminished access to these forested areas overall, also due to investors' encroachment on additional land (jatropha case) and the more limited availability of time (cassava case), meant that women in particular lost access to NTFPs. This had felt consequences for their family's food situation as well as for their income-generating possibilities.

Gender dimensions to labour issues from agricultural investments also emerged clearly in our focus group discussions. Perceptions of labour requirements within contract farming varied by gender and suggested that, on balance, as with jatropha, cassava and tobacco farming, it specifically increased the burdens on women's time. Women bore to a large extent the additional burdens of tending the new crops and also, in the case of tobacco, of managing and taking care of casual labourers hired to help them.

Labour issues also caused broader problems for poorer families, as one of our provincial government informants elaborated:

> 2+3 increases the labour requirements for farming which means farmers need to hire casual labourers and find the money to pay them every day before they receive any money from the crops. This is a big problem for poor households… They can't hire people to help farm cassava or tobacco if they don't even have enough food to eat – where would they get the money?
>
> (as first cited in Daley *et al.*, 2013: 32–33)

Some of our focus group participants from families who could not afford to use casual labourers reported having performed casual labour for others. However, the majority of participants in our focus groups said they were too busy with their own farming to undertake any casual labour for others. For one older widow, who was a tobacco contract farmer and whose children had all left home, not having enough cash to hire casual labourers had become a considerable problem as she felt she could no longer keep up with the labour-intensive tobacco farming. In this case, household structure and the number of active members thus had implications for the use of casual labour as much as the availability of cash income. More generally, the high start-up costs of tobacco farming also made it potentially out of reach for the poorest households – including the 5% of agricultural households in Laos headed by women – who would not have the capital themselves and might have difficulties in obtaining the necessary bank loans to start operations. Likewise, as we saw with women whose families were starting up cassava farming and who were concerned about not being able to repay the debts they had incurred for the investor's provision of land-clearing services, capital requirements are as much of an issue as land and labour needs for many poorer farmers considering engaging with agricultural investors, particularly in contract farming.

Conclusion

In this chapter we have explored some of the gendered changes and consequences that are unfolding in rural areas of Lao PDR as women and men engage with new agricultural investments. Our fieldwork enabled us to sketch a nuanced picture of how different groups of women and men experienced in different ways the four investments we looked at. Our findings suggest that existing land and labour relations, and especially access to land, labour and capital, are intersecting with social differences of gender, age and ethnicity to underwrite processes of agrarian transformation as corporate capital increasingly penetrates rural Laos.

Because of the strength of the household in rural Laos, many of the gender differences we found were quite subtle and difficult to disentangle and would merit further in-depth research to fully unpack. At the same time, however, it was evident that, while some women were clearly benefiting from the opportunities offered by new agricultural investments, women in general were more disadvantaged than men because they were more heavily affected by reduced access to NTFPs and by increased time and labour burdens as their families took up farming new crops. Our fieldwork also indicated that the gender dimensions of individual agricultural investments depend on multiple factors, including, but not limited to, the type and structure of the business model, the practices of the company, the labour requirements of the crop and amount of land utilized, the socio-economic and cultural status and circumstances of the participating family, and the complexities of intra-household relations.

While in general large-scale land acquisitions remain a threat to rural people across the globe, some agricultural investments do create (or have the potential to create) new opportunities, as we found in Laos. However, the difficulty lies in ensuring that women and men, especially those from poorer households, will be able to benefit equally from such opportunities. Although gender equality is heavily promoted at policy level in Laos, and gender issues have been broadly incorporated into agricultural and investment policies, this has not yet taken hold in practice at provincial, district and village government levels. There also remain broader governance issues around large-scale land acquisitions and agricultural investments in Laos, including of institutional capacity, which lay outwith the scope of this chapter. The implementation of the *Voluntary Guidelines on the Responsible Governance of Tenure of Land, Fisheries and Forests in the Context of National Food Security* may offer an opportunity to address relevant gender concerns and issues around land concessions and agricultural investments nationally, but the real prospect of this happening depends on too many political factors for it to be assured. In Laos, as elsewhere in the global debate on land grabbing, the 'silences' on gender need both a critical mass of gendered insights and evidence from the field and enough politically powerful 'agents' with sufficient 'voice' if they are to have any real chance of being broken.

Notes

1   Fieldwork was carried out by Elizabeth Daley, Clara Mi Young Park, Boualapanh
    Soumpholpakdy, Khamsai Inthavong, Martha Osorio and Khamphoui Vasavathdy.
    We gratefully acknowledge the work of our whole team. The next few pages of the
    present chapter draw heavily on Daley *et al.*, 2013.
2   US$ 1 = 8,000 kip at the time of our fieldwork.

References

ADB, (2011a) *Country Partnership Strategy: Lao PDR, 2012–2016 – Sector Assessment
(Summary): Agriculture and Natural Resources*, Manila, Philippines: ADB.

ADB, (2011b) *Country Partnership Strategy: Lao PDR, 2012–2016 – Poverty Analysis
(Summary)*, Manila, Philippines: ADB.

Anseeuw, W., Alden Wily, L., Cotula, L. & Taylor, M., (2012) *Land Rights and the Rush
for Land: Findings of the Global Commercial Pressures on Land Research Project*, Rome:
ILC.

Behrman, J., Meinzen-Dick, R. & Quisumbing, A., (2012) 'The Gender Implications of
Large-scale Land Deals', *The Journal of Peasant Studies*, vol. 39 no. 1, pp. 49–79.

Bernstein, H., (2010) *Class Dynamics of Agrarian Change (Agrarian Change and Peasant
Studies Series)*, Black Point, Nova Scotia/Sterling, VA: Fernwood Publishing/ Kumarian
Press.

Borras, S.M.J., (2010) 'The Politics of Transnational Agrarian Movements', *Development
and Change*, vol. 41, no. 5, pp. 771–803.

Cotula, L., (2012) 'The International Political Economy of the Global Land Rush: A
Critical Appraisal of Trends, Scale, Geography and Drivers', *Journal of Peasant Studies*,
vol. 39, no. 3–4, pp. 649–680.

Daley, E., (2011) *Gendered Impacts of Commercial Pressures on Land*, Rome: ILC.

Daley, E., Osorio, M. & Park, C.M.Y., (2013) *The Gender and Equity Implications of Land-
Related Investments on Land Access and Labour and Income-Generating Opportunities. A
Case Study of Selected Agricultural Investments in Lao PDR*, Rome: FAO.

Daley, E. & Pallas, S., (2014) 'Women and Land Deals in Africa and Asia: Weighing the
Implications and Changing the Game', *Feminist Economics*, vol. 20, no. 1,
pp. 178–201.

Doss, C., Summerfield, G. & Tsikata, D., (2014) 'Gender, Land and Food Security',
Feminist Economics, vol. 20, no. 1, pp. 1–23.

Edelman, M., Oya, C. & Borras, S.M., (2013) 'Global Land Grabs: Historical Processes,
Theoretical and Methodological Implications and Current Trajectories', *Third World
Quarterly*, vol. 34, no. 9, pp. 1517–1531.

Fairhead, J., Leach, M. & Scoones, I., (2012) 'Green Grabbing: A New Appropriation of
Nature?', *Journal of Peasant Studies*, vol. 39, no. 2, pp. 237–261.

FAO, (2012) *SD Dimensions: Lao PDR*, Available: www.fao.org/sd/WPdirect/WPre0109.
htm [20 Jan. 2012].

FAO & MAF, (2010) *National Gender Profile of Agricultural Households 2010: Report based
on the Lao Expenditure and Consumption Surveys, National Agricultural Census and the
National Population Census*, Vientiane, Lao PDR: FAO and MAF.

Fraser, A., (2009) *Lao People's Democratic Republic: Agriculture and Natural Resources Sector
Need Assessment*, Manila, Philippines: ADB.

Government of Lao PDR, (1997) *Land Law, No. 01/97/NA*, Vientiane, Lao PDR: National Assembly.

Government of Lao PDR, (2003a) *Law on Land, No. 04/NA*, Vientiane, Lao PDR: National Assembly.

Government of Lao PDR (2003b) *Constitution of the LAO People's Democratic Republic*, Vientiane, Lao PDR: National Assembly of the LAO PDR.

Government of Lao PDR, (2004) *Law on Development and Protection of Women*, Vientiane, Lao PDR: National Assembly.

Government of Lao PDR, (2006) *National Strategy for the Advancement of Women*, Vientiane, Lao PDR: Prime Minister's Office.

Government of Lao PDR, (2007) *Resolution of the National Land Meeting 7th-8th May 2007, No. 06/PMO, 30th May 2007*, Vientiane, Lao PDR: Prime Minister's Office.

Hall, D., (2011) 'Land Grabs, Land Control, and Southeast Asian Crop Booms', *Journal of Peasant Studies*, vol. 38, no. 4, pp. 837–857.

Julia & White, B., (2012) 'Gendered Experiences of Dispossession: Oil Palm Expansion in a Dayak Hibun Community in West Kalimantan', *Journal of Peasant Studies*, vol. 39, no. 3–4, pp. 995–1016.

Mann, E. & Luangkhot, N., (2008) *Study on Women's Land and Property Rights under Customary or Traditional Tenure Systems in Five Ethnic Groups in Lao PDR, Land Policy Study No.13 under LLTP II*, May 2008, Vientiane, Lao PDR: GTZ.

Montemayor, R., (2011) *Overseas Farmland Investments in Selected Asian Countries*, Quezon City, Philippines: East Asia Rice Working Group.

Oya, C., (2013) 'The Land Rush and Classic Agrarian Questions of Capital and Labour: A Systematic Scoping Review of the Socioeconomic Impact of Land Grabs in Africa', *Third World Quarterly*, vol. 34, no. 9, pp. 1532–1557.

Schoenweger, O. & Üllenberg, A., (2009) *Foreign Direct Investment (FDI) in Land in the Lao PDR*, Eschborn, Germany: GTZ.

Sihavong, S., (2007) *Lao PDR Country Paper – Decision-Makers Meeting on Good Administration of Land, Tokyo, 21–22 June 2007*, Vientiane, Lao PDR: Department of Land.

Sipaseuth, P. & Hunt, G., (n.d.) *Customary Land Rights in Laos – An Overview: Communities, Land, Forest and the Clash of Big Agri-Business in one of the Last Frontiers of South East Asian Wilderness*, Vientiane, Lao PDR: JVC Laos.

UNCTAD, (2013) *World Investment Report 2013. Global Value Chains: Investment and Trade for Development*, Geneva.

Vermeulen, S. & Cotula, L., (2010) 'Over the Heads of Local People: Consultation, Consent, and Recompense in Large-scale Land Deals for Biofuels Projects in Africa', *Journal of Peasant Studies*, vol. 37, no. 4, pp. 899–916.

Wehrmann, B., Souphida, P. & Sithipanhya, N., (2007) *Rural Land Markets in Lao PDR*, PowerPoint presentation for Lao–German Land Policy Development Project, Vientiane, Lao PDR, 22 May 2007.

White, B. *et al.*, (2012) 'The New Enclosures: Critical Perspectives on Corporate Land Deals', *Journal of Peasant Studies*, vol. 39, no. 3-4, pp. 619–647.

World Bank, (2009) *Lao PDR Economic Monitor 2009 End-Year Update: Lao PDR Recent Economic Developments*. Vientiane, Lao PDR: World Bank.

2 Women and benefit-sharing in large-scale land deals

A mining case study from Papua New Guinea

Nicholas Menzies and Georgia Harley[1]

Introduction

The global land rush has placed heightened attention on the impacts of large-scale land acquisition and use in developing countries, in particular for the communities who live on and near the land concerned (Deininger *et al.*, 2011). Large-scale mining activities in developing countries pre-date the global land rush, yet raise many of the same issues of asymmetric negotiations, rapid social change, environmental damage, and inequities in cost- and benefit-sharing within and between communities (Franks *et al.*, 2013). One axis of inequity in large-scale land acquisition is the differential experiences and outcomes for women and men. Unlike the gendered impacts of mining (World Bank, 2009; O'Faircheallaigh, 2012), the gendered impacts of the global land rush have been relatively understudied (Behrman *et al.*, 2011) and few examples exist of positive processes and outcomes for women.

We highlight here a *relatively* more promising example—from the Ok Tedi mine in Papua New Guinea (PNG)—which may serve to inform research, policy, and practice regarding large-scale land deals globally. Women affected by the operations of the Ok Tedi mine have been able to carve out a greater role in the negotiation process and a greater share of benefits than seen at other mines in PNG (and, as far as we can ascertain, anywhere else in the world). The Ok Tedi women have secured these rights in binding agreements, which is quite some achievement in the context of acute gender inequality in PNG and the prior experience of women in other mining communities. The reasons for the *relatively* more positive outcome for women on the negotiation side include a well-structured agreement-making process (established specifically to address a troubled history of community–mine relations) and the existence of strong female leadership. Despite the negotiation gains, the realization of these benefits into tangible development outcomes has been much more problematic, as it is with development more generally in the mine-impacted area, and indeed PNG broadly.

Globally, the requirement for formal agreements between large-scale land users and impacted residents, particularly in mining, is growing in law and regulation. These agreements are also increasingly understood by industry and government as useful in establishing durable governance arrangements, thus reducing the chance of violent conflict and improving the prospects for development. The experience with mining, in particular the case of Ok Tedi presented here, offers some lessons on how to establish such agreements and in particular to address the gendered impacts of large-scale land use. Among other things, the Ok Tedi case suggests the importance of: devoting considerable time to the agreement negotiation phase; making the "conflict and development" case to investors for involving women; using periodic renegotiation clauses to step up the position of women over time; and understanding the limitations of agreements in addressing the constraints of the underlying development context.

This chapter is based on qualitative research undertaken in mine-affected villages and with relevant government, company and nongovernment officials. Field research was undertaken in five of the nine CMCA trust regions in December 2011. Villages visited were "mine villages" (Finalbin); "river villages" (Atkamba, Moian, and Yogi); and "road villages" (Ningerum). All villages were in North Fly District (except for Moian, which is in Middle Fly) and impacts and conditions in the Middle and South Fly districts are understood to be different (Figure 2.1).

Research included document analysis, focus-group discussions and key informant interviews. Researchers interviewed facilitators and delegates who participated in the 2007 CMCA negotiations, impacted communities (including separate focus groups with women, men, and young people), government officials (at national, provincial, and local levels), civil society representatives, Ok Tedi Mining Limited (OTML) representatives (front-line staff and management), representatives of Ok Tedi Fly River Development Foundation/Ok Tedi Fly River Development Program (OTDF/OTFRDP) and the Papua New Guinea Sustainable Development Program (PNGSDP). Research was conducted by a multi-disciplinary team of local and international researchers of mixed genders. It is supplemented with observations of the community–company–state renegotiation process that took place in December 2012.

The chapter continues by providing a background to PNG, its dealings with mining agreements and the history of Ok Tedi. This is followed by a section on the 2007 agreement negotiation and implementation processes, which is succeeded by an analysis of the 2012 negotiation process. It ends with some suggestions for broader practice.

Background: PNG, Ok Tedi, communities, and gender

Since independence in 1975, PNG's cash economy has been heavily reliant on extractive industries. Papua New Guinea is rich in natural resources, particularly minerals (copper, gold, silver, and nickel), oil and gas. Alongside the fairly sophisticated extractives sector, the predominantly rural population relies largely on subsistence and semi-subsistence agriculture. As in many resource-dependent economies, high rates of economic growth, increased national revenues, and per capita GDP—especially over the past decade in PNG—have not translated into measurable improvements in incomes, livelihoods, and individual well-being for

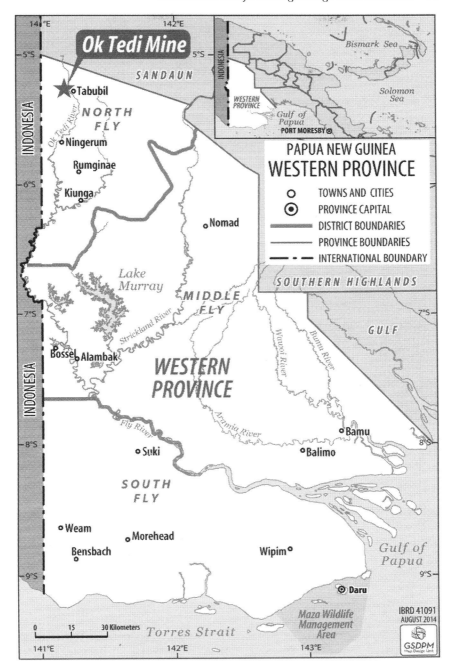

Figure 2.1 Ok Tedi Mine, Western Province, Papua New Guinea
Source: Menzies and Harley 2012

the vast majority of PNG's population, especially women. Human development outcomes, as indicated by material and food poverty rates, as well as childhood malnutrition, changed little between the mid 1990s and 2010, with PNG ranked 157th out of 187 countries in 2013 Human Development Index. Basic infrastructure and service delivery are severely limited, particularly in remote areas.

The mining regulatory regime in PNG provides a relatively strong position for communities affected by mining operations compared to many countries. Agreements (known as memoranda of agreement – MoAs) between the state (including local and provincial governments), companies, and impacted communities are required prior to an operation proceeding and commonly include significant community benefits, such as a share of royalties and an equity stake in the mining operation. Provinces and local governments also regularly receive sizeable shares of mining revenues, yet service delivery in mining-affected provinces remains weak and such provinces are some of the worst served in the country. The requirement for MoAs arose largely in response to conflict around the Panguna copper mine on the island of Bougainville during the period 1988–1997. The conflict began with localized acts of sabotage against the mine and escalated into a conflict with the state (as well as among different groups on Bougainville) resulting in an agreement for a referendum on whether the island should remain part of the state of PNG. Since the institution of the first MoA at the Porgera gold mine in Enga Province in 1989, subsequent agreements have been part of a process driving a greater share of revenues being distributed to the provinces, districts, local-level governments, and communities that host the projects from which the revenues are derived—in response to the national government's failure to deliver development and at the expense of the national government (Government of PNG, 2003).

Women in PNG face discrimination and lag behind men in most facets of life, with PNG ranked 135th out of 149 countries in 2013 Gender Inequality Index. Roughly two-thirds of women experience gender-based violence in their lifetimes, educational outcomes are limited, and maternal mortality rates are among the highest in the Asia-Pacific region. Only seven women have been elected to Parliament since 1975, and few sit on the boards of private corporate entities. Although laws allow women's representatives to be nominated to provincial and local governments, their representation is often tokenistic and their participation appears to be very limited (World Bank, 2012a). The Constitution provides for gender equity and equality, but customary law, recognized by the Constitution, as well as the application of state law, routinely discriminate against women in relation to rights and property (World Bank, 2012a). Unsurprisingly, therefore, women's voices are rarely represented in agreement-making around natural resources. Women control few, if any, benefits, while bearing a disproportionate burden of the social and environmental costs of mining (Macintyre, 2003; Macintyre, 2011).

The Ok Tedi mine is a very large open-pit copper and gold mine located in mountainous terrain in the far western corner of PNG's Western Province, near the border with West Papua (Indonesia). Residents impacted by the mine number more than 100,000 and are spread over a vast terrain of rivers and lakes; they are from many socio-linguistic groups with almost no road connections between them. Poverty rates are high and access to health and education low. The government is largely absent and the mining company—Ok Tedi Mining Limited—is often seen as "the only real government in town" (Burton, 2011). Collective action among impacted residents is challenging, given their dispersed nature, the lack of infrastructure and poor communications. The topographical and institutional landscape makes this an extremely challenging development context. And as noted above, gender inequality is particularly profound in this region (Ok Tedi Development Foundation, 2007; Cammack, 2009).

Ok Tedi commenced production in 1984. Relationships between the mine and affected communities have long been fractious. The dispute predominantly concerns the significant environmental damage caused by the mine's disposal of waste into the Ok Tedi and Fly River systems. Issues of concern include loss of fish stocks and water sources, increased flooding leading to forest and food crop destruction, a rise in mosquito-borne diseases and excessive dust from mining truck convoys on the road from the mine to the river port in Kiunga. According to independent experts, even if the mine were to stop using the river for tailings disposal, the riverine impacts would likely be felt for "several hundred years" (Tingay, 2007). These impacts are borne more heavily by women, who are traditionally responsible for crop production and water management. In 1994, affected communities, with the support of local and international environmental NGOs, mounted a class action lawsuit against the mine's then major shareholder, BHP Pty Ltd, in the Supreme Court of Victoria, Australia (where BHP is registered). The case was settled with a US$500 million payout and a commitment to contain mine waste disposal (Banks and Ballard, 1997). The case drew international interest at the time for its use of tort law to secure the accountability of a multinational company for environmental damages. (Since the Ok Tedi case, class actions have been pursued against Freeport-McMoRan's Grasberg mine in West Papua, Indonesia; Exxon-Mobil's natural gas installation in Aceh, Indonesia; Unocal's oil pipeline in Burma; Shell's petroleum operations in the Nigerian delta; Rio Tinto's copper mine on Bougainville; Texaco's petroleum operations in the Ecuadorian Amazon; and Thor Chemical's use of mercury-based chemicals in South Africa.) At Ok Tedi, mine waste continued to be disposed down the river systems, and community complaints persisted. Amidst concern about ongoing environmental liability, BHP queried whether the mine should close. As the single largest contributor to the national PNG economy, the national government and Western Province had (and still have), a strong interest in its continued operation. For example, in 2010, export earnings represented 18 percent of the country's GDP, and taxes and dividends to the national government represented 18 percent of tax revenue and 17 percent of government domestic revenue.

To address these issues a deal was put together with two key elements: first, in return for immunity from prosecution for the environmental damage, BHP would divest its shareholding to a development trust, the PNGSDP; second, the consent of all impacted communities would be sought and recorded in agreements (purportedly to be called "community mine closure agreements" but signed as "community mine continuation agreements" CMCAs). PNGSDP was registered in Singapore on the grounds that this would isolate it from day-to-day politics in PNG. What wasn't widely understood was that control of the trust remained in the hands of BHP through appointment of the trustees. The PNGSDP was set up to comprise a long-term fund and a development fund. The long-term fund invests two-thirds of the net income received from OTML in low-risk investments for the future benefit of the people of PNG following a mine closure. The development fund invests one-third of net income received from OTML in sustainable development projects. Two-thirds of those projects are national and one-third is focused in Western Province. The PNGSDP investments in Western Province include communities affected by the Ok Tedi mine, which, with other mine-related and government sources, creates a complex web of real and potential benefits for communities. In addition to five main sources under the CMCAs (discussed below), other sources of local projects include the Alice River Trust (set up after the class action lawsuit), mine charitable projects, mine-implemented tax-credit projects, member-of-parliament-controlled constituency development fund projects, and local government projects. These strands have been further complicated with legislation passed in 2013 under which the national government took over PNGSDP and its primary asset, OTML.

The first CMCAs were negotiated in 2001 and then revised in 2006–07. Most recently in 2012, they were revised again as Mine Life Extension Agreements. The agreements now cover more than 100,000 people in 156 villages stretching from the villages in the Highlands around the mine site near Tabubil, along the Ok Tedi and Fly Rivers, to the mouth of the Fly (see Figure 2.1).

Negotiation of the 2007 Agreement

This history of large- and small-scale conflict around mines across PNG (especially at Panguna), the particularly fraught history of dispute, litigation, and engagement at Ok Tedi, and the advanced stage of the mine's life were critical factors contributing to the negotiation process that emerged in 2007. For the 2007 negotiations, with over twenty years of experience in the area and production ongoing during negotiations, the mine operator suffered fewer of the time pressures that mining companies often face when negotiating agreements prior to the commencement of operations. Mine management also responded to the international pressure (from NGOs and multilateral organizations) that the environmental damage and litigation had brought, with a desire to leave an improved legacy.

Although not without its challenges, the 2007 CMCA negotiation was in many ways a model process, and the quality of the process was important to women's ability to secure the deal they did. Mine management engaged an Australian public affairs consulting firm, Pax Populous, to design the framework for an inclusive negotiation process. Independent international (the Keystone Center) and local (the Tanorama Network) facilitators were then selected jointly by the mine and community representatives to facilitate the process. Independent legal, environmental, and accounting advice was engaged for communities at no cost to them. Prominent former chief justice of the PNG Supreme Court, Sir Arnold Amet, was appointed as the independent legal observer; he became an adviser to the affected communities. The top-level negotiations were held in Tabubil, the township at the base of the mine. Regional-level meetings were held in each of three impacted sub-regions and village meetings in almost all the impacted villages. Delegates to regional meetings were directly elected by their village constituencies, and the representatives at the top-level negotiating table in Tabubil were elected from the regional meetings. The negotiation lasted eighteen months and cost K7 million (US$3.4 million), paid for by the mine. This broadly consultative process, the significant time set aside for it, and the independent facilitation and advice available all helped to ameliorate information asymmetries and build trust.

The negotiated outcome—the 2007 CMCA Agreement—created five main benefit streams for impacted communities:

1   cash compensation delivered in annual payments;
2   small-scale village projects (such as water tanks, outboard motors, and animal husbandry);
3   larger investments (such as passenger and cargo vessels that serve the Fly River, housing, and passenger planes);
4   school scholarships;
5   and a women and children's fund (the focus of this chapter).

To address what was seen by communities as poor implementation up to that point, key tenets of the 2007 Agreement were new structures to ensure "a high level of ownership and decision-making power over resources, programs, and projects" by impacted communities. In addition to existing village planning committees which suggest projects, and eight regional trusts which review and approve proposals, the 2007 Agreement created an overarching coordination body, the Ok Tedi Fly River Development Foundation (OTFRDF). OTFRDF was meant to be controlled by beneficiaries and assume final responsibility for assessing, implementing, and monitoring projects suggested by beneficiaries. In practice this did not happen, however, and control was maintained by OTML's Ok Tedi Development Foundation.

Women's engagement in the negotiations

The quality of the overall negotiation process provided an opening for women to exercise agency. Yet initially women were not included at all. In the negotiation's early stages, all of the community delegates were men. In deference to their understanding of local custom, the independent facilitators initially did not challenge this situation. As one facilitator noted: "we had to be very careful not to be perceived as undermining local authority or customs." Instead, facilitators asked the male representatives to ensure that they represented the views of their entire regional group, including women and children. The onsite nature of the discussions meant that, at least for the regional meetings, some women were able to sit outside the negotiations and listen. In PNG, it was common up to this point (and indeed subsequently) for mine negotiations to take place far from the site, often on far removed islands.

Several months into the negotiations, the facilitators realized that women's views were not being represented. Company managers also understood that the CMCAs would be more likely to achieve development outcomes if women were involved. One senior company representative reflected that: "there would be a payout at the end, and there was some concern that the men may drink that away, or buy jeeps, cigarettes etc." An observer noted that: "the women were so involved in health and education, they would end up being responsible for implementing social projects in the region." Mining company officials were also of the view that improved development outcomes could foster community support in favor of the mine and reduce the chances of mining-related complaints. For these reasons it was recognized that women's voices needed be heard. The combined support of the company and independent facilitators was critical in convincing the male delegates and the national government that women should be present in the negotiating process.

With negotiations at a midpoint, a women's delegation was established. The delegation was structured with a single delegate at the main negotiating table of more than thirty representatives and a twenty-member women's caucus that gathered outside of the meeting to formulate negotiating positions. As one facilitator noted: "the women were so happy that they had a seat at the table— they felt they had won something already."

Mrs. Ume Wainetti was identified as the women's delegate. Based in the PNG capital Port Moresby, Mrs. Wainetti was from the impacted region, yet also had a national profile as former chair of the National Council of Women and current convener of the national Family and Sexual Violence Action Committee. In negotiations, Wainetti used cultural cues and tactics, describing herself as a "sister and aunty" to other delegates. Coming from the impacted area, Wainetti could be both more assertive and employ a range of emotions with the male village representatives more freely than an outsider. Wainetti ensured that she sat next to the mining company Managing Director at key moments. Presentations of health statistics for women and children, combined with emotive personal stories, helped to influence the men involved in the discussions. One facilitator observed that Wainetti was "one of the best negotiators at the table." Her competence in this regard likely stemmed from a combination of tertiary education (when most of the other delegates had only primary level), national status and local roots, and substantial leadership and negotiation skills acquired in national and international settings.

The women's caucus brought together at least two women from each of nine impacted areas, along with the Provincial Government's women's officer. The caucus worked closely with the facilitators and the mine's gender desk, which had received prior assistance from a national-level World Bank-supported Women in Mining project and had already assessed women's development needs in the impact area. In a side workshop held over several days, mine staff and independent experts provided information about the overall mining operation, environmental impacts and the benefit envelope. Wainetti, the facilitators, and the mine outreach team also visited women in mine-affected villages, exchanging views and developing a shared negotiating position. As one facilitator put it: "they [the women's caucus] were great because they were great leaders, great negotiators, not just because they were women."

Initially, the women's key proposal was that a minimum of 5 percent of all funds be specifically set aside (i.e., ring-fenced) for the benefit of women and children. Wainetti described how women "wanted a separate pot to make sure that women and kids were not forgotten as usual." The proposal was not intended to exclude women from the remainder of the benefits, nor was it intended to be a maximum amount that women would receive. Rather it was designed to be a separate minimum amount of funding that would be managed by women and prioritized for specific initiatives for women and children. Drawing on personal relationships and networks, the women's caucus approached influential players out of session to seek their support for the proposal. Elder statesman and legal observer, Sir Arnold Amet, supported the idea and suggested that they raise the figure. The delegation also secured the support of the mine's senior management. A figure of 10 percent was ultimately chosen on the basis that the male beneficiaries would be unlikely to accept more and that 10 percent might fly "under the radar" at the negotiating table.

In tabling the proposal, Wainetti emphasized the complementary roles of women and men in the community and stressed that "we are not asking for much, only 10 percent." Following a silence, Amet spoke in support of the proposal, followed by a mining company representative. One facilitator described how "the backing of prestigious people was critical to the proposal being supported in the room." No questions or concerns were raised, and the proposal was adopted.

In addition to the earmarked fund, women secured further outcomes on an ad hoc basis throughout the negotiations. Cash compensation payments, which had previously been deposited into clan-level accounts controlled by men and subject to persistent concerns regarding misuse and leakage, were now required to be deposited into family bank accounts, to which women were encouraged by the mine to be signatories. Half of all educational scholarships for primary, secondary, and tertiary schooling were to be awarded to women and girls, and women were required to comprise half of the membership of the scholarship selection panels. Further, women were to be represented in the CMCA's key local governance bodies, called Village Planning Committees, which identify, plan, and allocate village-level CMCA projects funded by the CMCA. Each committee was now obliged to have two women representatives out of the five members (or three women out of a maximum of eight members). Lastly, women were to be represented on each of nine regional trusts and on the board of directors of the Ok Tedi Fly River Development Program, the foundation responsible for the agreement's implementation. The 2007 Agreement provides more explicit entitlements for women than any other mining agreement in PNG or, as far as can be discerned, globally.

However, the deal alone is not necessarily a success for women. Ring-fencing can be seen as "both a victory for women and a failure" (Sharp, 2008). On the upside, ring-fencing promises to improve the status of women by offering control over a specific allocation of funds, which could lead to stronger household decision-making. Research suggests that having women in decision-making positions can in itself generate positive spillover effects, such as changed investment priorities, changed attitudes toward women and girls, and differences in the reporting of crimes against women (Chattopadhyay and Duflo, 2004; Beaman *et al.*, 2008). On the other hand, it is hard to argue on its face that control of 10 percent of all benefits for more than two-thirds of the population (once children are included) is fair. Further, if ring-fencing entrenches norms that women are somehow undeserving of equal participation and equal benefit-sharing and excludes women from the remaining 90 percent of benefits, then its effectiveness should be questioned. This is, in part, an empirical question that can only be assessed in the context of implementation.

Implementation of the 2007 Agreement

The novelty of the deal secured for women in the 2007 Agreement raised high expectations but experience during implementation has been mixed.

Informed awareness of the women's deal is low

Field research in 2011, four years after the signing of the Agreement, revealed that in many villages, a wide cross-section of women and men had heard about "the women's 10 percent," but no beneficiaries were able to explain how much money was available, the process by which projects were selected, or what had been approved to date. Several women complained that they had not received guidance or training on how to access the benefits. "How do we get the money?... It is very hard…Since the launching, nobody knows what has happened with the 10 percent. There are no courses on how to apply for the money. Mothers are in a complete blackout." It did not appear as though men were resisting the new arrangement, with none expressing any resentment or complaints about the women's 10 percent other than a critique that the women "weren't using their money." This may suggest a "normalization" of women having control over some portion of resources.

The lack of understanding of the women's fund echoes broader confusion among communities about the CMCAs in general; *mipela no clia* ("We don't understand/we're not clear") being the most common refrain when asked about the Agreement. Few people could explain the process for CMCA project approval. Even members of the Village Planning Committees did not appear to understand how much money was available for CMCA projects in their village or region. Beneficiaries repeatedly expressed a desire for written information—"in black and white"—to dispel rumors and misinformation, build awareness, and foster accountability.

Representatives of the foundation note the information problem, but state that "we can't get information to 90,000 people." Indeed, the geographical challenges are considerable. The foundation relies on Village Planning Committee chairs to be conduits to the rest of their committee and the village at large, and minutes of regional meetings, notices and verbal updates are sent to the chairs for dissemination. One mine representative explained low levels of beneficiary awareness as a function of community "backwardness," perhaps reflecting an assumption that communities with little exposure to sophisticated financial topics are not able to understand the arrangements. This conclusion—that awareness is inherently and permanently constrained by the exotic novelty of trust funds and financial flows—is not uncommon on the part of community-development technocrats and resource-company staff. But global experience shows that targeted and skillful discussions at the community level can indeed empower village people to understand and engage effectively quite quickly (Nish and Bice, 2012).

The ring-fenced women's fund is operational, but impacts are not widely felt

In accordance with the Agreement, a separate process was established to make decisions about the women's ring-fenced benefits, governed by all-women groups elected by women from the beneficiary villages. From 2007 to 2010, K69.8 million (US$34 million) was set aside for the women's fund. As of 2012, the major spending decision was to invest in three learning centers, which are intended to build women's capacity to actively engage in development processes and ensure good use of their funds. As of 2011, only one learning center was open. Of the money that has been allocated, it is likely that much of it remains unspent—with underspending being a problem plaguing the general funds as well. In one region (covering eighteen villages), approximately US$20 million of general CMCA funds (that is, not the women's fund) remained unspent as of September 2011, and figures show up to half of individual village funds have also not been spent. One trustee attributed the chronic underspend to the failure of villagers to submit project proposals. Clearly, a targeted effort to improve, simplify, and streamline the proposal process could yield results. After all, underspending is plainly not due to lack of need as the region faces basic service failures and profound development challenges.

In the villages, however, very few women have heard of the training centers, and neither women nor men reported feeling any benefits from the 10 percent deal. Village women expressed concerns that they are not being faithfully represented in the women's bodies to decide on use of the money. Many of the women decision-makers are the wives of local ward councilors or Village Planning Committee chairmen, suggesting that elite divides may compound existing gender inequality. In one village, women complained that their representative on the regional women's group had moved away, was no longer resident in the village, and did not provide any feedback from meetings. Such an impression is reflected more broadly in the functioning of Village Planning Committees, which appear beset by challenges related to information, coordination, and representation. Communities report that committees do not faithfully represent community interests, "hoarding information and keeping benefits" for personal or family gain. Village Planning Committee chairs are frequently reported to have moved away into towns, limiting their ability to identify community needs, convey information, and be held accountable for decisions made.

Family bank accounts show promise

The introduction of family bank accounts has been somewhat of a success story in this otherwise sobering implementation tale. Disbursing the cash compensation component of the 2007 Agreement into family bank accounts—instead of clan accounts—appears to be having a positive impact, improving access to resources by both women and youth. Unlike the project component, there was general understanding of the entitlements, which varies per village, but was around K400 (US$200) per person per year (in 2011), including for children. There is also a fair understanding of the timing of the payments. In most of the villages visited for this research, families have opened bank accounts and women are cosignatories to those accounts. Women reported much greater access to money than under the previous system of clan accounts, where money would 'disappear.' Women also claim to spend more productively than men, though this has not been independently verified. Some youth also reported receiving their entitlements in cash from their parents.

Even so, villagers face high transaction costs in accessing their compensation. Like many parts of PNG, access to banking facilities in the CMCA area is extremely limited. Beneficiaries must travel to one of only three bank locations in the whole impacted area and travel costs are high. In one example, the cost of transport alone constitutes more than 15 percent of the annual compensation payment. Initial plans to provide banking in boats along the river were shelved due to security concerns. Mobile phone-facilitated payments have yet to reach the CMCA area, although the rollout of mobile towers offers promise for the future.

Despite the benefits of family bank accounts, they appear not to have increased formal savings. The foundation, mine, and villagers report that beneficiaries routinely withdraw the annual cash compensation amount in full as soon as it is deposited. Monthly account-keeping fees of K7 (US$3.40) reduce the incentive of families to save money through the banking system. The full withdrawal of funds also poses administrative burdens because this action automatically closes the account, which then needs to be reopened to receive the following year's payment.

Implementation of the scholarship scheme has been partially successful

The implementation of the scholarship program has occurred in accordance with the letter of the Agreement, but its impact has been less than foreshadowed. Scholarships have been awarded for primary, secondary, and tertiary education in PNG. Full scholarships are awarded to younger students; for older students, the amount is dependent on the student's scholastic achievement the previous year. This rubric is widely understood by beneficiaries and supported. At the time of the research, women made up half of the members on the scholarship selection panels covered. However, the selection process requires little discretion—in practice, the money set aside for scholarships each year has been greater than the number of applications, so the selection panel simply identifies whether an applicant is from a CMCA village. In practice, less than 50 percent of the scholarships are awarded to girls because fewer girls apply. Boys are often preferred for educational opportunities because a girl's productive capacity and eventual "bride price" payment regularly factor into the decision whether to send her a long distance for formal education. Furthermore, few schools have boarding facilities, and parents express reluctance to send young girls to stay with relatives due to security and financial concerns. More broadly, villagers expressed worry at the lack of economic opportunities in the region for all scholarship recipients (and others) after graduation. Few graduates return to the impacted area, raising concern for future local economic development.

Women continue to be under-represented in decision-making structures

In each village visited for the research in 2011, the Village Planning Committee included only one woman rather than the two (or three) required under the Agreement. As noted above, in most cases, the women's representative is the wife or family member of a ward councilor, Village Planning Committee chairman, or other elite male. No committee chairs were women. In the villages visited, few women reported being aware of what the Village Planning Committee does and only a handful participate in planning for CMCA village projects. Finally, the requisite three women have not been appointed to the board of the foundation. Indeed, prior to the national government assuming ownership of PNGSDP in 2013, there were no voting beneficiary representatives—male or female—on the board. Furthermore, the CMCA requirement for the mine to transfer equity to the foundation (for the benefit of the impacted communities) has not occurred. These missed opportunities prevent the foundation from realizing its commitment to ensure the "high level of community ownership" required in the 2007 Agreement.

The broader impacts of the deal have not yet accrued

The strong leadership demonstrated by women during the early negotiation phase has not been present during the implementation phase. After a change in women's leadership, interviews revealed that the CMCA area lacks a cadre of women who demonstrate a similar rigor and collective agency in implementation than the women's delegation demonstrated that one time in Tabubil in 2007. There are a few positive spillovers for women from the CMCAs, with representatives of the mine and foundation reporting increased attendance and assertiveness of women in community consultations. However, village women report few changes in their material circumstances, and there are few, if any, signs of greater entrepreneurship, participation in broader political life, or increased bargaining power. The anticipated empowerment gains appear not to have accrued.

This lack of spillovers is reflected in overall implementation of the agreement. Between 2001 and 2011, more than K1 billion (almost US$500 million at today's rates) accrued to CMCA communities (with another K1 billion to the six villages immediately surrounding the mine site). Regional coordinators for the foundation report being "treated like the MP" given the amounts of money they oversee. Despite the significant financial flows associated with the mine, there are few visible projects in CMCA villages, basic infrastructure and service delivery are severely limited, rates of poverty are high, and health and education indicators are poor—with women tending to be worse off than men. Some reasons for the lack of development are those that plague participatory and community development generally (see, for example, Mansuri and Rao, 2013), such as slow rollout of the foundation and underspending, intra-village divisions, poor village-level decision-making, and elite capture. There are, however, by way of context very few observable projects funded from other sources, such as local government or from MP-controlled constituency development funds.

2012 renegotiation: for better or worse?

In line with the original 2001 Agreement's provision for five-yearly reviews (a common aspect of many mining agreements), in 2012 the impacted communities came together to negotiate once more—this in the context of whether the life of the mine should be extended. The negotiating process differed somewhat from 2007. The nine regions that comprise the mine-affected communities each negotiated separate agreements. Thus instead of one negotiating table, there were nine.

However, continuity prevailed in other aspects, and the process was another example of good practice. In all, the negotiation process took three years with the final stage lasting five weeks, again being held on-site in Tabubil. Tanorama, the local company that helped facilitate the 2007 negotiation, facilitated the 2012 negotiations as well (this time without an international counterpart) and were thus able to draw on extensive corporate memory, knowledge of the 2007 process, and longstanding relationships with the negotiating parties. Independent observers were again brought in to ensure the process adhered to agreed guiding principles (though different individuals were used), but there was no access to independent professional advice.

Women's engagement in the negotiating process

This time around, women were represented in greater numbers. Unlike the one women's delegate in 2007, in 2012 three women represented each of eight affected regions (with the ninth region represented by six women). In total, thirty women sat around the nine negotiating tables in Tabubil to represent the interests of women and children in the negotiating process. These women had between six to ten years of education, and some had received additional vocational and technical training. The women present were the President and Vice-President of the women's fund regional associations, and the women's representative on each of the regional trusts. Despite the increase in the number of women, with 197 beneficiary negotiators in total, women made up only 15 percent of the representatives.

The negotiated outcome

At each negotiating table, the issue of the "women's 10 percent" was reopened and in all negotiations women sought an increase in the percentage. In seven of the nine mine life extension (MLE) Agreements, the quantum of ring-fenced funds dedicated to women increased, with the new average amount being 14 percent. In two of the nine regions, the figure rose as high as 18 percent and 18.24 percent. The women were careful to make arguments that the money would be for the benefit of the community as a whole, and often used male allies (whose participation had been secured ahead of the meetings) to make their case. The men also used the prospect of an increase in the proportion going to women and children to make the case to the mining company that the overall amount should be increased. It appears that the training women received, and the planning and budgeting experience gained from sitting on regional bodies as a result of the 2007 Agreement, increased the skill and boldness of the women negotiators. Further, the fact that the independent facilitators were women increased the comfort of the women's representatives to ask questions and speak out (Popoitai and Ofosu-Amaah, 2014).

So, was the renegotiation a success for these women? On the one hand, the increase in quantum reflects a better-negotiated outcome than that secured in 2007. One could see 2007 as a toehold that has been built on, with possibly further increases to come in future agreements. And in the context of entrenched gender inequality in PNG's Western Province, the women themselves described the outcome as a "hard-fought win" (Popoitai and Ofosu-Amaah, 2014). On the other hand, it could be seen as a pyrrhic victory. The MLE negotiations did not address the implementation challenges that have plagued the CMCA process to date. Implementation issues were recognized by the women negotiators, yet concrete changes to address elite capture, awareness and transparency, intra-community divisions, and other challenges failed to make it into the MLE agreement. Increasing quantum may be irrelevant to the lived experience of Ok Tedi's marginalized women, while existing funds remain under-spent and persistent implementation challenges prevent the realization of the fund's goals.

Suggestions for strengthening women's engagement in company–community agreements

With a view to informing future policy and practice that improves women's agency and development outcomes for all, the following suggestions from the Ok Tedi case are provided to those engaging in community–company natural resource agreements. A thorough analysis of the political dynamics peculiar to each context will reveal whether and how the following might be useful and feasible.

Guidance for the negotiation phase

First, industry operators can be powerful allies for women. Increasingly, companies see the business case for including and empowering women beneficiaries (Rio Tinto, 2010). Stronger roles for women—including as company employees—may be associated with reduced risk of conflict and increased stability of production. Women should focus on highlighting how their participation increases efficiency in the use of funds and fosters opportunities to generate positive development outcomes, while also reducing the risks of complaint, conflict, and disruption of production.

Second, educated women's representatives who are able to combine both local ties with national or international experience can be particularly effective, especially when supported by women's caucuses. Separate caucusing sessions for women, alongside the primary negotiating stream, allow information to be shared, capacity to be built, and negotiating strategy to be developed.

Third, independent facilitators and advisors (e.g. environmental, legal, and financial) can play an influential role. They can start to address asymmetries of information and power, build trust, and ultimately construct more equitable deals. Equitable deals can be more durable, thus creating more stable operating conditions for investors and benefit streams for the state (Franks *et al.*, 2014).

Fourth, simple agreements can have value in themselves. A complex web of benefit streams can undermine accountability by making it difficult for beneficiaries to understand their entitlements and know who is responsible for delivering what, let alone demanding performance if it is not delivered. Complexity provides space for elites to exploit community benefits for personal gain; and, over time, confusion and elite capture can breed tension and conflict.

Guidance for the implementation phase

First, family bank accounts (with women as cosignatories) for cash payments can enhance women's control within households. Opportunities exist to incentivize savings, for instance, by instituting a "bonus" compensation payment or matching grant to accounts that retain an operating balance. In countries like PNG that have an increasingly interested banking sector keen to exploit rapidly increasing teledensity and a regulator focused on financial inclusion the potential for pilot programs that address the constraints outlined here is significant.

Second, while educated women are critical, setting aside scholarships for girls, and having women on scholarship selection panels, may not be enough to overcome cultural and logistical barriers. Further incentives could be built in to enhance gender equality of educational opportunities, such as a requirement that boys' scholarships are conditional on a matching number of girls' scholarships, and supplementary financing for special provisions for girls' safety and security while attending school away from home.

Third, information cannot be expected to trickle down from local elites. Public, written information can quickly dispel myths and reinforce accountability. This can included information about benefit procedures, amounts, dates, and feedback/grievance channels posted in public places, such as community halls, health clinics, schools, and churches, and posters and pamphlets distributed widely, summarizing information in lay terms. Mobile phones can also to be used to convey information.

Fourth, establish effective pathways for redress. Structured feedback and grievance processes ensure that those responsible for project implementation have better information on activity performance and challenges. Processes with alternative channels allow beneficiaries to bypass their local representatives, who may be the subject of complaint.

Conclusion

The prevailing gender asset gap and the current global extractives boom highlight the need to engage women more proactively in agreement-making and support them to exercise greater agency over those resources. In this context, the processes and outcomes of the 2007 and 2012 negotiations for the Ok Tedi community–company–state agreements are an innovation. In 2007, women secured rights, including control over a portion of the total benefits, in legally enforceable mining agreements not seen anywhere in the world. This was achieved in the context of considerable underlying gender inequality. The positive evolution between the 2007 and 2012 agreements illustrates how an initial foothold can be exploited and improved upon in the context of agreements with built-in renegotiation clauses. The experience also highlights the importance of implementation challenges including logistical constraints, low administrative capacity, and elite capture. More attention to the principles and experiences of community-driven development as well as more local political analysis will likely benefit women's engagement and outcomes. The particular guidance for enhancing women's agency laid out above—in both the negotiation and the implementation phases—offers further opportunities to promote women's equality and through this, to achieve better development outcomes for all.

Note

1   This chapter is largely based on work already published as "'We Want What the Ok Tedi Women Have': Guidance from Papua New Guinea on Women's Engagement in Mining Deals," Nicholas Menzies and Georgia Harley (2012), J4P Briefing Note, World Bank. The authors would like to thank all those interlocutors and colleagues who gave their time and insights to the research underpinning this chapter, especially members of the impacted communities. Errors of fact and interpretation are those of the authors, as are the views expressed in this chapter, which should not be attributed to the World Bank, its executive directors, or the countries they represent.

References

Banks, G., & Ballard, C. (1997) *The Ok Tedi Settlement: Issues, Outcomes, and Implications*, Canberra: Asia Pacific Press.

Beaman, L., Chattopadhyay, R., Duflo, E., Pande, R., & Topalova, P. (2008) "Powerful Women: Does Exposure Reduce Bias?" Available: http://faculty.wcas.northwestern.edu/~lab823/powerfulwomen.pdf. Accessed 15 Dec 2014. Figures are also available here: http://hdr.undp.org/sites/all/themes/hdr_theme/country-notes/PNG.pdf. Article is available here: http://dspace.mit.edu/openaccess-disseminate/1721.1/57903.

Behrman, J., Meinzen-Dick, R., & Quisumbing, A. (2011) *The Gender Implications of Large-Scale Land Deals*, IFPRI Discussion Paper 01056, January.

Burton, J. (2011) *Understanding the Political Economic Context of Western Province, Papua New Guinea*, Canberra: Australian National University (on file with authors).

Cammack, D. (2009) *Chronic Poverty in Papua New Guinea*, Chronic Poverty Research Center.

Chattopadhyay, R., & Duflo. E. (2004) "Women as Policy Makers: Evidence from a Randomized Policy Experiment in India," *Econometrica*, vol. 72, no. 5, pp. 1409–1443, September.

Deininger, K., Byerlee, D., Lindsay, J., Norton, A., Selod, H., & Stickler, M. (2011) *Rising Global Interest in Farmland: Can It Yield Sustainable and Equitable Benefits?* World Bank, Available: https://openknowledge.worldbank.org/handle/10986/2263.

Dupuy, K. (2014) 'Community Development Requirements in Mining Laws: Global Dataset', (unpublished, on file with authors).

Franks, D. M., Brereton, D., & Moran, C. J. (2013) "The Cumulative Dimensions of Impact in Resource Regions," *Resources Policy*, vol. 38, no. 4, pp. 640–647.

Franks, D. M., Davis, R., Bebbington, A. J., Ali, S. H., Kemp, D., & Scurrah, M. (2014) "Conflict Translates Environmental and Social Risk into Business Costs," *Proceedings of the National Academy of Sciences*.

Government of Papua New Guinea (2003) *Green Paper*, Department of Mining, 1 February.

Macintyre, M. (2003) *Petztorme Women: Responding to Change in Lihir, Papua New Guinea*, *Women's Groups and Everyday Modernity in Melanesia* Oceania (Special Issue) vol. 74, no. 1&2, pp. 120–33.

Macintyre, M. (2011) "Modernity, Gender and Mining: Experiences from Papua New Guinea," in Kuntala Lahiri-Dutt, *Gendering the Field: Towards Sustainable Livelihoods for Mining Communities*, Canberra: ANU E-Press.

Mansuri, G. & Rao, V. (2013) *Localizing Development: Does Participation Work?* Washington, D.C.: World Bank

Newell, P. (2001) *Access to Environmental Justice? Litigation against TNCs in the South* 32(1) *Making Law Matter: Rules, Rights and Security in the Lives of the Poor*, IDS Bulletin, pp. 83–93.

Nish, S. & Bice, S. (2012) "Community-based agreement making with land-connected peoples," in Vanclay, F. & Esteves, A. M. (eds.) *New Directions in Social Impact Assessment: Conceptual and Methodological Advances*, Cheltenham: Edward Elgar Publishing.

O'Faircheallaigh, C. (2012) "Women's Absence, Women's Power: Indigenous Women and Negotiations with Mining Companies in Australia and Canada," *Ethnic and Racial Studies*, pp. 1–19.

Ok Tedi Development Foundation (2007) *CMCA Census Report Appendix: Basic Statistical Tables.*

Popoitai, Y., & Ofosu-Amaah, W. (2014) *Negotiating with the PNG Mining Industry for Women's Access to Resources and Voice: The Ok Tedi Mine Life Extension Negotiations for Mine Benefits Packages*, Washington, D.C.: World Bank.

Rio Tinto (2010) *Why Gender Matters: A Resource Guide for Integrating Gender Considerations into Communities Work at Rio Tinto*, London: Rio Tinto.

Sharp, B. (2008) "Renegotiating a Papua New Guinea Compensation Agreement: Applying an Informed Consensus Approach," Working paper 69, *Resource Management in the Asia Pacific.*

Tingay, A. (2007) *Letter of Endorsement from the Independent Scientist Appointed to the CMCA 2006/7 Review Process* (Attachment B to CMCAs).

Vanclay, F., & Esteves, A. M. (eds) (2011) *New Directions in Social Impact Assessment: Conceptual and Methodological Advances*, Cheltenham: Edward Elgar Publishing.

Ward, H. (2001) *Securing Transnational Corporate Accountability through National Courts: Implications and Policy Options* 24 Hastings Int. & Comp. L. Rev, pp. 451–474.

World Bank (2009) *Mining for Equity: Gender Dimensions of Extractive Industries*, Washington, D.C.: World Bank.

World Bank (2012a) *PNG Country Gender Assessment for the period 2011–2012*, Washington, D.C: World Bank.

World Bank (2012b), *World Development Report 2012 Gender Equality and Development*, Washington, D.C.: World Bank.

3 A women's world or the return of men?

The gendered impacts of residential tourism in Costa Rica

Femke van Noorloos

Introduction

Land is increasingly commercialized worldwide: in the past decade, land and real estate markets in the global South have shown much dynamism. While the debate on the "global land grab" has mostly focused on land investments for food supply and biofuels, it has now been widely accepted that the debate should be extended beyond food and fuel investments alone: for instance, large land acquisitions are taking place in the context of climate change mitigation and adaptation, mining concessions, urbanization, and speculation, and through the establishment of large-scale tourism complexes and residential tourism resorts (Borras Jr et al., 2012; Zoomers, 2010; Zoomers & Kaag, 2014).

While peri-urban and urban land deals are often smaller in scale than agricultural land grabs, such processes of rural–urban land conversion and speculation nonetheless contribute greatly to undermining local land rights through land price hikes, displacement, and gentrification (Roy, 2011; Janoschka et al., 2013; Phuc et al., 2014). The progressive integration of rural areas into the urban realm, both in terms of physical land conversion and in their lifestyles and cultures, engenders a large-scale transformation of rural landscapes, land-tenure systems, and ways of life. The consequences of such processes for different social groups have not been sufficiently studied to date.

Indeed, the gendered implications of land deals still receive only scant attention in academic realms, although there are some notable exceptions (Behrman et al., 2012; Collins, 2014; Verma, 2014; Wisborg, 2013). As Berhman et al. argue:

> A gender perspective is critical to truly understanding the impact of large-scale land deals because women and men have different social roles, rights, and opportunities and will be differentially affected by any major change in tenure regimes, especially land transfers to extra-local investors.
>
> (2012: 51)

The gendered consequences of more urban types of land pressures in particular remain largely invisible. This chapter will offer some first contributions to a gendered approach of urban and peri-urban land deals, particularly those related to tourism, real estate, and speculation.

It does so by analyzing increasing pressures on land in the northwest coastal region of Costa Rica (Guanacaste province), which has been one of Latin America's main areas of real estate and residential tourism growth in the past decade. On Costa Rica's coasts, as in many tourist destinations around the world, land is increasingly commercialized and commoditized. New types of tourism and mobility are generating mounting pressures on land. Tourism in many areas in the South is now deeply intertwined with real estate investment and urbanization: people buy property in the tourist destinations and stay there for shorter or longer periods, driven by the search for a better way of life, a lower cost of living, etc. This is known as "residential tourism." The residential tourism industry, with its focus on land transactions and urbanization, constitutes an urgent research topic in debates on land and development.

This chapter elaborates on the complex gendered dynamics created by residential tourism in the global South. By analyzing the causes, implications of and responses to residential tourism growth—and related real estate and speculation—from a gendered perspective, a more inclusive and complex picture emerges. It starts with a description of the development and characteristics of residential tourism in Costa Rica, followed by an analysis of the effects of residential tourism in terms of access to land and employment. Furthermore, the gendered responses to such profound transformations—such as environmental and water struggles—are highlighted. Finally, the focus is on the changing demographics and related power relations in residential tourism towns.

The empirical material for this chapter was collected through three periods of fieldwork in Guanacaste, Costa Rica, between 2008 and 2011, which included several types of data collection: interviews with various population groups; participant observation; and analysis of secondary data sources. In total, 17 in-depth qualitative interviews and 42 semi-structured interviews were held with local and labor migrant populations in 2008 and 2009 in Tamarindo, Villareal, Playas del Coco, and Ocotal. Analysis of national statistics, a survey among residential tourists, and an examination of land prices provide additional insights.

A private piece of paradise: residential tourism in Guanacaste, Costa Rica

Residential tourism and lifestyle migration have recently become more prominent in developing countries: both terms refer to the temporary or permanent mobility of relatively well-to-do citizens from mostly Western countries to a variety of tourist destinations, where they buy (or sometimes rent) property (Benson & O'Reilly, 2009; Janoschka & Haas, 2013). Most residential tourists or lifestyle migrants are Europeans or North Americans who migrate to the South in search of a more relaxed lifestyle, a lower cost of living, better weather, etc. Both the number of residential tourists and the size of the related land investments have increased markedly during the past ten years—and are expected to increase further—in various countries across Latin America, Africa, and Asia. A number of structural factors in North America and Europe are important for explaining the growth in residential tourism from North to South: demographic factors (e.g. ageing), increasing health costs, and decreasing retirement pensions; time–space compression through relatively inexpensive and rapid travel and improved and cheaper long-distance communication possibilities; and sociological factors such as more conscious lifestyle choices and need for social differentiation. Improved infrastructure, health services, and the liberalization of land markets in the South have also contributed to this growth. In contrast to short-term tourism, residential tourism focuses much more on real estate development and urbanization, and thus has important different repercussions socially but also for space, landscape and land use.

Costa Rica has been a well-known relocation destination for North Americans for decades, but these migration flows have recently intensified and extended geographically to new coastal areas, which has made them much more concentrated and visible. Costa Rica's fame as an ecotourism destination has been complemented by the image of a country "for sale," a real estate frontier and relocation "paradise" for increasing groups of North Americans. The northwest coastal region of Costa Rica (Guanacaste province) has been the country's main area of real estate and residential tourism growth in the past decade (Figure 3.1). In the 2000s, Guanacaste changed from a small-scale tourism destination to an area of exponential large-scale and residential tourism growth, including real estate investment. Rapid growth from 2002 to 2007 contrasts with the steep declines experienced during the worldwide economic crisis, particularly from 2008 to 2012, since when there has been a slow recovery.

Estimates of the number of residential tourists in the coastal area of Guanacaste range from about 7% to 14% of the total population, meaning there is a high concentration of residential tourists in a small area. However, permanent migrants are still in the minority and most people migrate for shorter periods or use their property as a second home or investment. The flow of residential tourists to Guanacaste has not only intensified, but also diversified considerably in recent times. Many different groups of people are involved: the majority come from the US and Canada, but there are also Costa Ricans from the Central Valley, from middle-income to elites and from permanent to temporary residents to short-term tourists. Individual house-buying has made way for an extensive real estate sector, where most properties are bought within residential projects and urbanizations.

The developers and investment capital mainly come from the US and Canada (two-thirds of the projects are partly or completely financed by North American capital), although there is also much domestic investment: 40% of the projects are either completely or partly financed by Costa Rican investors. Collaborations between North American and Costa Rican investors are common. Hence a 'foreignization' of land has clearly taken place, although domestic investors should not be overlooked.

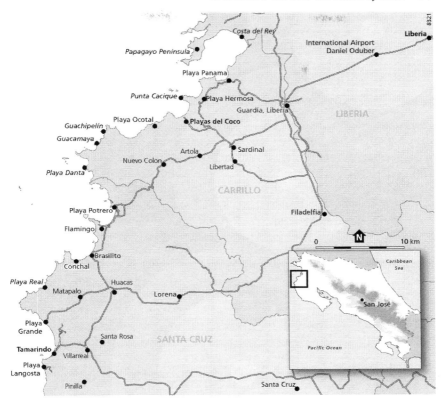

Figure 3.1 Research area: coastal region of Guanacaste, Costa Rica.

Losing access: land-use change and gentrification

In Latin America, land deals are not a new phenomenon: land grabs, the dispossession of rural communities, and deepening commercialization in rural areas have existed since colonial times. The northwest coast of Costa Rica has been subject to land grabs ever since colonization and particularly since the late nineteenth century (Edelman, 1998). From this point on, private individual land rights have prevailed in the area, although some parts are under state property or other property regimes, such as the narrow coastal strip, protected nature areas, a special tourism concession area, and agricultural reform land. We should thus regard current land deals as a continuation of historical processes, albeit with new foci, underlying reasons and a higher speed of change (van Noorloos, 2014).

The implications of land deals in the Guanacaste case center on the changes in *land use* brought about by the investments: the change from agriculture and cattle farming to a service economy based on tourism, construction, and real estate, has influenced people's access to land, labor, income, and gender relations.

Various researchers have stated that rapid development of residential tourism in developing countries can endanger local populations' access to land (e.g. indigenous and peasant groups) and may lead to direct or indirect displacement, for example in Mexico (Bastos, 2013; Torres & Momsen, 2005), Nicaragua (Bonilla & Mordt, 2011), Panama (Gómez et al., 2009), and South Africa (van Laar et al., 2013). Indeed, displacement of indigenous populations often takes place under great financial and political pressure resulting from real estate and tourism development, and in the context of inadequate recognition and demarcation of indigenous land rights. The gendered effects of such displacement remain under-researched. Land sale and displacement may have contradictory effects on women: it may cause a loss of livelihoods and access to important resources such as water, shells, and trees, while migration and employment may also provide them with new opportunities.

In Guanacaste, displacement, exclusion, and gentrification take place in rather indirect, mediated ways: there is no large-scale displacement. Voluntary land sale has driven the tourism and real estate development since the beginning. While land investors and speculators are mostly male, the Guanacastecans who sell their land include both men and women alike, with no important differences observed. Particularly at the beginning of the land investment boom, people often sold their properties for small sums and invested the money in consumer goods. While such land-sale processes were voluntary, many coastal low-income groups (including labor migrants) face processes of pre-emptive exclusion and economic hardship because of high land and housing prices (van Noorloos, 2011; van Noorloos, 2012). Land price inflation pushes new generations out of the region, and displaces alternative development trajectories such as small-scale tourism (Massey, 2005). Hence the spatial consequences of residential tourism in Guanacaste can be most adequately defined as gentrification (Janoschka et al., 2013): rising land and housing prices push poorer groups out of certain areas. The price of residential plots in Guanacaste increased by 17.7% annually between 2000 and 2009–11, to $187.50/m^2 in the latter period; for condominiums and houses, prices increased by 24.3% annually to $2717.30/m^2 (van Noorloos, 2012).[1] After the 2008 economic crisis, property prices in Guanacaste dropped somewhat, but not dramatically. Indeed, a large majority of local and Nicaraguan respondents agreed that housing, at least in the coastal towns, has become largely inaccessible for new buyers.

Rather than gender disparities, class, and (indirectly) nationality tend to determine access to land under the current gentrification process; in addition, there are age-based differences. New generations of young men and women growing up along the coast, as well as new immigrant laborers, cannot buy land in the coastal areas. Young people face difficulties in starting their own families; the price level makes them dependent on their parents for support. The interior rural area of Guanacaste still has affordable land, although this is slowly changing. Further frequent strategies are renting a small apartment, or taking care of absentee owners' property. Other young people depend on relatives to give them a piece of family land. Inheritance patterns seem rather gender-equal these days, with people passing on land to all children, regardless of gender. Indeed, in Latin America in general, inheritance of land has become more egalitarian and women mainly become landowners through inheritance, while men tend to buy land (Deere & León, 2003).

Thus gender disparities in access to land have not been directly affected by residential tourism; they are traditionally highly present in Costa Rica (as in all of Latin America), although in recent decades many improvements in family laws and land rights have been achieved, such as the recognition of dual-headed households and consensual unions, as well as joint-titling practices (Deere & León, 2003; Fuentes López et al., 2011). Hence women's bargaining power has increased in important ways, leading to a more gender equal land distribution. In addition, many laws and policies promoting gender equality and women's protection have been set up in Costa Rica during the 1990s, including family laws, subsidies, and protection against domestic violence (Chant, 2002; Preston-Werner, 2008). These developments have gone hand in hand with economic, technological, and sociological changes which have changed gender relations, including the downsizing of the public sector and the rise of tourism, which increased women's labor opportunities (Mannon, 2006). In Guanacaste in particular, significant changes in family life have been observed since the 1980s, for instance a growing incidence of lone motherhood and female-headed households, falling levels of legal marriage, rising numbers of out-of-wedlock births, greater rates of divorce and separation, and mounting involvement of women in the historically male preserve of family breadwinning (Chant, 2002).[2]

Arguably, all these changes have allowed women to acquire a new autonomy and empowerment, and this has also extended to land-related issues. However, as we will see, men still dominate the labor market in Guanacaste, and therefore have more opportunities to buy land. Hence, indirectly, increased land sale and the commoditization of land may favor men, even in the context of general increasing egalitarianism in inheritance patterns and state programs. At the same time, the demise of the traditional cattle sector and small-scale agriculture reduced the central role of land in the household economy: land has now acquired a more residential function and has become an object of speculation and investment.

Feminization of employment?

Since the 1990s, tourism growth in Guanacaste has benefited women's employment opportunities: their involvement in the workforce has increased considerably, as visualized in Figure 3.2 which shows data for the Santa Cruz and Carrillo cantons, the focus area of this research. This development continued up to 2011, during the boom of residential tourism: women's participation in the workforce continued to grow in absolute terms (from 4,943 in 2000 to 10,651 in 2011) and as part of the total female population (see Figure 3.2). Men's employment to population ratio has been declining rapidly since the 1970s, mainly due to the decline of the cattle sector in Guanacaste (Edelman, 1998) and general economic crisis of the late 1970s and 1980s, a process which was intertwined with important male out-migration patterns (Chant, 1991). However, male employment also recovered between 2000 and 2011: the new employment opportunities provided by construction and related industries have played an important role in that. Indeed, on a national level in Costa Rica tourism provides opportunities for men and women alike, and while women earn less income than men in the sector, it still represents an important part of their livelihoods (CEPAL, 2007).

The main difference between residential tourism and short-term tourism is the great relative importance of construction and real estate, compared to the traditional services sector. Currently in Guanacaste, however, short-term and residential tourism are still blended in such a way that all these sectors are still largely present, resulting in considerable employment and business opportunities for many groups in society.

Figure 3.3 shows that in the research area, many different tourism-related sectors experienced growth between 2000 and 2011. If we define tourism narrowly as lodging and food services, the number of people engaged in it increased by 8.8% annually between 2000 and 2011, making it the main economic activity in the area. Both men's and women's participation has increased to a great extent; for women, tourism is the main sector in terms of employment. Furthermore, women's employment in domestic work as well as commerce and vehicle repair grew rapidly, while men's employment increased particularly in commerce and vehicle repair, transport and storage, and construction (growth of the latter sector was particularly high between 2005–08, and as a result is not adequately reflected here).

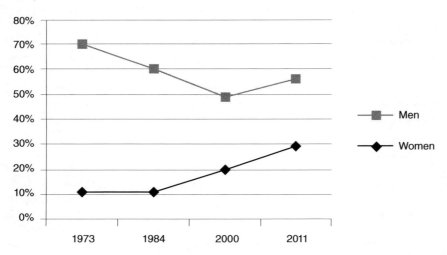

Figure 3.2 Employment to population ratio for men and women, 12+, Santa Cruz and Carrillo cantons, 1973, 1984, 2000, and 2011.
Source: Author's elaboration based on INEC Censo Nacional de Población y de Vivienda

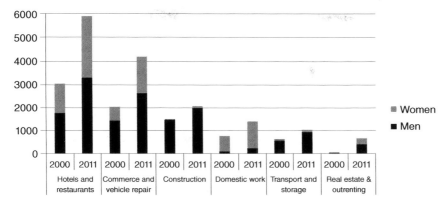

Figure 3.3 Number of men and women working in selected economic sectors, 2000–11.
Source: Author's elaboration based on INEC Censo Nacional de Población y de Vivienda

The local labor market on Guanacaste's coast clearly shows how gender differences intersect with ethnic and class differences. The booming tourism, real estate, and construction sectors have attracted a large number of migrants, particularly Nicaraguan and domestic migrants. Both Nicaraguan men's and women's involvement in Guanacaste's economy is vulnerable: they work mostly in low-skilled jobs in construction, gardening, and private security (men), domestic work (women), and tourism (both). Migrants from the US and from the Costa Rican center are more often occupied in high-skilled jobs such as tourism and real estate management, while local Guanacastecans are in the middle.

While tourism's employment effects in Guanacaste are generally positive, an analysis of the sector should also pay attention to quality of employment and vulnerability. Prostitution, a thriving sector in many tourism destinations such as Guanacaste, is a clear case in this regard. Also, a shift from short-term tourism to residential tourism probably reduces the quality of employment, with the increased importance of nonsecure and low-quality work in construction and domestic assistance, including cleaning and gardening. Both construction work and domestic work are typically irregular, temporary, and vulnerable: the ad hoc nature of the work, lack of social security provision, and health issues such as job-related accidents and sexual harassment, are major issues. The lower quality of employment is also reflected in low pay. Traditional tourism labor, while vulnerable, is relatively well paid. In the tourism sector narrowly defined as hotels and restaurants, per capita incomes where the head of household works in tourism are mostly found in the middle quintiles (for Costa Rica as a whole; see van Noorloos, 2012). On the other hand, construction workers' and domestic workers' households are largely in the lowest three quintiles (ibid).

Thus both men and women, particularly Nicaraguans and certain groups of Guanacastecans, face vulnerabilities in their work situation. However, the level of employment has improved generally for women in the research area: they are now better represented in high-level occupations such as managerial positions

(41% of these positions were filled by women in 2011, compared to 31% in 2000),[3] and intermediate and technical level positions (22% and 32% respectively)—although these are still to a large extent male domains. Women's participation in non-qualified positions has also increased but to a lesser extent (from 26% to 32%). Again, this increased representation in the higher echelons of the labor market might be particularly true for external women.

Broadly speaking, tourism has provided Guanacastecan women with important income generation opportunities, although the recent shift toward residential tourism seems to imply a decreasing quality of employment for both men and women. The 'feminization of employment' is not only related to the surge in tourism, however; declining birth rates and enhanced education have also played a role (Chant, 2002). Women's insertion in the labor market has allowed them more economic independence from men (Mannon, 2006), and indeed the feminization of employment seems related to a feminization of household headship (Chant, 2002), which has been on an upward trend since the 1990s; as of 2013, it was 36.5%.[4] Female employment in residential tourism has not necessarily been at the expense of men, who have recovered their employment position (at least in quantity) particularly in the period between 2000 and 2012, leading to a reduced need for out-migration—although certain groups of men have probably suffered considerably from the declining success of traditionally male occupations in agriculture, cattle farming, and fishery.

Gendered water and conservation struggles

While women have benefited economically from the growth of the service sector in Guanacaste, they are also among the main critics of residential tourism in recent years. In Costa Rica, conflict and criticism with regard to residential tourism often comes from an environmental perspective, and Guanacaste's main struggles are no different: besides land, they focus on water governance and nature conservation. Women have played key leading roles in these struggles, which often implicitly or explicitly draw on gendered discourses about development and conservation.

It is interesting to note how perceptions can differ on the 'beneficial infrastructure and social projects' that land deals can offer. Behrman *et al.* (2012) state that land investments which include 'social projects' such as improvements in water provision, can be particularly beneficial for women. However, in Guanacaste many women and men alike perceived such public–private investment in water infrastructure as a typical case of water grabbing and privatization, set up in a non-consultative way.

In 2005 the 'Nimboyores conflict' (Ramírez Cover, 2008; IPS, 2004) over water emerged in Lorena, and a female leader played an important role. The conflict focused on the planned extraction of large amounts of water in order to serve the golf courses and hotels of the coastal megaproject Reserva Conchal, which was located in a particularly arid area. The people of Lorena, where the water extraction would take place, were not consulted about these plans, and this prompted local people, led by a female schoolteacher, to object. Successful community protests and judicial action delayed the project, and ultimately the developer scrapped its plans. Other conflicts about water have followed since, particularly around the Sardinal–El Coco–Ocotal project in 2008, where women and men also played active roles in halting further water extraction for residential tourism development (van Noorloos, 2012).

Female and male leaders in interior towns thus fiercely defended their communities' continued access to water from the local aquifers, and often such struggles are framed in terms of 'defending water provision for our kids / the future generations' vs the 'short-term financial interests of the foreigners [developers].' Rapid residential tourism development is implicitly framed as a masculine capitalist invasion for quick profit, in contrast to the long-term intergenerational community values that women uphold. Indeed, the main reason for protests— apart from the lack of prior consultation—was the local residents' concern about *future* water access: although many wells were in the process of drying up, water access was not under any immediate threat. Critical visions of residential tourism and water privatization also draw on discourses on the public good vs private interests, which also has an implicit gendered perspective.

Other struggles around residential tourism in Guanacaste are related to nature conservation and environmental protection. One important example of such conflicts is the case of the leatherbacks of Guanacaste National Park, in the coastal town of Playa Grande. In this protected coastal area, which is a main nesting site for the critically endangered leatherback sea turtle, the combination of residential tourism development and rocketing land prices has triggered a typical development–conservation conflict. Women from the local women's association have played a key role in this conflict: the consolidation and protection of the national park in the face of potential encroachment by investors and politicians is a key objective of the association, and the leader frames it partly as a women's struggle against anti-conservationist husbands (although the 'conservationists' also include many men). The leader of the women's association blends her environmental activism with a particularly gendered discourse:

> Sometimes people tell me that I'm a fighter, for the environment and things like that. But I would say that it is because I'm a mother. They can say that there will be water for the next 20 years, but what happens after that with my kids? That's the main thing, I do everything for the boys and girls, I also consider the turtles to be my kids ... I would prefer my kids to say that I did everything to protect the turtles, even if they will become extinct, than saying that I didn't do anything. There needs to be a consciousness about the environment. A short time ago I talked to a man and he almost made me sick: he wants Playa Grande to become like a second Tamarindo ... When I told him that our kids would drown in alcoholism, he said that they are all lost anyway. It's incredible that he would say something like that.

Women are depicted as defenders of nature with reference to their motherhood and concern for the next generations, whereas men are portrayed as irresponsible and focused on short-term gains. Such gendered ideas and stereotypes reflect pre-existing ideas about men and women's roles in Guanacaste (see Chant, 2002) and convert them into advantages for women, who are increasingly claiming their space in the public domain. Via successful protest movements, as well as other mechanisms such as community development associations, water committees, and the like, women play important roles in decision-making on matters related to residential tourism on a local level. Other axes of differentiation such as class and ethnicity clearly play a role, with Nicaraguan women being particularly absent from community organization, while female US residents and domestic migrants are extremely active, although often in other types of organizations than those patronized by Guanacastecan women (van Noorloos, 2012).

In spite of these active roles, the power of communities and civil society to influence local affairs is still largely insufficient in Guanacaste, with the result that meaningful prior participation in land deals and related affairs is commonly absent in the residential tourism sector.

A new demographic: gendered identities in flux

The arrival of a large number of residential tourists, and the emergence of a powerful industry in real estate and construction which is also partly dominated by North Americans, has changed the local demographic and identity/power structures in Guanacaste. The gender, household, ethnic, and national characteristics of the coastal population have transformed considerably, and this has had important consequences for social hierarchies and gendered identities.

First, residential tourists have brought with them a particular age and household structure. Guanacaste's residential tourists are mostly older heterosexual couples. In a 2011 survey in Guanacaste (N=61) (see van Noorloos, 2012), most residential tourists were couples without children (49%), while 23% were families with children (including single people with children). The remainders were single people living alone (18%) or friends or other relatives living together (10%). The mean age was 52. Indeed, residential tourists in Guanacaste have diversified in recent years, and there is a general upward trend among older, more middle-income groups, while the number of young, single people (both male and female) has waned relatively. Guanacaste has become an established, accessible destination with American-style services.

With such characteristics, Guanacaste's current residential tourists arguably form less of a challenge to traditional family structures and gender roles than is the case in other areas (Croucher, 2013; Frohlick, 2007); and the 'gender demonstration effect' might also be smaller today that it was during the 1970s and 1980s, when the first wave of single adventurous men and women from North America relocated to Guanacaste and had more intensive contact with the local population than is now the case (see van Noorloos, 2012). While the total number of residential tourists is not enough to contribute to a general ageing of the population, the North American resident and tourist population in

Guanacaste has clearly become older. Among the native population, young people are still a large majority.

A second notable change is the 'return of men' in Guanacaste: improved labor opportunities for men emanating from residential tourism have attracted former out-migrants and new migrants alike. The implications of this process for residential and marital dynamics are complex, and will probably become apparent only in the longer term. We have seen that the increase in female household headship has not been halted; Guanacastecan women's independence seems only to have grown in recent years. Thus a return of men to marriage as solid economic providers is not yet observable. What is clear is that Guanacaste's population in general has become more temporary, mobile, and flexible, leading to decreasing social cohesion (van Noorloos, 2012). Hence there are larger groups of flexible, single laborers, rather than a return to the traditional family.

Increased diversity in national and ethnic terms is a third demographic change, and one that has consequences for power structures. As noted above, Guanacaste's residential tourists are predominately North American, while people from Europe and Costa Rica's urban areas are also present. On the other hand, Nicaraguans comprise a large labor migrant group in Guanacaste, as do domestic migrants. Such increased variety among the population has clear consequences for local social hierarchies. Even Guanacaste's public space, with its real estate advertisements in English showing white middle-class couples buying property, reflects the spatial power and elite status of western residential tourists (see Torkington, 2013). They form a powerful, highly esteemed group in Costa Rica, set apart through their high economic, human, social, and cultural capital. On the other hand, the local population has relatively little economic and human capital, but makes up for that with social and political connections. Nicaraguan labor migrants are generally lowest on the local hierarchy.

Such power positions and identities intertwine in often contradictory ways with gender relations and identities. Indeed, research on gender and mobility has highlighted the complex intersection of hierarchies and identities during and after women's migration; and such intersections acquire a different meaning when dealing with 'privileged mobilities' such as residential tourism and lifestyle migration. For example, female lifestyle migrants in Mexico frequently experience contradictions between their privileged status as relatively rich and well-regarded North Americans and their marginalization as typically single women in a patriarchal society (Croucher, 2013). Indeed, North American women—as well as local and Nicaraguan men—have encountered complex contradictions in their local social position in Guanacaste. Female residential tourists may have been on the wrong end of verbal assaults by men, and may be aware of certain 'no go' areas for women (e.g. local bars). Poor Guanacastecan and Nicaraguan males see their positions in the local hierarchy further decreasing, which may add to marginalization, family instability, and even violence (ibid). Age is another aspect of power that is important: the younger generation of Guanacastecans— male and female—has gained economic and decision-making power, but young people are also marginalized in terms of access to land.

Furthermore, some changes in gendered identities are noticeable. The real estate and construction industry related to residential tourism has sparked a type of 'wild west capitalism' aimed at making a quick profit, which is stereotypically associated with masculinity, and often with North American culture. Indeed, many of the project developers and investors in the area are male and North American. We have seen how this conceptualization of residential tourism as an implicitly masculine capitalist invasion for quick profit, has inspired local engendered activism against such developments, with various women positioning themselves as defenders of 'life' and the environment. However, this is not a uniquely female position, and men are also involved in such activism. More importantly, large populations—male and female—remain indifferent, accepting, or inactive with regards to new developments.

Conclusions

This chapter has shed light on the gendered dynamics of current land deals in the global South. The focus was on smaller-scale peri-urban land deals and rural–urban land conversion, an under-researched topic in the debate on land deals. It has provided some first approximations to a gendered approach of urban and peri-urban land deals, particularly those related to tourism, real estate, and speculation, by examining residential tourism growth in northwest Costa Rica. By analyzing the causes, implications of and responses to residential tourism growth in one of the main residential tourism destinations of Latin America from a gendered perspective, a more inclusive and complex picture has emerged. Such a perspective offers additional insights.

A more subtle and differential understanding emerges of the actual and possible long-term implications of residential tourism, for example, in terms of access to land and employment. The rapid development of residential tourism in developing countries can endanger local populations' access to land and may lead to direct or indirect displacement, with contradictory consequences for women. In Guananacaste, however, rather than direct displacement, processes of land-price inflation and gentrification are profoundly reshaping the local area. Housing, at least in the coastal towns, has become largely inaccessible for new buyers. This has differential consequences for men and women, but particularly across class and ethnic groups. Women are represented among the people who voluntarily sell their land to investors in a private land market. However, increased land sale activity and a growth in the commoditization of land locally may indirectly favor men because of their ongoing advantages in terms of income and employment, even in the context of general increasing egalitarianism in inheritance patterns and state programs (Deere & León, 2003).

In general, tourism has provided Guanacastecan women with important income generation opportunities, although the recent shift toward residential tourism seems to imply a decreasing quality of employment, both for men and women, and a shift toward migrant labor. Hence both men and women face vulnerabilities in their work situation. However, in general women are inserting themselves more in the higher domains of the labor market than in the lowest ones. Women's insertion in the labor market has allowed them more economic independence from men. These findings are in line with other research on gender and land deals: female paid employment can have a transformative effect on women's autonomy, independence, and bargaining power within the household, especially for younger generations; however, low-skilled, temporary, and vulnerable work is a mixed blessing for women (Behrman *et al.*, 2012).

Behrman *et al.* (2012) also indicate that economic change does not lead to automatic improvements in male–female relations. Indeed, the shift toward a service sector in Guanacaste may have been empowering for women, but if men experience marginalization, household relations and levels of violence could actually worsen. Female household headship is still on the rise. While female employment in residential tourism has not necessarily been at the expense of men, in the context of changing power relations and rapid change, poor Guanacastecan and Nicaraguan males may still see their positions in the local hierarchy decreasing, which may add to marginalization.

The responses to profound social and economic transformations take on particularly gendered forms and discourses. While women have been benefiting economically from the growth of the service sector in Guanacaste, they are also among the main critics of residential tourism in recent years, and play important roles in decision-making on matters related to residential tourism on a local level. Environmental activism is blended with gendered discourses.

A gendered view of residential tourism finally highlights the changing demographics of the area, which has important implications for power relations. Residential tourism has brought in many older couples; men have found labor opportunities and returned to the area; and the population is increasingly diverse, fragmented, and temporary. The variety of ethnic and national groups has changed the local power structure in Guanacaste. Such power positions and identities intertwine in often contradictory ways with gender and generational relations and identities.

The Guanacaste case is obviously very specific, and there are strong state institutions and legal frameworks in place which protect women and prevent rapid investments from causing large-scale societal impacts; a largely private individualized land market is also in place. In other contexts, residential tourism and other types of rural–urban land conversion may take on very different meanings and implications for men and women. Nevertheless, this case illustrates that implications of land deals vary widely depending on which group we look at: the intersections of gender, age, ethnicity, nationality, and class result in contradictory outcomes. Demographic change is important to take into account. It also shows that short-term evaluations fall short in analyzing the full implications of land deals. Finally, adequate female representation in decision-making and action related to land deals is necessary and can be successful in mediating the impacts of such investments.

68 *Femke van Noorloos*

Notes

1   While these prices refer generally to land and housing aimed at the residential tourist market, general housing prices can be assumed to have increased significantly also (van Noorloos, 2012).
2   Gender relations are traditionally unequal in rural Costa Rica and particularly so in Guanacaste: in the northwest of Costa Rica, male out-migration for agricultural labor was common until the 1990s, which reinforced a traditional spatial and sexual division of labor (Chant, 1991).
3   All data in this section adapted from INEC Censo Nacional de Población y de Vivienda 2000 and 2011.
4   INEC Encuesta Nacional de Hogares, data for Chorotega region.

References

Bastos, S. (2013) "Territorial dispossession and indigenous rearticulation in the Chapala lakeshore," in Janoschka, M., & Haas, H. (eds), *Contested Spatialities: Lifestyle Migration and Residential Tourism* (pp. 47–59). London: Routledge.
Behrman, J., Meinzen-Dick, R., & Quisumbing, A. (2012) "The gender implications of large-scale land deals," *Journal of Peasant Studies*, vol. 39, no. 1, pp. 49–79.
Benson, M., & O'Reilly, K. (2009) "Migration and the search for a better way of life: A critical exploration of lifestyle migration," *Sociological Review*, vol. 57, no. 4, pp. 608–625.
Bonilla, A., & Mordt, M. (2011) "Turismo en el municipio de tola (Nicaragua): Exclusión y resistencia local," *Opiniones En Desarrollo (Programa Turismo Responsable)*, no. 11, pp. 2–28.
Borras Jr, S. M., Franco, J. C., Gomez, S., Kay, C., & Spoor, M. (2012) "Land grabbing in Latin America and the Caribbean," *Journal of Peasant Studies*, vol. 39, no. 3–4, pp. 845–872.
CEPAL. (2007) *Turismo y condiciones sociales en centroamérica: Las experiencias en Costa Rica y Nicaragua*. Santiago, Chile: CEPAL.
Chant, S. (1991) "Gender, migration and urban development in Costa Rica: The case of Guanacaste," *Geoforum*, vol. 22, no. 3, pp. 237–253.
Chant, S. (2002) "Families on the verge of breakdown? Views on contemporary trends in family life in guanacaste, Costa Rica," *Journal of Developing Societies*, vol. 18, no. 2–3, pp. 109–148.
Collins, A. M. (2014) "Governing the global land grab: What role for gender in the voluntary guidelines and the principles for responsible investment?," *Globalizations*, vol. 11, no. 2, pp. 189–203.
Croucher, S. (2013) "The gendered spatialities of lifestyle migration," in Janoschka, M. & Haas, H. (eds), *Contested Spatialities, Lifestyle Migration and Residential Tourism* (pp. 15–28). London: Routledge.
Deere, C. D., & León, M. (2003) "The gender asset gap: Land in Latin America,'" *World Development*, vol. 31, no. 6, pp. 925–947.
Edelman, M. (1998) *La lógica del latifundio: Las grandes propiedades del noroeste de Costa Rica desde fines del siglo XIX*. San José, Costa Rica: Editorial Universidad de Costa Rica.
Frohlick, S. (2007) "Fluid exchanges: The negotiation of intimacy between tourist women and local men in a transnational town in Caribbean Costa Rica," *City & Society*, vol. 19, no. 1, pp. 139–168.

Fuentes López, A. P., Medina Bernal, J. L., & Coronado Delgado, S. A. (2011) *Mujeres rurales, tierra y producción: Propiedad, acceso y control de la tierra para las mujeres, tomo I*. San José, Costa Rica: Asociación para el Desarrollo de las Mujeres Negras Costarricenses.

Gómez, I., Kandel, S., & Morán, W. (2009) *Conflictos y respuestas territoriales ante el auge inmobiliario del turismo. el caso del archipiélago de bocas del toro*. San Salvador, El Salvador: PRISMA.

Janoschka, M., & Haas, H. (2013) *Contested Spatialities, Lifestyle Migration and Residential Tourism*. London: Routledge.

Janoschka, M., Sequera, J., & Salinas, L. (2013) "Gentrification in Spain and Latin America: A critical dialogue," *International Journal of Urban and Regional Research*, doi:10.1111/1468-2427.12030

Mannon, S. E. (2006) "Love in the time of neo-liberalism: gender, work, and power in a Costa Rican marriage," *Gender & Society*, vol. 20, no. 4, pp. 511–530.

Massey, D. (2005) *For Space*. London: Sage.

Phuc, N. Q., van Westen, A., & Zoomers, A. (2014) "Agricultural land for urban development: The process of land conversion in central Vietnam," *Habitat International*, vol. 41, pp. 1–7.

Preston-Werner, T. (2008) "In the kitchen: Negotiating changing family roles in Costa Rica," *Journal of Folklore Research*, vol. 45, no. 3, pp. 329–359.

Roy, A. (2011) "Re-forming the megacity: Calcutta and the rural–urban interface," in *Megacities* (pp. 93–109). London: Springer.

Torkington, K. (2013) "Lifestyle migrants, the linguistic landscape and the politics of place," in Janoschka, M., & Haas, H. (eds), *Contested Spatialities: Lifestyle Migration and Residential Tourism* (pp. 77–95). London: Routledge.

Torres, R. M., & Momsen, J. D. (2005) "Gringolandia: The construction of a new tourist space in Mexico," *Annals of the Association of American Geographers*, vol. 95, no. 2, pp. 314–335. doi:10.1111/j.1467-8306.2005.00462.x

van Laar, S., Cottyn, I., Donaldson, R., Zoomers, A., & Ferreira, S. (2013) "'Living apart together' in Franschhoek, South Africa: The implications of second-home development for equitable and sustainable development," in Janoschka, M., & Haas, H. (eds), *Contested Spatialities: Lifestyle Migration and Residential Tourism* (pp. 190–204). London: Routledge.

van Noorloos, F. (2011) "Residential tourism causing land privatization and alienation: New pressures on Costa Rica's coasts," *Development*, vol. 54, no. 1, pp. 85–90.

van Noorloos, F. (2012) *Whose place in the sun? residential tourism and its implications for equitable and sustainable development in Guanacaste, Costa Rica*, (PhD, Utrecht University). *Eburon*, Available: http://dspace.library.uu.nl/handle/1874/257921

van Noorloos, F. (2014) "Transnational land investment in Costa Rica: Tracing residential tourism and its implications for development," in Kaag, M., & Zoomers, A. (eds), *The Global Land Grab: Beyond the Hype* (pp. 86–99). London: Zed Books.

Verma, R. (2014) "Land grabs, power, and gender in East and Southern Africa: So, what's new?," *Feminist Economics*, vol. 20, no. 1, pp. 52–75.

Wisborg, P. (2013) "Transnational land deals and gender equality: Utilitarian and human rights approaches," *Feminist Economics*, pp. 1–28.

Zoomers, A. (2010) "Globalisation and the foreignisation of space: Seven processes driving the current global land grab," *Journal of Peasant Studies*, vol. 37, no. 2, pp. 429–447.

Zoomers, A., & Kaag, M. (2014) "Conclusion: Beyond the global land grab hype: ways forward in research and action," in Kaag, M., & Zoomers, A. (eds), *The Global Land Grab: Beyond the Hype* (pp. 201–216). London: Zed Books.

Part II

From *de facto* to *de jure*

Formalizing patriarchy in the codification of customary tenure?

Caroline S. Archambault and Annelies Zoomers

Customary land tenure regimes are regimes wherein a community of members rather than a state or state laws establishes the rules governing access and use. Membership of the community regulating land is often driven by ethnic identity, clan, or family. Rights within the systems are typically inheritable and land sales are usually prohibited. Traditional authorities govern the customary system and act as repositories of knowledge around membership. Rules are not usually recorded and flexibility and adaptability provide these systems with resilience to adapt to changing times (Lawry 2013). Customary systems are dynamic and responsive systems as "[t]he arbiter of norms is always the living community" (Wily 2012: 5)..

Customary tenure systems are found in a diversity of ecological settings, including agricultural lands, pasturelands, forests, and marshlands. It is a major system of landholding across the world, which can even be found in industrial economies such as Spain and Switzerland. In sub-Saharan Africa, but also in large areas of Latin America and Asia, customary tenure is the most predominant land tenure system. In most African countries, rural privately titled landholdings account for only 1–2% of land (ibid). In some African countries, like Kenya, Zimbabwe, and South Africa, the proportion of private titled lands is much higher but still not the majority. Legally and officially, customary systems are often defined as public, state, national, or government land. Typically, these systems have little or weak recognition in statutory law.

After more than two decades when emphasis was given to stimulating individual land-titling and the creation of modern land markets, governments are now increasingly engaging in processes of recognizing and formalizing customary land rights (Cuskelly 2011). Customary tenure, once seen as the greatest obstacle to agricultural modernization, is now embraced by many as a well-adapted system, closely connected to changing rural realities and capable of providing secure land rights (Orebech *et al.* 2005). The change in perception, evident among policy-makers, development agencies, and academics, stems from a variety of forces including popular demands for democratization, general processes of decentralization, the influence of rights-based movements, and growing evidence that the introduction of individual freehold title in many contexts was not bringing about the anticipated benefits in terms of production and development (World Bank 2001; Quan 2000; Bruce and Migot-Adholla 1994).

Consequently, there appears now to be a growing consensus advocating statutory rights of customary ownership. In 2011, 60% of 190 constitutions provided some degree of recognition of customary law and 20% specifically recognized customary law regarding land and natural resources (Cuskelly 2011). There is, however, considerable variation in the degree of legal protection afforded to different customary tenure regimes. For the most part, legal recognition of customary land rights requires formalization via registration and mapping at the individual or group/community level. Typically this involves registering territory and membership, as well as the usual regulatory and governance systems.

This process brings with it many challenges, also with regard to gender equity. Customary tenure regimes are often not egalitarian and are rarely equitable systems as regards to gender, age, and social status, among other differences. Thus, while formalizing customary systems may provide important protections to marginalized groups, it also runs the risk of further entrenching inequalities as well as the institutions that perpetuate them. Feminist scholars, for example, have raised concern about the implications of legalizing customary systems on women's land tenure security (Whitehead and Tsikata 2003; Deere and León 2001). Customary systems are very often governed by male traditional authorities or male-run local institutions and commonly exclude women as members. Finding ways to design systems that are inclusive to women and to their needs is a major challenge deserving of more attention and research, not least into the gendered nature of complex customary tenure systems.

The second section of this book, with case studies from Cameroon, Argentina, Madagascar, and India, explores the various ways in which tenure reforms aimed at formalizing customary rights have important gendered impacts.

In Cameroon, the establishment of community forests, managed by (largely male) local governance bodies, have not only sidelined women's non-forest timber product commercialization to focus on the male-controlled timber industry, but have also created onerous regulatory requirements that serve to empower wealthy and educated men at the expense of women and minorities.

In Argentina, the procedure for claiming indigenous communal land is also arduous and results in very few successful claims. However, the process of political mobilization around communal rights includes an important role for women and may provide, in the near future, an entry for women into political leadership in land struggles and political engagement outside of the realm of land advocacy.

In Madagascar, a comprehensive land-tenure reform designed to formalize and secure the rural population's customary claims has included the possibility for joint certification of lands held by couples. That said, very few joint certificates have been issued to date, reflecting a lack of political priority, a weak system of implementation, and a persistent unitary view of the household among civil servants and rural households.

By contrast, a very recent program in India's West Bengal to distribute land to poor and landless households was relatively successful in ensuring the joint titling of parcels of land. This was likely due to the political commitment to the program, the politicized nature of the program—which had a high level of civic engagement of women—and a "deep" partnership with the external organization responsible for implementation. The joint titling appears to have resulted in women's enhanced decision-making authority over household production and spending.

References

Bruce, John W. and Shem E. Migot-Adholla (eds) (1994) *Searching for Land Tenure Security in Africa.* Dubuque, IA: Kendall Hunt Publishing Company.

Cuskelly, K. (2011) *Customs and Constitutions: State Recognition of Customary Law around the World.* Bangkok, Thailand: IUCN.

Deere C. and C. León (2001) *Empowering Women: Land and Property Rights in Latin America.* Pittsburgh, PA: University of Pittsburgh Press.

Lawry, Steven (2013) "Customary Land Rights in sub-Saharan Africa as Systems of Economic, Social, and Cultural Rights." Paper Presented at the World Bank Conference on Land and Poverty, Washington, D.C.

Orebech, Peter, Fred Bosselman, Jes Bjarup, David Callies, Martin Chanock, and Hanne Petersen (2005) *The Role of Customary Law in Sustainable Development.* Cambridge: Cambridge University Press.

Quan, J. (2000) "Land Tenure, Economic Growth and Poverty in sub-Saharan Africa." In C. Toulmin and J. Quan (eds), *Evolving Land Rights, Policy and Tenure in Africa,* pp. 31–50. London: IIED with DFID and NRI.

Whitehead, Ann and Dzodzi Tsikata (2003) "Policy Discourses on Women's Land Rights in sub-Saharan Africa: The Implications of the Re-turn to the Customary." *Journal of Agrarian Change,* 3(1,2): 67–112.

Wily, Liz Alden (2012) "Customary Land Tenure in the Modern World: Rights to Resources in Crisis: Reviewing the Fate of Customary Tenure in Africa". Brief #1 of 5. Research Papers. International Land Coalition.

World Bank (2001) *Land Policy and Administration: Lessons Learned and New Challenges for the Bank's Development Agenda.* Washington, D.C.: World Bank.

4 Cameroon's community forests program and women's income generation from non-timber forest products

Negative impacts and potential solutions

Marguerite Belobo Belibi, Judith van Eijnatten, and Nicholas Barber

Introduction

The five and a half decades since independence have witnessed an increasing formalization of land tenure in Cameroon. The country's 1994 Forestry Law is among the most important pieces of legislation in advancing this process. Building on previous initiatives of sedentarization and land titling, the 1994 law imposed a system of classification that proclaimed state ownership of nearly all Cameroon's vast forestlands. This legal categorization was at odds with local open access and common property land-tenure regimes, as part of which customary rules and traditional authorities regulated access to forest resources.

The 1994 law does, however, include some provisions for local control over forest resources. Specifically, it provides for the establishment of "community forests," overseen by local management bodies, wherein communities can commercially exploit timber and non-timber forest products (NTFPs). The community forest provisions of the 1994 law, however, lack the flexibility of customary land tenure systems. In addition to greatly circumscribing the extent and type of forest territory that local communities can control, the onerous regulatory requirements imposed by the Forestry Law and related pieces of legislation serve to empower wealthy, educated community members—almost always men—at the expense of women and minorities. This inequality is particularly apparent in community forest management bodies' focus on timber exploitation, traditionally performed by men, rather than on the commercialization of NTFPs, the collection and processing of which is most often the domain of women.

This chapter traces the impacts of land tenure reforms in Cameroon on local populations in the forestlands of the country's southeast, with particular attention to the impact of the 1994 Forestry Law on women's commercialization of NTFPs. The result of a novel collaboration between two staff members of SNV

Netherlands Development Organisation, and an anthropologist working on issues of indigenous rights and identity in southeast Cameroon, the chapter draws on the results of a recent SNV project in order to discuss a potential solution to the aforementioned problems. The SNV project demonstrates the ways in which improved local organization and access to market information can help marginalized community members—in particular women—benefit from the commercial exploitation of NTFPs under the provision of the Forest Law.

Background: changing land and resource tenure in southeast Cameroon

Spanning more than 2 million square kilometers across six Central African countries, the Congo Basin rainforest is the world's second largest contiguous tropical forest. Along with the Amazon and the rainforests of Southeast Asia, it houses the majority of the world's biodiversity, and is a vital "carbon sink" regulating the global climate. The forest is also an important economic resource for the countries that it traverses, producing high-quality timber and other goods for export. For populations living in and around the forest, NTFPs provide food, water, shelter, and medicine. The forest also has important cultural and spiritual significance for local communities, especially for indigenous groups such as the Baka and Bagyeli (sometimes grouped with other, related groups under the label "pygmies," considered by many to be pejorative).

In Cameroon, the Congo Basin rainforest covers more than 40 percent of the country's total territory and is home to approximately 2.5 million people out of a national population of 19.5 million (USAID, 2011). The densest portion of the forest, and the majority of forest inhabitants, are located in the southeastern part of the country. This region has, and continues to be, economically and politically marginalized compared to the rest of the country (Ango, 1982; Rupp, 2011).

The population of southeast Cameroon is divided between Bantu agriculturalists and groups such as the Baka, who have traditionally been hunter-gatherers.[1] In one survey of a segment of this region, Bantu constituted 60 percent of the population, Baka 25 percent, and traders and other migrants that did not belong to either group 15 percent (Njounan Tegomo *et al.*, 2012: 46). Prior to the colonial era, both Baka and Bantu lived deep in the forest. The Bantu resided in permanent villages, while the Baka were nomadic, moving between temporary settlements in search of game and other forest resources, such as wild yams and honey.

Traditional Baka and Bantu conceptions of property rights involved a mix of "open access" and "common property" regimes. Under open-access regimes "no one has the legal right to exclude anyone from using a resource," whereas in common property regimes "the members of a clearly demarcated group" have access to a resource, but "exclude non-members of that group from using [it]" (Ostrom and Hess, 2007: 6).

Owing to their nomadism, the Baka have not traditionally had any conception of "ownership" over land. While the Baka did maintain a sense that certain areas of the forest were the territory of specific bands or kinship groups, these boundaries were flexible, temporary, and porous. Thus, in actuality, Baka were free to exploit forest resources more or less without restriction.

Unlike the Baka, Bantu groups in southeast Cameroon were relatively sedentary, and thus maintained a more fixed concept of "territory" than the Baka did. Village lands and surrounding cultivated areas were held as common property by entire villages or segments thereof. In spite of this, however, Bantu also considered the majority of uncultivated forest lands to be an open-access resource in which anyone was free to hunt and collect forest products (Nguiffo, 1998: 105). The above-described customary systems of forest land tenure among Baka and Bantu groups in southeast Cameroon did not entail perfect equality between the two groups or among group members. While Baka and Bantu did not consider most forest territory to "belong" to any one group or individual to the exclusion of others, both groups maintained "well-known rules," governed by traditional systems of authority, which determined who could exploit which forest resources (Nguiffo, 1998: 105). These rules often involved a gendered division of labor. While there were important differences between the two groups, in general men performed hunting activities, while, with some exceptions, women were responsible for the (arguably more onerous) work of gathering and processing NTFPs.

Land-related attitudes and laws in southeast Cameroon began to change in the late nineteenth century, when the country's German colonial masters undertook a project of road construction and sedentarization for forest populations. While this project was cloaked in expressions of altruism, such as the desire to provide education and health services to rural peoples, the "real objective" likely had more to do with making forest residents "more accessible to the administration for tax collection" and increasing the pool of workers available as forced labor for activities such as rubber collection (Nguiffo, 1998: 105). Given the fact that they already resided in permanent settlements, and thus were both more accessible to government officials and more habituated to a sedentary lifestyle, the Bantu were the first to become subject to this projection of colonial authority. Some Bantu communities found themselves alongside newly built roads, while others migrated to roadside areas.[2]

This period also witnessed a drastic change in the legal status of forest lands. An 1896 imperial decree proclaimed all lands that were not clearly "occupied" to be "vacant and ownerless" and thus property of the German crown. The decree defined "occupation" very narrowly, considering only clearly inhabited or cultivated territory to be "occupied." This excluded vast expanses of forest used by local populations for hunting, gathering and other activities (Nguiffo et al., 2009: 3–4).

The colonial state's claim of ownership over uncultivated lands would underwrite massive land expropriations over the course of the twentieth century, as the colonial, and later Cameroonian, governments transferred control of the "uncultivated," "uninhabited" forest commons to private companies (Nguiffo, 1998: 108). At the same time, the sheer expansiveness of the Congo Basin rainforest rendered it difficult for the state to project its authority in remote, difficult-to-access areas. In many such locations local populations were able to maintain customary, open-access regimes involving fundamentally different conceptualizations of ownership and territory as compared to state laws (Karsenty, 1999).

Cameroon gained its independence in 1960. Far from abandoning the destructive land policies of the colonial government, the post-colonial state maintained the concept of state ownership of forest lands. Indeed, owing to severe economic problems, "there was a considerable rise in forest resource exports, exploitation and destruction" after independence (Nguiffo, 1998: 108). Cameroon's primary land law, enacted in 1974, formalized the notion of state ownership of "uncultivated lands." This law mandated the registration and titling of all privately held lands, with active "occupation" or cultivation a prerequisite for proving landownership. This stipulation "enabled the state to reclaim the bulk of communities' land as it forbade registration of unexploited land which was under customary ownership" (Nguiffo, Kenfack, and Mballa, 2009: 10).

Given the cost and complexity of obtaining land titles in Cameroon, only a very few local elites have been able to obtain titles and the concomitant rights to commercialize resources extracted from their lands. Today, the vast majority of Cameroonians still do not have a formal title for their land (Ashley and Mbile, 2005: 8). The requirement that landholdings be titled was particularly disadvantageous for women. While in customary land-tenure systems "different rights to land are distributed among different groups and individuals," in formal, written, privatized systems, "most land rights are concentrated in the hands of a minority that, due to economic factors, ideology, and the influence of powerholders, almost never includes women" (Lastarria-Cornhiel, 1997: 1317).

The 1994 Forestry Law

Cameroon's 1994 Forestry Law further complicated local communities' relation to forest lands. Largely drafted by officials from the World Bank under the terms of a Structural Adjustment Program, the Forestry Law ostensibly encompassed three principal considerations:

1   Fuelling economic growth through the industrial exploitation of timber;
2   Protecting biodiversity;
3   Recognizing and guaranteeing popular participation in forest management and ensuring the distribution of benefits from logging and other activities to local communities (Nguiffo *et al.*, 2012: 12).

In reality, however, a number of researchers and civil society organizations have argued that the specifics of the law, as well as the fashion of its implementation, have privileged the first of these goals at the expense of the third (Nguiffo *et al.*, 2012: 14).

The Forestry Law divides the entire expanse of Cameroon's forests into two broad categories: permanent forest estate (PFE)—areas which will be maintained as forest areas (although some "sustainable" logging is permitted); and non-permanent forest estate (NPFE)—areas designated for eventual transformation into agricultural lands (Nguiffo *et al.*, 2012: 23). Each of these categories is further subdivided. The PFE consists of state and commune forest areas (*"forêts dominales,"* and *"forêts communales"*). The national government directly manages state forests, which encompass national parks and other protected areas as well as major logging concessions (*"unités forestières d'aménagement"* or "UFAs"), while local, sub-regional governments manage commune forests. The NPFE consists of community forests (see below), privately held lands, and "national forest domain" (*"forêt du domain national"*). "National forest domain" areas officially belong to the state, but are "largely made up of secondary forest that lacks titles but clearly belongs to individuals, families, and clans" (Ashley and Mbile, 2005: 5). In addition to granting long-term logging UFAs in the PFE, the state often sells short-term *"ventes de coupe"* logging rights in the national domain forest area. Table 4.1 summarises land classification and rights according to the 1994 forestry law.

Some have viewed this formal categorization of forest lands, and in particular the provision for local management of forest resources through commune and community forests, as empowering local actors vis-à-vis the national government. While the Forestry Law does grant communities the right to *manage* some forest resources, however, it does not give them formal title to forest lands. Indeed, one of the key aspects of the 1994 Forestry Law is the divorcing of land rights from *usage rights*. While communities have their rights to use resources in certain segments of the forest formally recognized, the lands on which these resources lie can be expropriated by the state at any time for "vaguely defined reasons of 'public interest'" (OKANI, CED, and FPP, 2013). Furthermore, the recognition of local usage rights applies to subsistence activities only. Any commercialization of forest resources "can only be done in delimited territories and requires special permits" (Nguiffo *et al.*, 2012: 27). Overall, while it appears to involve a devolution of responsibility to local governments and communities, the 1994 Forestry Law maintains the key characteristic of colonial and independence-era policies: the ownership of forests by the state, rather than local people or communities (Nguiffo *et al.*, 2012: 13).

Table 4.1 Land classification and rights according to 1994 Forestry Law

| | Permanent Forest Estate (PFE) | | | | Non-Permanent Forest Estate (NPFE) | | |
| | State forest | | Commune forests | Community forests | National domain forest | Private lands |
	Protected areas	Logging concessions (UFAs)				
Title holder (land rights)	State	State	State (via sub-regional gov't)	State	State	Individual/corporation
Usage rights for local populations?	No (with some exceptions)	Unclear/varies	Yes	Yes	Yes	No
Timber and NTFP commercial'n rights for local populations?	No	No	No	Yes, with proper permits	No	No

Community forest provisions under the 1994 Forestry Law

In spite of its focus on increasing state profits from timber extraction, the 1994 Forestry Law did contain measures aimed at protecting biodiversity (most importantly a goal of classifying 30% of Cameroon's territory as protected areas) and at devolving power to local communities. Reacting to World Bank pressure, and influenced by a growing trend in the field of international development, which touted the benefits of local management of renewable resources such as forests, the government of Cameroon enacted provisions for the establishment of locally managed "community forests" (Karsenty, 1999: 147).

The establishment of a community forest gives participant "communities" (which may comprise one or more villages) exclusive rights to commercialize "all products derived from the forest, including timber, NTFPs, wildlife, and fisheries" (Ashley and Mbile, 2005: 9). Land rights, however, remain with the state. The law also includes a number of restrictions on the size and location of community forests. Most importantly, all community forests must be situated in the non-permanent forest estate (NPFE). As the NPFE consists primarily of second-growth forest, timber in these areas is of a much lesser value than timber in the PFE. Community forests are also restricted in size to 5,000 hectares, an area "far below the size of what is considered a village forest" according to most customary tenure practices (Nguiffo, 1998: 116). Other forest areas, which were previously managed according to traditional common property or open access regimes, were re-categorized as national domain, state, or commune forests under the jurisdiction of the state. Villagers maintain usage rights in some of these areas, but have no territorial or commercialization rights. According to Phil René Oyono (2010: 124) community forests are thus an example of "the institutionalization of prohibitions and restrictions in access to historically common resources."

The 1994 Forestry Law and related pieces of legislation also enact a number of bureaucratic requirements for the creation and operation of community forests. In order to apply to create a community forest, a group of villagers must form a "common initiative group" (*"groupe d'intérêt communautaire*," or GIC). The GIC is required to have a constitution which "prescribes criteria for membership" (Rupp, 2011: 29). Not all residents of villages bordering a community forest will be members of that forest's GIC, and thus not all community members have an equal say in management decisions (Nguiffo *et al.*, 2012).

Once established, a GIC must enter into a formal agreement with the national forest service and submit a management plan outlining logging, agriculture, agroforestry, and conservation activities to be undertaken in the community forest (Ashley and Mbile, 2005: 9). The maximum duration of such agreements is 25 years. Further stipulations mandate that any timber exploitation must be "artisanal," and involve the "manual removal of boards from the forest," and that any proceeds realized by the GIC from the sale of timber and NTFPs must be reinvested in community-development infrastructure (Ashley and Mbile, 2005: 9). Decisions about what infrastructure to invest in are taken by the GIC. The government also requires a permit in order to transport a forest product (timber and/or NTFP) away from a community forest for commercial sale.

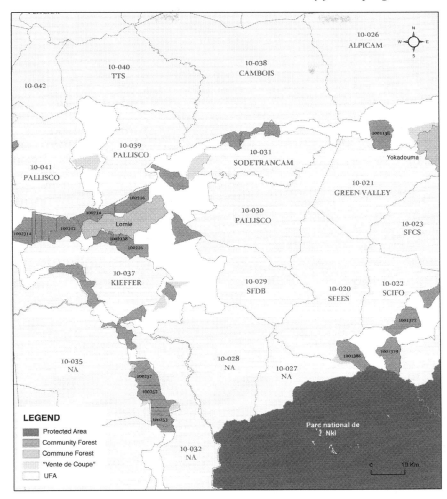

Figure 4.1 Land demarcations near Lomié, Eastern Cameroon.
Source: World Resources Institute *Atlas Forestier du Cameroun 2012*; Projection: WGS 1984 Zone 33 Nord

Establishing a community forest requires significant organizational skills and financial resources. In order to develop a forest management plan, the community is required to map forest boundaries and inventory forest resources, which can take up to two years. A 2009 survey of 20 community forests in Cameroon calculated that the required financial investment for establishing a forest amounted to between US$12,000 and $24,000 (Mbile *et al.*, 2009). In part because of this, in 1999, five years after the promulgation of the Forestry Law, no community forests had yet been legally established (Rupp, 2011: 30). This situation has, however, changed in recent years. By December 2009, 174 community forests had been registered, out of which 135 had signed conventions. The attributed forests covered 620,000 hectares and included 340 villages (Mbile *et al.*, 2009). Figure 4.1 shows demarcations for land classified in different categories, including community forests, near Lomié in East Cameroon.

The Cameroonian government framed the community forests provision of the 1994 Forestry Law as a way to "revive traditional and endogenous common management institutions" (Nguiffo, 1998: 116). While not completely egalitarian, these local institutions were nevertheless seen as more democratic and inclusive than state-centered, "top-down" approaches. "Decentralization is expected to give marginalized groups more influence on local policy and forest resource management because open, participatory decision-making works in favour of equality" (Bandiaky and Tiani, 2010: 144). Perhaps because of this logic, the community forest sections of the 1994 Forestry Law do not include any specific provisions for the equitable representation of women and minorities such as the Baka in GICs, nor for the equitable distribution of benefits from community forest activities (Assembe Mvondo, 2006: 687).

Unfortunately, while, in some cases local residents have succeeded in establishing community forests, often with the aid of national or international NGOs, there has also been a major problem of "elite capture," wherein "elites with political connections," who often have only a distant relation to the local community, control community forest GICs (Leonhardt, 2006: 93–4 n. 6). The cost and complexity of the process for establishing a community forest has the effect of advantaging better educated and politically connected community members (usually Bantu men) at the expense of less educated, less connected individuals (women and Baka). Compounding this problem of elite capture, there is often weak oversight relating to the requirement that community forest profits be reinvested in development projects. Most community forests thus operate without full community participation, and with low levels of transparency and accountability. Benefit sharing is low, and a predominantly male elite captures the majority of rents and profits (Assembe Mvondo, 2006).

Gender, community forests, and NTFPs

A recent report by the African Women's Network for Community Management of Forests (REFACOF) (Karpe *et al.*, 2013) identified "the persistence of a grave situation of discrimination" against women in rural areas in Cameroon "especially concerning access and management of land and forests" (1). Indeed, there is persistent underrepresentation of women and Baka on community forest GICs (with Baka women thus being doubly marginalized).

According to a 2006 study (Tobith and Cuny, 2006), while women do attend meetings related to the establishment of community forests, their numbers tend to be greatly inferior as compared to men. The same study also shows that women's influence in the community forest decision-making process remains weak, especially in relation to the election of the executive members of the community forest GIC. When women obtain executive positions themselves, it is often in the role of treasurer or cashier, a post that is typically thought to be "women's work" and which entails little formal decision-making power. This limited presence of women in community forest management committees means that their needs and interests are less likely to be taken into account during the creation and implementation of forest management plans.

Community forest GICs' emphasis on the exploitation of timber, as opposed to NTFPs, is both a reason for and a product of women's marginalization and underrepresentation on these committees. Men traditionally manage timber-related activities, which are usually more financially lucrative than NTFP exploitation. Men often consider NTFP harvesting to be a women's affair and thus of secondary importance. This gendered division of responsibility when it comes to forest resources, combined with community forest management committees' focus on timber at the expense of NTFPs, further reduces women's influence in decisions regarding the utilization of community forest revenues (Tobith and Cuny, 2006). While NTFP harvesting has a place in the Forestry Law, the law too focuses much more heavily on timber exploitation. Although less profitable than timber exploitation, however, NTFP collection and sales nevertheless constitute an important income strategy for women and their families.

Generally, NTFP collection by women involves gathering fruits and seeds from the forest floor. Depending on the biodiversity of the forest, the product sought, and the quantities desired, a trip to the forest might take a few hours or several days. A longer excursion would involve overnight camping—often with primary processing, such as the removal of seeds from fruits—taking place in the forest in order to reduce the weight of product that has to be carried. The work is heavy: women must penetrate the forest with cutlasses, sometimes for significant distances, wearing little protective clothing and carrying basic supplies. The work also carries a high risk of injuries through accidents, attacks by wild animals, or losing one's way. Good knowledge of the forest, the location of resources, and their seasonal availability are important attributes for successful NTFP collection. Woman may work individually or in groups. Collection groups can be ethnically homogeneous or mixed. In areas where Baka and Bantu live in proximity, Bantu may seek the services of Baka, not only as guides but also as labor to collect and/or process the product. The collected NTFPs are most often destined for local consumption, thus contributing substantially to food accessibility and security. Other NTFPs have medicinal properties or are used to fulfill other basic needs.

Structural obstacles to women's commercialization of NTFPs

According to Section 8 of the 1994 Forestry Law, forest communities are entitled "to collect all forest, wildlife, and fisheries products freely *for their personal use*, except protected species" (emphasis added). While the law is thus fairly liberal in permitting subsistence activities, it is very restrictive when it comes to the *commercialization* of NTFPs. Commercial sales of NTFPs require that the seller obtain a permit, quota, or have an agreement with the Ministry of Forests (Ingram,

2014). In order to obtain a permit, the seller must navigate multiple levels of bureaucracy, spread across several government bodies. This process can often take several months to a year. Furthermore, in terms of cost, NTFP commercialization permits do not differentiate between local, small-scale sales by collectors and large-scale commercialization by companies and syndicates. The high transaction costs involved in obtaining these permits thus work to the disadvantage of local populations, favoring those with sufficient political and economic power to gather the necessary paperwork and follow up their dossier in the capital (Mbile *et al.*, 2009). Further exacerbating this inequality, NTFP harvesters are often ill informed about permit requirements. As part of a 2014 study, for instance, 95% of Cameroonian NTFP harvesters interviewed were uninformed about the permitting system and legal harvest rights (Ingram, 2014: 117).

Given the difficulty of obtaining commercialization permits, most NTFP collectors must choose between selling their products to middlemen (*"buyum-sellum"*), or transporting their products without the proper paperwork from supply zones to market. The latter option leaves NTFP collectors open to unscrupulous gendarmes, police, forest guards, and custom agents, who may demand the payment of informal fees or "taxes" in return for allowing goods to pass through various checkpoints. According to a recent study (Ingram, 2011) there were an average of 22 roadblocks and checkpoints between southwest Cameroon and major markets in Nigeria, and ten between collection zones in the Littoral region and major markets in the city of Douala. The high prevalence of corruption thus creates significant costs during transport to market. For instance, Awono *et al.* (2013: 11) estimate that the cost of corruption for bush mango transported from source zones in southern Cameroon constitutes 33% of total transportation costs.

The above-described situation renders it nearly impossible for NTFP collectors, who are predominantly poor women, to operate within the law. Large-scale NTFP commercialization is instead left to wealthy traders who are able to purchase permits and operate teams of middlemen to buy and transport products from supply zones to major markets. During the harvesting season, these middlemen go door-to-door to buy products, imposing prices that are far below market value. Women are forced to accept the prices proposed by the middlemen for a number of reasons: First, NTFP prices are volatile and women are uninformed of market prices. Second, the collection season for the majority of NTFPs follows a period of food insecurity between December and June (van Eijnatten and Belobo Belibi, 2013), and coincides with the beginning of the school year (early September). This means that women selling NTFPs are often short of money to purchase food and/or pay school fees for their children.

A lack of market transparency also inhibits trade. Information for potential customers regarding locations, volumes, and quality of products and regularity of supply is not available. Community suppliers lack information about customers and are unable to rate and appropriately price and grade their products. A lack of regular, reliable customers causes NTFPs to degrade and rot and thus become unmarketable.

Potential solutions: community organization and market information

Improved local organization and market information-sharing between communities and potential customers represents one potential solution to empower local community NTFP collectors to overcome some of the difficulties discussed above. The remainder of this chapter discusses one such effort, undertaken by SNV Netherlands Development Organisation in community forests in the South and East regions of Cameroon. The project took place between 2007 and 2013 and targeted 20 community forests in three principal geographic areas: six community forests in and around Yokadouma in the East region; nine community forests in and around Lomié, also in the East; and five forests in and around Djoum, in the South region.

The SNV project took a value chain approach, focusing on improving organization among local women NTFP collectors, boosting product quality and value addition of products, increasing transparency through market information on prices and product availability, and establishing commercial linkages between collectors and traders.

To build local capacity, SNV provided training on improved collection and processing techniques for specific NTFPs, including bush mango, njansang, koutou, ebaye, cola, and talala. The training also included modules on responding to market demand, grading product quality, understanding the "purchase tricks" of middlemen, standardizing units of measurement, and using spring balances for weighing products. The training employed a "trickle-down" approach. SNV held an initial training with a core of "group trainers," who then transferred the skills they had acquired to local "collections groups."

At its base, the SNV project organized women into local "collection groups" (CGs). It was important that women became organized at the lowest level because NTFP collection and processing is tedious, labor-intensive, and time-consuming. Working in a group meant that women stimulated and motivated each other and thus were able to increase their production. The formation of community collections groups also allowed women to "bulk" their products, constituting large stocks, which had the effect of decreasing dependency on middlemen and encouraging the building of direct and fair commercial relationships with wholesalers.

Collection groups in the same and neighboring villages were then brought together in "collection group networks" (CGNs). These networks aimed to promote collaboration and organization at a higher level, and also served to facilitate group sales. Representatives from the CGs met regularly at the level of their network to monitor the evolution of the bulking process in the different groups. The meetings helped to generate a spirit of competition between the groups regarding the amount and quality of product collected.

The NCFO, or Network of Community Forest Organizations, occupied the highest level of the project organizational schema. The NCFO had a designated person (focal point) to support NTFP commercialization. It helped to identify and develop relationships with traders in towns and cities, surveyed the market for prices, assisted in the building of capacity for organizing group sales, and provided support in price negotiations if the CGNs so desired. Figure 4.2 shows the basic structure of NTFP commercialization networks as described here.

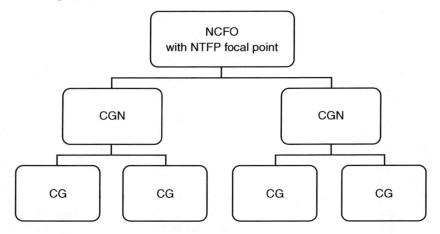

Figure 4.2 Basic structure of NTFP commercialization networks.

NCFOs met regularly with the CGNs to support and guide their work. At the end of a season the NCFOs compiled the information from the collection group registers, which provided insight into the total quantities of products extracted from the forest, the quantities/qualities sold, the prices, and the total income generated. This information allowed NCFOs and CGNs to begin planning for the following NTFP season.

For organizing the collective sales it was important that CGNs and buyers reach a consensus on the type, quality, and quantity of NTFPs to be traded, the unit of measurement to be used, and the price, date, and place of the sale. If there were two or more sales on the same day in different villages, it was also important that the CGNs and the NCFOs ensured that the same prices and units of measurement were applied in both instances.

To improve transparency, the project designed a market information system (MIS) based on communications technologies accessible to both collectors and traders. Several towns in the project area had community radio stations. These stations could broadcast over distances of up to 30 kilometers and were widely listened to by NTFP collectors living in forest areas, as well as traders living in town centers.

The MIS functioned as follows: CGNs collected and compiled information on NTFP supply, including the volume and quality of products available for sale, as well as contact details for sellers. They then transmitted this information by mobile phone to the NTFP focal point. The NTFP focal point compiled information from different community forests and transmitted it to the radio station by Internet.

Traders followed a similar procedure, transmitting information on market demand, including the volume and quality of NTFPs they were willing to purchase, by mobile phone to the radio station. The radio station then broadcast the information on a weekly basis. Collectors and traders could listen to the broadcast and obtain the information they needed to contact one another and to negotiate commercial deals. The MIS thus gradually reduced reliance on middlemen.

Project results

During the SNV project, incomes from NTFP collection rose dramatically. While collectors reported that, in previous years, incomes from NTFPs had been so low as to be almost negligible, during the NTFP seasons of 2011 in Yokadouma and 2012 in Lomié and Djoum, for instance, 765 (out of 817) collectors participating in the project earned a total of €94,468, for an average income of €123 per collector.

While this figure represents an important increase, however, it masks significant differences between different genders and ethnicities. Most importantly, while women constituted 91% of project participants, the few male participants earned significantly higher incomes. The average income for women was €114, while for men it was €260.

The income disparity between Bantu and Baka participants was even more troubling. The small minority of Baka participants (overall, 96% of collectors were Bantu and 4% were Baka) earned far less than their Bantu counterparts. Baka women earned eight times less than Bantu women (€14 vs €122) and Baka men earned fifteen times less than Bantu men (€17 vs €270). Thus, while the project did benefit women (and to a lesser extent Baka), it did so primarily by increasing overall prices and sales of NTFPs, rather than by eliminating ethnic and gender inequalities.

In fact, conversations with project participants indicated that, as NTFP exploitation has become more lucrative, men were increasingly taking up what had traditionally been viewed as "women's work." Reflecting persistent gender inequalities in local communities, men selling NTFPs tended to focus on those goods that were easily processed, leaving products such as njansang, for which processing is very labor intensive, to women. More study is needed in order to determine the ways in which future, similar projects can seek to address and counter the above-described inequalities.

In spite of these shortcomings, however, there is no question that the improved commercialization of NTFPs benefited local women and their families. Indeed, one principal attraction of income-generation projects for women is that they have a trickle-down benefit for their families, and in particular their children. Certainly this was the case for the SNV project. Table 4.2 shows the composition of the population benefiting from project activities. In Lomié and Yokadouma, project activities reached a total of 4833 family members, of whom 30% were female children, 32% male children, 20% women, and 17% men. The average income per beneficiary worked out to €19.25 per year.

Table 4.2 Make-up of the population, in terms of gender and adult/child (under the age of 16), benefiting from project activities in the Lomié and Yokadouma areas, as well as overall

Type of beneficiary	Lomié		Yokadouma		Total averages	
	No.	%	No.	%	No.	%
Female child	825	34	643	27	1468	30
Male child	784	32	757	32	1541	32
Female adult	457	19	530	22	987	20
Male adult	379	16	458	19	837	17
Total	2445	100	2388	100	4833	100

Table 4.3 shows how the overall income, earned by project beneficiaries from NTFP sales, was invested. The project was particularly successful in allowing women the means to pay for their children's education. For instance, the 306 collectors in Lomié spent 41% of their project income on school uniforms and supplies for their children. This works out to €15.76 per child per year, which is enough to cover the cost of primary education in rural Cameroon. (Primary school education itself is free but the authors estimate the cost of uniforms, books, and occasional extra fees to be around €15/year.)[3]

Table 4.3 Investment of NTFP income as percentages of total income

Investment of income	% of total income
Education	41
Enterprise	20
Food	9
Health	8
Construction	8
Birth of child	3
Kitchen utensils	3
Savings	2
Miscellaneous	6
Community projects	0
Total	100

To gain insight into the contribution of NTFP commercialization to household food security, the project sought to determine the quantity of NTFPs consumed by households as a percentage of the total production. Results from Lomié and Yokadouma indicate that an average of 9% of the NTFPs produced were not commercialized but kept to ensure household food security. This figure amounts to just over one kilogram of NTFPs per person per year. Considering that major NTFPs, such as bush mango and njangsang are not usually stored for longer than four months because their high oil content causes them to spoil quickly, this figure implies a daily intake of about 9 grams per person per day for project participants and their families during the four-month season. Most NTFPs are used in the preparation of meals. They supply nutrients and contribute to dietary diversity.

The large number of community members who participated in NTFP collection and commercialization across the project areas demonstrates the relatively low entry barriers to the NTFP market once collectors are organized and market access is established. Indeed, many project participants indicated that NTFP commercialization was more attractive to them than was timber commercialization as the latter requires long and expensive bureaucratic procedures, capital, sophisticated equipment, and skilled labor. Because of these barriers, community forests often abandon timber exploitation projects before completion. Furthermore, as previously mentioned, when community forests do succeed in selling timber the benefits are often limited to a select, elite group. In the current context, despite the shortcomings in the legal provisions of the Forestry Law, NTFP commercialization as a micro-industry, is capable of providing significant incomes to a wider group of community members.

Interestingly, none of the project income was allocated to community development projects as prescribed by the community forest section of the Forestry Law. While this may reflect, on the one hand, the weak enforcement of the law, it also demonstrates the lack of congruence between the law and prevailing customs and habits in forest areas, where women have traditionally collected NTFPs for household food security rather than as a means of realizing community development goals.

Conclusion

The SNV project allowed NTFP collectors to greatly improve their bargaining position in the NTFP value chain. Women are now producing more NTFPs, of better quality, and are demanding and receiving higher prices for their products. Consequently their incomes have increased. These benefits, however, have occurred in the context of a restrictive Forestry Law. The provisions of the 1994 Law, and the complex policies and procedures regulating the creation and management of community forests, continue to benefit elites at the expense of women and ethnic minorities. So long as the bodies governing community forests are dominated by wealthy, Bantu men, the financial benefits that women, and Baka, will be able to derive from NTFPs will be greatly circumscribed.

Notably, a process for reforming the 1994 Forestry Law is currently underway. While the revised law has yet to be formalized, draft versions indicate some progress toward enabling local communities to benefit more from NTFP commercialization. Drafts of the law do not, however, go so far as to accept civil society recommendations (e.g. Nguiffo *et al.*, 2012) to return property rights over forest areas to local communities, or to turn over management of community forests to local, democratically elected village government, as opposed to unelected GICs.

Notes

1   Contrary to simplistic dichotomies that portray Bantu as "farmers" and Baka as "hunter-gatherers," in reality there has always been "movement between farming and hunting and gathering for both Baka and non-Baka" (Leonhardt 2006: 74). Bantu also often ventured into the forest to hunt or collect NTFPs, although they ranged over a much smaller expanse of forest territory than did the Baka. Baka have also increasingly taken up agriculture as a means of supplementing hunting and gathering.
2   The Baka were subject to a similar sedentarization initiative beginning in the 1960s, which resulted in their settling along roadsides, often next to Bantu villages (Oyono 2010).
3   It should be noted that, while project participants in Lomié and Yokadouma were almost exclusively Bantu, in Djoum, where participants were mostly Baka, education costs constituted a much smaller percentage of investment of income. In Djoum project participants spent about half of their income on food and household items like soap and kerosene, and another third of income on clothes.

References

Ango, M. (1982) *L'est Camerounais: Une Géographie de Sous-Peuplement et de La Marginalité*, Ph.D., Université de Bordeaux II.

Ashley, R., and Mbile, P. (2005) "The Policy Terrain in Protected Area Landscapes," *Agroforestry in Landscape Mosaics Working Paper Series*, World Agroforestry Centre, Tropical Resources Institute of Yale University, and University of Georgia.

Assembe Mvondo, S. A. (2006) "Decentralized Forest Resources and Access of Minorities to Environmental Justice: An Analysis of the Case of the Baka in Southern Cameroon," *International Journal of Environmental Studies* vol. 63, no. 5, pp. 681–89. Available: 10.1080/00207230600963825

Awono, A., Ingram, V., Schure, J., and Levang, P. (2013) "Guide for Small and Medium Enterprises in the Sustainable Non-Timber Forest Product Trade in Central Africa," Bogor, Indonesia: CIFOR. Available: www.cifor.org/publications/pdf_files/Books/BAwono1301.pdf

Bandiaky, S., and Tiani, A.M. (2010) "Gendered Representation and Participation in Decentralized Forest Management: Case Studies from Cameroon and Senegal," in German, L.A., Karsenty, A., and Tiani, A.M. (eds) *Governing Africa's Forests in a Globalized World*, pp. 144–59. Sterling, VA: Earthscan.

Carlos, de W., Devers, D., de Marcken, P., Atya, R.E., Nasi, R., and Mayaux, P. (2009) *The Forests of the Congo Basin: State of the Forest 2008*. Luxembourg: Publications Office of the European Union.

Ingram, V. (2011) "Governing Forest Commons in the Congo Basin: Non-Timber Forest Product Value Chains," paper presented at 13th Biennial Conference of the International Association for Studies of the Commons, Hyderabad, India.

—— (2014) *Win-Wins in Forest Product Value Chains?: How Governance Impacts the Sustainability of Livelihoods Based on Non-Timber Forest Products from Cameroon*, Leiden:

African Studies Centre. Available: https://openaccess.leidenuniv.nl/handle/18 87/24875

Karpe, P., Ndjebet, C., and Edoa, C.W. (2013) *Forêt, REDD et Participation Des Femmes Au Cameroun*. Edéa: Réseau des Femmes Africaines pour la gestion Communautaire des Forêts (REFACOF). Available: www.gender-climate.org/Content/Docs/ Publications/refacof_Participation_Cmr_v3_FINAL.pdf

Karsenty, A. (1999) "Vers la fin de l'État forestier?," *Politique africaine*, vol. 75, no. 3, pp. 147–61. Available: 10.3917/polaf.075.0147

Lastarria-Cornhiel, S. (1997) "Impact of Privatization on Gender and Property Rights in Africa," *World Development*, vol. 25, no. 8, pp. 1317–33.

Leonhardt, A. (2006) "Baka and the Magic of the State: Between Autochthony and Citizenship," *African Studies Review*, vol. 49, no. 2, pp. 69–94.

Mbile, P., Ndzomo-Abanda, G., Essoumba, E., and Misouma, A. (2009) "Alternate Tenure and Enterprise Models in Cameroon: Community Forests in the Context of Community Rights and Forest Landscapes," Gigiri: World Agroforestry Centre.

Nguiffo, S. (1998) "In Defence of the Commons: Forest Battles in Southern Cameroon," in Goldman, M. (ed.) *Privatizing Nature: Political Struggles for the Global Commons*, pp. 102–19. London: Pluto Press.

Nguiffo, Samuel, Pierre Étienne Kenfack, and Nadine Mballa. (2009) "Historical and Contemporary Land Laws and Their Impact on Indigenous Peoples' Land Rights in Cameroon," 2. Land Rights and the Forest Peoples of Africa. Moreton-in-Marsh: Forest Peoples Programme.

Nguiffo, S., Waouo, J., Kamkuimo, P., and Effa, M.F. (2012) *Quelle Loi Pour La Forêt: Propositions de La Société Civile Pour La Réforme de La Loi Forestière Au Camerous*. Yaoundé: Centre pour l'Environnement et le Développement.

Njounan Tegomo, O., Defo, L., and Usongo, L. (2012) "Mapping of Resource Use Area by the Baka Pygmies Inside and Around Boumba-Bek National Park in Southeast Cameroon, with Special Reference to Baka's Customary Rights," *African Studies Monographs*, vol. 43, pp. 45–59.

OKANI, CED, and FPP (2013) *Demande D'examen Des Implications de L'adoption Imminente D'une Nouvelle Loi Forestière Racialement Discriminatoire Pour Les Peuples Autochtones Tributaires de La Forêt Du Cameroun Au Titre Des Procédures D'alerte Rapide et D'intervention D'urgence et Des Procédures de Suivi*, Formal complaint submitted to the United National Committee on the Elimination of Racial Discrimination. Geneva.

Ostrom, E., and Hess, C. (2007) "Private and Common Property Rights," *SSRN Scholarly Paper* ID 1304699. Rochester, NY: Social Science Research Network. Available: http:// papers.ssrn.com/abstract=1304699

Oyono, P.R. (2005) "The Foundations of the 'Conflit de Langage' over Land and Forests in Southern Cameroon," *African Studies Monographs*, vol. 26, no. 3, pp. 115–44.

——— (20100 "From Diversity to Exclusion for Forest Minorities in Cameroon." in Colfer, C.J. (ed.) *The Equitable Forest: Diversity, Community, and Resource Management*, pp. 113–29. New York: Routledge.

Rainforest Foundation (2003) *Forest Law Enforcement and Governance: Rights and Poverty Alleviation in the Congo Basin*, London.

Rupp, S. (2011) *Forests of Belonging: Identities, Ethnicities, and Stereotypes in the Congo River Basin*. Seattle: University of Washington Press.

Tobith, C., and Cuny, P. (2006) "Genre et Foresterie Communautaire Au Cameroun. Quelles Perspectives Pour Les Femmes?, " *Bois et Forêts Tropiques*, vol. 289, no. 3, pp. 17–26.

USAID (2011) *Country Profile: Property Rights and Resource Governance – Cameroon*, Washington: USAID. Available: http://usaidlandtenure.net/sites/default/files/country-profiles/full-reports/USAID_Land_Tenure_Cameroon_Profile.pdf

Van Eijnatten, J., and Belibi, M.B. (2013) *Food Accessibility in Six Community Forests in the Yokadouma Area, Eastern Cameroon*. Yaoundé: SNV.

5 Gendered mobilization

Women and the politics of indigenous land claims in Argentina

Matthias vom Hau

Postcolonial Latin America experienced recurrent mass mobilizations for land distribution, with well-known examples including the Zapatistas in early 20th century Mexico or the Brazilian Landless Workers' Movement (MST) in contemporary Brazil. The region also witnessed several large-scale land reform projects with the aim of redistributing land in a more equitable manner, such as the reforms enacted under Lázaro Cárdenas in Mexico during the 1930s and under the Velasco regime in Peru during the 1970s. At the same time, Latin America continues to be marked by extreme land inequality (de Ferranti *et al.*, 2004; Hoffman and Centeno, 2003). Large swathes of land tend to be concentrated in the hands of a few large landowners. And the last decades have done nothing to break this pattern. Trade liberalization, in tandem with the large-scale commercialization of agriculture and a dramatically expanding "frontier of extraction" have increased pressures on established landholding patterns, ultimately reinforcing the unequal distribution of land across the region (Bebbington *et al.*, 2008; Zoomers, 2000).

The current pressures on land have affected indigenous people in a particularly severe manner. Historically one of the poorest and most marginalized sectors in Latin America (Hall and Patrinos, 2005; Mahoney, 2010; Psacharopoulos and Patrinos, 1994), rural indigenous communities often lack tenure rights and do not have the title of the land they work and live on.[1] This land insecurity means that indigenous communities are vulnerable to evictions pursued by the current legal titleholders and the enclosure of territories they use for subsistence activities (e.g., for cattle pasture or hunting).[2]

At the same time, Latin America recently saw a dramatic transformation. Since the 1990s most countries in the region have introduced new multicultural rights in their respective constitutions, and these usually include the recognition of indigenous communal lands (Van Cott, 2000). In other words, for the first time since independence 200 years ago, indigenous communities gained the constitutional right to make demands for land they consider historically their own. These legal changes were closely entwined with the rise of indigenous people as a political force in their own right. Across the region, indigenous movements (and in some cases ethnic-based political parties) demand self-determination and autonomy and envision more inclusive nations that recognize ethnic, cultural and linguistic differences. They also push for the implementation of the new communal land rights (Sieder, 2002; Yashar, 2005).

This chapter explores indigenous land claims in Argentina from a gender perspective. The country is particularly suitable for such an analysis because it has been largely ignored by students of indigenous politics in Latin America (Gordillo and Hirsch, 2003), not least because dominant discourses about national identity and history describe Argentina as a "white nation" of European immigrants (Bastia and vom Hau, 2014). Yet the country largely follows the overall regional pattern. Indigenous people tend to be among the most destitute citizens of Argentina, and they tend to be concentrated in rural areas, territories disproportionally affected by recent economic transformations. The country also experienced legal changes similar to the rest of the region. The 1994 Constitution established the right to communal lands for any self-identified indigenous community. The actual claiming of indigenous communal land is difficult and protracted because of the legal proofs needed. Nonetheless, local indigenous movements have adopted communal land rights as one of their central demands.

The main focus of the chapter is on the role of women in indigenous land rights movements. It does so by exploring the *Diaguita Calchaquí* in the Argentine province of Tucumán. Diaguita land claims (so far) did not entail greater access to land for indigenous women. As a matter of fact, Diaguita communities have obtained the formal titling of communal lands only rarely. Yet a focus on women's land access alone overlooks the broader consequences of indigenous activism for gender relations. The chapter highlights the gendered nature of indigenous mobilization for land rights. Evidence from Tucumán illustrates that Diaguita women frequently join indigenous land struggles, and that their participation is to an important extent shaped by relatively small gender differences in education between Diaguita men and women, indigenous women's labor market incorporation, and their migration experiences.

Yet only a few Diaguita women have ascended into leadership positions. The chapter argues that the relative absence of women as movement leaders is related to the fact that for most of them, indigenous land struggles represent an initiation into political activism. By contrast, most male activists were already part of class-based *campesino* or union movements, or held political office. This prior political experience contributes to establishing men in leadership roles, and thereby reinforces within-movement gender hierarchies.

Simultaneously, the lack of prior political experience has led to distinct forms of female leadership. While male leaders often use their previously established contacts for patronage politics, Diaguita women cannot rely on this option and therefore choose to build their powerbase differently, by working on the socialization and recruitment especially of younger community members into the land rights movement. In some cases, women's leadership also spills over into other forms of political participation, especially in gender politics.

In short, the chapter demonstrates the importance of analyzing not just indigenous women's land access, but also the gendered implications of indigenous mobilization for land rights. Drawing on a qualitative approach the chapter combines semi-structured interviews and ethnographic observation. While drawing on the activist biographies of two female Diaguita leaders in particular, the analysis as a whole is based on more than 60 interviews with indigenous activists, non-activists, state officials, and economic elites in Tucumán that were conducted in October/November 2008 and February 2009, and in July 2012 and August 2013. These interviews were complemented by frequent consultations with anthropologists and sociologists from various universities and research institutions in San Miguel de Tucumán, Salta, and Buenos Aires.

Indigenous mobilization for land rights in Northwestern Argentina[3]

A variety of interrelated factors has shaped indigenous land struggles in Northwestern Argentina. First, changes in global and national *opportunity structures*—most prominently the rise of a global human rights regime and constitutional multiculturalism—set the stage for indigenous organizing around land rights. From the 1990s onwards, documents such as the International Labour Organization (ILO) Convention 169 or the United Nations Declaration on the Rights of Indigenous Peoples have provided local activists with new legal frameworks and normative resources to demand indigenous self-determination and the recovery of communal territories (Carrasco, 2000). The adoption of these frameworks was reinforced by the rise of transnational activist networks and NGOs concerned with indigenous issues (Brysk, 2000). At the national level, the 1994 constitutional reform confirmed these new legal norms by depicting Argentina as a pluricultural nation and encoding the ethnic and cultural pre-existence of indigenous peoples. This "multicultural constitutionalism" (Van Cott, 2000) established distinct indigenous forms of political authority and self-organization, and—at least in theory—recognized indigenous communal landholdings.[4]

The constitutional reform also established new forms of governance that shaped the relationship between the central state, provincial states, and indigenous communities. The *Instituto Nacional de Asuntos Indígenas* (INAI) was confirmed as the main national state agency responsible for the implementation of the new legal norms. Most prominently, in 2006 a new national law (*Ley 26,160*) stopped the expropriation of lands occupied by indigenous communities and mandated a nationwide land survey. As a consequence the INAI, in collaboration with provincial-level state agencies, became responsible to collect relevant information on indigenous land use for the assessment of current and future land claims.

Diaguita land claims in Tucumán

The majority of citizens who self-identify as Diaguita live in the Andean valleys of Northwestern Argentina. National census data from 2004 indicate that 31,753 individuals declare themselves as belonging to this group (INDEC, 2004/2005). Roughly half of those, around 15,000, are concentrated in Tucumán. Each of the sixteen Diaguita communities located in this province includes between several hundred and 2,000 comuneros, or members with voting rights and (potential) entitlements to communal lands.

The main *motivation* for local indigenous activists to make use of the new multicultural rights comes from economic restructuring. Historically, the economy of Tucumán was primarily oriented toward agriculture. Sugarcane and citrus fruits dominated in the lowlands, while in the Andean valleys corn farming and cattle herding constituted the main economic activities. Over the last two decades the lowlands have experienced the large-scale mechanization of sugarcane production, while in the highlands tourism has increasingly complemented the dominant agricultural sector. A growing demand for summer homes and a booming hotel industry intensifies land sales, and often entails the fencing of historically open pastures. Not having a title also exposes communities to the risk of possible eviction, even from lands they have lived on for generations. While mining has not (yet) become a major economic force in Tucumán, mining activities in neighboring provinces such as Catamarca and in Chile had severe ecological consequences, the most importance of which is increased water scarcity. Land commodification thus constitutes a crucial backdrop for recent indigenous land claims in Tucumán.

Securing land titling is a protracted process that required legal proofs to demonstrate a continued history of land occupation. A dominant framing strategy employed by indigenous activists is to represent the Diaguita as original inhabitants who occupied the territory long before the onset of Spanish colonialism. Land claims usually draw on historical records or archeological studies. The preparation of maps is also common. In many Diaguita communities, the *cacique* (the elected community leader) and various council members craft a map that shows the settlements, ceremonial centers, and pasture areas historically used by the community. Other forms of evidence include legal documents, kinship trees, genealogies of landmark names, and the projection of spatial memories onto satellite images and GPS-generated maps facilitated by the INAI land survey team.

Women's role in the Diaguita land rights movement

At a first glance, Diaguita activism for land rights involves both men and women. For example, in August 2013 I was able to observe a major demonstration in Santiago del Tucumán. The more than 1,400 protesters that marched along the major avenues of the city center and stopped the traffic for hours on end included male and female protesters in almost equal numbers, an observation that was later confirmed in conversations with the organizers and bystanding police officers. More generally, an analysis of local newspapers in Northwestern Argentina reveals no significant gender differences in indigenous militancy.[5] Whether analyzing images and descriptions of marches, vigils, or road blockades, the rank and file protesters usually include male and female activists on equal terms.

Upon a closer look, however, indigenous mobilization for land claims is highly gendered. Male and female activists perform different roles that reflect and reinforce the established gender order. The protest march across Santiago del Tucumán frequently stopped in front of the state agencies that were of particular relevance to Diaguita land struggles, most prominently the provincial government, the Ombudsman's Office, and the provincial supreme court. Participants then made short public statements and engaged with the local media. These representative tasks were predominantly conducted by indigenous men. Male activists thus constituted the "public face" of the demonstration. Diaguita women, by contrast, were more involved in background tasks, such as the cutting and painting of banners and signs. They were also the ones responsible for preparing the food to be consumed in the aftermath of the march, something that both male and female activists I talked to did not find particularly noteworthy or surprising.[6]

Gender differences are even more paramount when analyzing Diaguita leadership. The majority of the caciques and community representatives are men, as is the general secretary of the *Unión de Pueblos de la Nación Diaguita* (UPND), the main umbrella organization of indigenous activism in the province. Yet it is important to note that this male predominance does not preclude female leadership. Since 2004 at least three of the sixteen Diaguita communities in Tucumán have elected a woman as *cacica*, and many more women have served as council representatives for their respective local community.

Teresa, the first cacica in Tucumán

Teresa is one of these female leaders.[7] In her late forties and a primary schoolteacher by profession, she became the first Diaguita *cacica* in Tucumán. In 2004 she was elected by the community of La Honda, a Diaguita settlement of about 120 families located in one of the province's major Andean valleys, and was reelected for a second term in 2007. Teresa drew a direct connection between her office and the land struggles she was involved in. Specifically, she saw her main role as a *cacica* in making sure that community members retained the possibility of small-scale farming and livestock agriculture, and that the land plots used for these purposes remained in communal hands to ensure that future generations could continue to do so, even if they chose to live and work outside La Honda for some time. Teresa contrasted this "sustainable development" with other forms of development introduced by the expansion of tourism and increasing land commodification. "Construction is not progress! ... It is not progress that you sell your land so that a vast number of chalets can be built and there just remains a little house, like a shack in the middle of all the chalets, and they say 'Look at this progress,' but this is not development."

Teresa's perspective on development had direct practical implications. As a *cacica* she sharply opposed any sales of individual plots of the land claimed by her community. She justified her position by directly referring to the 1994 Constitution.

> There was a huge confrontation, I had to be strict with the people [of La Honda] that they don't sell what's there. The law is very clear in this regard, the laws are there, but what you write you erase with the elbow, so to speak. The law says that [indigenous] lands are not for sale, are not transferable, and are free of charge. This is what … the national constitution says. It is very clear, land can't be sold. We have to try and preserve our socioeconomic space [as indigenous peoples] in which we can feel comfortable in the future and do not have to leave.

And indeed, even a short walk around La Honda revealed a striking absence of new buildings and construction sites, a pattern that stood in sharp contrast to the multitudes of new summer homes and hotels that were built in neighboring towns during the 2000s.

The pivotal moment in Teresa's activist biography, and, in her view, also the immediate reason for her election as the *cacica* of La Honda, were Diaguita protests against the grazing rents paid to landowners. Most of the land in the valley was formally in the hands of several large landholding families, who had fenced off their territory and then charged livestock-owning peasants for passage and pasture access. During the early 2000s, after decades of compliance, these practices became a focal point of indigenous protest, and local communities started resisting these payments. As Teresa recounted, community members of La Honda stopped paying grazing rents in 2004—not without conflict:

> The landlord was called Rodrigo Sánchez [name changed]. We started strong, we met with him and told him we were not going to pay more [grazing rents]. He responded by threatening me, telling me that he was going to denounce me because I was a social agitator who broke the peace, who had stirred them up [La Honda, Teresa's community] for the wrong cause to produce a social disaster … I told him to go ahead, that I knew my rights, and that it was a gross injustice that pasture rents were paid and that the hills [Teresa refers here to pasture areas in higher altitudes above the valley] had been fenced even though they have always been open to everyone for all my life, I grew up playing in those hills and they were free.

Teresa links her leadership role in Diaguita land struggles to the inherent qualities of women:

> We have something that men sometimes do not have. Men usually do not have this inner strength. We are much stronger, because we are able to be mothers, do the housework on our own, work to support the family, wash dishes, do the laundry, clean, and so on, so we have the power to lead.

In other words, Teresa perceives women as generally better prepared for community leadership because of all the different roles they had to fulfill simultaneously, as mothers, breadwinners, and homemakers.

This leadership potential in women often goes unrealized, however. Teresa identifies significant opposition among Diaguita men, even among male activists who want women to participate in indigenous land struggles. From the perspective of these men, women are not capable of projecting leadership and strength: "They [the men] do not to accept a woman easily, they are all machos. In their view a woman should be at home and raise her children." Dominant gender norms thus constitute a major challenge to female activists within the movement, not just because these attitudes and expectations help men to demarcate the political space available to women, but also because women themselves internalize these norms.[8]

This poses the question of how Teresa managed to become a *cacica*. She emphasizes two pivotal factors. For one thing, Teresa observes a recent change in gender attitudes that she directly attributes to growing pressures on indigenous land. "They [Diaguita men] see different necessities now, with the shrinking of our space … and the dwindling of animals. They will listen when someone is prepared and wants to help. It is convenient for them, so they show more confidence [in women]." Moreover, Teresa also emphasizes her experience of leaving the valley, migrating to a larger city, and receiving a university-level education as crucial for becoming accepted as a leader among men in La Honda and beyond. Obtaining their acceptance was an uphill battle.

> In my case I see how they [her community, and especially men in La Honda] respect my background, especially because I left, I can read, I was trained as a teacher, and that was something that was almost impossible in my time, it was impossible to study because there was no school, so you had to leave. And it was expensive and you had to work on top of your studies and most people my age group could not do this, so I was an exception in La Honda and this brought me admiration and respect.

Teresa's activist biography, and the link between education and political activism it illustrates, conforms with well-established arguments on the expansion of higher education, the acquisition of cultural capital among previously marginalized groups (whether women or ethnic minorities more generally), and the possibilities of political activism.[9]

Clara, community council member and artisan

Another female Diaguita leader I interviewed in 2009 was Clara. In her early fifties, she had been recently elected as a council member for the Diaguita community of Los Pinos. Clara's activist biography again highlights the importance of migration for female involvement in indigenous land rights movements. Only three years before, in 2006, Clara had returned to Tucumán from Buenos Aires, where she had spent most of her working life in a variety of different jobs, including domestic work.

Yet in contrast to the close link between migration, the acquisition of formal cultural capital, and female activism exemplified by Teresa, Clara's experience demonstrates the crucial role of migration in shaping internally held and externally ascribed identities that often underpin micro-level dynamics of mobilization (see Viterna 2013, Chapter 3). During her years in the capital, Clara imagined returning to Los Pinos, adopting a rural lifestyle again, and her annual visits home did nothing but reinforce this longing. "I always dreamed of when I would go back with my savings, riding horses, tending sheep; every time I returned [to Buenos Aires] I would start to cry and mourn." Her strong identification with Los Pinos merged with a growing sense of being Diaguita and an Argentine of indigenous origins, a reactive process that was to an important extent driven by Clara's experience of discrimination as an *indígena* in Buenos Aires.[10]

Once Clara had resettled in Los Pinos, she encountered the reality of intensified pressures on the land used by her community. The looming threat of eviction and enclosure motivated Clara to become involved. Echoing Teresa, Clara drew a direct connection between indigenous land struggles and the 1994 Constitution:

> They [the current legal titleholders] wanted to kick us out with the provincial law that they have, but we do not recognize this [law], because we were the first ones here, we existed even before the arrival of Columbus, it's as simple as that, and the nation [national government] made this law, they gave us Article 75, 12.

And, again similar to Teresa, Clara emphasized a specific protest (in her case against the fencing of a lake close by her community) that she experienced as both a personal and collective success and that convinced her to take on a leadership role thereafter.

> Two years ago they [the provincial government] wanted to fence the entire dam [and the artificial lake created by it]. Yet we as indigenous communities told them no, that they will not close off [the lake] even though the government already had the poles ready and wanted to fence, with wire, a public resource! But we told them that we are not going to allow this. We have animals and the highway and other fences already cut their paths, the animals need to come down and drink water ... We said that, as indigenous peoples of the area, we will not allow them to close the dam. But they said that it was a decision taken by law, and we said that regardless of the decision they made and all the posts they already put in, we did not let them close the dam.

Simultaneously, Clara's activism and community leadership was shaped by ethnic development projects and the work of NGOs. Even when still in Buenos Aires, she played a central role in setting up a group of local female artisans that produced and sold textiles made with traditional weaving techniques. During the early 2000s the World Bank funded the so-called Indigenous Communities

Development Project (ICD) across a variety of different settings, including Tucumán, in order to strengthen local indigenous communities and foster their capacities to identify collective needs, with the ultimate aim of facilitating the initiation of community-run projects. Simultaneously, NGOs such as the Catholic Church-supported *Equipo Nacional de Pastoral Aborigen* (ENDEPA) provided local activists with legal training about indigenous rights, but also ran workshops on conflict mediation and proposal-writing. Projects that resulted from these initiatives included a range of activities, such as the construction of new wells and irrigation channels, training in tourism management, and the preservation of Diaguita artisanship. As Clara explains, "we put this project together thinking about empowerment and the preservation of ancestral weaving techniques, because there were only a few people left who still knew how to do them."

Based on this rationale, she applied and received funding for weaving materials and the construction of a stall along the main road leading from the valley to the provincial capital. Yet Clara's success, and the status this project brought her, need to be put into context. When asked about the long-term impact of the ICD, a former project manager indicated that indigenous artisan projects were especially attractive to donors because these initiatives were supposed to combine the preservation (and consumption) of ethnic diversity with female entrepreneurship and labor market incorporation.[11]

In sum, the biographies of Teresa and Clara show that indigenous women can and do exert agency and obtained leadership roles in land struggles, even though the upper echelons of indigenous activism remain dominated by men. I also identified some of the factors that enable and motivate indigenous women to engage in land rights movements. Crucial are preexisting patterns of gender inequality and the historical relationship between indigenous groups and the larger society. In Tucumán both Diaguita men and women have been incorporated into wider social and economic transformations, most importantly the expansion of mass education, urbanization, and market participation. In other words, relative gender equality in educational attainment, the prevalence of female labor migration, as well as development projects focused on women's market incorporation have facilitated female activism. The next section compares the biographies of male and female Diaguita activists to further develop and nuance this argument.

Comparing male and female Diaguita leadership

At a first glance, the recruitment of female leaders such as Teresa and Clara is not that different from the situation with men. Similar to Teresa, a substantial number of male activists left the valley to pursue university-level education and obtain an advanced degree. Diego Solar followed precisely this route. Prior to being elected the *cacique* of Las Palapas, he studied law in Buenos Aires and returned to Tucumán as a qualified lawyer. During his years in the capital, he also became involved in a wider transnational network of indigenous lawyers in

Argentina and other countries. While Diego himself was reluctant to talk about his educational background, several other activists repeatedly emphasized his formal credentials. For example, Teresa drew a close connection between his professional status and his standing among indigenous communities when she described how her community confronted the local landlord over grazing rents.

> I told them [Teresa's community La Honda] not to pay because there were laws, and I showed them the laws. Then I brought in Diego Solar, who is a lawyer, and told him to explain it to the people ... Diego Solar told them that these laws do exist and that he had been to other places in the world where indigenous peoples had managed to obtain benefits at the international level, and that they should not to be afraid but have faith in themselves, and that nothing was going to happen to them. Then the families in La Honda started to tell our "alleged" landlord that they would not pay the grazing rents anymore, and in the following year they did the same, so we are not paying anymore. Diego Solar came on various occasions and the people felt that if the police grabbed them, Diego Solar would bail them out.

Public development projects and NGOs played a similar role in mobilizing indigenous men. While Clara's artisan initiative had the explicit goal of fostering female entrepreneurship, several more general employment- and infrastructure-focused ICD projects contributed to the mobilization of male activists as well, largely because these projects included leadership-strengthening and community-building components, and ultimately fostered new networks beyond individual communities that helped to develop a collective identity as Diaguita. Even the instigation of new communal conflicts over the access and control of these development programs probably contributed to rather than undermined indigenous activism.[12]

At the same time, there was also a major difference in the recruitment of male and female leaders. Indigenous land struggles were usually the first time women engaged in any form of activism, while men often brought prior political experience. Most of the male leaders I interviewed were already politically active before their participation in Diaguita land struggles. Most prominently, an older generation of male *caciques* participated in an earlier episode of indigenous activism in Tucumán that surged briefly during the early 1970s, before the military dictatorship seized power. Other male leaders such as Alejandro López held positions in the municipal government before joining the land rights movement. Another group of men acted as local party officials or neighborhood brokers (*punteros*) for the Peronist Party, building a clientele and then exchanging votes for access to state and party resources. For example, Sergio Arenas, the *cacique* of El Fortunado, claims that "I have always been a Peronist" and that he seeks to form a "renovating movement" from within Peronism to obtain land titles for members of his community.

Participation in non-indigenous politics remains a matter of intense debate among Diaguita leaders. Yet irrespective of their position on the issue, activists with prior political experience certainly benefited from it. Alejandro, for instance, suggests that his position as the elected *delegado* (a position comparable to a mayor of a small town), and the control over municipal resources it gave him, was crucial in obtaining the communal land title for Las Palapas:

> I was able to get the land title because I was the authority of the community ... I held the position of cacique during this time period and was also the delegado. If I had not used my position as a public official as a springboard, I would have never managed to obtain the titling of the land.

Other male activists similarly credited their political experience for ascending to leadership roles. For men, prior involvement—whether in government office, political parties, or other movements—thus constitutes a critical resource in establishing themselves as leaders within the Diaguita movement. Seen in this light, the almost exclusive confinement of this kind of experience to indigenous men helps to explain the relative absence of indigenous women from positions of power within the movement. As the next section will develop in more detail, the lack of indigenous women's prior political experience has also contributed to the formation of a distinct style of female leadership.

The gendered implications of indigenous land rights activism

What are the consequences of indigenous land claims? And what are their implications for female leadership and gender relations? When the analytical focus is on land titling, success has been limited. The majority of indigenous communities in Argentina have sought communal land, yet to date only a fraction have made a successful claim.

In Tucumán, only one out of sixteen recognized Diaguita communities, Las Palapas, has obtained formal titling and received around 52,000 hectares of land. What Alejandro López does not mention in our conversation is that indigenous leaders in Las Palapas had the peculiar advantage of being able to support their claims with a written legal document from the colonial period, a *Cédula Real*, which established the precise boundaries of a land title granted by the Spanish Crown. In turn, the land title enabled Las Palapas to receive further benefits. The community became a frontrunner in obtaining funds for improving potable water provision and irrigation systems, largely because many development agencies, whether national or international, only support infrastructure projects in case of tenure security. Interviews with non-activist community members from Las Palapas suggest that formal land rights also provide "psychological security," especially because the formalization of tenure ensures the free movement of animals and facilitates investments in tourism-related projects.

Moreover, from a gender perspective, tenure security in Las Palapas has not transformed the domestic and productive roles of men and women. I could not detect any significant differences between the economic activities of men and women in Las Palapas and other communities. Up to a generation ago, most of those who identify as Diaguita were engaged in a combination of livestock agriculture and farming, and produced primarily for self-consumption. To obtain some cash, male household members also tended to migrate for temporary work to the sugarcane harvest in the lowlands of Tucumán and neighboring provinces. Over the last three decades, the importance of farming and cattle herding declined and subsistence strategies became primarily built around salaries and wages, whether in Las Palapas or other Diaguita communities. Today, men tend to engage primarily in construction work, public employment, or fixed-term contracts in tourism or development projects, while women are more likely to derive income from a combination of social assistance programs, handicrafts, and agriculture, which includes the tending of small plots of land and the making of dairy products. This gendered division of labor might help to explain why female indigenous leaders such as Teresa and Marta are particularly concerned about the threats posed by eviction and land fragmentation, whereas male leaders such as Diego and Sergio are more concerned about the symbolic meanings of communal land rights.

Yet focusing on the *outcome*—land access—alone overlooks important gender implications of the *process* of indigenous mobilization. For one thing, male and female leaders differ in their leadership style and the priorities they set for movement organization and further membership recruitment. Teresa and Clara are more concerned than their male counterparts about the identity commitments found among younger community members (*comuneros*). Both women worried that the next generation might not know enough about its roots or be too afraid to develop a strong identification as Diaguita. In Clara's words:

> I think it is a process to get to say "I am Indian." Often there is discrimination. A girl from Los Pinos told me that in secondary school, they ask who is a descendant of indigenous peoples and only she raised her hand, all the others did not assume this [identity]. So it's a process. I also analyze those who are studying outside [of Los Pinos] and what they know about their roots, because at some point they will be in the majority.[13]

Consequently, the two women spent significant efforts on mobilizing younger community members. Teresa, for example, offered afternoon classes on local history and regularly convened excursions to visit archeological sites showcasing Diaguita precolonial heritage. Marta combined regular visits to the families of Los Pinos with the organization of youth-specific events. Seen through the lens of social movement theory, those activities were clearly aimed at fostering "participation identities," so that younger *comuneros* come to see their involvement as something that would be natural and almost necessary to pursue for "people like me" (Stryker, 2000).

The importance female leaders assign to youth participation is at least partially a result of their own distinctive recruitment into the land rights movement. One of the distinguishing features of women in leadership positions is that—in sharp contrast to male leaders such as Sergio or Alejandro—female activists such as

Teresa and Clara are largely new to political mobilization. Therefore they cannot rely on previously established political networks and access to state and party resources in order to mobilize support for their (re)election as *cacicas* or council members. Consequently, these women do not pursue an option many of the male leaders frequently rely on: the establishment of clientelist ties with their constituencies and the delivery of targeted public benefits, a basic ingredient of indigenous politics in Argentina.[14]

Clientelism is obviously not a male domain. Yet the lack of prior political linkages makes it a difficult strategy to use for female leaders. This puts a different spin on Teresa and Clara's preoccupation with the identity and involvement of young *comuneros*. When clientelist exchanges are not an option, then mobilizing youths with the aim to foster commitment and pride in indigenous identity constitutes an alternative pathway to establish a political powerbase. In doing so, female leaders draw on externally assigned ascriptions and stereotypes about women as mothers and caregivers, predestined to engage in the socialization of the young. Clara, for example, emphasizes that her main electoral support came from the younger community members when she ran for *cacique* of Los Pinos in 2010 (she ultimately lost the election by a small margin). She also highlights that "the young people said they felt comfortable working with me" because of her identity as a woman.

Indigenous mobilization is not only gendered with respect to the leadership style pursued by men and women. Another crucial implication are potential spillovers from women's land rights activism into other forms of political participation. Teresa and Clara's biographies again provide important insights. Teresa eventually withdrew from the indigenous land rights movement, and from political participation altogether. The reasons for her demobilization are multi-faceted, but what stands out is that her rather confrontational "male" leadership style, combined with her hardliner stance on the sale of any communal lands claimed by La Honda, provoked opposition from within her community and other (male) indigenous leaders in the UPND, and eventually even alienated her key allies, indigenous women and young people in her community, leading her to step down from office in 2010.

By contrast, Clara's initial involvement in Diaguita land rights activism acted as a stepping stone toward other forms of political engagement. Tired of the lack of female representation in Los Pinos and the male-dominated meetings of the UPND, Clara initiated the foundation of the *Organización de Mujeres Diaguitas* and became the association's first president. Set up in 2010 with more than 70 members, this organization seeks to provide Diaguita women with a space to deliberate and accommodate their specific situation as women within the movement and as *indígenas* in wider society, while establishing an organizational platform to foster female leadership. Clara emphasizes that "we are not feminists, we want to work alongside the men and do not want to compete with them" (in Leiva, 2011: 36). The statement echoes other research on indigenous gender politics, which finds that indigenous women reject feminism as a Western concept that misrepresents their position in society and that has potentially divisive implications (Richards, 2005). This said, Clara's growing engagement in gender politics illustrates that women's initial involvement in indigenous land struggles does establish a possible pathway towards other forms of political participation.

Conclusion

Based on the comparison of Diaguita activism in the Argentine province of Tucumán, this chapter has explored the impact of indigenous land claims on gender relations. Both Diaguita men and women viewed the possibility of claiming indigenous communal land established by the 1994 Constitution as a crucial resource in their efforts to contain mounting pressures on the land they use and live on. So far only one out of sixteen Diaguita communities in the province managed to obtain a communal land title.

Yet this is not the whole story. This chapter moved the analytical spotlight from the *outcome* to the *process* of indigenous land claims, and found that in Tucumán women actively participate in the land rights movement. Their involvement has expanded women's social networks and fostered their identification as Diaguita and indigenous Argentines. The chapter further demonstrated that a small number of Diaguita women ascended to become movement leaders. Mobilization for land claims often constitutes women's first entry point into political leadership roles and in some cases has led to involvement in gender politics and other forms of political participation.

As leaders, indigenous women also set different priorities and pursue distinct goals. The chapter showed that female Diaguita leaders prioritize working with youth and seek to foster an indigenous identification especially among younger community members. Such a focus is at least partially related to the gendered mobilization patterns. Male leaders can often rely on prior political experiences for building their powerbase. By contrast, female activists usually have not engaged in politics beforehand and lack these kinds of resources, leading them to establish political support through youth mobilization.

It also merits attention that indigenous women's activism is highly context-dependent. In the case of Diaguita land struggles in Tucumán, relative gender equality in terms of educational attainment and the prevalence of female labor migration, as well as development projects focused on women's market incorporation, greatly facilitated women's activism. These factors are put into sharp relief when comparing Diaguita land claims to those of other indigenous groups in Argentina. For example, the in many ways radically different Mbya communities in Misiones provide a dramatic contrast (vom Hau and Wilde 2010). There, indigenous activism around land rights remains confined to men; women are excluded from politics. These rigid gender boundaries are to an important extent linked to very different histories of engaging the state and larger society. Diaguita communities are former pastoralists with a long history of interaction with outsiders and lost their original language generations ago, while Mbya communities are historically highly mobile horticulturalists who had only sparse outside contact and continue to speak Guarani.[15] Mbya women are far more bound by their role as the embodiment of community. They are frequently prevented from completing even primary schooling or becoming wage laborers. The Mbya "traditional" way of life is also guarded by a number of NGOs concerned with cultural preservation. As this brief comparative sketch illustrates, it is important to pay close attention to the broader scope conditions that foster (or undermine) the political activism of indigenous women.

Taken together, the analysis of the Diaguita land rights movement in Tucumán suggests that it is crucial to move beyond women's access to land and focus on gendered patterns of land-related activism more broadly. Indigenous women's involvement in land claims constitutes a potential entry into leadership roles within the movement and political engagement more generally. Seen in this light, indigenous mobilization for land rights thus can have empowering effects and might even contribute to future transformations of gender hierarchies, even in the absence of successful land claims.

Acknowledgements

I would like to thank the *Ministerio de Ciencia e Innovación* (MICINN) in Spain for its generous funding of fieldwork leading up to this study (Grant No. CSO2011-28387, INDIMOVE project). I am also grateful to Caroline Archambault and Annelies Zoomers for their excellent comments and suggestions on a first draft of this chapter. Any remaining errors are mine.

Notes

1   A significant part of the indigenous population lives concentrated in urban areas. Their activism around communal land rights is an understudied area, yet unfortunately beyond the scope of this chapter.
2   This is true for both private and public lands. Latin American states often sell or reassign the use of public lands to foster export-oriented agriculture (e.g., wine, soy beans) or extractive industries, usually in the name of a vaguely defined "national interest."
3   Parts of this section have already been published in vom Hau and Wilde (2010).
4   The 1994 Constitution also established important limitations to indigenous land claims. First, the constitution speaks of land rights, and not territory. Specifically, the constitutional focus on land does not specify the rights of indigenous communities to control the exploitation of resources found within their territories, for example minerals or medical plants, and the potential future uses of these resources (Carrasco, 2000). Second, the right to claim communal lands is associated with indigenous communities, defined as "groups of families," and thus ultimately linked to a specific location or settlement. Such a focus on local communities more broadly, and not on indigenous groups, prevents land claims covering large surfaces—that might crosscut national boundaries.
5   The larger project this chapter draws on combines in-depth interviews with indigenous activists, non-activists, state officials, civil society actors, and economic elites with an analysis of contentious activities and indigenous claims-making based on local newspapers in Tucumán.

6   This gendered division of labor is not specific to indigenous land rights activism or
    Diaguitas in Tucumán. Women doing what some have dubbed the "shitwork" of
    activism is in fact common across a variety of social movements (McAdam, 1992).
7   The names and locations used for the case narratives have been changed in order to
    guarantee the anonymity of interviewees.
8   Leiva (2011) and Méndez (2011) come to similar conclusions.
9   See Wimmer (2002), Gutierrez (1999), and Stavenhagen (2002) on the nexus
    between the expansion of mass education and the rise of indigenous movements in
    Latin America.
10 See Jenkins (1997) on identity theory and reactive ethnicity.
11 Interview with Jorge Aimaro, former project manager for the ICD and currently
    working for the INAI in Tucumán.
12 See Woolcock and Gibson (2008) for a more general theoretical framework on the
    role of conflict in communal empowerment.
13 This and the following citation are taken from an interview with Clara conducted by
    another researcher in 2010 (Leiva 2011: 34–38).
14 See Gordillo (2008) on the nexus between clientelism and indigenous politics, and
    Auyero (2000) and Levitsky (2003) on clientelism in Argentina more generally.
15 The two groups also differ in how they are categorized. Outsiders tend to describe the
    Mbya as "real Indians," whereas the Diaguita are often depicted as "fake Indians" that
    lack authenticity.

References

Auyero, J. (2000) "The Logic of Clientelism in Argentina: An Ethnographic Account,"
    Latin American Research Review, vol. 35, no. 3, pp. 55–81.
Bastia, T., and Hau, M. vom (2014) "Migration, Race and Nationhood in Argentina,"
    Journal of Ethnic and Migration Studies, vol. 40, no. 3, pp. 475–92.
Bebbington, A., Humphreys Bebbington, D., Bury, J., Lingand, J., Muñoz, J.P. and Scurrah,
    M. (2008) "Mining and Social Movements: Struggles Over Livelihood and Rural
    Territorial Development in the Andes," *World Development*, vol. 36, pp. 2888–2905.
Brysk, A. (2000) "Democratizing Civil Society in Latin America," *Journal of Democracy*,
    vol. 11, pp. 151–166.
Carrasco, M. (2000) *Los Derechos de los Pueblos Indígenas en Argentina*. Buenos Aires:
    Vinciguerra.
de Ferranti, D. de, Perry, G.E., Ferreira, F.H.G., and Walton M. (eds) (2004) *Inequality in
    Latin America: Breaking with History?* Washington, D.C.: World Bank.
Gordillo, G. (2008) "The Clientelization of Ethnicity: Party Hegemony and Indigenous
    Political Subjectivities," *Journal of Latin American Cultural Studies*, vol. 17, no. 3,
    pp. 335–48.
Gordillo, G. and Hirsch, S. (2003) "Indigenous Struggles and Contested Identities in
    Argentina Histories of Invisibilization and Reemergence," *Journal of Latin American
    Anthropology*, vol. 8, pp. 4–30.
Gutiérrez, N. (1999) *Nationalist Myths and Ethnic Identities: Indigenous Intellectuals and the
    Mexican State*. Lincoln, NE: University of Nebraska Press.
Hall, G. and Patrinos, H.A. (2005) *Pueblos indígenas, pobreza y desarrollo humano en América
    Latina: 1994-2004*. Washington, D.C.: World Bank.
Hoffman, K. and Centeno, M.A. (2003) "The Lopsided Continent: Inequality in Latin
    America," *Annual Review of Sociology*, vol. 29, no. 1, pp. 363–90.

Instituto Nacional de Estadísticas y Censos de la República Argentina (2004/5) Encuesta Complementaria de Pueblos Indígenas. Internet source available at www.indec.mecon.ar/webcenso/ECPI/index_ecpi.asp. Accessed 12 April 2014.

Jenkins, R. (1997) *Rethinking Ethnicity: Arguments and Explorations*. Thousand Oaks, CA: Sage.

Leiva, E.C. (2011) "Mujeres Diaguitas en Lucha: Testimonios de Resistencia." (Cartagena de Indias, Colombia: CIESAS-Sureste), Diploma para el Fortalecimiento del Liderazgo de las Mujeres Indígenas.

Levitsky, S. (2003) *Transforming Labor-Based Parties in Latin America: Argentine Peronism in Comparative Perspective*. New York: Cambridge University Press.

McAdam, D. (1992) "Gender as a Mediator of the Activist Experience: The Case of Freedom Summer," *American Journal of Sociology*, vol. 97, no. 5, pp. 1211–40.

Mahoney, J. (2010) *Colonialism and Postcolonial Development: Spanish America in Comparative Perspective*. Cambridge, UK: Cambridge University Press.

Méndez, M.B. (2011) "Mujeres Indígenas en Cargos del Gobierno Comunitario del Pueblo Diaguita del Valle de Tafí. " (San Cristóbal de las Casas, Chiapas, México: CIESAS-Sureste), Diploma para el Fortalecimiento del Liderazgo de las Mujeres Indígenas.

Psacharopoulos, G. and Patrinos, H.A. (1994). *Indigenous People and Poverty in Latin America: An Empirical Analysis*. Washington, D.C.: World Bank.

Richards, P. (2005) "The Politics of Gender, Human Rights, and Being Indigenous in Chile," *Gender & Society*, vol. 19, no. 2, pp. 199–220.

Sieder, R. (ed) (2002) *Multiculturalism in Latin America: Indigenous Rights, Diversity and Democracy*. New York: Palgrave Macmillan.

Stavenhagen, R. (2002) "Indigenous Peoples and the State in Latin America: An Ongoing Debate," in Sieder, R. (ed.) *Multiculturalism in Latin America: Indigenous Rights, Diversity, and Democracy*, pp. 24–44. New York: Palgrave Macmillan,

Stryker, S. (2000) "Identity Competition: Key to Differential Social Movement Participation?," in Stryker, S., Owens, T. J., and White, R. W. (eds) *Self, Identity, and Social Movements*, pp. 21–40. Minneapolis, MN: University of Minnesota Press.

Van Cott, D.L. (2000) *The Friendly Liquidation of the Past: The Politics of Diversity in Latin America*. Pittsburgh, PA: University of Pittsburgh Press.

Viterna, J. (2013) *Women in War: The Micro-Processes of Mobilization in El Salvador*. New York: Oxford University Press.

vom Hau, M. and Wilde, G. (2010) "'We Have Always Lived Here': Indigenous Movements, Citizenship and Poverty in Argentina," *Journal of Development Studies*, vol. 46, no. 7, pp. 1283–1303.

Wimmer, A. (2002) *Nationalist Exclusion and Ethnic Conflict: Shadows of Modernity*. New York: Cambridge University Press.

Woolcock, M. and Gibson, C. (2008) "Empowerment, Deliberative Development, and Local-Level Politics in Indonesia: Participatory Projects as a Source of Countervailing Power," *Studies in Comparative International Development*, vol. 43, no. 2, pp. 151–80.

Yashar, D. (2005) *Contesting Citizenship: Indigenous Movements, the State, and the Postliberal Challenge in Latin America*. Cambridge, UK: Cambridge University Press.

Zoomers, A. (2000) *Current Land Policy in Latin America: Regulating Land Tenure under Neo-Liberalism*. Amsterdam: Royal Tropical Institute.

6 Joint land certificates in Madagascar

The gendered outcome of a "gender-neutral" policy

Marit Widman

Introduction

For a century, two systems of land management coexisted in Madagascar—the colonial system for land titling on one hand, and customary land tenure on the other. The land-titling system suffered from low capacity and elite capture. Disputes over inheritance and boundaries amplified as pressure on arable land increased due to commercial interest, migration, population growth, and soil erosion. In response to these issues, Madagascar instituted a comprehensive land tenure reform in 2005, in line with the World Bank privatization agenda to encourage investments. The reform aimed at improving access to formal property rights to land for the rural population, modernizing land services, and reforming the land legislation. A key element was the establishment of local land offices assigned to issue land certificates.

No gender equality principles were adopted in the reform and no reference made to intra-household allocation of land rights. In order to secure women's rights to jointly held land, the Millennium Challenge Corporation (MCC), acting as donor, advocated mandatory joint certification for couples' co-owned property. However, joint certification remained a voluntary measure and few couples have used the opportunity; the majority of the land certificates are issued to men individually. Resourceful women seem to have opted for individual certificates rather than joint.

This chapter investigates the reasons for the low number of joint certificates during the first years of the Malagasy land tenure reform. The analysis builds on fieldwork conducted in Madagascar in 2011. The rural municipality Soavinandriana is studied in detail, using survey data and focus group interviews. The analysis points out three main factors contributing to the weak role of joint certification. First, it has not been a political priority. The problems of access, long waiting times, high costs, etc. in the titling system were considered more important to address in the reform process than gender issues. The land legislation was considered to be gender-neutral, and there was no strong national women's movement to push the agenda of joint certificates. Second, the political crisis in 2009 resulted in underfunding and weak implementation. Since the donor most concerned with gender issues—MCC—left the project there has been little information and effort to promote joint certificates. Third, a "traditional view" of the household, where the husband represents the household, dominates both among civil servants and rural households.

Securing shared property rights for women is crucial, particularly since widows do not have the legal right to keep land that is certified in their husbands' names only. In 2013 Madagascar held the first general election since the 2009 *coup d'état*, and the new government may take the opportunity to address the weaknesses in the land tenure reform.

This study serves as a reminder of the importance of effective measures to secure women's land rights.

History of Malagasy land tenure

Madagascar is the fourth-largest island in the world, with a surface area of 587,000 km², and a population of approximately 20 million. It is one of the poorest countries in the world, and three-quarters of the population live below the national poverty line (World Bank, 2010). About 80 percent of the households rely on agriculture for their livelihoods, mainly rice production and raising livestock. Farm sizes are typically small, on average less than one hectare (ha) (Andrianarina-Ratisialonana and Burnod, 2012). Traditions vary between groups and regions, but there are some common features of customary land tenure as described by Andrianarina-Ratisialonana and Burnod (2012). First, the collective nature of ownership and managements structures. Second, the first person to clear and work the land was allocated the use right. Third, there was no written formalization of land rights. The clan leaders, *ray-amandrena* (Leisz *et al.*, 1994), had an important role in land management and allocation. Land holds significant cultural and social value and is thought to belong to the ancestors. In general, land was passed on in a patrilineal descent system (Leisz *et al.*, 1994).

In the 18th century, the monarchy stipulated that it owned all land, while the population had usufruct rights. The first written code governing land was formulated in 1881. When France colonized Madagascar in 1896, the monarchy's property was turned into colonial state property. The colonial administration introduced private property rights, aiming to secure colonial interests, through a titling system (Maldidier, 2000). Large concessions—in total about one million hectares, or roughly 12 percent of arable land[1]—were allocated to colonial settlers and companies in return for growing export crops such as coffee and vanilla. Most of the concessions were located in relative proximity to the capital Antananarivo, in the east and north-west parts of the country (Brès, 2007; Maldidier, 2000). The most fertile lands were expropriated by the colonial state, whereas the Malagasy peasants were pushed into indigenous reserves and areas of collective registration (*cadastre*) in the close surroundings of the concessions, also covering about 1 million ha. In order to protect community lands from colonial settlers, villages sometimes registered a collective title in the name of the community leader. In practice these measures implied that land was still governed by customary rules (Teyssier *et al.*, 2006; Andrianarina-Ratisialonana and Burnod 2012; Maldidier, 2000; Leisz, 1994).

At independence in 1960, most of the French colonial settlers left Madagascar but their land titles were still valid and often the land itself continued to be cultivated by former workers (Brès, 2007). A clause for decolonizing land, which had been abandoned by the legal owners, was enforced by the socialist Second Republic. Between 1977 and 1982, about 10 percent of former colonial concessions were returned to the Malagasy state (Brès, 2007). Teyssier *et al.* (2006) describe how the land-titling system remained in place, but the administrative process was expensive, long, and the land services were difficult to access for the rural population. There is no complete, accurate, and up-to-date information about existing titles, but approximate numbers indicate that a total of 330,000 private titles, corresponding to less than 10 percent of agricultural plots, were issued and that about 5 percent underwent collective registration, which implied a first step toward a private title. The majority of titles were registered prior to independence. Teyssier *et al.* (2006) further state that there are many pending requests for titles, and explain that when owners did not pursue the collective registration process, the legal status became unclear. It is typically those Malagasy with resources that have benefited from the titling system, and who have sometimes abused the system by titling land that is occupied by someone else (Teyssier *et al.*, 2006; Maldidier, 2000).

Across all of Madagascar, the state system and customary land management co-exist to some degree. Customary tenure systems have evolved due to increasing pressure on land, new rules, and new actors (Leisz *et al.*, 1994; Jacoby and Minten, 2007). Rice fields are typically individually held whereas pasture lands and forests fall under common management. Very generally, the central highlands and the lowland rice basins with fertile soils, where pressure on land has been high since colonial times, have a more market-oriented and individualized tenure system, while areas located further away from markets and main roads, typically in the south and coastal areas, are managed under customary tenure (Maldidier, 2000). In response to the discrepancy between the formal system and the local situation, a semi-formal system of *petits papiers* ("little documents") issued by local authorities developed (Teyssier *et al.*, 2006).

Rising income inequality in rural Madagascar is accentuated by increasing inequality in access to land. As the decolonization of former colonial land has not been completed, many Malagasy peasants do not have formal ownership of land which they have cultivated for generations. (Maldidier, 2000; Teyssier *et al.*, 2008). According to the principle "the land belongs to those who cultivate it,"[2] they are however the legitimate landowners. Descendants of colonial settlers have in some cases sold land to commercial investors and evicted the occupants, resulting in violent conflicts. Disputes also arise when the descendants of community leaders claim private ownership of collective land titles which had been registered in the name of a community leader in order to keep land under customary tenure (Maldidier, 2000). On a local level, pressure from immigration and commercial interests also contributes to conflicts over land. Within village boundaries, conflicts and disputes between sharecroppers, landlords, and tenants are common. Undivided inheritance and disagreement over the content of verbal contracts between parents and children are grounds for many conflicts between heirs. Although community and family control over land is still important, local systems for dispute settlements are weakened (Maldidier, 2000).

Land-tenure reform

The superposition of two systems of land rights—the system of land titles and state institutions on one hand, and the customary systems on the other—created a good deal of uncertainty and insecurity in rural Madagascar. These difficulties, coupled with the increasing pressure on arable land from commercial investments, migration and population growth, resulted in a rising number of conflicts with which neither local systems for conflict management nor courts could cope. The World Bank-supported development plan adopted by Madagascar suggested market-oriented reforms to encourage investment. In 2004, a task force was assigned to prepare a land-tenure reform.

The Letter for Land Policy, established to guide the development of the reform, and the new government agency in charge of land management, the National Land Program (PNF), were launched a year later. The World Bank, the Food and Agriculture Association of the United Nations (FAO), and other donors contributed to the funding of the reform. The US government-financed MCC provided 85 percent of the funding (or about USD 90 million) through its implementing unit, the Millennium Challenge Account Madagascar or MCA (MCC, 2009). There is a trend of land-tenure reforms in sub-Saharan Africa in which formalization of customary land rights is a key feature. Tripp (2004) describes how World Bank-supported land policies, which aimed to increase market integration and to attract foreign investors, have evolved to recognize customary systems of land management. In Madagascar, the formalization of land rights also implies privatization. Private land now includes both titled and untitled occupied property (*propriété privée non-titrée* (PPNT)) (*Loi 2006-031*).

The Letter for Land Policy (2005) identifies four axes of the reform:

1   to restructure and modernize the land service administration;
2   to improve and decentralize land management by creating local land offices (LLOs) at commune level that are authorized to issue and manage the innovation "land certificates," formal ownership documents complementing the land titles;
3   to renew land-related legislation;
4   a national training program for land administration staff.

The initiative to start an LLO should come from the commune and it should become a self-financed commune service. However, to date international donors have played an important role. The staff, known as "LLO agents," should have attained a level of secondary education at minimum and are on average young.

Citizens apply for a land certificate—whether for one or several plots—by visiting the LLO and presenting proof of ownership through purchase or inheritance, as a gift, or by having cleared or used the land in a productive way (*mise-en-valeur*). A digital map with the legal status of land indicated, called a *plan local d'occupation foncière* (PLOF), is consulted to verify that the land is not already titled. Thereafter, a local recognition session on the ground verifies ownership and delimitation of the plot, attended by a committee consisting of representatives of the commune and fokontany (administrative unit/village), the LLO agent, and neighbors. The fee for the certificate is based on the size and type of land. There are two opposition periods during which it's possible to make a complaint if anyone else has legal claims to the plot. A land certificate can be issued individually, to a couple (joint certificate), in the name of several persons, for instance a group of siblings (consortium certificate), or to public entities. The land rights provided by a land certificate are practically identical to the rights provided by a land title (Teyssier *et al.*, 2006).

The development of the reform was relatively strong until the *coup d'état* in 2009. The land deals with two agribusiness investors—South Korean Daewoo and Indian Varunco—concerning almost half of all agricultural land in Madagascar, have been seen as the trigger of the political crises. The contracts would last for more than 50 years and the farmers already using the land in question were not consulted. When the deals became public, massive protests ensued and ultimately the projects were cancelled (Andrianarina-Ratsialonana *et al.*, 2011). After the military coup Madagascar was governed by an interim regime until the first elections in late 2013. The interim regime was not recognized by the international community, which implied that the MCC did not renew their contract, and indeed it withdrew all funding in 2009 (MCA, 2009). This was unforeseen by many of the communes dependent on the funding to run their LLOs. The political crisis had negative effects on the wider economy, including infrastructure development and the functioning of public services. Newly established LLOs were particularly vulnerable; they lost their electricity supply and lacked crucial resources, such as gasoline, printer ink, and computer software. Poor infrastructure was exacerbated by incompetent (and inadequate) staffing, and LLO employees were often badly trained, under-paid, or irregularly paid. There was also a lack of supervision and control, which opened up possibilities for corruption. In sum, the certification program has been largely ineffective, although in comparison to the titling system it seems to have greater potential to deliver formal tenure rights to the rural population. Of Madagascar's 1,550 communes 420 have established LLOs. Approximately 105,000 certificates have been issued since 2005, covering about 125,000 ha. However, there are another 90,000 pending applications for certificates (Land Observatory, 2014).

Gender dimensions of land governance

The Malagasy constitution grants women and men equal rights, and prohibits discrimination based on sex (Government of Madagascar, 1992). Madagascar ratified the UN Convention on Elimination of Discrimination Against Women, CEDAW, in 1989 (UN, 2008). However, the marriage code still assigns the husband the role as household head (*Loi 2007-022*). Women participate less in political institutions and local decision-making bodies than men and have difficulties accessing public administration and services (Noaroarisoa, 2009).

The marriage code stipulates a partial common property regime (*Loi 2007-022*), which means that assets acquired during marriage are common property, whereas assets acquired before marriage and inherited assets are individual property. In the case of divorce, common property is divided equally between the spouses, whereas individual property is kept by the spouses respectively. Widows are a vulnerable group since women often follow their husbands and work on his land. A widow can keep half of the common property, but is only sixth in order of inheritance to the rest of the property[3] (*Loi 1968-012*). The legislation applies to civil marriage including registered traditional marriages but, particularly in rural Madagascar, traditional marriage without registration is widespread (Noroarisoa, 2009). The customary division of common property in case of separation is that the husband keeps two-thirds and the wife one-third. This practice prevails, but there are also cases when the wife does not receive any of the common property (Noroarisoa, 2009; Widman, 2014).

The custom of patrilineal descent still dominates in many communities, although the legislation on succession and inheritance has been gender-neutral since 1968 (*Loi 1968-012*; Noroarisoa, 2009). There is no legal portion for children or spouse, but in absence of a will children are the primary heirs irrespective of gender. However, it is possible to give female heirs their share of the inheritance as a sum of money instead of physical assets.

Gendered norms and customs with regard to land vary across regions and socio-cultural groups, but usually women have only secondary rights to land. This implies a right to use the land but not to bequeath, donate, or sell it. In the most patriarchal contexts, the coastal and south-east regions, a woman cannot inherit land, and gains user rights only if she is unmarried and has no brothers (Leisz *et al.*, 1994; Noroarisoa, 2009).

Gender inequality was not considered an important problem in Madagascar according to one of the "architects" of the land-tenure reform (personal message). In most sub-Saharan African countries, as explained by Joireman (2008), co-ownership of land property is "an alien concept" and few countries have legislation that provide for co-ownership of marital property. The Malagasy legislation on marriage and inheritance are comparatively progressive, and the land legislation act of 1960 (*Ordonnance* n°60-146) does not make any distinction between men's and women's opportunities to own land. The option of making a joint title in the name of both spouses existed in the titling system introduced in the colonial period, although it was little used (Leisz *et al.*, 1994). The new land policy of 2005 also makes provision for joint certificates (*Loi 2005-019*), but there is no specific reference to women's land rights in the policy. Other issues, such as the low capacity of land services in terms of processing applications, long waiting times etc., were given priority over gender equality in the land-reform process.

However, the donor MCC's internal rules obliged them to make a gender assessment of the reform before funding it. Hence, a gender evaluation was conducted in 2006, and showed that:

- information about joint certificates had not reached the beneficiaries;
- staff at LLOs did not know about this option and therefore spread misinformation;
- there were no systematic questions on civil status when a person applied for a certificate (Giovarelli, 2006).

Women raised concerns about having only their husband's name registered on the certificate, since some had found that their spouses had sold land without their consent. The MCC advocated mandatory registration of joint property in the name of both spouses, or at the very minimum the inclusion of an extra line in the application form (Giovarelli, 2006) to encourage joint certification. These concerns and recommendations given short shrift by the PNF, whose policy response was simply to add an extra line for the spouse's name in the application form.

Information on the number of joint certificates is not collected at national level, but available numbers indicate that very few joint certificates had been applied for before 2011, when the fieldwork for this study was conducted. The numbers of joint certificates issued as compared to the total number of certificates at the best-performing LLOs in three different regions were as follows:

- Soavinandriana—twelve out of 2,237;[4]
- Amparafaravola— two out of 1,605;[5]
- Antetezambaro[6]—one out of 80.

Civil society observers also noted this trend, and identified the lack of joint certificates as a problem for women's land-tenure security (interviews with NGO HARDI, Programme SAHA).

Case study site

In order to investigate gender dimensions of the land-tenure reform, as part of a doctoral research project, the author conducted fieldwork in Madagascar from December 2010 to May 2011. Interviews were undertaken with key informants at the PNF and with the persons who had been drafting the policy (André Teyssier in particular). LLO agents and users were also interviewed during visits at about fifteen LLOs in different parts of the country.

Based on information collected in the first stage of the fieldwork, a case study site was chosen: the commune of Soavinandriana. It was one of the very first LLOs, and has received the highest number of applications for certificates. The FAO, which had identified the need for secure land rights in order for other agricultural extension services to be successful, funded the LLO (Brès, 2007). The LLO is inter-communale with the neighboring commune Ampary, which however has large areas of already titled land that is ineligible for certification. The data collection was therefore conducted in Soavinandriana only.

Soavinandriana is located in the Itasy region in the central highlands of Madagascar. The fertile land, with its volcanic soils, and the relative proximity to the capital, attracted colonial settlers and migrants. Soavinandriana consists of thirty-three *fokontany* (villages) and has about 50,000 inhabitants. The population density is comparatively high (180 inhabitants/km^2) and population growth has been attributed to relatively high fertility among local people as well as continued migration to the area. Eighty-five percent of the population is involved in agricultural production. The most important crops are rice, manioc, maize, and some cash crops such as coffee, tomatoes, and beans. Fishing is another important activity (Brès, 2007). Both men and women participate in agricultural production and the work on the land, although there is a gendered division of tasks. Men typically work with cattle and preparation of soils, while women are typically responsible for tasks such as weeding and transplanting as well as household work and childcare (Jarosz, 1997). In Soavinandriana, as in most of the central highlands, women's literacy rates are higher than in other regions, women are better informed about their rights to common property (ILC *et al.*, 2009), inheritance regimes are more gender equal, and civil marriage is more common (ROR, 2008).

Methods

The fieldwork and data collection in Soavinandriana took place in March and April 2011. First, information about the applications for certificates at the LLO was registered in what is called the Soavinandriana Land Certificate Database 2011. It included 2,237 applications made by 1,207 different persons, of which a random selection of 360 persons, including both men and women, were drawn. The sampling procedure used to select 148 households without certificates, used as counterfactual, was random walk (UN, 2005; Martin, 2005).[7] In addition, all households with a joint certificate were interviewed. Deere and Doss (2006) stress that individual-level data is necessary to capture gender differences in asset ownership within households, and therefore both partners in a couple were interviewed separately. In total 455 men and 514 women in 511 households were interviewed. The data used in this chapter includes the 378 couples in the dataset.

The household survey instrument included questions about all members of the households, the individual and household inheritance, assets, and livelihoods. Furthermore, there were land-related questions about the characteristics of the plots, the rights to sell and rent etc., as well as questions about motivations and facts about land certification. The survey was held by the enumerators in Malagasy, and translated into French.

Moreover, focus group interviews were conducted with women and men respectively, as well as local leaders and village elders (*ray aman-drena*), in two different villages with different characteristics with regards to pressure on land, distance to the commune center etc. There was also one focus group with local leaders from different *fokontany*.

Data on joint certificates and motivations

Of the plots in the Land Certificate Database 76.5 percent are registered in the name of a man, 20.8 percent in the name of a woman (which is also the average percentage for the whole country (Land Observatory, 2014)), and 2.2 percent in the name of a consortium (i.e. two or more persons, not forming a couple); 0.5 percent of the certificates (12 certificates) are joint, and registered in the names of both partners in a couple. Surprisingly, the number of joint certificates reported in the household survey was 31. This discrepancy with the Land Certificate Database is due to five households with one certificate each reporting several of their plots to be jointly certified; and 11 households having no joint certificate at the LLO reporting to have a total of 20 joint certificates. This over-reporting indicates that information about the reform has not yet reached potential beneficiaries. Focus group discussions revealed that women sometimes considered a certificate in their husband's name as belonging to the whole household.

In line with the partial common property marital regime, couples should certify land individually or jointly depending on the origin of the plot. However, Table 6.1 shows that less than 3 percent of the plots acquired jointly by couples are jointly certified. Land acquired by couples is most often registered in the name of the husband (72 percent), although a surprisingly large share of couples' plots are certified in the name of the wife (25 percent). However, there is an oversampling of women with land certificates in the survey.[8] Widman (2014) investigates the characteristics of these women and finds that they have fewer children, have an income source outside the farm, and their husband has lower education as compared to women who do not hold certificates to common property. All of these factors can be associated with stronger bargaining power (see for instance Kabeer, 1999). This suggests that women with more influence in household decisions seem to opt for individual certificates rather than joint ones.

Land certificates are valued by men and women alike, but not all are able to afford them. The most important reason to apply for a certificate reported by both men and women is "protection from appropriation," followed by the ability they confer to protect the land as inheritance. The most important reason for *not* applying for a certificate is lack of economic resources; the average cost for a

Table 6.1 Plots acquired by couples

	Percentage	Frequency
No certificate	68.7	792
Certificates	31.3	361
Total number of plots	100	1153
Certificates:		
In the name of a man	72.0	260
In the name of a woman	25.2	91
Joint certificate	2.8	10
Total number of certificates	100	361

Source: Soavinandriana Household Survey (2011) Collected by the author

certificate is 25,000 Ariary (about USD 15). The second most important reason stated is "I don't have the power to apply," which indicates secondary land rights. A few men and women state that they do not see the benefit of land certificates or have no confidence in them. No men, but a few women, state that the LLO is too far away (Widman, 2014).

With regard to the type of certificate chosen, Table 6.2 shows that the most important reason for certifying a plot in the name of the husband is simply that "he is the household head." The main reason stated for certifying jointly acquired land in the name of the wife is that it would make division of inheritance easier, by ensuring that the children will inherit the land after both parents are deceased. In focus group discussions, it was mentioned that it works like insurance for the wife and children, in case something happens to the husband. Among the couples who have actually applied for joint certificates, four respondents state that the reason is to make a division of inheritance easier;[9] another three felt it reflected the fact that the land had been acquired by the couple together.

Table 6.3 indicates that the eleven households with joint certificates share some common characteristics that distinguish them from couples without joint certificates. All joint certificates belong to couples that have been through a civil marriage ceremony with the exception of one that belongs to a widow. Of the couples without joint certificates, 73 percent are civilly married. Both men and women in couples with joint certificates are on average younger than those without joint certificates. Couples with joint certificates have on average more plots, and a large majority of the plots have been acquired jointly, whereas the other households have larger shares of individually acquired land. And, although the numbers are very low, there is some indication that men and women in couples with joint certificates have a slightly higher level of education than other couples.

Table 6.2 Reason to register in husband's name/wife's name/jointly (plots acquired by couple)

Reason	Husband's name		Wife's name		Jointly	
	Freq.	*Percentage*	*Freq.*	*Percentage*	*Freq.*	*Percentage*
His/her inheritance	5	3.2	4	10.5		
He/she has purchased it	13	8.4	2	5.3	3	37.5
He/she is the household head	107	69.0	5	13.2	1	12.5
To make division of inheritance easier	18	11.6	17	44.7	4	50
Other	12	7.7	10	26.3		
Total	155	100.00	38	100.00	8	100.00

Source: Soavinandriana household survey (2011), collected by the author

Table 6.3 Characteristics of couples with and without joint land certificates (LC)

	Couple with joint LC N=11[1]		Couple without joint LC (but with at least one individual LC) N=268	
	Frequency	Percentage	Frequency	Percentage
Civil marriage	10[1]	100	196	73
More than primary education (woman)	2	20	27	10
More than primary education (man)	2	20	45	17
Median age (woman)	40		42	
Median age (man)	44.5		47	
Average number of plots	6.9		6.3	
Share of land that is jointly acquired		71		43
Share of land that is acquired by man		21		42
Share of land that is acquired by woman		8		15

Source: Soavinandriana household survey (2011), collected by the author
Note: 1. One of the households with a joint certificate is a widow

As discussed above, one of the households with a joint certificate is that of a widow, who reported that when she was bereaved she kept all the land that had been acquired within the household. Note that if land is registered in the name of her husband only, the widow would not have had the legal right to keep it.

Explanations for the lack of joint certificates

This section presents the three main interacting factors that have resulted in the low number of joint land certificates issued in Madagascar. In broad strokes, they are as follows:

1   the lack of political interest in gender issues in general, and in joint certificates in particular, which resulted in the government implementing only voluntary measures;
2   lack of funding and poor implementation of land-reform initiatives, which have led to insufficient promotion of joint certificates;
3   customary rules on land tenure, inheritance, and marriage, which continue to dominate in many regions and families.

In Madagascar a large part of agricultural land is jointly owned by couples. The experience from land-tenure reforms in other countries (Deere and León, 2003; Walker, 2003) shows that when joint-titling is not mandatory, male household heads tend to receive individual land titles. Therefore joint-titling is a measure necessary to guarantee married women effective ownership rights to land which has been jointly acquired (Deere and León, 2003). The presence of strong women's rights movements seems to played a crucial role in the strengthening women's land rights in general and joint-titling in particular in land-reform processes, as has been the case in Nicaragua and Columbia (Deere and León, 2003) as well as Peru (Glavin *et al.*, 2013). Women's groups have also played an important role in African countries such as Uganda and Tanzania, as described by Tripp (2004) but the struggle has been harder. Tripp (2004) highlights these groups' focus on the revision of statutory law to protect women's land. In Madagascar, there was no strong women's movement pushing the joint certificate agenda. Adelski (2002) observes that civil society in Madagascar remains weak and dominated by the urban elite, and has little advocacy capacity as compared to neighboring countries. Women in particular do not enjoy equal participation in democratic governance. This can be related to the influence of French development cooperation, which could do more to support the organization of civil society and gender equality (OECD, 2014).

In Madagascar the problems of access to land administrations, corruption, high costs, and long waiting times for titles—not to mention outdated registers and maps etc.—were given priority over women's access to land in the land-reform process, partly because the Malagasy context was considered less discriminatory towards women than that in many other African countries. However, the presumed "gender neutrality" of the Malagasy legislation does not mean that discrimination does not exist. In fact, there are clear gender norms and expectations on men and women with regard to land, which are reflected in the legislation related to marriage that assigns husbands the role of household head.

Civil servants often have a conservative idea of how households should run. In an interview conducted by the author in 2011, one government employee expressed the view that:

> The "risk" with a mandatory system is that it is seen as interference in family life. ... Malagasy households consider the HH [household] as a "unit"... whose head is the husband. Registering the land title or the land certificate in the name of the father/husband is not necessarily considered as if the land is the individual property of the father/husband. Comparing welfare distribution may not be relevant since everything owned by the HH is owned by the family.
>
> (personal message)

Staff at the PNF argued informally that pushing for women to be registered in a joint certificate may cause unrest both within family units and within wider society. In the same vein, one of the leading women in the resistance movement aiming to defend land in Madagascar against foreign investors stated that: "forcing joint ownership will disturb the order in families..." (discussion on the land-tenure reform organized by ILC, Sep. 2011).

In focus group discussions women stated that asking to be registered on a joint certificate may be interpreted as not having confidence in one's husband, which could cause conflicts within the family and be socially controversial. The same idea was reflected in the survey responses. Even though the partial common property regime has been in place since 1994, the husband is typically regarded as manager of the household's resources and administrative matters. This relates to gender norms and division of labor. In focus group discussions some men stated that it was easier for them to make the four-hour walk to the LLO than it would be for their wives, who had to stay home and take care of the children; in the survey, women stated that the LLO was situated too far away.

The MCA, the biggest funder of the reform, was also the donor most concerned with gender issues. The overall problems of implementation and sustainability of Madagascar's land-tenure reform seem to have overlooked these aspects, and as noted above, the only measure taken to encourage joint certification was the inclusion of a second line for the spouse's name in the application form. The design of the application form can impact joint-titling, as shown by Deininger *et al.* (2008) who studied the Ethiopian land-tenure reform. In regions where the names and photos of both spouses were required, joint-titling was more common than in locations where there was only one line for an applicant's name and one photo required.

In Madagascar there was evident confusion at the PNF, and consequently at LLOs, about which application form to use. A multitude of different (and outdated) forms were circulating at the LLOs. In places where the correct forms *were* being used, some LLO staff members did not know what the second line was for. Staff at the PNF stressed that joint certification was not a prioritized issue. Furthermore, there was confusion among LLO staff and applicants about how to fill out the application form, which has resulted in couples wanting a joint certificate ending up with a certificate in the name of the husband only. The crucial role of well-informed LLO agents is also illustrated by the man who had first applied for an individual certificate for a plot belonging to him and his wife, but when the LLO agent (a new staff member) had asked him why he did not include his wife in the certificate, he decided to do so. At least in Soavinandriana the idea of joint ownership is not necessarily controversial per se. One main obstacle is lack of information about joint certificates and the consequences thereof in case of, for instance, death of the other spouse. The few couples with joint certificates are familiar with the formal legal system and are would seem to be better informed about legal implications (see Table 6.3).

It is possible to appeal a decision at the LLO, hence a wife could claim to be included on a land certificate for co-owned property. To date there are no known attempts by women to appeal certification, and it seems unlikely to happen. Legal knowledge is generally low among women and there is no obligation to inform the spouse about certification (Noroarisoa, 2009). Given that it is controversial for some women to even ask their husbands about a joint certificate, to challenge them in an official process and thereby bring a household conflict into the open seems like a big step.

Conclusion

The land-tenure reform in Madagascar instituted in 2005 is aimed at reducing land-tenure insecurity through issuing land certificates on privately held land. The problems of access, long waiting times, high costs, and elite capture were given priority over gender equality in the policy design, however. Mandatory joint certification for couples' common property was promoted by the biggest donor, the MCC, but received scant attention from policy-makers and remained a voluntary measure. Since the MCC left the project, few efforts have been made to promote joint certificates and little information circulated about the issue. Civil servants and households in general maintain a unitary model of the household which assigns men the role of head and thereby manager of joint property. With regard to women's land rights, individual certificates have been the focus of attention by the land services and beneficiaries.

The 2009 political and economic crisis halted the reform process; two-thirds of the communes do not have an LLO and of the LLOs that do exist, many are dysfunctional. However, since the 2013 elections Madagascar is no longer ostracized by the international community, which gives legislators an opportunity to continue and develop the reform. Joint certificates play a crucial role in securing widowed and divorced women's rights to common property. A mandatory mechanism for joint certification of jointly held property would be ideal. The experience from Peru shows that stringent, enforceable rules for marital property can effectively provide women with such titles (Glavin *et al.*, 2013). In Madagascar, a partial common property regime is already in place, hence mandatory joint certification would involve (in principle at least) bringing land legislation in line with the marriage code. However, this would not comprise traditional marriages; hence information about the benefits of civil marriage and the opportunity for joint certification for traditionally married couples would also be extremely important.

Civil society in Madagascar has started to pay more attention to the issue of joint certificates recently. The issue is now much more on the radar for the Land Observatory which, since the fieldwork for this study was completed, has noted that the majority of plots jointly held by couples is registered in the name of the man, and recommends that gender equality should be supported more fully (Land Observatory, 2014). The future of the reform hinges on donors and their priorities. One example is the World Bank, which is likely to contribute to attempts to accelerate land reform and has recently focused on joint ownership of land globally (World Bank, 2011).

Whether the recent interest in joint certification will translate into a mechanism for mandatory joint certification is uncertain. Realistic expectations are that joint certification will be highlighted in future information campaigns. The problems of weak infrastructure and poor information flows are still urgent, and need to be addressed in order to successfully disseminate information to LLOs and the rural population.

Notes

1   This approximation is based on recent estimates of arable land—8 million hectares—made by the Ministry of Agriculture (Andrianirina-Ratsialonana *et al.* 2011). The cultivated land area is estimated to be 2 million hectares.
2   An important principle under the socialist Second Republic, and also according to custom.
3   Surviving spouses have the right to stay on the property for one year following their bereavement. The situation for a widow typically depends on the relation to her late husband's family (Nororarisoa, 2009).
4   Soavinandriana Land Certificate Database, 2011, collected by the author.
5   Amparafaravola Land Certificate Database, 2010, collected by master's student Randrianarimanarivo Faniry Anja.
6   Antetezambaro Land Certificate Database, 2011, collected by author and NGO EFA.
7   This is not a probability sampling method strictly speaking, but has been shown to give accurate and precise estimates, and has been widely used by for instance the World Health Organization (Milligan *et al.*, 2004).
8   Ninety-one of the certificates for jointly held land included in the survey are certified to a woman; 387 certificates are registered to a total of 299 women at the LLO.
9   Only eight of the eleven households with joint certificates have answered this question.

References

Adelski, E. (2002) *Strategy Outline: Mainstreaming Gender in USAID/Madagascar's 2003–2008 Integrated Strategic Plan. Draft.* USAID. Available: http://pdf.usaid.gov/pdf_docs/Pnada399.pdf [10 June 2014].

Andrianarinina-Ratsialonana, R., and Burnod, P. (2012). *Between the Legal and the Legitimate: Status of Land Governance in Madagascar.* World Bank. Available: http://siteresources.worldbank.org/INTLGA/Resources/Final_Synthesis_Report.pdf [1 Apr. 2014].

Andrianarinina-Ratsialonana, R., Ramarojohn, L., Burnod, P., and Teyssier, A. (2011) *After Daewoo? Current Status and Perspectives of Large-scale Land Acquisitions in Madagascar,* International Land Coalition. Available: www.landcoalition.org/sites/default/files/publication/905/CIRAD_OF_Mada_ENG_web_16.03.11.pdf [1 Apr. 2014]

Brès, A. (2007) *Logiques de Production et Stratégies de Sécurisation Foncière Paysannes: Quelles Perspectives de Suivi – Évaluation des Impacts du Guichet Foncier de Soavinandriana – Ampary (Madagascar).* Master's thesis, Centre National d'Études Agronomiques des Régions Chaudes (CNEARC).

Deere, C.D., and Doss, C.R. (2006) "The Gender Asset Gap: What Do We Know and Why Does It Matter?", *Feminist Economics*, vol. 12, no. 1–2, pp. 1–50.

Deere, C.D., and León, M. (2003) "The Gender Asset Gap: Land in Latin America," *World Development*, vol. 31, no. 6, pp. 925–947.

Deininger, K., Ali, D.A., Holden, S., and Zevenbergen, J. (2008) "Rural Land Certification in Ethiopia: Process, Initial Impact, and Implications for Other African Countries," *World Development*, vol. 36, no. 10, pp. 1786–1812.

Giovarelli, R. (2006) MCC *Madagascar Projet Foncier Matières Relatives au Genre en Prendre en Compte*, Mission Report from Madagascar. Available: www.landcoalition.org/sites/default/files/legacy/legacypdf/08_Giovarelli_Gender_Madagascar_MCC.pdf?q=pdf/08_Giovarelli_Gender_Madagascar_MCC.pdf [21 Feb. 2012].

Glavin, G., Stokke, K., and Wiig, H. (2013) "The Impact of Women's Mobilisation: Civil Society Organisations and the Implementation of Land Titling in Peru," *Forum for Development Studies*, vol. 40, no. 1. Available: www.tandfonline.com/doi/abs/10.1080/08039410.2012.691108

Government of Madagascar, (1960) *Ordonnance n° 60-146 du 3 octobre 1960 relative au régime foncier de l'immatriculation.*

——(1968) *Loi 68-012 du 4 Juillet 1968 relative aux successions, testaments et donations.*

——(1992/2007) *Constitution of Madagascar.*

——(2005) *Lettre de Politique Foncière [Land Policy Letter]*, Ministère de l'Agriculture, de l'Elevage et de la Pêche.

——(2005) *Loi 2005-019 du 17 octobre 2005 fixant les principes régissant les statuts des terres.*

——(2006) *Loi 2006-031 du 24 Novembre 2006 fixant le régime juridique de la propriéte foncière privée non titrée.*

——(2007) *Loi 2007-022 du 20 août 2007 relative au mariage et aux régimes matrimoniaux.*

ILC, Intercooperation/SAHA and PNF, (2009) *L'aspect genre dans le processus de réforme foncière – Version préliminaire.* Available: http://landportal.info/sites/default/fi les/08_09 _madagenre_version_preliminaire_0.pdf [15 Apr. 2014].

ILC, online discussion http://landportal.info/content/land-reform-madagascar-model-replication [21 Sep. 2011] Access date Nov 15 2014.

Jacoby, H. G., and Minten, B. (2007) "Is Land Titling in sub-Saharan Africa Cost-Effective? Evidence from Madagascar," *World Bank Economic Review*, vol. 21, no. 3, pp. 461–485.

Jarosz, L. (1997) "Women as Share Croppers in Madagascar," in Sachs, C.E. (ed.), *Women Working in the Environment*. New York: Taylor & Francis, pp. 127–138.

Joireman, S.F. (2008) "The Mystery of Capital Formation in sub-Saharan Africa: Women, Property Rights and Customary Law," *World Development*, vol. 36, no. 7, pp. 1233–1246.

Kabeer, N.(1999) "Resources, Agency, Achievements: Reflections on the Measurement of Women Empowerment," *Development & Change*, vol. 30, pp. 435–464.

Land Observatory, (2014) *Statistiques Guichets Fonciers*, Available: www.observatoire-foncier.mg/ [14 April 2014]

——(2014) « La Femme et le Foncier » à l'honneur www.observatoire-foncier.mg/event-71/ [14 June 2014].

Leisz, S., Robles, A., and Gage, J. (1994) *Land and Natural Resource Tenure and Security in Madagascar*, USAID/Madagascar, Land Tenure Center, University of Wisconsin-Madison.

Martin, O. (2005) *L'enquête et ses méthodes: L'analyse de données quantitatives.* Paris: Armand Colin.

Maldidier, C. (2000) *Le Foncier à Madagascar (introduction des actes de l'Atelier Foncier de 2000)*. Communications présentées à l'atelier sur le foncier à Madagascar, 8 et 9 avril 1999, Ambohimanambola, Ministère de l'aménagement de la ville et des territoires de la ville. http://benjamin.lisan.free.fr/projetsreforestation/FoncierMadagascarMaldidier2000.pdf [14 April 2014].

Millennium Challenge Corporation (MCC) (2009) *MCC Board Authorizes Termination of Program with Madagascar.* Available: www.mcc.gov/pages/press/release/release-051909-mccboardauthorizes [1 May 2011].

Milligan, P., Njie, A., and Bennett, S. (2004) "Comparison of Two Cluster Sampling Methods for Health Surveys in Developing Countries," *International Journal of Epidemiology*, vol. 33, no. 3, pp. 469–76.

Noroarisoa, R. (2009) *Southern African Development Community Gender Protocol Barometer Baseline Study, Madagascar*. *www.genderlinks.org.za/attachment.php?aa_id=10134* [14 April 2014].

OECD (2014) *France - a good donor but must ensure that poor countries get the aid they need*. Available:www.oecd.org/dac/france-a-good-donor-but-must-ensure-that-poor-countries-get-the-aid-they-need.htm [14 June 2014].

ROR (2008) *Reseau Observatoires Ruraux Madagascar*. "Enquête periodique auprès des ménages."

Teyssier, A., Andrianirina-Ratsialonana, R., Razafindralambo, R., and Razafindrakoto, Y. (2008) *Decentralization of Land Management in Madagascar: Process, Innovations, and Observation of the First Outcome*. Available: http://siteresources.worldbank.org/INTIE/Resources/475495-202322503179/LandDecentralizationinMadagascar.pdf [Accessed 1 May 2011].

Tripp, A.M. (2004) "Women's Movements, Customary Law, and Land Rights in Africa: The Case of Uganda," *African Studies Quarterly*, vol. 7, pp. 1–19.

United Nations (2005) *Designing Household Survey Samples: Practical Guidelines*, Department of Economic and Social Affairs Statistics Division, Studies in Methods Series F 98, United Nations.

——2008. *Examen des Rapports Présentés par les États parties en Application de l'Article 18 de la Convention sur l'Elimination de Toutes les formes de Discrimination à l'Egard des Femmes. Cinquième rapport périodique des États parties. Madagascar*

Walker, C. (2003) "Piety in the Sky? Gender Policy and Land Reform in South Africa," *Journal of Agrarian Change*, vol. 3, no. 1–2, pp. 113–148.

Widman, M. (2014) "Land Tenure Insecurity and Formalizing Land Rights in Madagascar: A Gender Perspective on the Certification Program," *Feminist Economics*, vol. 20, no. 1, pp. 130–154.

World Bank, (2010) Available: http://data.worldbank.org/indicator/SI.POV.NAHC/countries [19 April 2014].

——(2011) *Helping Women Achieve Equal Treatment in Obtaining Land Rights: Gender in Land Administration and Land Certification Projects*. Available: http://siteresources.worldbank.org/EXTPREMNET/Resources/Results2011-PREM-SB-new-Gender-LandTitling.pdf [14 June 2014].

7 Land titling and women's decision-making in West Bengal

Vivien Savath, Diana Fletschner, and Florence Santos

Introduction

The 2012 World Development Report on Gender Equality and Development identified women's voice, agency and participation as major priorities, both for their economic implications and because of the intrinsic value of equality among genders. At the same moment, India continues to grapple with its status as one of the most gender-unequal nations in the world, coupled with stagnant economic development particularly in its rural regions.

This study is motivated by the hypothesis that formal land rights in rural developing regions can bolster women's agency and thereby unlock aspects of both the gender equality and economic development conundrums. We examine a program, Nijo Griha Nijo Bhumi (NGNB) (formerly known as the Cultivation Dwelling Plot Allocation program), that has allotted over 250,000 titles, or *pattas*, to homesteadless households in West Bengal with an explicit priority to include women's names. Beyond title, we further explore the extent of the relationship between women's entitlement to land and their agency in the household. This program experience provides lessons for joint-titling programs and evidence to support continued efforts to empower women through land.

Women's agency and land title

Women's agency has come to be considered a fundamental precondition to many development aims, and a critical end in itself for those concerned with gender equality. Beyond this recognition, however, lies the issue of how to capture expressions of agency and what influences individuals' agency. Land and property ownership has long been a prominent hypothesis but there has been little empirical evidence to support it until now.

Empirical studies are beginning to emerge with evidence for land and property theories. Swaminathan *et al.* (2012) use multivariate analysis to examine men's and women's decision-making power over individual employment choices and the ability to control earnings in Karnataka state. The team found that property ownership (land and/or house) improves women's autonomy in these decisions, but not the egalitarianism of decision-making between couples. Doss *et al.* (2014)

find evidence across three African countries (Malawi, Mali, and Tanzania) for women's entitlement to land being associated with greater input into household decision-making. Furthermore, their results suggest that individual title is associated with greater input than joint title. They performed a similar analysis in Orissa, India, and found no significant relationship. We hope to contribute more to this nascent body of empirical work with data from a neighboring, but substantially distinct, state in India.

We set the stage with a description of West Bengal's unique land context and the NGNB program. Following that introduction, we conduct an empirical examination of women's inclusion on the title and differences in their intra-household agency. We then conclude with policy lessons relevant to the ongoing dialogue on land rights and women's agency.

Introduction to West Bengal

Land and families

West Bengal covers 86,841 square kilometers oriented in a north–south strip, bordered by Bangladesh to the east, Nepal and Bhutan to the north, and Orissa to the south. Roughly 64% of the total land area is arable. The state has two major geographic zones, the southern Gangetic plain, which is dominated by the urban state capital, Kolkata, and the northern Himalayan and sub-Himalayan zone where the state abuts Nepal and Bhutan. While agriculture accounts for only 24% of the state economy, it is still the primary income-generating activity for the population and 70% of households are at least partially dependent on agriculture. Agricultural wage labor on others' land is a very common livelihood activity as is other wage labor in brick kilns or on road construction. These activities are dominated by men, but women do participate at rates higher than seen in many other states of India. More common livelihood activities for women include cottage industries such as sewing, bidi-rolling, or fence-making. Families that own even marginal land (less than one hectare) will commonly cultivate a backyard garden and/or raise fowl or livestock to supplement their food budget. Poor households without land in this context are much more heavily dependent on unreliable wage labor opportunities, and vulnerable to economic shocks.

According to the 2011 Indian census, West Bengal has a population density of 1,029 per km², second only to the State of Bihar. 68% of the population is in rural areas where the poverty rate is 22% (Government of India Planning Commission, 2013). Muslims make up a large minority in West Bengal, accounting for over 25% of the population. The presence of this large religious minority is notable in the context of land because the Government of India uses a system of plural family laws according to religion to determine land rights in marriage and inheritance. Approximately 23% of West Bengal's population is Scheduled Caste (SC) and there is a very small population of Scheduled Tribes (ST), who tend to live in small isolated pockets. ST and SC are designations laid out in the Indian Constitution to identify historically disadvantaged groups in India and determine their eligibility for government entitlements. Physical scarcity of land in the face of the burgeoning population and immigration remains one of the largest challenges to addressing landlessness in West Bengal, setting it apart from other Indian states. Landholdings are highly fragmented; 82% of farmers hold less than 1 hectare, and another 14% hold between 1–2 hectares (Government of West Bengal, 2011).

Land policy and administration

Integral to economic development and socio-cultural identities, land has long been a central fixture in Indian policy. The British colonial land legacy was a semifeudal system whereby land was highly concentrated in the hands of landlords and intermediaries, an arrangement designed to extract rents from tenants and pass revenue on to the British Empire. One dominant system was known as the *zamindari* system whereby land was administrated by *zamindars* or a class of Indian aristocratic landlords and cultivated by agricultural laborers or sharecroppers called *bargadars*. The *zamindar* system was characterized by a series of intermediaries responsible for tax collection and this hierarchy was preserved when the British instated the *zamindars* as the land proprietors under their Permanent Settlement.

In the lead-up to India's full independence in 1947, the Government of India Act 1935 devolved much authority to the country's states. Many of the powers given to the states in this Act were held over in independent India and enshrined in its Constitution, including those relating to land reform. Thus, the national land reform strategy was to provide country-wide guidance that was then interpreted, legislated, and implemented by the states.

Indian land reforms continued to be guided by the central government, but implemented by the states in the post-independence era. The national strategy after independence was designed around two new objectives: increased productivity and more equitable distribution. To these ends, India's central Planning Commission encouraged the promulgation of a few key tactics:

1   abolition of intermediaries;
2   protection of tenants;
3   rationalization of different tenure systems;
4   land redistribution via "ceiling surplus" laws.

Ceiling surplus laws define a maximum holding for private landowners; any holdings above that ceiling could legally be vested by the government for redistribution.

At the state level, West Bengal is widely recognized as one of the most progressive states with regard to redistributive land reform, and one of the more successful implementers of the prescribed strategies to return "land to the tillers." Beginning in 1978, the Marxist Left Front-led government launched Operation Barga, a state-wide effort to document and enumerate West Bengal's *bargadar* agricultural laborers, thus providing them with greater tenure security (mainly relating to rent control and anti-eviction protection) under the law. A large share of these arrangements would eventually convert to full ownership under the *bargardars'* preemptory purchase rights (Hanstad & Brown, 2001). In practice, Operation Barga essentially registered only men, although occasionally single women were also registered.

West Bengal was also at the fore among states in terms of effective distribution of ceiling-surplus land, having vested and allocated 1.04 million acres by 2001. The speed of redistribution in West Bengal in more recent years has slowed greatly, hampered by the availability of surplus land coupled with the large numbers of homesteadless households. The most recent National Sample Survey estimates 550,000 people are absolutely landless in West Bengal, while government-owned land for redistribution totals only about 40,000 hectares, with much of it tied up in litigation. West Bengal's government land reform programs are turning increasingly to purchases of land from private landowners and land banks to accommodate the landless. The Indian tradition of wealthy landowners transferring land at less than market price, or as a gift, is rooted in the Bhoodan movement of 1951, as part of which Vinoba Bhave traveled across India on foot campaigning for these donations to take place.

This sequence of reforms largely ignored women's individual needs. The prevailing view was of a unitary household in which all members, men and women, pooled resources and risks. In this historically patriarchal society, women were assumed to be "taken care of" under the auspices of their male relations. Only more recently has the West Bengal government adopted an explicit policy of joint-titling when allocating land under these acts, as is the case for the program under study (Brown & Das Chowdhury, 2002). A 1992 national-level chief minister's conference presided over by Prime Minister N.T. Rama Rao was the catalyst for Indian states to begin targeting women in their individual land reform programs. Rao was a women's rights advocate whose administration presided over changes improving women's rights to inheriting property, rights to their spouse's earnings, and representation in local government, among others. West Bengal established joint-titling as mandatory soon after this meeting in an administrative notification. The edict largely existed in theory only, however, with a 2003 survey revealing that only 11% of government distributed land in West Bengal was indeed allocated with a joint title.

Following decades of state-level programming in this manner with mixed results, the Government of India introduced a National Land Reform policy to reinvigorate land reform efforts at the central level. The policy was released for public comment in 2013 with stated goals to:

1   distribute land to all rural landless poor;
2   restore land unjustly taken from vulnerable communities such as *Dalits* and Tribals;
3   protect *Dalit* and Tribal land including the commons on which they depend;
4   liberalize land leasing laws;
5   improve land rights for women.

Women's rights to land

Gender adds yet another layer to the land question in India. Women's rights to land have long been subject to different practices than their male counterparts. Whether the applicable source of law is Hindu scripture, Muslim *sharia*, or Tribal custom, women's rights over land have typically been circumscribed.

The population in West Bengal is majority Hindu (encompassing the Scheduled Caste groups), and therefore subject to family laws that derive from ancient Hindu scripture. Ancient Hindu source codes explicitly restrict a woman's right to own property, especially inherited property. At the same time, these source texts establish the concept of *stridhan*, literally "women's property or fortune," properties to which a woman has absolute right. Separate schools of thought have placed different definitions of what types of property constitute *stridhan*, with the *Mitakshara* school dominating in most of modern day India, but the *Dayabhaga* prevalent in West Bengal. The schools agree that *stridhan* includes seven possible types of property:

1   gifts and bequests from strangers;
2   gifts and bequests from relations;
3   property acquired through self-exertion and mechanical arts;
4   property purchased with *stridhan*;
5   property acquired by compromise;
6   property obtained by adverse possession;
7   property obtained in lieu of maintenance.

The inclusion of an additional two forms—property acquired by inheritance and that acquired by partition as potential *stridhan*—remain controversial to this day (Halder & Jaishankar, 2008–2009).

During the British colonial period, social reform pressure from Europe and from within India, as well as a desire to have a uniform law supersede the diverse Hindu practices, spurred the Hindu Women's Right to Property Act (1937). Though the act had many flaws, it finally codified the characteristics of *stridhan* and made progress in recognizing the rights of widows. Many of those flaws were rectified post-independence with the new Hindu Code Bills. The law made further departures from scripture in 1956 with the Hindu Succession Act, which established that women's inheritances would be considered absolute property as was the case for male inheritors. Women's rightful shares, however, continued to be lesser than their brothers' because they were not considered part of the "coparcenary," a familial group that governed ancestral land (Halder & Jaishankar, 2008–2009).

Between the 11th and 17th centuries, repeated Muslim incursions and periods of Muslim rule left a long-standing legacy of Islamic traditions and influence intermingled with the Hindu tradition, especially in Northern India. West Bengal's large Muslim population is governed by a multitude of diverse local interpretations of Islamic law (*shariat*). Very broadly, *shariat* specifies shares for certain individuals and limits bequests to one-third of the estate. The right of women to inherit land is explicit, although their share is limited to one-half that of their male counterparts. Islamic law also established the concept of *mehr*, a payment of property made to the bride by the groom at the time of marriage that becomes hers alone, as a woman's right. In West Bengal, however, centuries of coexistence with Hindus have weakened the tradition of *mehr* so much so that many Muslim families practice dowry instead. In 1937, concurrent with the reformist debates that spurred the Hindu Women's Right to Property Act, the Muslim Personal Law was envisioned as a unifying code for all Muslims and a major push for Muslim women's rights by delineating their rights of possession.

The Scheduled Tribe minorities in West Bengal are anecdotally known to be more gender-egalitarian within the household. In regard to land, many tribal traditions do not recognize that anyone owns the land, often managing land communally. In this sense, men and women in the household are more equal as non-owners, and the entire household, or community, can be more vulnerable in a context where formal, individual titles have legitimacy over communally recognized use rights.

The West Bengal NGNB program

Within this unique context, the Government of West Bengal launched a homestead-allocation program in 2009 with the primary aim of allocating land to homesteadless agricultural laborer households. While many other states in India have land reform programs, the NGNB program is distinct in its ambition, because of its statewide scope, the fact that it allocates land (rather than just titles), and post-move support. The land for the program is taken either from available government land or purchases of land from private landowners at program-defined rates. NGNB operates on a large scale through the Department of Land and Land Reforms, and coordinates with Block Development Offices and locally elected self-government bodies called *Panchayati Raj*. This program has allocated nearly 250,000 titles and land parcels since inception. At the time of writing, an additional 115,000 families have been identified as eligible for future allocation.

The program works through focused efforts in one geographic administrative area (block) at a time. It establishes a Land Purchase and Land Distribution Committee in the block to identify land available for purchase at the program-defined rate. The acquired land is demarcated to be allocated to selected households in clusters of plots that are at least five decimals (a decimal is a hundredth of an acre) in size. The same committee collaborates with local leaders from the *Panchayat Raj* to identify potential beneficiary families. These families are evaluated according to program guidelines, which prioritize impoverished homesteadless agricultural-labor and rural artisan families, female-headed households, and households with only daughters and no sons. Selected families are then shown their potential land in the new cluster, and if they agree to the program terms, are given a title to that land and allowed to move. The program

Figure 7.1 Ruma Sardar with her daughter showing her NGNB *patta*. A house and the sanitary toilet coordinated with NGNB (housing through Indira Awas Yojana (IAY) program and toilet from Total Sanitation campaign) are visible at the back.
Photographer: Mr. Salim Paul

terms restrict the plot from alienation, sharecropping, or the use of hired labor, but inheritance follows the same terms as any other private property. Housing is not guaranteed through this program, but implementing officers coordinate funds for housing from other government programs at the national and state levels, or beneficiaries take loans from a microfinance organization such as Bandhan. Similarly, the Committee coordinates a variety of after-move support activities, such as agricultural extension visits, or electrification via other government departments as needed.

Gender-sensitive aspects of NGNB

Aside from being a massive poverty alleviation program, NGNB is significant in its commitment to include women. Measures for inclusion are present in the process of land selection and allocation, inclusion of women's names on the title, and support to make sure they understand their individual rights over the allocated property. When the NGNB program rolls out in a new area, its advertising purposely uses images of women. Officials involved in the program attend gender-sensitization trainings and receive official documentation materials with images of women. These guidelines specifically list an order of priority for beneficiaries, with female-headed households and widows at the top. Members of the *Panchayat Raj* are responsible for the initial identification of households and made aware of the program's priority focus on women. The West Bengal Panchayat Act reserved one-third of *Panchayat* seats for women; this quota was later raised in 2011 to 50%, ensuring the initial enumeration is sensitive to women.

The guidelines expected the title to include the names of both spouses and list the woman's name first. This required changing the format of the documents—adding one line to explicitly make room for a second name on the title—and bringing the importance of this detail to the attention of government officials.

Figure 7.2 *Patta* distribution ceremony in Coochbehar District, November 2010.
Photographer: Mr. Salim Paul

Figure 7.3 Mrs. Jhana Sarkar signs her *patta*, November 2010.
Photographer: Mr. Salim Paul

In more recent variations of the program, titles were conferred in public *patta* ceremonies that required the participation of both title holders. *Patta* ceremonies are low-cost interventions expected to reinforce women's status as landowners because:

1   having women sign the documents and handing them the *pattas* directly ensures that women know they own a plot;
2   granting these documents publicly provides legitimacy by ensuring that their respective families, communities, government agents, and service providers are aware of their new status;
3   doing it through a collective ceremony can prompt their communities, who see a sizeable group of women become landowners, to update their gender-based perceptions and norms.

A simple stage is erected in a public location with decorations. Local officials deliver speeches about the meaning of secure land rights, the government program, and why women's names are listed first on the title. Recipients, women and men, file through a table set up for distribution, receive the *patta* and sign the record of rights. In some cases they also receive *tiffin*, small refreshments and gifts. The success of the early *patta* ceremonies inspired the government to coordinate state-wide "mega" ceremonies in which multiple locations would distribute *patta* on a single day. On February 16, 2014 alone, over 55,000 titles were distributed statewide.

As the program moves forward, government officials have been collecting sex-disaggregated data, including whose names are on the title and the marital status of beneficiaries. This data, in turn, allows gender-sensitive program monitoring.

NGNB *program outcomes*

Program-monitoring data indicates that 77% of *pattas* have been given in joint name with the woman's name first, 15% of land titles are in the name of women only, and 8% of land titles are in the name of men only. This is a high success rate especially compared to the 2003 survey, which found only an 11% rate of joint-titling on government *pattas*, and compared to many other examples in India and around the world.

This rate of success is probably due to several overlapping factors. First, NGNB is a flagship program of the current Chief Minister Mamata Banerjee, who has a parallel political priority of women's empowerment. The state is notable for its investment in, and success of, women's self-help group programs. Second, West Bengal is a highly politicized state with strong Marxist influences where women have long played a part in rural partisan politics. This political environment has led to the courting of women's votes and women being more civically engaged than their counterparts in many other Indian states. Third, an external advocate and "watch dog," Landesa, has provided technical assistance, capacity-building, and accountability measures to help ensure that, in the field, joint-titling is willingly and correctly implemented. This is a multi-year, committed partnership with the government that has spanned administrations to ensure that women's land rights do not fall off the agenda.

Despite the high rates of political engagement and awareness among women in West Bengal, our qualitative data suggests that in terms of land allocation there was little self-selection on the part of the women. Eligible female non-beneficiaries assumed that *pattas* would be distributed only to husbands by default and were incredulous when we suggested the possibility of a joint title, although they quickly recognized the benefits of such an arrangement. Female beneficiaries we interviewed indicated that their *pattas* had been jointly titled automatically, meaning that they did not have to ask their husbands for their names to be included and leaving both parties satisfied that it was simply the government's decision. The following is excerpted from a focus group discussion conducted with program-eligible non-beneficiaries on September 10, 2012:

> *Interviewer:* Suppose the government is giving land and officers are preparing the documents for that land—who should be the owner of that land according to you?
> *Respondent:* Of course, my husband.
> *Interviewer:* Why? How that is better than any other options?
> *Respondent:* Will they give [land] in my name? [in disbelief]

Given the high rate of women's titling, we use the remainder of this chapter to explore whether title can be more than just a name on a piece of paper. We examine whether it might be related to a woman's agency and decision-making power within the household.

Empirical exploration of joint title and women's agency

Data

We gathered quantitative data from 1,150 partnered NGNB-eligible households in three districts of West Bengal in October 2012, one to two years after *pattas* were distributed. The data, gathered as part of the NGNB program evaluation, was reported by women and includes plot-level information on landownership and decision-making, as well as a wide range of information at the individual and household level. Of the women interviewed, 649 are from households who became NGNB beneficiaries in 2010 and another 501 eligible, non-beneficiary women provide a comparison group. Because of our interest in exploring intra-household dynamics, all the women we included in the study are partnered.

The average woman in our sample is 35 years old and 41% of the women interviewed are literate. Since the composition of their households is likely to affect their ability to make decisions, it is important to report that among the women in our sample, 19% live with their extended families, 51% have sons and, taken as a group, they have an average of 1.3 children under 14. Decision-making patterns are also bound to vary with social and cultural norms, so we should note that the sample includes Scheduled Caste households (59%), Scheduled Tribe households (11%), General Caste households (10%), Muslim households (15%), Christian households (3%) and Other Backward Caste households (2%). The sample is roughly evenly distributed among three districts: Bankura (34%), Coochbehar (39%), and Jalpaiguri (27%).

Qualitative data collection took place in September 2012. We conducted eight focus group discussions with beneficiaries and eligible non-beneficiaries. The focus groups included a participatory activity that involved household decisions by gender roles.

Types of decisions

We consider four types of household decisions. The first category includes *regular production* decisions, which in this rural area entails decisions about how plots are going to be used, what will be grown on the plots, and whether the crops they yield will be sold. The second category comprises decisions related to *market transactions of land*—whether plots will be rented, mortgaged, or sold. The third category refers to *intra-family transfers* of land, or decisions over who will inherit the household's plots. Finally, the fourth category is made of *household spending* decisions related to the household's food consumption, its purchase of furniture or other productive assets, and whether or not it takes out loans.

Primary decision-makers

We asked each woman to list two primary decision-makers. We considered her to be a primary decision-maker if she listed herself. Similarly, we counted her husband as a primary decision-maker if she included his name. As such, our indicators do not distinguish whether these decisions are made jointly or independently. However, because we are interested in women's overall relative agency, when she reported that "everybody" in the household participates on a given decision, we do not consider her or her husband as a decision-maker.

Women as primary decision-makers in West Bengal

The graphs that follow provide visual insights into the decision-making patterns of resource-poor rural households in West Bengal. In each graph, we use horizontal lines to represent the eleven types of decisions covered by this study and rely on geometric symbols to signal how the prevalence of decision-makers varies depending on the demographics considered.

Figure 7.4 shows that while not all women view themselves as primary decision-makers in every decision, they are involved in those related to what the household produces on the vast majority of household plots and the sale of those products. Women are also very likely to be involved in their households' consumption and investment decisions. The high rate of decision-making is somewhat particular to

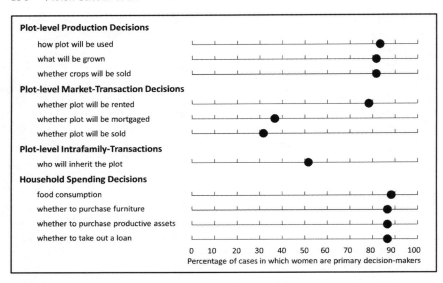

Figure 7.4 Percentage of cases in which women are primary decision-makers in West Bengal.

West Bengal, as noted above, is a left-leaning state with a high level of political awareness among women, and particularly in relation to the types of decisions that have to do with running the household and rearing children. This is illustrated below by one of the focus group discussions conducted on September 10, 2012:

> *Respondent:* We can understand children's health matters better. Husband goes to workplace in the morning, nobody is there to take such decisions other than us.
>
> *Respondent:* [Children's education] are mothers' responsibilities, fathers remain busy with their work and in search of work. Children's responsibilities are on mothers. Visiting doctor's place with sick children is also mothers' responsibility. At the end of their school or playing they will come to us and demand food—we need to keep in mind about their hunger, how they will need to eat and what will they eat—fathers will never decide those.

Women's participation is noticeably lower with regard to land transactions, particularly decisions that could have lasting consequences. Only half of the women interviewed reported participating in decisions to bequeath land—a vitally important issue given that inheritance is one of the most common routes to acquiring land in this region and those with the power to bequeath land can use it as a *de facto* intra-family insurance for when they are no longer able to provide for themselves. Even fewer reported being a key player in household decisions to mortgage or sell land.

Arguably, some of these patterns may be driven by constraints that are not specific to women. This would be the case, for example, if: a number of the women interviewed lived in multigenerational households where consequential decisions were made by the elders; the land market were very flat; or inheritance decisions were mostly determined by cultural norms. Fortunately, the information women provided reveals the extent to which their husbands are primary decision-makers. Because husbands and wives come from the same households, deal with the same plots of land, and are exposed to the same markets and the same culture, a simple comparison of their decision-making patterns allows us to identify gender-specific differences. We do this in Figure 7.5.

As hypothesized, the decision-making patterns for women are very similar to those of their husbands, suggesting that, indeed, other factors may drive the extent to which they can be primary decision-makers. Still, while the gender gap is not large, it is important to note that for each and every type of decision men are more likely than women to be primary decision-makers—a pattern that is consistent with evidence from other regions (see Santos *et al.*, 2014).

Because our sample was designed to evaluate the NGNB land program, it is important to remember that close to 40% of the women interviewed are from non-beneficiary households that remained landless at the time of the survey. Their families are living on, and possibly using, someone else's land. Thus, a more informative analysis of plot-level decisions should focus on NGNB beneficiary households which, as described, were expected to have received a plot of land jointly titled to husband and wife in the previous twelve to eighteen months and to have benefited from other complementary government programs.

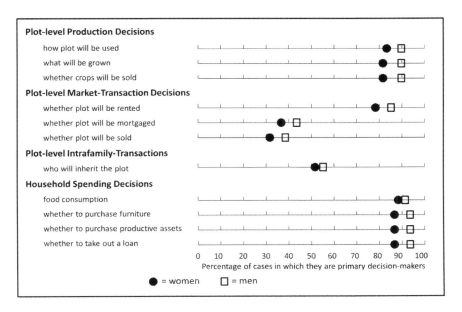

Figure 7.5 Gender gap in primary decision-making.

As discussed above, NGNB guidelines include a provision for joint-titling. Despite best intentions, however, complex realities on the ground often result in considerable implementation departures from even the most carefully designed framework. The most common departure from joint-titling occurs if the initial enumeration of potential beneficiary households by the *Panchayat* failed to name the woman of the household, an exogenous occurrence. This allows us to compare women in NGNB beneficiary households with and without their names on title.

Figure 7.6 suggests that joint-titling can have important consequences for women's agency, over and above any other program benefits that generally accrued to the whole household (like housing, electricity, and agricultural extension). As can be easily observed among landowning households, women whose rights to the plots have been formalized by the inclusion of their names on the titles reported decision-making levels that closely match those of their husbands—the gender gap in intra-household decision-making essentially disappears. This result is corroborated by qualitative evidence from the focus groups where beneficiary women were more likely to report joint decision-making than non-beneficiary women, who clearly delineated men's decisions and women's decisions. In stark contrast, beneficiary women who indicated that their newly received plots were documented without their names report noticeably lower agency: these women are 20 to 40 percent less likely to be primary decision-makers. The gender gap in intra-household decision-making is larger across all types of decisions, as illustrated by the interview below during a focus group discussion on September 15th, 2012:

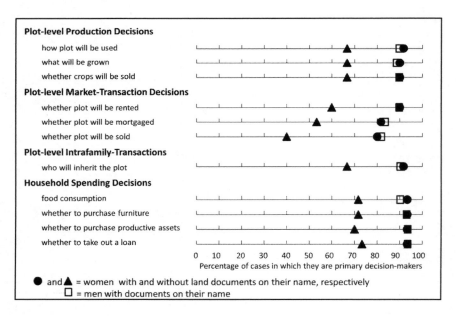

Figure 7.6 Percentage of cases in which men and women with and without title are primary decision-makers.

Respondent: After receiving this land our courage and strengths has become different now. We received a big piece of land—we can plant trees here—those will be our own trees—we could not claim that so far. We could not claim things as mine even if we planted those, because then we use to stay at others land. If I plant a chili plant, I can say "This is mine." If I wish, I can pluck chilies any time from that plant. This is our courage now, our joy.

Interviewer: When you built the house on this plot, who took decisions like where to build a kitchen, where the toilet will be, and where you will plant trees?

Respondent: We took joint decision.

Respondent: We also took joint decision. Nothing is possible to plan without discussion, we discussed, then we decided how to use our land.

These encouraging results show that land allocation programs can not only be successful in establishing joint titles, but that including women's names on titles is indeed associated with increases in their decision-making power, overall and relative to their husbands. We mentioned earlier qualitative evidence that self-selection was not a major factor at play, we now turn to a regression to rule out some potential confounding factors on women's decision-making.

Influencing factors on women's decision-making power

Statistical framework

As described earlier the ability of a woman (i) to make decisions (WD_i) can be affected by her own characteristics (WC_i) as well as by the characteristics of her household (HHC_i) and her community ($DIST_i$). Furthermore, her ability to make decisions may depend on whether her household has a title ($NGNB_i$). Households that are program beneficiaries acquired a fundamental new asset and are expected to have gained access to other government programs and services, to have moved to a new location and possibly redefined their social networks, and to have gained status in the community. In addition, if the gendered provisions of the program were implemented properly (in that the plot's title included her name—WNT_i), her decision-making ability may have received a boost. The latter two effects are the ones we seek to identify and thus we estimate:

$$WD_i = \beta_0 + \beta_1 NGNB_i + \beta_2 WNT_i + \beta_3 WC_i + \beta_4 HHC_i + \beta_5 DIST_i \in_i$$

and we will focus our attention on β_1 and β_2.

To simplify the analysis we combine the fourteen decisions into the four categories described earlier, using the woman's average response for each category and using Ordinary Least Squares (OLS) regression for all decisions except the inheritance category which contains only one decision and was estimated using a logit model.

Results

In Figure 7.7, we list all the factors we have considered as possible drivers of decision-making and, for each of the four categories, we use bars to indicate those that we found to influence women's ability to be primary decision-makers.[1] Not included in the figure are additional control variables for geography (district) as well as the value of the plot. Rectangles to the right (left) of the vertical lines indicate that the factor has a positive (negative) influence on women's decision-making.

As predicted, a number of factors combine to shape women's agency. While results vary depending on the category of decisions being considered, women are more likely to be decision-makers if they are literate, and in some cases if they come from Scheduled Tribe or Christian households. Not surprisingly, women are less likely to be primary decision-makers when they live with their extended families. Somewhat counterintuitively, the number of dependants women have does not seem to affect or be affected by their decision-making power. Sons in particular, however, appear to be negatively associated with a woman's decision-making power over inheritance, but positively associated with her ability to make decisions on household spending.

More importantly, given the questions we are exploring, the multivariate statistical exercises demonstrate that the program had a positive effect on women's agency. Even after controlling for a host of concurrent demographic and socio-economic factors that could affect women's relative position, we find that women whose households received a plot of land through the NGNB program are

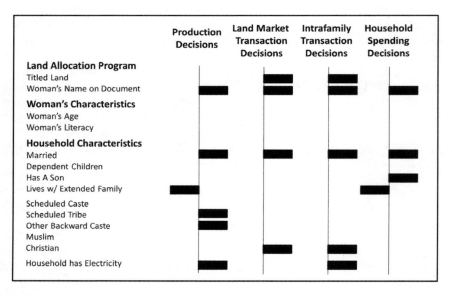

Figure 7.7 Possible drivers of decision-making for women.

more likely to be involved in decisions to transfer rights to land, be it through market transactions (renting, mortgaging, or selling) or bequest. It should be noted, however, that this finding may largely reflect the fact that, as landowners, members of these households—regardless of their gender—are more likely to consider and to make decisions about land transactions. We note the additional caveat that given the short timeframe since *patta* allocation, many economic or livelihood impacts are yet to be measured and the women are responding mostly in the hypothetical about major decisions. However, our qualitative interviews suggest that high rates of titled women's self-reported decision-making power stem from positive shifts toward feelings of confidence and security, as exemplified from the focus group discussion conducted on September 15th, 2012. These changes in mental attitude can happen almost immediately.

> *Respondent:* [Having land in my name] is good, it is a good feeling. We do not find ourselves very helpless when our husbands get angry with us. Land works as mental support.
> *Respondent:* Similarly in our old age land will be my shelter and our son will not evict us from this land. This is our secured place.
> *Respondent:* We shall not allow our husbands to sell this land; they can't sell that without our permission. And we can stay here in any adverse situation—we shall never become homeless again. This land is secured shelter not only for us but for our children too.

Recommendations

The evidence thus far offers strong endorsement for joint-titling in land reform. In particular, in cases where the joint-titling provisions of the NGNB program have been properly implemented, women are significantly more likely to be primary decision-makers across a number of critical household issues. In contrast, when there were deviations from the guidelines and documents included only the men, or the women were unaware of their entitlement, women have noticeably lower involvement in their households' decisions.

The NGNB case in West Bengal contains several lessons. First, it is essential to sensitize and train all government officials responsible for program implementation. Landesa's role in training and coordinating officers has been credited by government officials as a reason behind the success of joint-titling. Field officers need to not only have full understanding of the gendered guidelines of the program and of their responsibility to implement them, but must also see women as landowners and worthy of becoming beneficiaries in their own right. Second, it is essential to audit the NGNB processes, paperwork, and documents required to identify eligible beneficiaries, allocate land, issue documents, and promote the convergence of other government services in order to understand the reasons behind deviations from the program guidelines. The NGNB program learned about women missing from titles and remediated the process and the situation. Third, the guidelines need to unambiguously establish that for plots allocated to couples, women's names must be included in the documents. In the case of the NGNB, having a political champion in the Chief Minister gave significant weight to the joint-titling mandate, as well as the momentum and resources to see it through. Fourth, the program should more uniformly include mechanisms, such as the *patta* ceremonies, to increase the visibility and social acceptance of women's as landowners in their own right.

As our results show, when the NGNB joint-titling and other gender-sensitive mechanisms are implemented in accordance to the design, we see that women approach parity with men in the rate of being a primary decision-maker over critical household decisions. We recommend building on these successes in future implementation of the NGNB by feeding these outcomes back into the ongoing program sensitization, showing how these measures change the lives of women and their families. Based on these early indicators of positive program outcomes, land-allocation programming and policy should also build in incentives for field officers' gender-sensitive performance, and continue gender-sensitive monitoring of the program's implementation to understand where deviations from the program guidelines might occur.

To be fully effective, program and policy designers should look "beyond" the program, and consider complementary interventions or partnerships such as community sensitization and capacity-building activities, legal awareness programs, or grassroots-level behavioral-change campaigns.

Notes

1   We report results that are statistically significant at the 5% level.

References

Brown, J., & Das Chowdhury, S. (2002) *Women's Land Rights in West Bengal: A Field Study.* RDI Reports on Foreign Aid and Development, No. 116., Seattle.

Doss, C., Kim, S., Njuki, J., Hillenbrand, E., & Miruka, M. (2014) *Women's Individual and Joint Property Ownership: Effects on Household Decisionmaking.* Washington, D.C.: IFPRI.

Government of India Planning Commission. (2013) *Press Note on Poverty Estimates, 2011–12.* New Delhi: Government of India Press Information Bureau.

Government of West Bengal. (2011) *Agricultural Census.* Calcutta.

Halder, D., & Jaishankar, K. (2008–2009) "Property Rights of Hindu Women: A Feminist Review of Succession Laws of Ancient, Medieval, and Modern India," *Journal of Law and Religion,* vol. 24, no. 2, pp. 663–687.

Hanstad, T., & Brown, J. (2001) *Land Reform Law and Implementation in West Bengal: Lessons and Recommendations.* Seattle: RDI Reports of Foreign Aid and Development No. 112.

Santos, F., Fletschner, D., & Savath, V. (2014) "An Intrahousehold Analysis of Access to and Control Over Land in the Northern Province, Rwanda," *2014 World Bank Conference on Land and Poverty.* Washington, D.C.: World Bank.

Swaminathan, H., Suchitra, J. Y., & Lahoti, R. (2012) *Individual Property Rights and Bargaining Outcomes: Evidence from Intra-Household Asset Data.* Bangalore: Indian Institute of Management Bangalore.

Part III

From common property to private holdings

A tragedy for the "commoners"?

Caroline S. Archambault and Annelies Zoomers

A common property regime is an institutional arrangement for the cooperative use, management, and sometimes ownership of natural resources. While it is most often associated with collective governance of common-pool resources (CPRs), such as grasslands, forests, wetlands, and fisheries, such systems can also more broadly include collective agriculture in centrally planned economies. Recent literature on the new commons has expanded conventional notions of the commons to include, for example, sidewalks and playgrounds, knowledge, or even to stretch as far as outer space (Hess, 2008).

Focusing here on a narrower field of common property, namely that pertaining to collective governance of farmlands, rangelands, and forests, it is evident that these systems of tenure are pervasive and found throughout the world. It is difficult to estimate the extent of land covered by common property regimes. Rough estimates based on the presence of national forests, permanent wetlands, shrublands, savannas, grasslands, and sparsely vegetated and barren lands and excluding terrestrial protected areas, suggest that 52% of the global land area is covered by people's commons (Wily, 2011). Of this total, sub-Saharan Africa has the largest estimated area of commons. Typically commons have overlapping (and competing) statutory and customary rights. In the majority of cases these lands are legally vested in the state.

Rural households heavily rely upon commons for their livelihoods. Commons provide critical safety nets for poor households; beyond the provision of subsistence, they can generate significant income. For example, Beck and Nesmith (2001) found that common property resources accounted for some 12% of household incomes in India and estimated a comparable contribution to incomes in West Africa.

Lands held under collective tenure are being reduced for a number of reasons. They are particularly vulnerable to commercial pressure and appropriations as they often lack the protection of occupancy. They are sometimes perceived as unoccupied or "empty" (as is often mentioned in the context of the land-grab debate), unowned, and available. They tend to offer vast, intact, resource-rich areas that are attractive for large-scale commercial development, such as plantation, mining, logging, or ranching enterprises. This threat has escalated recently with the onset of the global land rush.

Furthermore, the subdivision of lands held under collective tenure into individual private holdings is also widespread, for example, within communal rangelands and woodlands, and sometimes even occurs as a way of protecting against commercial pressures. Persistent notions that private holdings are superior to those under collective tenure with regard to economic efficiency, modernization, and development have encouraged the acceptance of such policies to privatize the commons (Ho and Spoor, 2006; Catley *et al.* 2013). The notion of the tragedy of the commons, although misleading in its conflation of common property and open access, has been incredibly persuasive in associating communal tenure regimes with poor environmental stewardship and ecological degradation (Hardin, 1968). In the 1990s, prolific research and writing on common-pool resources presented a vast body of empirical studies that demonstrated the efficiency and environmental advantages of communal tenure (Ostrom, 1991; Berks, 1989). Parallel movements occurred with regard to social inclusion, social justice, and bottom-up approaches to development, and were accompanied by an increasing recognition of the failures of private property arrangements as ways to equitably and sustainably protect natural resources (Bromley, 1992). This in turn led to renewed policy commitments to collective tenure and ushered in a movement supporting community-based conservation (Agrawal, 2005).

Nevertheless, the commons continue to undergo subdivision as various pressures lead "commoners" to seek private rights. These pressures include population growth, heightened competition for land, increasing threats of appropriation, failures of and frustrations with institutions of collective governance, as well as expectations for and ideas about the role of private property in modernization and development (Archambault *et al.* 2014).

Collective farming is also an important, distinctive, and often state-imposed form of communal land management that recently has undergone extensive privatization. Many socialist and communist states organized, in a wide variety of forms, agricultural production in large-scale collective and state cooperative farms. This was the case in most of the countries in the Soviet Union and East Central Europe as well as the Baltic States, some countries in Asia, parts of North and sub-Saharan Africa, and Latin America. The break-up of these agricultural collectives, which began in earnest in the late 1980s but continues today, is often a fundamental part of the transition process from a centrally planned to a market economy. The range of processes employed to facilitate such break-ups differ considerably between countries—and even across regions within the same country—resulting in a mix of farms types, although decollectivization into individual private holdings is common (Mathijs and Swinnen, 1998; Spoor and Visser, 2001; Ho and Spoor, 2006).

Privatizing collective holdings, whether rangelands, cooperative farms, or forests, raises important distributional challenges. To whom should private rights be vested? Which types of rights should be granted and for how long? And which resources (land alone or also natural resources found on or beneath the land) should be included (McKean, 1998)? Literature on the impacts of privatization of communal lands suggests that in many contexts these issues are not well thought through prior to reforms. The privatization of collective holdings may bring about important benefits, but may also risk exacerbating inequalities and dispossessing common holders, thus stimulating social stratification as well as enclosure or exclusion.

The poor and marginalized not only have a difficult time securing shares, as they are often excluded from membership in collectivities and are too poor to access land through markets, but they also struggle to retain access and at times of distress face great pressure to sell or lease their lands, which can result in dispossession (Razavi, 2007). While women are often included as a category among the landless and marginal, explicit research attention to the gender dynamics and impacts of these tenure transformations is often lacking. Important exceptions include the work of Thelen (2003), Scott (2003), and Kandiyoti (2003) on the processes of decollectivization in farming. There is an important body of literature on the gendered implications of land-titling, but this is not specific to the subdivision of commons (see for example, Deere and León, 2001, Englert and Daley, 2008). Gendered analyses of communal and collective tenure systems can contribute important insights into creative institutional arrangements that allow commoners to reap benefits associated with privatization while mitigating the costs. And in situations where privatization persists, the distributional challenges need to be thought through in relation to men and women's capacities, priorities, and vulnerabilities to help facilitate equitable social and economic outcomes of such reforms.

The third part of this book, with contributions from Morocco, Mexico, China, and Kenya demonstrates the far-reaching gendered impacts on social and economic life of the wave of initiatives aimed at privatizing formerly collective landholdings.

In Morocco, the privatization of former agricultural state cooperatives has led to the alienation of land from families as the commoditization of land has propelled a professionalization and masculinization of agriculture, further relegating women to the domestic domain and often excluding them from being able to inherit.

In Mexico, following the dissolution and privatization of *ejidos*, only a small population of (often elder) women are left with full property rights over their family land. These women struggle to maintain productive lands as they face a long history of discriminatory land reforms, policies that have underinvested in rural agricultural development, and the loss of critical labor due to youth outmigration.

In Kenya, among the pastoral Maasai, men and women, often with differing priorities, are trying to reap the benefits of rangeland subdivision while minimizing the costs. On the one hand, private titles to land can facilitate new economic opportunities and investments in housing, yet, on the other hand, subdivision provokes social tension and vulnerabilities to land dispossession through enclosure, exclusion, and land sales."

And in China, the recent decollectivization of the country's forests has failed to confer secure rights to forest lands and resources for women and thus has prevented them from reaping the potential benefits entailed in privatization. In the context of high rates of male outmigration, where women are left to manage family farms and forests, this has been detrimental to family and community welfare.

References

Agrawal, A. (2005) *Environmentality: Technologies of Government and the Making of Subjects*, Durham, NC: Duke University Press.

Archambault, C., Matter, S., Ole Riamit, S. K. and Galaty, J. (2014) "Maasai Livelihood Pathways in Kenya: Macro-level Factors in Diversifying Diversification," in Sick, D. (ed.), *Rural Livelihoods, Regional Economies and Processes of Change*, New York: Routledge.

Beck, T. and Nesmith, C. (2001) "Building on Poor People's Capacities: The Case of Common Property Resources in India and West Africa," *World Development*, vol. 29, no. 1, pp. 119–133.

Berks, F. (ed.) (1989) *Common Property Resources: Ecology and Community-Based Sustainable Development*, London: Belhaven Press.

Bromley, D. (ed.) (1992) *Making the Commons Work: Theory, Practice, Policy*, San Francisco: Institute for Contemporary Studies.

Catley, A., Lind, J. and Scoones, I. (eds) (2013) *Pastoralism and Development in Africa: Dynamic Change at the Margins*, London: Routledge.

Deere, C. D., & León, M. (2001) "Who Owns the Land? Gender and Land: Titling Programmes in Latin America," *Journal of Agrarian Change*, vol. 1, no. 3, pp. 440–467.

Englert, B., & Daley, E. (eds) (2008) *Women's Land Rights and Privatization in Eastern Africa*, London: James Curry: Eastern Africa Series.

Hardin, G. (1968) "The Tragedy of the Commons," *Science*, vol. 162, no. 3859, pp. 1243–1248.

Hess, C. (2008) "Mapping the New Commons," presented at the 12th Biennial Conference of the International Association of the Commons, Cheltenham, UK, 14–18 July.

Ho, P. and Spoor, M. (2006) "Whose Land? The Political Economy of Land Titling in Transitional Economies," *Land Use Policy*, vol. 23, pp. 580–587.

Kandiyoti, D. (2003) "The Cry for Land: Agrarian Reform, Gender and Land Rights in Uzbekistan," *Journal of Agrarian Change*, vol. 3, no. 1–2, pp. 225–256.

McKean, M. A. (1998) "Common Property: What Is It, What Is It Good For, and What Makes It Work?" in Gibson, C., McKean, M. A. and Ostrom, E. (eds) *Forest Resources and Institutions: Forests, Trees and People Programme*, Rome: FAO.

Mathijs, E. and Swinnen, J. F. M. (1998) "The Economics of Agricultural Decollectivization in East Central Europe and the Former Soviet Union," *Economic Development and Cultural Change*, vol. 47, no. 1, pp. 1–26.

Ostrom, E. (1991) *Governing the Commons: The Evolution of Institutions for Collective Action*, Cambridge: Cambridge University Press.

Razavi, S. (2007) "Liberalisation and the Debates on Women's Access to Land," *Third World Quarterly*, vol. 28, no. 8, pp. 1479–1500.

Scott, S. (2003) "Gender, Household Headship and Entitlements to Land: New Vulnerabilities in Vietnam's Decollectivization," *Gender Technology and Development*, vol. 7, no. 2, pp. 233–263.

Spoor, M. and Visser, O. (2001) "The State of Agrarian Reform in the Former Soviet Union," *Europe–Asia Studies*, vol. 53, no. 6, pp. 885–901.

Thelen, T. (2003) "The New Power of Old Men: Privatisation and Family Relations in Mesterszallas (Hungary)," *Anthropology of East Europe Review*, vol. 21, no. 2, pp. 15–21.

Wily, L. A. (2011) *The Tragedy of Public Lands: The Fate of the Commons under Global Commercial Pressure*, Rome: International Land Coalition.

8 'One doesn't sell one's parents'

Gendered experiences of shifting tenure regimes in the agricultural plain of the Sais in Morocco

Lisa Bossenbroek and Margreet Zwarteveen

Introduction

In 2006, the government of Morocco decided to privatize the land of the former socialist-inspired collective state cooperatives because the restrictions on their transferability were seen as hampering their profitability. The resulting shift in land control is happening alongside, but is also provoking, wider processes of agrarian change, manifested among others things in the introduction of new high-value crops, the use of new technologies (such as tubewells and drip irrigation) and alterations in labour relations. In this chapter we want to explore what the shift from a collective to a private tenure system means for gender relations. We base our analysis on one year of in-depth ethnographic fieldwork done in 2011–13 in the former cooperative of Ait Ali, which is situated in the agricultural plain of the Sais in Morocco. Our findings suggest that the privatization of land results in the disarticulation of land rights from wider kinship-based relations of dependency and reciprocity and erodes the historical, territorial and family values land used to embody. The disarticulation of land rights from wider kinship-based relations happens in tandem with and through a renegotiation of gender relations and subjectivities. By tracing the history of the state cooperative, we show how land-use rights used to epitomize post-colonial collective struggles against the colonial regime and later against the Moroccan state. In the state cooperative, land was used through gendered family, kinship, and community relations based on the institutions of inheritance and marriage, with farms and families being deeply intertwined through labour arrangements and how land was used. Conversely, gendered subjectivities and institutions importantly manifested themselves, and became enacted, through how land was used and managed. Today, farming increasingly is becoming a professional activity and identity, premised on a growing division between a private family domain associated with women and a public professional domain associated with men. This opens up new possibilities for becoming a modern farmer to some rural male youngsters, but makes it increasingly difficult for many women to negotiate and justify their farming activities and subjectivities. Changes in the monetary value of land, as well as changes in the inheritance system, are symptomatic of the changing meanings of land, something that may provoke protracted intra-family negotiations over land in which the position of women is particularly weak. In sum, our analysis shows how the current privatization of land in the region of the Sais is shaped and in turn shapes existing identities and institutions, transforming the gendered spaces and subjectivities in often constraining ways for women.

Methodology

The research on which this chapter is based was conducted (by the first author) during a period of one year, stretching over May to October 2012 and May to October 2013. As part of our methodology, we describe the realities of land privatization experienced by the people concerned, and question and address the processes of unfairness and injustice linked to land and farming realities.

After obtaining a general overview of the agrarian dynamics in the region of the Sais, where the research was conducted, we selected the dissolving state cooperative Ait Ali for an in-depth analysis of current privatization dynamics. Most of the 36 people living in this state cooperative together with their families are originally from the *douar*[1] Ait Ali, which is situated next to the state cooperative, and consists approximately of 80 extended households. Most of these people are Berber and belong to the tribe also called Ait Ali.

We used a combination of methods and interview techniques, including life histories, in-depth interviews and topic interviews (drawing on personal views of an event or the change process, or perception of the future) and group discussions. Many people, especially women, were reluctant at first to share their often intimate – and sometimes sad – stories about the land with the researchers. To gain trust, therefore, much time was spent simply visiting people on short courtesy visits and participating in social events. We soon discovered that land transactions can be the source of pain, sadness and shame, which is why talking about the issue required patience and subtlety. When conducting individual interviews, we therefore not only paid attention to the content of the story of the interviewee, but also considered the tone of the voice, the silences induced, the imaginaries mobilized and the conduct of the interviewee.

Political history of land-tenure relations in Morocco: land privatization as a historical process

The land question and the formation of property rights in Morocco are central to the political agrarian history of the country. This is partly due to the fact that Morocco is considered an agrarian country, where 44% (2000)[2] of its habitants live rurally; agriculture contributes of 15–20% of the country's GDP (Jouve, 2002). The political economy of land privatization in Morocco is a process that has been marked by roughly three phases of change: the pre-colonial situation before 1912; the colonial period from 1912–56, when Morocco was a French protectorate; and the post-colonial period. Rather than signifying radical ruptures, changes on the ground are often marked by continuity and a gradual transition from one land-tenure regime to another (see Bernstein, 2010).

Land tenure relations in pre-colonial Morocco were characterized by four predominant categories of land (Bouderbala, 1999; Raki, 1980):

1   collective lands that were collectively held by tribal groups and used for cultivation and grazing;
2   *Guich* lands, which were military lands that had been given out by the *Makhzen*[3] to tribal groups;
3   *Habous* lands, religious landed property often used to build mosques or schools;
4   *Melk* lands, which were individually owned.

In 1912, the French introduced the notion of privately registered landownership to legitimize and facilitate foreign land acquisitions. This created huge inequalities in landownership. Towards the end of the French protectorate, the total area of agricultural lands was ± 7.8 million hectares, of which ± 13%[4] was in the hands of 5,900 Europeans and ±4% belonged to 1,700 Moroccans, who owned the best lands with an average farm size of 170 hectares. This group of landowners engaged predominantly in lucrative, mechanized farming (Swearingen, 1987). In contrast, the remaining 83% of agricultural lands, considered as 'traditional land', belonged to 1.4 million Moroccan families. These numbers hide the 500,000 families who owned less than 0.5 hectares or no land at all, as well as the landless farmers who often worked as labourers on the colonial farms.

Morocco obtained its independence in 1956, which coincided with the independence of other former colonies. Independence struggles sparked off a national debate during the decades that followed, in which agriculture, land reforms and the future of the ± 13% of colonized land figured prominently.

The majority of the left-wing parties agreed that a *real* land reform was what was needed. This entailed the dismantling of large farms and estates and the redistribution of the colonized land among small and landless farmers, thereby altering the existing agrarian structures and the established political power (Ben Barka, 1963; Bouami, 1980). The sitting government, whose power rested among others on the wealthy Moroccans who had acquired large landholdings during the French protectorate, was reluctant to engage in such reforms. Hence, barely anything changed with regard to the existing landownership inequalities in the countryside. Most of the lands that were part of the official colonization became state enterprises, and the lands that once belong privately to colonizers were gradually sold to Moroccan nationals. In the early 1970s, because of the growing political unrest caused by, inter alia, a worsening economic crisis, increasing socio-economic inequalities in the country side, land reclamations by peasants (see also El Yazami and Wallon, 1991) and the threat of a rural exodus that endangered the existing power structures, the government embarked on a limited land-reform programme. Because of private land sales and the establishment of state enterprises on land formerly owned by the colons, only 30% of the initial 1 million hectares remained to be distributed to small and landless farmers (Bouderbala, 2001; Pascon, 1977). The reform consisted of redistributing these lands to state cooperatives, which fell under the responsibility of the ministry of agriculture. Cooperative members – who had to either be former labourers of a French colonial farm, landless or own a small parcel of land – were often recruited from different parts of the country and were forced to work together, without having any cropping freedom.[5] Cooperative members thus became clients coerced by the government (Pascon, 1977: 185) in an apparently socialist structure. Land remained state property and the members of state cooperatives simply received use rights and remained officially unable to rent or sell the land. The land reforms were an isolated act that did not challenge the existing political power or change the dominant modes of production (Pascon, 1977).

From the 1980s onwards, the government of Morocco chose a path of economic liberation, which was considered necessary to alleviate the country's financial deficits. It adopted two structural adjustments programmes, which resulted in a repositioning of the state and the opening up of the agricultural sector to the market. These policies favoured a productive and competitive agricultural sector over the reduction of existing inequalities (Jouve, 2002). The existing patchwork of different coexisting property regimes was considered to stand in the way of the full development of the agrarian sector and restrict investments (ibid; Akesbi et al., 2007).

In addition, the lands of the state cooperatives were considered to be 'frozen', as they could not be exchanged in markets and thus remained outside the economy. This in turn was seen to limit the productivity and efficiency with which they were used. State cooperatives also faced many other problems that lead to low production figures. Although the government financially supported the state cooperatives, the development of the cooperatives depended on how well members worked together. In practice however, some members preferred farming individually and chose to sell their produce outside the structures of the cooperatives (see also Mahdi and Allali, 2001). This, together with reductions in the financial support received by the government after the structural adjustments of the 1980s, explains why cooperatives were no longer able to cover their expenses – such as acquiring machinery – with the proceeds generated by produce sales, which plunged them into a financial crisis. The government thus decided in 2006 to 'liberalize the sector', or as stated in a statement of the Ministry of Agriculture to 'remove all barriers that can hamper investments' (2007). On the condition that they paid off their debts, members of state cooperatives could now become owners of the land they used to work on in return for a symbolic fee of approximately 70,000 Dirham (approximately €6,250), depending on the size of the land and the quality of the soil. Former members of the cooperative could thus become private landowners, with the land becoming private property.

The context of the Sais agricultural plain

The cooperative where we carried out our research is situated in the agricultural plain of the Sais: it comprises 220,000 hectares, of which 49,677 hectares are irrigated, mainly with groundwater (Ministry of Agriculture 2012). In this region, 93 state cooperatives were created, representing roughly 12% of the total number of cooperatives in the country (Mahdi and Allali, 2001). Of these cooperatives, initially three were *coopératives de production*, each of c. 3,000 hectares. In these particular cooperatives, all land and capital was held in co-property[6] and the members worked as labourers who were remunerated on a yearly basis. In the early 1990s the three *coopératives de production* were divided in smaller entities and became either *coopératives de service* or *coopératives mixtes*, where members received an individual land plot, but where the supply and marketing of agricultural goods was done collectively.

Agriculture is the main activity in the region, which became progressively more dynamic from the 1980s onwards as the result of a combination of liberalization policies, the increased access of individual farmers to groundwater and resulting changes in cropping patterns, the integration of markets that were previously not connected and the use of new technologies (such as deep tubewells and drip irrigation). In 2008, the agricultural sector received a new impetus in the form of *Le plan Maroc Vert*, a comprehensive strategy whose aim was to facilitate rapid modernization and intensification of agriculture. A first critical analysis of *Le Plan Maroc Vert* reveals that the plan strongly favours and promotes a 'modern' way of farming that is based on high-value crops, new technologies and intensive inputs (Errahj, 2013; Akesbi, 2012).

Land as symbol of resistance and struggle against the colons and the Moroccan state

Tracing the history of the cooperative Ait Ali – which used to be part of the large *coopérative de production* Ait Naamen (comprising 3,000 hectares and with 178 members) – reveals much about the value that land used to embody. Historically land has symbolized the post-colonial struggle, as well as the resistance to the Moroccan state and the collective character of the cooperative. During our interviews with former members, they recalled bitterly how members of other cooperatives received an individual land plot with land-use rights on which they could work with their families, whereas they had become labourers, working under the government's control and being remunerated on a yearly basis or in kind. They used to be picked up in cars, sometimes with their family members, from their *douars* and brought to the cooperative to work for the day. They remembered their despair about still not owning any land and recalled how they had been workers on the farms of colonizers, managed with a heavy hand and had been left disappointed with how little had changed since the French left. They regarded this as the continuation of state repression, something that prevented them from being independent peasants. Some vividly recalled the distrust that existed between them and the state.

These *coopératives de production* functioned poorly and members were increasingly dissatisfied with their situation. Many feared that they would receive little or no remuneration for their work because of the cooperative's increasing debts, which is why they kept back parts of the harvest so that they could sell it themselves as a means of guaranteeing at least some income. As a result, however, large swathes of harvested produce disappeared, further reducing the income of the cooperative. Also, conflicts among the different tribes who had been forced to work together under the same structure of the state cooperative were common. Some members withdrew altogether, while others started to organize sit-ins in Rabat, Morocco's capital, demanding the division of the state cooperatives and individual land plots. As the only time in Moroccans' land tenure history that farmers went to Rabat to protest, this was a clear sign of dissatisfaction with the existing model. Eventually, this led to the division (in 1991–92) of the *coopérative de production* Ait Naamen into five smaller state cooperatives each of approximately 350 hectares and with 30 to 40 members. One of them was the *cooperative* Ait Ali.

Within this cooperative, each member received an individual land plot of between 7 and 13 hectares, depending on the quality of the land. The plots were distributed through a lottery system:

> [I]t was like a lottery, you pick a number and get a plot assigned. You could not choose which plot you wanted. Some were closer to the *douar*, others a bit further away.
>
> (interview with Aziz,[7] 25 July 2012)

The plots were not irrigated initially, but each member eventually received another 0.5 hectares that could be irrigated with water from a canal, and where vegetables were grown. All members also received a plot of 1,000m² intended for housing, which prompted many to move from the *douar* where they were living to the state cooperative.

The family farm as the cornerstone of the state cooperative: membership criteria and inheritance practices

In Ait Ali's early days, the reconstitution of the family farm formed the cornerstone of the functioning and the continuity of the state cooperative, with land assuring both the material as well as the ideological 'reproduction' of farms and families. The intimate relations between the family and the land were, for instance, expressed in the formal obligations and rights of the members of the state cooperative. These were codified in the *Dahir de la Réforme Agraire*, the law of the land reform, dated 29 December 1972. To be eligible as a member, not only must one be a landowner and be a farmer or be a salaried agricultural worker (Article 5, *Dahir de la Réforme Agraire*, 1972), we were told that in practice that people's personal circumstances were also taken into account: being a father was viewed as being a positive qualifier for potential membership. Women could also become members of a state cooperative in theory; in practice, however, if they did apply they were selected only if their husbands were not eligible. In our case study, only three of the 36 initial members were women. We encountered, for example, a woman who had applied for a plot of land because her husband had migrated to France. Other female members had obtained membership when their husband passed away as a result of the specific requirements of the inheritance system that we discuss in detail below. Today, the number of registered female members has increased to nine. The actual number of female members may even be higher, as land transfers were not always registered or communicated to the *Rais*, the president of the state cooperative. At the time we completed our research, most initial members were between 50 and 70 years old. In addition to the general membership rules, there were also certain rules regarding the organization of the work on the individual parcels of land, which again underscored the family-based character of farming. The members were, for instance, supposed to work on their individual plots with the help of family members 'living under the same roof' (Article 22, *Dahir de la Réforme Agraire*, 1972).

The particular inheritance practices that existed in the state cooperatives, and which differ from Sharia law, are another clear expression of how land contributed to and assured the social reproduction of families. When land-use titles were registered with the male head of the household, upon his death the land use right were often transferred to his wife. When discussing the reasons for this, many people referred to the particular role of the mother in the family and in the Moroccan (rural) society: as the backbone of the family, she is greatly honoured, revered and perceived as strong and responsible (see also Rassam, 1980). Registering the land in her name was a peace-keeping strategy; as it prevented the land being divided up into smaller parcels, it thus avoided conflicts between siblings and generations:

> the woman is the one who controls everything. If the son takes over the land, he will force his mother and other brothers to leave the land, because he will marry and his spouse will say that she doesn't want to live with your brothers and with your mother.
>
> (interview with former director of a state farm
> in the Sais region, 7 May 2012)

In order to assure the social reproduction of the family, if a mother was not eligible to inherit the land,[8] the land use right would instead often be transferred to an unmarried son who still lived in the parental house. This would mean that the use and ownership of the land stayed within the family: if the rights were transferred to a married male sibling, the family would run the risk of losing it upon his death, since the land would then be transferred to his wife (the daughter-in-law). The important objective of keeping the family together was thus partly achieved through the careful crafting of particular land inheritance practices, with land serving as the 'glue' in family ties.

The enactment of land use rights through marriage and gendered labour relations: the reaffirmation of gendered identities

The historical trajectories of the different family farms in the state cooperative reveal that as soon as the members received their individual land plot, land-tenure relations became embedded in wider household-, kinship- and community-based gendered relations. In addition to the membership rules and inheritance practices, marriage and labour arrangements mediated and expressed the gendered social relations and dependencies around land, simultaneously carving out gendered subjectivities and spaces. Although most land-use rights were registered in men's names, the intimate connections between families and farms worked to acknowledge the centrality and importance of women, something that positively influences their bargaining power. At the same time, the fuzziness of the boundaries between farm and family allowed women to extend and negotiate their mobility and agency by constructing farm work as an extension of their domestic activities.

Although marriage practices in rural Morocco are currently changing, marriage used to be an important strategy to forge alliances, as well as a central institution that safeguarded and controlled the chastity of women. Upon marriage, the newly wed wife usually leaves her parents' home and land, and moves to her in-laws' house. If the wife bears children, while her offspring grow up she will gradually become more involved in farm activities, usually on the land owned by her husband or in-laws. Through her everyday domestic work, and by helping with the collective work on the land, she confirms her commitment to her marriage and becomes part of the reproduction of the family farm, simultaneously enacting her identity as a wife, mother and farmer. The work on the farm thus is an almost logical extension of the work in the house, with the boundaries between the house and the farm being fluid and permeable. The case of Rabha, 50 years old, illustrates this. Rabha married Hassan, whose brother – at that time unmarried – had inherited the land-use title upon the death of their father in 1983. Their 9-hectare plot is situated about one kilometre from their house. Rabha is originally from another state cooperative 40 kilometres away. She tried maintaining her claim to her natal land by sending her son to work on that land, and explained to us that she had done so to be able to pass it on to her children. She was responsible for all the household chores, like cooking the meals for her five children (ranging at that time between 11 and 20 years of age) and sometimes also for the individuals who were working on the land, as well as baking bread, doing laundry and cleaning the house (with the help of her two daughters). She also took care of their three cows. Initially, like everyone else in the early days of the cooperative, Rabha's family cultivated cereals, barley and peas. The growing and harvesting of these crops is considered a man's job, and was normally carried out by the brothers who were sometimes helped by their sons or other male relatives. Rabha, together with other female family members and sometimes female neighbours, would help with the sorting and cleaning of the wheat, barley and peas once they had been harvested. After a couple years, the brothers collectively invested in the digging of a well and started to cultivate different irrigated crops – such as onions, potatoes, carrots and tomatoes – on c. 3 hectares of the plot. Rabha started to help more frequently on the land from this point, sometimes with her sisters-in-law or other relatives. She worked alongside her husband, her brothers-in-law and sons. The cultivation and preparation of the soil, and the irrigation of the onions and potatoes, were considered tasks for the men, while the women were responsible for the planting (and later weeding) of the carrots, tomatoes and sometimes also of the onions; at harvest time, men and women, at points assisted by labourers (mostly family members, neighbours and individuals living in the *douar* Ait Ali), worked together to bring the crops in safely.

The example of Monsieur Molud further reflects how gendered identities are partly enacted and affirmed through a gendered division of farm activities. He is 65 years old and received a land plot of 8.5 hectares. He has two sons and one daughter, who are now in their late twenties. They initially cultivated rain-fed crops, which was done with the help of hired labourers living in the surrounding *douars*. A few years later, they dug a well. Soon after, Monsieur Molud and his family moved to the plot, which was situated two kilometres away from the 1,000m² that they received for building their house upon the division of the large cooperative. As soon as they moved, Monsieur Molud's two oldest sons left school and actively began to farm. They planted onions on 3 hectares, tomatoes on 1.5 hectares and wheat on the rest of the plot. They divided the activities: the oldest son was responsible for irrigation and organizing the labourers. He also monitored the farming activities on the land. His younger brother drove the tractor on the family's plot and also those of their neighbours. During an interview, the brothers explained that they discussed everything with their father and that their mother, who was in poor health, hardly worked on the land. One of the sons is married and his wife was responsible for the household chores, and also looked after a couple of cows. Their sister was living with an aunt in a nearby town and was going to school.

The above examples illustrate how the use of the land is embedded in wider household, kinship- and community relations, serving the reproduction of the family farm by means of activities through which gendered subjectivities are enacted and reproduced. Rabha explained that keeping the ties to her natal land was important for her; she regarded it as a way to secure the future of her children. Holding on to the land also contributed to her personal autonomy and bargaining power within her own family. Simultaneously, her activities on her brother-in-law's land are important in affirming her social position in the family; through her labour investments, she invests in her reputation and her identity as a good wife and mother. The fact that farm work is (seen as) an extension of domestic work and because most farm activities are done with family members, women like Rabha are able to stretch the boundaries of the private sphere – the space to which women are culturally and traditionally confined in rural Morocco – thus extending their mobility without losing their credibility as women, mothers and wives. Moreover, these collective activities were also important moments of interactions and exchange about personal events and village concerns. For men, as the case of

Monsieur Molud demonstrates, subjectivities are much more clearly tied to landownership, their occupational position as farmer and their work on the farm. Where women's subjectivities were more tied to the marital contract and associated with the private sphere of the house, men's subjectivities were defined by their position as head of the family and or the farm (see also Brandth, 2002).

Land privatization and dynamics in Ait Ali: changing meaning of land and the gradual disarticulation of land rights and family relations

During the final years of the state cooperative, the family farm – as an amalgam of gendered activities and identities formed around the fluid boundaries between the house, the farm and the land – gradually changed. Land became ever more disarticulated and dis-embedded from family and kinship relations, and dis-associated from memories of struggle and territory. Our evidence suggests that this process has accelerated since the land privatization of 2006. The stories of the people who sold their land provide particularly vivid witness to this; their regret and sorrow about the separation from their land illustrate both that land used to signify much more than just a resource, and also that the land's meanings are changing. Many were reluctant to openly discuss their decision to sell their land. They often tried to hide this information from us, diverting the conversation to their future plans in agriculture whenever we brought up the topic. When invited to visit their fields to see the crops planted or the drip-irrigation systems installed, we often found ourselves waiting in vain for anyone to arrive at the agreed time. Such appointments were also often postponed, or turned out very differently than expected – we ended up visiting another *douar*, for example, or another farmer, or even went to the city for a coffee. Deeply puzzled at first, we gradually came to understand that the reluctance of our interlocutors to share experiences of selling their land reflected the social importance attached to land and the shame many people feel in admitting to having disposed of it. For them, as for many of the first members of the cooperatives, landownership is much more than property; it is the result of years of struggle by parents and grandparents to obtain the right to own the land many of them used to work on as labourers under an authoritative foreign ruler. Owned land is also a repository of years of labour and other investments. When we were asking our friends in the state cooperative why so many people were unwilling to admit that they sold their land, they replied, 'selling land is like selling your parents, or your mother – you don't do that' (interview with Mohammed and Aziza, 1 November 2012).

In comparison with ten years ago, the value of land is now increasingly determined by its market price, which has drastically increased since 2006. The price today (2013) of a hectare of land is between 500,000 Dirham (c. €45,000) and 600,000 Dirham (c. €55,000). In 2006, at the beginning of the land-privatization process, the same lands were worth around 120,000 Dirham (€11,000) per hectare. Depending on the location of the land (close to the city or close to a hard road) and the water availability (the presence of wells), the price per hectare can be even higher. We were told by our interviewees, both by families who sold the land as well as by recent buyers, that only the rich can afford to pay such prices. Or, as a female former landowner indicated, 'people who can buy the land did not earn their money through working', which refers to some land transactions that are used to launder drug money, as is carried out mostly by individuals from the North Moroccan Rif region.

The land market is far from a 'neutral space', where intermediaries connect willing buyers and sellers and help them negotiate the best price for all parties involved. Instead, this institution is highly gendered: the negotiations and transactions are predominantly conducted between men and take place in cafes, spaces that are typically not accessible to women. That this effectively works to limit women's opportunities to buy or sell land became apparent during our fieldwork: women sometimes approached us to ask if we knew anyone who was interested in buying their land, or they requested our help in finding potential buyers. In addition, although forming part of a policy of economic liberalization that entails the withdrawal of the state, the Moroccan government is deeply involved in land-transfer dynamics. By offering tax exemptions and subsidies to support new investments, it actively steers the privatization outcome into a specific direction: that of supposedly efficient, productive and competitive agricultural production that can be realized by a very specific type of entrepreneurial farmer. This in turn leads to the increase of 'entrepreneurial' farming, which can be characterized among other things by investing heavily in the land, the introduction of mechanization (e.g. drip irrigation) and the cultivation of high-value crops (mainly fruit trees and grapes).

The professionalization and masculinization of farming activities

The gradual dis-articulation of the family from the farm and the associated land further manifests itself through the gradual professionalization and masculinization of farming. For some young men, this offers attractive new opportunities to demonstrate their masculinity, as the activity of farming is redefined from something associated with backwardness and tradition to something associated with modernity and progress. In our case study these newly emerging masculinities are epitomized by the new farming projects undertaken by the investors and entrepreneurs who buy up the land. Their farming style often starkly contrasts with that seen on the lands that are not sold. In our case study, eight members of the cooperative sold their land and 18 obtained their individual land rights by paying the symbolic price. Approximately ten members continue as members of the state cooperative.[9] Many of the buyers come from other regions in Morocco; they do not settle in the area but live either abroad or in the city. In our case, six of the eight buyers made large investments in their land that visibly altered the landscape: they demarcated their newly acquired property with high fences; planted semi-permanent high-value crops, as noted above; started producing for the national market. The other two buyers continued with a mix of irrigated agriculture and rain-fed agriculture. We were told that these were 'pending projects': the buyer waits until he has sufficient money to pursue his potential project.

There are differences in how members of families who did not sell their lands appreciate these changes, and these vary in line with generation and socio-economic background. The older generation, many of whom were the original members of the state farm, perceive the new land buyers as *barrani*, which literally means 'outsiders': statements such as 'they are different', 'they think differently', 'he doesn't come to you, so why should you go to him?' were used to express the social distance they perceived as existing between themselves and these newcomers. Many specifically referred to the new enclosures of the land with fences, seeing these as clear markers of how society is changing for the worse. To them, the replacement of the old rows of olive trees – often the result of a joint investment of neighbouring farmers – with cement poles and barbed wire, guards and sometimes dogs to mark and forcefully delineate plot boundaries is a stark expression of changing property relations. The younger generation, who are between the age of 18 and 35, have a slightly more positive perception of the new buyers. During group discussions with young women and young men, both groups mentioned that instead of using the negative word *barrani* they would prefer to use the more neutral term *mostatmir*, which means investor. Many youngsters, although noting how the arrival of newcomers was accompanied by land sales arising from financial distress, and while regretting that new fences make the free grazing of animals more difficult, positively appreciate the economic opportunities that new foreign investors are creating, including modern technologies and different opportunities for employment and development (see also Bossenbroek *et al.*, 2014). Likewise, the agricultural projects undertaken by newcomers serve as a source of inspiration to some former cooperative members, even if they do not have any direct contacts with them. For instance, many of those who managed to obtain their private land title have now started digging new wells to expand irrigation across their plot and cultivate more vegetables. Many have plans for, or are installing, drip irrigation and some are also starting to fence their lands and are thinking of planting a couple of hectares of fruit trees in the near future.

Taken together, these new initiatives can be characterized as a gradual 'professionalization' of farming, with farming identities increasingly becoming reserved for, and actively taken up by, some ambitious young male farmers whose fathers or mothers used to be members of the state cooperative. Their positive appreciation of the opportunities offered by mechanization, higher value crops and drip irrigation is based on a labelling of these changes as 'new' and 'modern'. They mark a new era, and allow male youngsters to positively distinguish themselves from their old-fashioned 'peasant' parents, and to become new, clean and entrepreneurial farmers. Their idea of farming, for which hard physical labour is required while becoming dirty in the mud, is giving way to a more technical, less physical demanding way of farming that requires more managerial skills. This change also marks a clear masculinization of the profession.

The eroding fluidity of the boundaries between private and public spheres

The dis-articulation of the family from the farm and the land also occurs partly via a gradual erosion of the social relations in which women's activities used to be embedded. This is accompanied with a clearer distinction – and a more marked symbolic boundary – between the private home domain and the public professional domain. This is first and foremost due to the changing labour relations that are part of the process of agricultural intensification, as well as the transformation in cropping patterns that has drastically increased the demand for agricultural labour. Ever more farmers are seeking these labourers from the wider community, and outside kinship and community relations. The presence of 'outside' labourers, especially when they are male, makes female family members reluctant to continue working on the land, as indicated by the following quote:

> we used to work on the land and help out when it was needed; for example, during the harvest of the onions I used to fill the boxes with onions. Today we hardly do it any more because the harvest is done by male workers. We do not work together with them.
>
> (interview with Hind, 24 March 2014)

Moreover, as a result of fencing, land is increasingly becoming individual property – a personal business and space – in which it is difficult for women to find a place. This also affects community interactions: when talking with different cooperative members, all of them felt that 'there is no cooperative any more; it is now every man for himself'. Intra-community relations are now being replaced with new property demarcations, with male managers who oversee the projects of the absentee investors or entrepreneurs and young male farmers. New farming styles and fences thus also mark a seem to solidify new frontiers, which besides regulating certain forms of mobility, also affect the social exchanges among the people living in the state cooperative; face-to-face meetings and informal chats are reduced.

Changing inheritance practices

Gradual changes in inheritance practices further reflect and illustrate how land becomes increasingly disconnected from families, histories and identities. Following the changes in land privatization, inheritance practices shifted into the direction of Sharia law and its linked customs. In theory this means that instead of appointing one single heir, sons now receive two-thirds of an inheritance, daughters one-third and the wife or mother one-sixth. We witnessed several cases in which families had not yet obtained the private land title before the initial cooperative member passed away. Such situations provoked sometimes heated and protracted quarrels between siblings about how to divide the land. In cases where the individual land title was issued in the name of the youngest son, often all brothers (their sisters usually move out of the house upon marriage and cease work on their parents' land) used to work on it. Rather than collectively managing the land, or allowing the one heir to do so, families instead often choose to sell the land so as to avoid conflicts between brothers and generations. Yet the decision about whether or not to sell also itself sometimes was a cause of intense disagreement.

In these contentious intra-family negotiations about land inheritance issues, women have a particularly weak bargaining position. Although theoretically (according to the Sharia) they are entitled to a share of the inheritance, it is customary practice that they leave their part to their brothers. This is first of all related to the fact that often one or several brothers are in charge of farming and in order to keep the peace, and to keep the land (and the family) together, sisters used to renounce their land share. Also, as land did not have the same monetary value as it has today, the stakes were lower. That women do not receive any share of the family land is often justified by the fact that they will be moving out of the parents' home – and leaving the family – upon marriage. Aziza's story serves as an example here. She married a member of the state farm and moved out of her parent's house. We were told that her husband was the first person in the cooperative who sold his land. Aziza's father used to be a member of the state cooperative but had recently (in 2012) passed away. We talked briefly with Aziza and asked her how her father's land was going to be divided. She explained that it would be done according to the Sharia: she would get 1 or 1.5 hectares and her brothers 3 hectares or slightly more. She was thinking of installing drip irrigation on the land that she would inherit, seeing the land as insurance for the future of herself and her children. A couple of months later we talked with her brother, Aziz. We asked if the division had already been done. He said that they would not divide the land and would continue working on it with all the seven brothers, like they always had done. When asked 'What about your sisters?', Aziz answered 'they all have their own houses, we will just give them something in memory of father' (interview conducted on 13 October 2012). When we dug deeper and asked specifically about Aziza, who was still living in the state cooperative, Aziz explained that he did not see the point of giving her land, since her husband had sold his land only to squander all his money. He added that if Aziza claimed her part of the inheritance, he would buy her out. Knowing the price per hectare, we thought that this would be better than nothing; the money would still allow her to provide for her children's future. However, when we asked Aziz how much he was thinking to give his sister, he answered 'the price per hectare is 380,000 [Dirham] (€34,000), but since we are family, we will see'. We frequently heard stories like this, where sisters were excluded from their rightful inheritance in order to maintain peace among their brothers.

An interview with a notary in the region suggested that there are many women, like Aziza, who aspire to claim their inheritance rights. Apparently, the increasing monetary value and meaning of land is also leading to a re-appreciation of customary inheritance practices.

Conclusion

Our analysis shows how changes in land-tenure regimes in the region of the Sais are co-shaped by changing gender relations and subjectivities. Situating our analysis in the land-tenure history of the region reveals how the value of land once symbolized resistance as well as a collective struggle for independence and freedom in which kinship relations were important resources. For as long as state cooperatives existed, the organization of farming was closely interwoven with land tenure and family relations. Complementary gendered labour divisions and farming identities muddled the boundaries between families and farms, with the latter being a logical extension of the former and the two shaping each other in intimate ways. Today, however, as part of the privatization process, there is a gradual disarticulation of farms and wider kinship and community relations. We have identified and described three processes that manifest and mark this uncoupling of the meaning of land from the livelihoods and meaning of farming families. The first is a professionalization and masculinization of farming identities; processes which offer new and exciting opportunities for some young men to combine the activity of farming with modern ideals of manhood. The second is the gradual emergence of stronger symbolic and spatial gendered distinctions. Women are increasingly confined to the domestic sphere (sometimes encompassing the newly fenced land) and removed from the public, professional one. For male farmers, newly fenced land becomes an important space for enacting their new identity as 'professionals'. The third way in which the separation of land from families and territories occurs is through changes in inheritance: from inheritance practices in the state cooperative that honoured and reinforced the centrality of mothers in both farms and families, to the customs surrounding the Sharia that allow women (at least in principle) to claim a share of the land as inheritance. Within the ideological context of rural Morocco, characterized by the strict control of female chastity, these processes together work to reconfigure female mobility and subjectivity. Within the shifting meanings of place and subjectivities, some women are confined to a new home-bound traditionalism, while increasing their dependence on men as income earners and employers. Others, especially the younger generations, attempt to negotiate the changing order of meaning and seek new activities in farming and sometimes in the city. These attempts remain scattered and emerge at the margins of the increasing masculinization of the agricultural sector. Nevertheless, these aspirations need to be followed closely as they might be indicators of changing and new femininities.

Notes

1   In the Moroccan rural society the *douar*, which can be translated as 'village' (Rachik, 2000: 40), is the most important socio-cultural unit after the family. It is often based on kinship ties and has strong territorial and historical roots.
2   In 1960, 71% of the Moroccan population was living in the countryside (Haut Commissariat au Plan 1960).

3   Until the end of the protectorate, the *Makhzen* refers to the apparatus of state domination and power. Until the protectorate the *Makhzen* used to denote a bureaucratic establishment founded on the court surrounding the Sultan, his administration and his local representatives. The term is still used today and refers to a mode of governance that determines the relationship between the ruler and those who are ruled (Tozy, 1991).

4   The colonization of land during the French protectorate consisted of 56% private colonization, 22 % state colonization, and 22% acquisition by Moroccan notables.

5   The members of the state cooperatives initially did not have a free choice regarding cropping. Although this rule did not change in theory, in practice we have observed how, from the mid-1980s onwards, this rule was applied only loosely and members gradually started to cultivate what they wanted.

6   Although it was stated in the official documents on the state cooperatives that the land was held in co-property, e.g. collective ownership, and thus owned by all the members of the state cooperative, in practice the land remained state owned. The assets (for example machinery) bought by all the members, were held as collective property.

7   To protect the privacy of our informants, the original names of all the interviewees referred to above have been changed.

8   According to the rules of the state cooperative, she was not allowed to be older than 55 years. This rule was abolished in 2006 upon the privatization of the land of the state cooperatives. From that point on, mothers and/or wives older than 55 could also inherit the land.

9   These numbers are based on the land sales up to September 2013. According to the Ministry of Agriculture, when the state cooperative has fewer than seven members, it is officially dissolved.

References

Akesbi, N. (2012) 'Une nouvelle stratégie pour l'agriculture marocaine : Le «Plan Maroc Vert»', *New Medit*, vol. 11, no. 2 pp. 12–23.

Akesbi, N., Benatya, D., El Aoufi, N. (2007) *Les implications structurelles de la libéralisation sur l'agriculture et le développement au Maroc*, Colloque International: Enjeux économiques, sociaux et environnementaux de la libéralisation commerciale des pays du Maghreb et du Proche-Orient. Rabat, Morocco.

Ben Barka, E.N. (1963) 'Les conditions d'une véritable réforme agraire au Maroc', in Dresch *et al.* (ed.) *Réforme agraire au Maghreb: colloque sur les conditions d'une véritable réforme agraire au Maroc*, Édition Francois Maspero, Paris, pp. 107–141.

Bernstein, H. (2010) *Class Dynamics of Agrarian Change*, Fernwood Publishing.

Bossenbroek, L., Errahj, E., and El Alime, N. (2014) 'Les nouvelles modalités du travail agricole dans le Sais au Maroc. L'émergence des inégalités identitaires entre l'ouvrier et l'ouvrière?', Farzyat, Available: http://farzyat.cjb.ma/les-nouvelles-modalites-du-travail-agricole-dans-le-sais-au-maroc-lemergence-des-inegalites-identitaires-entre-louvrier-et-louvriere (forthcoming in: Le Maroc au Présent, Rabat)

Bouami, A. (1980) 'L'Etat et la question agraire', in *Parti du Progres et du Socialisme, La question agraire au Maroc*. Rabat, Morocco, Édition Al-Bayane: pp. 87–129.

Bouderbala, N. (1999) 'Les systèmes de propriété foncière au Maghreb. Le cas du Maroc', *Cahiers Options Méditerranéennes* vol. 36, pp. 47–66.

Bouderbala, N. (2001) 'La lutte contre le morcellement au Maroc: un thème idéologique', in Anne-Marie Jouve (ed.) *Terres méditerranéennes. Le morcellement, richesse ou danger?* Paris, Karthala-Ciheam.

Brandth, B. (2002) 'Gender identity in European family farming: A literature review', *Sociologica Ruralis* vol. 42, no. 3, pp. 181–200.

El Yazami, D., and Wallon, B. (1991) 'Le livre blanc sur les droits de l'homme au Maroc', *EDI, Études et Documentation Internationales*, Paris.

Errahj, M. (December 2013) *Presentation at the seminar (Re-) Engaging with agrarian transformation: The rural, a battlefield of new social hierarchies?*, Wageningen University.

Jouve, A.M. (2002) 'Cinquante ans d'agriculture marocaine', in Blanc, P. (ed.) *Du Maghreb au Proche Orient: les défis de l'agriculture*. Harmattan, pp. 51–71.

Mahdi, A. and Allali, A. (2001) 'Les coopératives de la réforme agraires: trente ans après', *Publication of the Bulletin Economique et Social du Maroc*, Rabat, Morocco, Société d'Études Économiques Sociales et Statistiques, pp. 109–125.

Ministère de l'Agriculture, (2007) « Note sur le secteur de la Réforme Agraire », Circulaire n°209 du 15/10/2007 qui fixe les modalités d'application de la loi 06.01, Disponible au Ministère de l'Agriculture du Développement Rural et des Pêches Maritimes, Division des Affaires Juridiques.

Ministère de l'Agriculture et de la Pêche Maritime (MAPM) (2012) *Situation de l'agriculture marocaine*. Rabat, Morocco.

Pascon, P. (1977) 'Interrogations autour de la réforme agraire', in N. Bouderbala, Chraïbi, M., and Pascon, P. (eds) *La question agraire au Maroc 2*. Publication du bulletin economique et social du Maroc, pp. 183–200.

Rachik, H. (2000) 'Les usages politiques des notions de tribu et de nation au Maroc', *Identity, Culture and Politics*, vol. 1, no. 1, pp. 35–47.

Raki, M. (1980) 'Stratégie de l'Etat et classes sociales dans la société rurale', in *Le Parti du Progres et du Socialisme: La question agraire au Maroc*. Rabat, Morocco, Édition Al Bayane, pp. 47–85.

Swearingen, W.D. (1987) 'Terre, politique et pouvoir au Maroc', *Revue de l'Occident musulman et de la Méditerranée* vol. 45, no. 45, pp. 41–54.

Tozy, M. (1991) 'Les enjeux de pouvoir dans les « champs politiques désamorcés » au Maroc', in Michel, C. (ed.) *Changements politiques au Maghreb*. Paris, Éditions du CNRS, pp. 153–168.

9 Aging ejidos in the wake of neo-liberal reform

Livelihood predicaments of Mexican ejidatarias

Verónica Vázquez-García

Introduction

The 1910 revolution led to dramatic transformations in Mexico's land-tenure structure largely due to the involvement of peasant leader Emiliano Zapata in the armed struggle. The expropriation of land from rich hacendados in order to distribute it among landless peasants legitimated the project of social justice of the emerging nation state (Warman, 2001). Article 27 of the 1917 Constitution recognized the need to distribute such land under the modality of ejidos. Each household within the ejido would receive a plot for cultivation and have access to communal lands such as pastures and forests, and to collective resources such as water. Heads of households were called ejidatarios. Only one person per household could become ejidatario or ejidataria; this person was specified in law as a male aged 18 and above, or a widow with a family to support. His or her land right had to be transferred within the family, with spouses legally designated as the principal heir for ejiditarios and son as the heirs of ejidatarias. Land plots were considered a family patrimony, and the communal lands and collective resources of ejidos were to be governed by an assembly of ejidatarios represented by the Comisariado de Bienes Ejidales.

One hundred years later, ejidos continue to be the major form of property in rural Mexico. According to the agrarian census of 2007, 54.1% (105,949,097 hectares) of the total surface of Mexico are either ejidos or agrarian communities, with a clear predominance of the first (91.9% are ejidos, the rest are agrarian communities).[1] These lands belong to 5.6 million people, accounting for 75.7% of all landholders (De María & Campos, 2005; Robles, 2012).

The agrarian law inspired by article 27 of the Mexican constitution was modified several times during the twentieth century (1927, 1934, 1971, 1992). The most important change occurred in 1992, when the government declared an end to the state's constitutional obligation to distribute land to the landless rural poor, and promoted a package of reforms aimed at the commercialization of ejidos. These reforms were accompanied by a wide range of neo-liberal policies, including trade liberalization (i.e. joining NAFTA, which came into effect in January 1994) and the withdrawal of state support for national agricultural production in the form of technology and subsidies. The government renounced its role as regulator and facilitator of land tenure. Instead, it sought to create the legal mechanisms that would enable private capital to expand into ejido lands, with the aim that such investment would increase agricultural production with aggregated value (Flores, 2009).

Unlike other Latin American countries, such as Bolivia and Ecuador, where left-wing governments have recently fought neo-liberalism by strengthening family agriculture with measures such as land redistribution, protection of local genetic resources, creation of peasant cooperatives, and changes to the constitution to guarantee the rights of nature, Mexico's right-wing governments have dismantled the public institutions originally designed to support agricultural production (i.e. INMECAFE and BANRURAL). This has caused the loss of food sovereignty that has resulted in a dramatic increase in imported foodstuffs, which has rocketed from 19% in 1993 to 42% in 2013 (Pérez, 2013). This percentage is 17 points higher than the 25% recommended by the Food and Agriculture Association of the United Nations (FAO).

The package of neo-liberal policies implemented during the last two decades has led to a fall in three vital areas: first, the use of technology among rural food producers; second, the number of organizations supporting the rural poor; and third, the number of credits given to this community.[2] Government subsidies that were meant to support production (i.e. PROCAMPO) have financed export-oriented agriculture and concentrated wealth in the hands of the few: 10% of agricultural producers receive 45% of PROCAMPO monies, the program with the largest amount of financial resources handled by the Ministry of Agriculture (Carrillo, 2011). By contrast, peasant families have been enrolled in programs such as OPORTUNIDADES, whose main objective is to reduce poverty by financing consumption rather than production (i.e. by giving money to women so that their children stay in school) (Rubio, 2009; Merino, 2010). Instead of receiving support for their productive endeavors, peasant families have become targets of social assistance programs handled by the Ministry for Social Development (Rubio, 2003; Scott, 2010; Fox & Haight, 2010).

In spite of these efforts, rural poverty continues to be a major problem in Mexico. The annual GDP of rural areas (US$2,310) is six times lower than that of urban areas. Between 2006 and 2008, rural poverty increased 6.1%, affecting 2.3 million people. One third of the heads of rural households cannot read or write (Haro, 2011). Half of the people living in the countryside (14 million of 29.7 million) are under 20 years of age, and they have few employment opportunities. In approximately half (13,000) of all ejidos, most young people have left (Robles, 2012). Consequently, ejido lands remain in the hands of the elderly: 53% of landholders are 50 years and older, while 24.5% are over 65 years of age. Female landholders are even older than male ones: 66.9% are 50 years and above and 34.7% are over 65 of age, compared to 52.7% and 22.3% of men respectively (Robles, 2007).

This chapter analyzes rural women's access to land and their ability to sustain their livelihoods in the context of these transformations. The argument is twofold. First, it shows that, due to a long history of discriminatory legal policies, the 1992 agrarian reform has had no beneficial effect for women. Drawing on a case study on cacao production conducted with elderly female landholders in Cárdenas, Tabasco, the second part of the chapter examines the difficulties they face in maintaining livelihoods in a rural setting. Women have suffered more than men from neo-liberal policies because, as widows, they inherited a cacao plantation initiated by men, and in their old age they have little access to household labor. The chapter argues that, in a context of adverse economic policies, poverty, and youth out-migration, the government has failed to empower women and has not invested in their property rights and agricultural capabilities so that they might cope with the demographic and economic implications of neo-liberal policies.

The Mexican agrarian law: one hundred years of gender discrimination

A significant amount of research has been conducted on the gender bias of the agrarian law (Vázquez-García, 1996, 2001; Baitenmann, 1997; Deere & León, 2001, 2003; Hamilton, 2002; Lastarria-Cornhiel, 2011; Almeida, 2009, 2012). Scholars have shown that the law discriminated against women because they could receive ejido lands only if they were heads of households with children to support even though all adult men were eligible for land rights regardless of their marital status and/or number of children. Changes were made to the regulations in 1927 and 1934 concerning their eligible age (Table 9.1).

It was not until 1971 that women could receive land regardless of their marital status, as the table above shows. These changes responded to a global trend pushing for the advancement of women's rights at that time, and coincided with

Table 9.1 Eligibility criteria in the agrarian law regarding ejido lands

Year	Men	Women	Sole heir priority (by law)
1917	Article 27 recognizes the state's obligation to distribute land		
1920	Heads of households		Not specified
1927	18 years of age	Widows and single mothers with children	Not specified
1934	16 years of age; any age if they have children	Widows and single mothers with children	Spouse takes precedence
1971	16 years of age; any age if they have children	16 years of age regardless of marital status; any age if they have children	Spouse or a child
1992	18 years of age; any age if they have children	18 years of age regardless of marital status; any age if they have children	Spouse loses priority; land can be bequeathed to any person or sold within the ejido

Sources: own elaboration based on Baitenmann (1997); Botey (2000); Deere & León (2001); UN-Habitat (2005); Almeida (2009).

Mexico preparing to host the first Word Conference on Women in 1975. However, the changes were implemented very late, since most land had already been distributed during the Lázaro Cárdenas administration (1934–1940). The 1971 reform meant progress on paper rather than real agrarian justice for women (Botey, 2000). While in 1971 only 1.4% of ejidatarios were female, nine years after this reform females still accounted for just 15% of ejido landowners (Arizpe & Botey, 1986).

The 1992 reform opened up the possibility of privatizing ejido lands by allowing ejidatarios to assume full ownership of individual parcels and enter into business partnerships with private capital. If approved by the Comisariado de Bienes Ejidales, communal lands could also be privatized. The government that pushed for this reform argued that it would increase productivity and the rural economy's contribution to the GNP by securing individual ejido property. Thus, ejidatarios were granted the right to sell their parcels of land. Given that ejidatarios were overwhelmingly male, however, this reform increased women's vulnerabilities. The only form of protection against dispossession through land sales by their husbands then and now is a "derecho de tanto," or priority to buy from the spouse within 30 days of his announcing an official intention to sell. In practice, though, this is rarely used as women's lack of access to financial resources. Wives also lost the priority of inheritance, as now land could be bequeathed to anyone within or outside of the family (Esparza et al., 1996).

The Programa de Certificación de Derechos Ejidales (PROCEDE) was implemented in order to formalize individual landownership. It recognized three types of landholders:

1   Ejidatarios. The only fully fledged ejido members, ejidatarios own agricultural parcels of land, can vote in ejido assemblies and hold positions in ejido governance structures.
2   Possessors (posesionarios) also have individual agricultural parcels. Ejidatarios saw in PROCEDE a practical way to transfer part of their land rights to their offspring while still alive; their children (mostly male) thus became possessors. Posesionarios do not have the right to vote, however, nor can they hold positions in assemblies.
3   Settlers (avecindados) own only housing plots (the piece of land in the rural village on which their dwellings are built) within the ejido. Due to their location and size, these plots are considered unfit for cultivation. Like possessors, settlers cannot vote in assemblies nor hold positions therein (United Nations-Habitat, 2005).

These three groups are not mutually exclusive—ejidatarios and possessors usually own both agricultural lands and housing plots, whereas settlers own only the latter. As a result of the 1992 reform, all three may sell or bequeath their property to anyone of their choice.

PROCEDE was not a land redistribution program; it was a land certification program. The extension of the ejido and the list of eligible ejidatarios were established in most cases during the first half of the 20th century, shortly after the Mexican revolution. With PROCEDE, the total extension of each ejido was not modified. The number of landholders changed only because deceased ejidatarios were replaced by their wives or sons, and those who were still alive had the chance to divide their property among their sons. For example, a parcel of 20 hectares would be split among three sons (each gaining 5 hectares) who would thus become possessors. Their father (an ejidatario) would keep the remaining 5 hectares. Settlers simply received a property title for the house in which they had always lived.

By 1999, when the PROCEDE titling process was almost complete, 17.7% of ejidatarios, 22.8% of possessors, and 30.8% of settlers were female. By 2011, these percentages had increased to 20.6%, 25.8%, and 34.6%, respectively (Table 9.2). The largest group of female landholders are the settlers who own small housing plots within the ejido—the dwellings that, before PROCEDE, was untitled. On such plots, female settlers may have fruit trees and plants (edible, medicinal, and ornamental), raise domestic animals (mostly poultry; pigs, sheep, and goats in some regions), and even grow tiny amounts of corn. Female settlers are considerably younger than ejidatarias, with an average age of 53 years (Procuraduría Agraria, 2011).

The second most important group in terms of numbers is that of possessors, as Table 9.2 shows. These are women who received agricultural land during the PROCEDE titling process either as inheritance (fathers would bequeath while still alive because PROCEDE gave them the opportunity to do so) or when they bought land—no information is available on the proportions of each subgroup. Córdova (2000) and Almeida (2012) describe female possessors in Veracruz as being more educated than the norm and as having a history of income-generating activities. Some of these women have remained single; they live with their parents and take care of them during old age. Their male siblings were denied land because they may have abused alcohol, argued with their parents, or left the ejido for good. The average age of female possessors is very similar to that of settlers: 54 years of age (Procuraduría Agraria, 2011).

Finally, the smallest group of female landholders, again shown in Table 9.2, is that of ejidatarias. Their average age is 61 (Procuraduría Agraria, 2011). Most ejidatarias (66.9%) are 50 years or above, 34.7% are older than 65 (Robles, 2007). Most are widows and as such are the "keepers" of a family patrimony that will eventually be transferred to one or various adult sons. These elderly ejidatarias are left with the responsibility for managing and maintaining agricultural

Table 9.2 Number of landholders by sex (%)

	Ejidatarios	Ejidatarias	Total	Male possessors	Female possessors	Total	Male settlers	Female settlers	Total
1999	82.3	17.7	100	77.2	22.8	100	69.2	30.8	100
2011	79.4	20.6	100	74.2	25.8	100	65.4	34.6	100

Source: own elaboration based on Procuraduría Agraria (2011) and Costa & Velasco (2012).

production on everything from cattle ranches to commercial plantations of avocado, coffee, sugarcane, or cacao (depending on the region), in addition to subsistence-level corn farming.

Ejidatarias are the only group of women with full rights in ejidos: they can vote in assemblies and hold positions in governance structures. However, between 1998 and 2012, only 2.6% of all ejidos had a woman in the highest possible position of authority (president of the Comisariado de Bienes Ejidales) (Costa & Velasco, 2012). The lack of participation by ejidatarias in the decision-making relating to land and natural resources underscores that these female landholders are merely in place to transfer land from fathers to sons, thus maintaining succession within the family. However, this patrimony is under threat, not only because the 1992 reform allowed lands to be bequeathed outside of the nuclear family, but also because aging ejidatarias are struggling to generate a livelihood livelihoods from these lands in the context of little access to family labor and a lack of investments in their own agricultural capacities. A case study of ejidatarias in the cacao-producing region of Tabasco illustrates these dynamics.

Elderly ejidatarias struggling to produce cacao in La Natividad, Tabasco

Cacao is a pre-Hispanic crop used by native peoples to prepare their famous chocolate. Before the Spanish invasion, it was so highly regarded that people also used it as a trading currency. Eighty percent of Mexico's national cacao production is concentrated in the state of Tabasco, where around 20,000 families own 60,324 hectares (Ramírez-Martínez, 2007). The municipality of Cárdenas has registered 10,654 hectares and 4,293 tons of annual cacao production, thereby occupying second place in the state (SAGARPA, 2010).

Throughout the centuries, Mexico has continued to be an important cacao producer internationally. However, the Cacao National Commission disappeared in the 1990s and the country has fallen from ninth to fourteenth place in a list of global producers over the last two decades (Priego-Castillo *et al.*, 2009). Presently, eight agroindustries handle 60% of all cacao operations (Pérez, 2011). Scholars have attributed this situation to producers' lack of access to technology, government subsidies, and fair prices. Presently, 95% of cacao producers are ejido families who complement their earnings from cacao with other low-paid income-generating activities, such as masonry, domestic work, and informal trade, such as food stands, in addition to benefits received from programs like OPORTUNIDADES (Martínez, 2007; Córdova Ávalos *et al.*, 2001; Córdova Ávalos, 2005). Lack of access to household labor is a problem. Much manual work (weeding, fertilizing, and maintaining proper levels of humidity and shade) is required to keep plantations in good shape. Cacao plantations have gone well beyond their productive cycle (c. 30 years) and their aging owners have been unable to replant and maintain them, since young men in the community prefer to leave the ejido in order to find work with PEMEX, the state-owned industry whose main extractive and administrative operations take place in southeast Mexico (Pérez, 2011).

Research was conducted in 2009 and 2010 in Miguel Hidalgo Segunda Sección B, an ejido locally known as La Natividad, belonging to the municipality of Cárdenas. With a total population of 889 people, La Natividad has a very high marginalization index (CONAPO, 2010). Its main activity is cacao production. While 72 producers are registered by the state office for rural development, the first visits to the ejido confirmed only 50 active producers. Eight had recently sold their lands. Another eight had left and a further two had died. In other words, 25% of registered producers had stopped producing cacao. Unfortunately, we do not exactly know how or why this happened. What we do know, however, is that the abandonment of cacao plantations is fairly common in Tabasco. In the last two decades, production has declined both in terms of hectares and tons being produced. Cacao plantations have been replaced by sugarcane, corn, and cattle, because these activities produce higher revenues and receive government subsidies (Pérez, 2011).

Data were collected using two research methods. First, a participatory workshop allowed us to identify the gender division of labor and the major problems involved in local cacao production. Second, a questionnaire was created from the workshop information and supplied to all remaining cacao producers (36 men and 14 women), with the purpose of comparing the relationship between men and women's land-tenure and production strategies.

Only one (7.1%) of the 14 female producers had a spouse, as opposed to 86.1% of men (Table 9.3). All of the female producers are ejidatarias. More than half (nine out of 14) had inherited their parcel of land from their husbands, two had inherited from other relatives and only three bought it, thus confirming that, in spite of the 1971 and 1992 reforms, inheritance continues to be the most important means for rural women to acquire land, as documented in other studies (Robles *et al.*, 2000; Govela, 2009; Almeida, 2012; Ruiz, 2012).

Approximately one third of female and male ejidatarios live in extended households, while 14.3% of women and 5.5% of men live alone (Table 9.3). Women are 65.1 years of age while men are 58.5 years old on average. Not only are female landholders older than men, but they are also more likely to have no partner and to live by themselves, thus confirming the national presence of an aging population of ejidatarias (Vázquez, 2003; Robles, 2007; Bartra, 2011).

Table 9.3　Cacao producers in La Natividad, Tabasco

	Women (N=14) %				Men (N=36) %			
Marital status	Married 7.1	Single 14.3	Widow 64.3	Separated 14.3	Married 86.1	Single 5.5	Widower 5.5	Separated 2.8
Type of household	Nuclear 50		Extended 35.7	Lives alone 14.3	Nuclear 61.1		Extended 33.6	Lives alone 5.5
Is agriculture his/her main activity?	Yes 7.1		No 92.9		Yes 83.3		No 16.7	
Does she/he have additional income?	Yes 92.9		No 7.1		Yes 75		No 25	

A strict gender division of labor shapes all activities of Mexican rural households. As the main breadwinners, men take care of agriculture and also generate income in male-defined professions (i.e. masonry). Women perform all reproductive work, generate income (mostly in small trade) and "help out" in agricultural activities when the male head decides that their labor is required. Cacao cultivation is no exception. Workshop participants stated that cacao trees must be trimmed, and the underneath soils carefully weeded and swept. Plantations are frequently fertilized and fumigated against ants and fungus. Harvesting is done by hand and pods must be cleaned before being sold. Women participate in weeding, sweeping, harvesting, and pod-cleaning as required by the male head. Cacao production is culturally defined as a male activity, as demonstrated by the fact that all 50 plantations under study were initiated by men. Evidently, these cultural norms are being reframed by wider processes such as the lack of access to training and agricultural inputs as well as changes in the household's life cycle resulting from the aging process of household heads and youth out-migration.

Not surprisingly, ejidatarios in La Natividad find it easier than ejidatarias to work the plantations initiated by other men in the family. Table 9.3 shows that 83.3% of men and 7.1% of women consider agriculture their main activity. Men perform most agricultural activities and resort to engaging family members and/or paid labor for specific, more time-consuming tasks, i.e. fertilizing and harvesting. By contrast, most women have additional sources of income (old age pensions, small-scale trading, i.e. clothes, food) and delegate agricultural activities to their adult, married sons. Those who cannot rely on relatives to assist must resort to hired labor to sustain cacao production.

Ejidatarias earn little and less than their male counterparts. They also invest less money in productive inputs like pesticides and fertilizers because they rely more on hired labor (Table 9.4). The government has been unable to address this situation. The PROMUSAG (Programa de la Mujer en el Sector Agrario) is the only program in the country specifically designed to finance the productive activities of female landholders. Even though its budget almost doubled between 2007 and 2012 (from 556 to 941 million pesos), only 18% of the demand was covered (Costa & Velasco, 2012). Moreover, just 24.4% of all recipients were women who actually owned agricultural lands, and only 4% of the total amount of money was invested in agriculture (Martínez, 2005).

To summarize, cacao production in Tabasco has declined severely due to a number of factors. The crop is sold to a few agroindustries at low prices and with no value added. Ejidatarios have not received government support (such as subsidies or technological innovations) to maintain their plantations and increase their earnings; in fact, the state agency originally designed to provide such support disappeared in the 1990s. Plantations are old and require a lot of manual work besides investment in pesticides and fertilizers. Aging ejidatarios have been unable to replant and maintain their cacao plants partly because young men have preferred to obtain paid employment with PEMEX to working the land with their parents.

Table 9.4 Cacao earnings and reinvestments

	Women (N=14) %				Men (N=36) %			
Earnings	Less than $1,000*	$1,000–$3,000	More than $3,000	No earnings	Less than $1,000	$1,000–$3,000	More than $3,000	No earnings
	64.3	14.3	7.1	14.3	25	19.4	36.1	19.4
Cacao reinvestments	Labor 57.1	Pesticides 42.8	Fertilizers 35.7		Labor 52.7	Pesticides 55.5		Fertilizers 52.7

*Exchange rate: 13 pesos per U.S. dollar.

Ejidatarias have suffered from this situation more than men because, as elderly widows, they have even less access to labor. Even though they own agricultural land, the only program in the country designed to support female landholders cannot cope with the demand. In other words, the government has failed to empower ejidatarias to take over this traditionally male crop by addressing their specific needs as elderly women; the ejidatarias must contend with no access to credit and technology as well as the aforementioned labor shortage at home.

Land rentals by female landholders were not the focus of this case study. However, research conducted elsewhere in the country has shown that women rent out their land when they see themselves in situations very similar to those seen in La Natividad. For example, female landholders in Veracruz have no money to invest; they have no access to household labor; they have a full-time job (and hence no time to work on the land) (Almeida, 2012). Women in Tlaxcala actively change eligible tenants every one or two years in order to avoid land claims by the people who are actually working on the plots. When women own land, rental periods for tenants tend to be longer, as the inability to work the land is a more permanent issue (as opposed to men who migrate and come back), and they lack agricultural machinery (i.e. tractors) (Zapata et al., 2006). In the irrigated ejidos of the Frailesca region of Chiapas, between 28.5 and 100% of female landholders had rented their land to either neighbors (small parcels) or external agents (larger ones) (Ruiz, 2012). In fact, as a result of rental procedures large agribusiness companies control approximately 25% of the best lands and 80% of all agricultural production in the country. Between 1991 and 2007, the extension of rented land increased from 4.6 million to 6.3 million hectares (Robles, 2007, 2010, and 2012).

Land sales are less frequent than rentals. They are the last option to which people resort in case of sickness or emergencies, and only after selling other assets (i.e. animals). However, some women have lost their land to debts incurred in financing male out-migration, or have sold it so that male family members can buy trucks and start businesses (Zapata et al., 2006, 2010; Calderón, 2009; Almeida, 2012). Land sales are frequent in Tlaxcala (three out of ten households), although very often they involve only fractions of the parcel (Zapata et al., 2006). In the Frailesca region of Chiapas, between 14.3 and 27.3% of women have sold land, in most cases to other people within the ejido (Ruiz, 2012). Although this is a considerable amount, it is lower than the land rentals reported above for the same region, thus confirming the fact that female landholders prefer renting rather than selling. In fact, 72% of the women who live in households with land titles in Tlaxcala (although the land title generally is not theirs) would not like to sell the land. The same percentage considers having a land title "important" or "very important" (Zapata *et al.*, 2006).

The attachment to ejido lands can be found elsewhere in the country, among both men and women. In spite of the 1992 reform, rural landholders still own 105 million hectares, a similar amount owned in 1991. Land sales occur in two out of three ejidos, but the amount of land sold accounts for only 2.9% of all social property existing in the country, and 82.4% of all transactions take place among ejidos members (Robles, 2012). The most important questions at his point are: what will happen to ejido lands when this generation of elderly landholders passes away? Will their children (many of whom have left the community) be as interested as their parents in keeping the land? Ejidos are not only being controlled by agroindustries through land rentals; they are being forced into changes of land use by urbanization as well as tourism, hydroelectric, and mining companies. Ironically, conservation programs (i.e. Payment for Environmental Services) are also creating changes in land use, thus separating rural people from agricultural activities even further. The long-term impact of these forces on ejidos—the most important legacy of the revolution for rural Mexico—still remains to be seen.

Conclusions

Approximately half of Mexico's territory belongs to ejidos and agrarian communities, the two forms of land tenure that emerged from the revolution of 1910. In 1992, the agrarian law was changed in order to allow for the privatization and individualization of ejido lands, by far the most predominant category. This constitutional reform was accompanied by a wide range of neo-liberal policies, including trade liberalization and the withdrawal of state support to agricultural production. These changes brought about the loss of food sovereignty, rural poverty, and youth outmigration. The purpose of this chapter was to analyze rural women's access to land and their ability to sustain their livelihoods in the context of all these transformations. This last section summarizes its main findings and reflects upon them.

The chapter examined the ways in which the various versions of the agrarian law discriminated against women. Up until 1971, women had to be widows with children to receive land from the state; alternatively, the most important venue for women to access land was inheritance from deceased husbands in their capacity as primary heirs to ejido lands. The 1992 reform created a land market and changed the criteria for land transfers. None of these changes benefited women, however, for two reasons. First, their economic power to buy land is very limited. Second, allowing ejidatarios to bequeath land outside the immediate family decreased women's legal chances to inherit and widened the possibility for land dispossession.

Presently, about one-quarter of landholders are women, either as settlers, possessors, or ejidatarias. The predominant form is that of settlers with urban plots in the village, followed by possessors, who are typically middle-aged women who received agricultural land from their fathers or managed to buy it with their own savings. Finally, ejidatarias comprise the only group of women with full rights in ejido governance structures. However, they also are the smallest in terms of numbers, and the oldest in terms of age. Their participation in ejido decision-making is minimal and their patrimony is under threat due to a lack of access to agricultural services, inputs, and labor.

The case study on ejidatarias in Tabasco showed that cacao production has faced a severe decline due to producers' lack of access to technology, subsidies, fair prices, and labor due to youth out-migration. However, ejidatarias face more difficulties than men, because, as elderly widows, they have even less access to household labor, earn less, and spend more money on hired labor. The only government program specifically designed to support female landholders has been unable to strengthen women's productive capacities. It covers only one-fifth of the demand and most of the financed activities do not even involve agriculture in ejido lands.

The lack of investment in women's capacities will compromise the property rights of Mexican families for generations to come, because aging ejidatarias face difficulties in making their land fulfil its potential yield. Elsewhere in Mexico, similar circumstances are forcing women into renting or selling land. Sales occur when an emergency arises or male economic endeavors (such as out-migration of the setting up of businesses) need to be financed. The good news is that land rentals are more frequent than sales, and sales involve only parts of the parcel.

Land stands out as an important asset for the women who still own it. However, as discussed above, ejidos face pressure from a wide range of sources—including urbanization as well as mining and conservation projects—which are causing changes in land-use through rentals, concessions, sales, and payments for environmental services. More efforts are needed to support women's productive capacities and abilities to save the family patrimony. We know fairly well the characteristics of female settlers, possessors, and ejidatarias in terms of numbers, age, parcel size, and location. We also know a reasonable amount about the composition of ejidatarias' households, and their marital status, but need to collect more information on female possessors and settlers regarding these matters. The data should be used to create land-use programs that are both able to cope with demand, and capable of addressing the specific needs of each group of female landholders. These programs should help women to take over the productive domains affected by youth out-migration, and traditionally defined as male. The only way to do so is to recognize that women are not only consumers but also food producers; that many own agricultural lands; that they are the repositories of enormous knowledge regarding land and natural resource management; that they need more access to credits, technology, fair prices, and labor to make their lands operate effectively; and that their participation in ejido governance structures needs to be strengthened for ejidos to survive. In short, women must become central actors in rural policy design if we want to reverse the loss of food sovereignty and counteract the demographic and economic effects of neo-liberalism.

Acknowledgements

I would like to thank Heidy Guadalupe Sánchez Interiano and Nélyda Solana Villanueva for their help in fieldwork data gathering and processing. Octavio Ruiz Rosado, Juan José Obrador Olán, and Julián Pérez Flores were very helpful in administering the funds provided by the "Línea Prioritaria de Investigación Agroecosistemas Sustentables" of the Colegio de Postgraduados. María de los Ángeles Pérez Villar gathered and organized extremely useful information for the case study. Caroline Archambault provided exceptionally helpful comments to earlier versions of this chapter.

Notes

1   No disaggregated data are available. Generally, agrarian communities are made up by indigenous people whose ancestral rights to land were acknowledged by the state; no land was donated to them. Since agrarian communities were not affected by the 1992 reform, they will not be the focus of this chapter.
2   Credits decreased from 744,400 in 1991 to 172,585 in 2007. The number of units withdrawing from agricultural production increased from 584,817 in 1991 to 1.4 million in 2009 (Robles, 2012).

References

Almeida, E., (2009) *Ejidatarias, posesionarias y avecindadas. Mujeres frente a sus derechos de propiedad en tierras ejidales de México*, La Paz, Bolivia: International Land Coalition y Centro de Estudios Mexicanos y Centroamericanos.
Almeida, E., (2012) "Herencia y donación: prácticas intra-familiares de trasmisión de la tierra. El caso de un ejido veracruzano," *Cuicuilco*, mayo-agosto, vol. 19, no. 54, pp. 55–79.
Arizpe, L. & Botey, C., (1986) "Las políticas de desarrollo agrario y su impacto sobre la mujer campesina en México," in Deere, C. D. & León de Leal, M., (eds) *La mujer y la política agraria en América Latina*. Bogotá, Colombia: Siglo XXI Editores y ACEP, pp. 133–149.
Baitenmann, H., (1997) *Rural Agency and State Formation in Postrevolutionary México: The Agrarian Reform in Central Veracruz (1915–1992)*. New York: New School for Social Research.
Bartra, A., (2011) "Erosión que no cesa," *La Jornada del Campo* 48, 17 Sep., vol. 48.
Botey, C., (2000) "Mujer rural: reforma agraria y contrarreforma," in Aranda J., Botey C., & Robles, R., (eds) *Tiempo de crisis, tiempo de mujeres*. México D.F.: Universidad Autónoma Benito Juárez y Centro de Estudios de la Cuestión Agraria Mexicana, pp. 95–154.
Calderón Cisneros, A., (2009) "El impacto de la crisis alimentaria sobre la tierra y los recursos naturales", in Rubio, B., (ed) *El impacto de la crisis alimentaria en las mujeres*

rurales de bajos ingresos en México 2008–2009. México D.F.: Red Nacional de Asesoras y Promotoras Rurales, INDESOL y Cámara de Diputados , pp. 47–57.

Carrillo Meza, O., (2011) "Presupuesto rural, ¿continuidad o cambios de fondo?", 17 Sep., vol. 48.

CONAPO, (2010) *Indice de de marginación por localidad 2010*, México D.F.: CONAPO.

Córdova Ávalos, V., (2005) "Organización campesina en la reconversión del cacao tradicional a cacao orgánico en Tabasco, México," in Aragón García, A., López-Olguín, F., & Tapia, A. M., (ed.) *Manejo agroecológico de sistemas*. Puebla: Benemérita Universidad Autónoma de Puebla.

Córdova Ávalos, V. *et al.*, (2001) "Factores que afectan la producción de cacao (Theobroma cacao L.) en el ejido Francisco I. Madero del Plan Chontalpa, Tabasco, México," *Universidad y ciencia*, vol. 17, no. 34, pp. 93–100.

Córdova Plaza, R., (2000) "Género, poder y tenencia de la tierra en un ejido de Veracruz," *Sotavento*, Issue 5, pp. 107–127.

Costa Leonardo, N. & Velasco Ocampo, M. G., (2012) *Perfil de la mujer rural en México*. México D.F.: Secretaría de la Reforma Agraria.

De María, A. & Campos, O., (2005) "El acceso de las mujeres rurales a la tierra: el caso de México," *Estudios Agrarios*, vol. 30, pp. 79–90.

Deere, C. D. & León de Leal, M., (2001) "¿De quién es la tierra? Género y titulación de tierras en América Latina," *Humánitas. Portal Temático*, vol. 18, no. 48, pp. 43–69.

Deere, C. D. & León de Leal, M., (2003) "The Gender Asset Gap: Land in Latin America," *World Development*, vol. 31, no. 6, p. 925–947.

Esparza Salinas, R., Suárez, B. & Bonfil, P., (1996) *Las mujeres campesinas ante las reformas al artículo 27 de la constitución*. México D.F.: GIMTRAP.

Flores Hernández, A., (2009) "Género y migración en dos sistemas de organización de la tierra en Tlaxcala, México," *Agricultura, Sociedad y Desarrollo*, enero-abril, vol. 6, no. 1, pp. 1–31.

Fox, J. & Haight, L., (2010) "La política agrícola mexicana: metas múltiples e intereses en conflicto" in Fox, J. & Haight, L., (eds) *Subsidios para la desigualdad. Las políticas públicas del maíz a partir del libre comercio*. Santa Cruz: University of California, pp. 9–54.

Govela, R., (2009) "Las políticas públicas hacia las mujeres rurales y la crisis alimentaria: más garrote y menos tortilla," in Rubio, B., (ed.) *El impacto de la crisis alimentaria en las mujeres rurales de bajos ingresos en México 2008–2009*. México D.F.: Red Nacional de Asesoras y Promotoras Rurales, INDESOL y Cámara de Diputados, pp. 39–46.

Hamilton, S., (2002) "Neocolonialism, Gender and Property Rights in Rural Mexico," *Latin American Research Review*, vol. 37, no. 1, pp. 119–143.

Haro Encinas , L. F., (2011) "Agricultura campesina, agricultura comercial, ¿un dilema?," *La Jornada del Campo* 48, 17 September.

Lastarria-Cornhiel, S., (2011) "Women and Access to Communal Land in Latin America," in Costas, P., (ed.) *Women's Land. Reflections on Rural Women's Access to Land in Latin America*. La Paz, Bolivia: International Land Coalition, pp. 19–40.

Martínez Arboleya , H., (2007) *Los medios de vida sostenibles de las familias productoras de cacao orgnánico en el municipio de Cunduacán, Tabasco*. Cárdenas: Tesis de Maestría, Colegio de Postgraduados.

Martínez Corona, B., (2005) "Mujeres de núcleos agrarios, liderazgo y proyectos productivos," in Martelo Z., & López Zavala, J., (eds) *La integración económica de las mujeres rurales: un enfoque de género*. México D.F.: Secretaría de Reforma Agraria, pp. 235–288.

Merino, M., (2010) "Los programas de subsidios al campo: las razones y las sinrazones de una política mal diseñada," in Fox, J. & Haight, L., (eds) *Subsidios para la desigualdad. Las políticas públicas para el maíz a partir del libre comercio*. Santa Cruz, California: Woodrow Wilson International Center for Scholars, pp. 55–72.

Pérez, M., (2011) "Cambio climático, plagas y PEMEX ponen en riesgo el cultivo del cacao en México," *La Jornada*, 7 August.

Pérez, M., (2013) "Campo desmantelado, saldo de los 20 años de vigencia del TLCAN: expertos," *La Jornada*, 11 November, p. 18.

Priego-Castillo, G. A. *et al.*, (2009) "Evaluación de la sustentabilidad de dos sistemas de producción de cacao: estudios de caso en unidades de producción rural en Comalcalco, Tabasco," *Universidad y Ciencia Trópico Húmedo*, vol. 25, no. 1, pp. 39–57.

Procuraduría Agraria, (2011) *Estadísticas agrarias. Información seleccionada*. México D.F.: Procuraduría Agraria.

Ramírez-Martínez, M. A., (2007) "Los productores de cacao de pequeña escala en el contexto de la globalización" *Hitos de Cciencias Económico-Administrativas*, vol. 13, no. 37, pp. 103–112.

Robles Berlanga, H. M., (2007) *El sector rural en el siglo XXI. Un mundo de realidades y posibilidades*. México D.F.: Centro de Estudios para el Desarrollo Rural Sustentable y la Soberanía Alimentaria.

Robles Berlanga, H. M., (2010) *Dinámicas en el mercado de la tierra en América Latina*, México: FAO.

Robles Berlanga, H. M., (2012) "El caso de México," in *Dinámicas del mercado de la tierra en América Latina y El Caribe: concentración y extranjerización*. Roma: FAO, pp. 307–342.

Robles Berlanga, H. M., Artis, G., Salazar, J. & Muñoz, L., (2000) *Y ando yo también en el campo. Presencia de la mujer en el agro mexicano*. México D.F.: Procuraduria Agraria.

Rubio, B., (2003) *Explotados y excluidos. Los campesinos latinoamericanos en la fase agroexportadora neoliberal*. México: Universidad Autónoma Chapingo y Plaza y Valdés.

Rubio, B., (2009) "El impacto de la crisis alimentaria en la situación económica de las mujeres rurales," in Rubio, B., (ed.) *El impacto de la crisis alimentaria en las mujeres rurales de bajos ingresos*. México D.F.: REDPAR, INDESOL y Cámara de Diputados, pp. 31–39.

Ruiz Meza, L. E., (2012) "Relaciones de género y mercados de derechos de agua y tierra en Chiapas," *Región y Sociedad*, vol. 24, no. 53, p. 55–89.

SAGARPA, (2010) *Base de datos producción de cacao 2007–2010*. Cárdenas: CADER Cárdenas y Benito Juárez.

Scott, J., (2010) 'Subsidios agrícolas en México: ¿quién gana y cuánto?," in Fox, J., & Haight, L., (eds) *Subsidios para la desigualdad. Las políticas públicas del maíz en México a partir del libre comercio*. Santa Cruz: University of California, pp. 73–128.

United Nations-Habitat, (2005) *Law, Land Tenure and Gender Review: Latin America*. Nairobi: United Nations Human Settlements Programme (UN-HABITAT).

Vázquez-García, V., (1996) "Donde manda el hombre, no manda la mujer. Género y tenencia de la tierra en el México rural," *Cuadernos Agrarios*, enero-junio, Issue 13, pp. 63–83.

Vázquez-García, V., (2001) "Género y tenencia de la tierra en el ejido mexicano: ¿La costumbre o la ley del Estado?," *Estudios Agrarios*, vol. 7, no. 18, pp. 117–146.

Vázquez Palacios, F., (2003) *Envejecer ente cultivos del campo mexicano*. Santiago de Chile, 51 Congreso de Americanistas.

Warman, A., (2001) *El campo mexicano en el siglo XX*. México D.F.: Fondo de Cultura Económica.

Zapata Martelo , E., Gutiérrez García , B. M. & Flores Hernández, A., (2006) *Caminar por los tepetates. La visión de las mujeres de Hueyotlipan, Tlaxcala, México.* Texcoco: Colegio de Postgraduados.

Zapata Martelo, E., Suárez San Román , B. & Flores Hernández, A., (2010) *Se van muchos y regresan pocos. Economía política feminista, acercamiento a la migración.* México D.F.: GIMTRAP, INDESOL y Colegio de Postgraduados.

10 Women's forestland rights in the collective forestland reforms in China

Fieldwork findings and policy recommendations

Xiaobei Wang, Elisa Scalise, and Renee Giovarelli

Introduction

After nearly 30 years of forestland tenure reform in China, the Chinese government initiated a new round of reforms in 2008 to further clarify and secure farmers' rights to collectively owned forestland. The reforms cover rights to the 182.47 million hectares of China's forestland owned by administrative villages (also called village collectives), which constitutes 60.06% of China's total forestland area (State Forestry Bureau, 2009). The reforms are expected to reduce poverty and directly improve the livelihoods of 400 million farmers (State Forestry Bureau, 2007).

With the continuing increase of male urban labor migration, women have become key agricultural laborers, accounting for more than 65% of the rural labor force in China (Chen, 2012). Therefore, whether women have benefited to the same extent as men from the forestland reform and whether women's forestland rights are as secure as men's are crucial questions that must be answered if China's forestland tenure reform can be regarded as a success. This solutions-focused qualitative research conducted by Landesa is aimed at understanding the implications of the current forestland reform for rural women in China, which generally has not secured women's land rights, and recommending a gender-sensitive forestland strategy to the government of China.

This chapter is arranged in seven sections. Following this introduction is a brief description of the history of collective forestland tenure reforms in China. Section three introduces gender equality in Chinese law. The fourth section is a description of the research methodology. The fifth section describes field findings. The report ends with policy recommendations and the conclusion.

Collective forestland tenure reform in China

Initiation of collective forestland tenure reform

Forestland provides a major source of income for the famers living in mountainous areas, who account for 56% of China's total population (Jia, 2011). Collective management of forestland began in the 1950s, and over the 20 years it existed was inefficient due to its inability to motivate labour. While the forestland was nominally owned and managed by the collectives, the decision-making was centralized and the central government had almost complete control over the management, sales, and purchase of collectively owned forests. Farmers worked on forestland under the supervision of the collective and were paid according to how many work hours they accumulated, irrespective of the output they produced. They did not have any property rights over the forestland, and they lacked incentive to work hard, which consequently led to high supervision costs and low efficiency.

By the late 1970s China's forestry sector was facing serious problems, including severe deforestation, low plantation of trees, increasing imbalance of supply and demand of timber and forest products, and further deterioration of the environment (Central Committee of CPC and the State Council, 1981). At the same time, poor management of the collective forests caused farmers in mountainous areas to fall deeper into poverty and made their communities among the poorest in China. Among the 331 poverty-stricken counties identified by the Chinese government in 1985, 82.5% of them were mountainous counties, where forestland is typically located (He & Wang, 2013).

In the early 1980s, China underwent profound reform of arable land management and use in rural areas by establishing the Household Responsibility System. Under the Household Responsibility System, village collectives retained ownership of the land, but use rights were allocated to farmer "households" based on the number of people in the household. These reforms were significant and marked the beginning of successful economic reform for rural farmers (Zhu, 2006). The dramatic increase in agricultural productivity in China since the 1980s is attributable to efficiency gains created by moving from collective to household farming (Prosterman et al., 1998).

The Chinese government was greatly encouraged by the success of the arable land reform and conducted similar reform in the early 1980s on collective forestland. Following the same principles as the arable land reform, ownership rights remained with the collective while use rights were allocated by the collective to farmer households within the collective, on a per capita basis, for individual farming. By allocating use rights and responsibility to individual households, the reforms sought to create incentives for farmers to better manage their forestland, thus increasing efficiency and improving environmental stewardship (Zhang & Xu, 2009).

The issuance of the "The Decision on the Protection of the Forest and the Development of Forestry" by the central government in 1981 marked the beginning of forestland tenure reform in China (Central Committee of CPC and the State Council, 1981). The primary objective of the policy was to establish the household as the basic legal unit for forestland under village collective ownership. The Decision required that the collective designate part of the collectively owned forestland as "Private Mountains" and allocate to each farmer's household a small plot of this land for permanent, inheritable private use. It also required the collective to contract the management of the remaining forestland to interested villager groups, households, and individual farmers as "Responsibility Mountains" with negotiated terms and remuneration linked to the forest's output. The Decision also called for issuing forest certificates to affirm ownership rights to trees and use rights to forestland. Moreover, a cutting permit was required for harvesting trees.

The issuance of this Decision marked the beginning of a long legislative and policy process aimed at progressively strengthening forestland use rights among farmers' households. By 1986, 69% of the collectively-owned forestland had either been allocated to farmer households for private use or contracted to villages, households, or individuals for management (Xu et al., 2008). This progress was significant, but the remaining land was still managed by the collective.

Legal framework for collective forestland

Until 1998, the land reform (for both arable and forest land) had been conducted through the issuance of central-level decisions. After almost 20 years, a more formal legal framework for rural land, including forestland, began to take shape in China with the revision of the Forest Law in 1998, and the adoption of the Land Management Law in 1998, the Rural Land Contracting Law in 2002, and the Property Law in 2007.

Under the terms of these revisions, farmers are legally granted use rights to the forestland allocated to their households for a term of 70 years.[1] They are entitled to use, profit from, transfer the use right, and inherit the forestland within the contracting term.[2] The law requires that the government issue forestland rights certificates to households that document their use rights.[3]

However, certain restrictions apply, depending on the type of forest. There are two types of collective forestland, each approximately 50% of the land: ecological and commercial. For ecological forests, farmers are strictly prohibited from harvesting trees and the use right to the land is not transferable.[4] They are able to profit from non-timber products. Commercial forests may be harvested, but a farmer must apply for a cutting permit.[5]

Launch of a new round of collective forestland reform

A new round of reforms began in 2008 with the policy "The Decision on Promoting the Reform of Collective Forest Tenure Regime." The Decision emphasized the issuance of land rights certificates and expanded farmers' rights by allowing subcontracting, leasing, and mortgaging of contracted forestland (Central Committee of CPC and the State Council, 2008).

According to the State Forestry Bureau, by the end of 2013 rights to over 99% of collective forestland had been clarified and 90 million households were issued forestland certificates, marking the completion of the clarification and verification process (People's Daily, 2014).

With broader and more secure forestland rights allocated to households, farmers' motivation for engaging in forestry production increased greatly (FAO, 2012). They enjoyed a large increase in household income generated from sales of timber and non-timber forest products or from subcontracting, leasing, or mortgaging the contracted forestland. Forestland has become an important asset and productive resource for famers. Moreover, the forestry industry creates about 45 million employment opportunities every year and provides jobs for 37.5% of the rural labor force (State Forestry Bureau, 2012).

According to incomplete statistics from 30 provinces, in 2011 farmers living in forest areas that had implemented forestland reform had an average per capita income of RMB 6,435. On average, RMB 1,203 was generated by forestry activities, accounting for 18.69% of farmers' total income. Forestry-related income can reach as high as over 60% of total household income (State Forestry Bureau, 2012). Collective forestland reform brought rapid forestry development after its implementation, which lifted many farmers out of poverty.

Village self-governance in collective forestland reform

Forestland reforms are strongly influenced by village-level administration and governance. The introduction of the Household Responsibility System signaled the end of the People's Commune System, a political and administrative production unit formed to govern rural areas that had been adopted in the 1950s. With the move to the Household Responsibility System, the functions of the people's commune were transferred to the newly established township government, and the "production brigades" of the peoples' communes became the administrative village. "Self-governance" of the administrative village became the new pattern of administration in rural China.

The Organic Law of the Villagers Committee, issued in 1998 and revised in 2010, provides the legal foundation for village self-governance in China. Under village self-governance, the directly elected village committee is responsible for overseeing the village's day-to-day affairs. Major decisions are made by the villagers' assembly and must be ratified by a majority vote.[6] Village affairs are subject to rules and regulations passed by the assembly, and the committee is supposed to be transparent and accept villager supervision.[7]

The latest forestland reforms support the right of the villagers' assembly to specify local reform plans, as long as they respect central and local government policy and law. The new policies emphasize farmers' rights to know, participate in, and make decisions on forestland matters (Central Committee of CPC & the State Council, 2008). These principles are in line with the requirements of the Organic Law of Villagers Committee (hereafter "the Organic Law"), which dictate that collectively owned land and related benefits can be allocated only by a majority vote of the villagers' assembly.[8]

It is worth noting that although the villagers' autonomy in their own village has many benefits, one adverse effect of the process is its potential infringement on the rights of vulnerable, underrepresented classes, including divorced and married-out women.

Gender equality in Chinese law

With respect to gender equality, China has surpassed many other countries in creating a gender-sensitive legal framework for land rights (Li & Bruce, 2005). A series of laws and policies in China grants equal land rights to women and men, and the Constitution of the PRC (1982) asserts equality between the sexes.[9] This constitutional principle is reflected in the Law Protecting Women's Rights and Interests (2005), which states that women shall enjoy equal rights with men in all aspects of political, economic, cultural, social, and family life.[10] This law further explicitly states that women shall enjoy equal rights with men in the contracted management of rural land, distribution of proceeds of collective economic organizations, use of land requisition and occupation compensations, and use of house sites.[11] The constitutional principle is also embodied in the Rural Land Contracting Law (2002), the law governing land-use rights for rural land in China, which prohibits infringement on women's legitimate rights and interests in the land use contract.[12] And, under the Marriage Law (2001), husbands and wives have equal status in the household; unless otherwise agreed, property is held jointly between them.[13]

In over 30 years of forestland tenure reform in China, relevant laws and policies appear to be either neutral or positive for women. Yet patriarchal traditions are still dominant in rural areas, and the implementation of these seemingly unbiased laws and policies has not been favorable to women's rights and interests in practice. Women are still disadvantaged when it comes to land tenure in rural China. According to the 3rd Survey on the Status of Chinese Women, land-rights issues have been one of the four key issues faced by rural women in the past ten years (All China Women's Federation, 2011).

Gender equality is actively promoted in Chinese law but is still not well recognized in rural Chinese society. In practice, the discretion permitted to the village committee under the Organic Law, coupled with traditional practices, beliefs, and norms such as patrilocal residence and patrilineal inheritance, all work to make women's land rights insecure and begs the question of whether women and men benefitted equally from the forestland tenure reforms in China.

Chinese law provides that former collective land is distributed to households on a per capita basis and allows the collective to decide who counts in the household—who is a member of the collective, thus, determines who has a right to the land. We know from experience and research around the world that it matters who within the household has rights to land. Women are more likely than men to spend income from family resources (including land) on children's nutrition and education (Quisumbing, 1996), and rights to land can provide an important fallback position in cases of divorce or the death of a spouse.

Methodology

Conducted in 2011, the research for this chapter combined desk and field research. The literature review preceded the field research, providing an overview of forestland reform in China from a gender perspective. The literature review included information on China's collective forestland reform, its history and development and relevant laws, regulations, and policies, and on laws and regulations related to women's land rights and the status of women's land rights issues in China. Although there is significant literature regarding forestland reform and a growing body of literature regarding land reform and women, little has been written on the impact of forestland reform on women, thus confirming the importance of these research efforts.

Field research was conducted from July to September 2011 in three of the most forested Chinese provinces: Hunan, Fujian, and Yunnan. In each of these provinces, ten randomly selected villages were visited. Seventy local people were interviewed either in the form of key informant interviews or focus group discussions, which included one female villager from each of the thirty villages, one male villager from each of six villages randomly selected from among the thirty villages, one village committee leader from each of the thirty villages, one local official of the forestry department, and a forestry company staff person from each of the three respective provinces.

Field findings on women's forestland rights

China's urbanization has caused male out-migration from rural villages, leaving women in charge of the land. By the end of 2012, migrant workers constitute respectively 30%, 40%, and 55% of the rural working-age population in western, middle, and eastern China (State Statistics Bureau, 2013). In each of the villages we visited, 50–70% of the villagers leave home to work in urban areas for most of the year. Usually it is the husband and adult children of a family who out-migrate in order to seek income-generating employment. Women are left behind in the villages to work on the land, take care of children and the elderly, and raise livestock and the like. Although the migrant workers make contributions to the household income, women are the main agricultural managers.

The contracted forestland area per household in Yunnan, Fujian, and Hunan provinces is respectively 2.93ha, 2.31ha, and 1.42ha, which is six to ten times greater than the arable land per household in these areas (State Forestry Bureau, 2013). Although the income of the migrant workers constitutes an important part of the total household income in these areas—for some families interviewed it can be as high as 70%—the contracted forestland is still regarded by farmers in the forested regions as an important productive asset and source of income for their household. Farmers choose either to make long-term investments in planting timber or to invest in non-timber forest products like Chinese medicinal plants, mushrooms, or vegetables, which are suitable for local natural and climatic conditions. In some places, farmers raise chicken or pigs in the forest. For those interviewed in our fieldwork, forestry income typically accounts for about 20% of all household income.

Women play a crucial role in forestland use and management, and their efforts determine the amount of income that a household can generate from the forestland. Yet this research shows that the role of women in forest management is not recognized in the policy or practice that governs forestland in China. Women may not benefit from forestland rights to the same extent as men: they are not involved in decision-making, which affects their use of the forest, they are neither consulted about nor informed of important policy changes, and they are unable to use their forestland rights as an asset that can be transferred, exchanged, or used as collateral. Ultimately, because women's role in forestland use is not legally recognized and protected, they are unable to invest in or leverage the land in ways that confer long-term benefits. Their benefits are instead restricted to short-term income from forestry labor.

Women's rights in the allocation of collective forestland

Many women are excluded from the allocation of collective forestland use rights and the benefit generated from forestland rights

In the forestland reform, the village collective distributes forestland use rights to each village household on a per capita basis. However, only those who are regarded as "members" of a village collective are counted. Under current Chinese law, membership in a collective is not defined or standardized among villages, leaving the question to the determination of each village committee.

In rural China, women overwhelmingly follow the tradition of patrilocal residence. Traditionally, once they marry, they are no longer seen as members of their birth village but are also often viewed as outsiders in their new village. No matter where a woman resides or where she was born, her "membership" is not set—depending on how each village defines membership, she may be a member of both villages or of neither. Women, deprived of village membership, are excluded from the allocation of collective forestland and the benefits that accrue to those who are included. For example, women who are not members would not have their names listed on the household document, giving them very limited ability to manage the land and negotiate their share of its benefits. Membership is deprived in the following scenarios.

Some married-out women are deprived of the right to contract forestland in their birth village

Generally, a woman works on the land in her husband's village, not her birth village, and the value of being counted and having documented rights to land is greatest in the location where she lives. However, if she does not have rights to land in her marital village, having rights in her birth village provides a fallback position in case of abandonment, divorce, or death of her spouse; a woman's retainment of a valuable right in her birth village makes it easier for her to return there.

Nearly all collectives set a start date for the allocation of the forestland to each household in the collective. Generally, rules provide that women who married out after this start date have the right to receive a share of forestland in their birth village; women who married out before this start date do not.

However, our research showed that each village defines the date of marriage differently. Some villages use the issuance of a marriage certificate by the civil administration department as a marker. Because not every married couple in rural China has a marriage certificate, especially in remote areas, some villages recognize a marriage at its ceremony regardless of any civil certificate. Yet other villages set a firm date and will permit a married-out woman to retain her membership for one year after her marriage to an outsider. Women who do not meet the membership requirements as defined by the village committee will not be included in allocation of forestland rights in their village of birth.

Some married-in women are not defined as village members and do not enjoy forestland rights in their husbands' village

Those married-out women who lose their forestland rights in their birth village are not necessarily able to acquire a share of forestland in the village they married into. Villages set varying rules to accept married-in women as their village members. Some villages, for example, require that married-in women provide three documents to establish their residency: their marriage certificate, their registered residence migration card, and their birth-control approval certificate. Other villages require a marriage certificate and the registered residence migration card. Finally, a few villages require only the marriage certificate.

However, for many rural women, especially the poorest, acquiring marriage certificates or other required documents is not a simple exercise. Because the women's birth village is often far away, the preparation of these documents requires traveling great distances at considerable expense. Some villages resolve this by recognizing married-in women from distant villages as members once they give birth to their first child, but others do not.

Whether or when a woman can be accepted as a member of the collective when she has married in is thus not only determined by her residence in a village but also by factors that may be beyond her control. If she is denied membership in the village before the start date of forestland allocation, then her new household will receive a reduced land allocation. Perhaps more importantly, the village and her husband will not consider her as having any claim to the land, which means she is essentially a laborer on it, and has no right to make decisions about investment in or use of the land or the income derived from it. Moreover, if the household breaks down, she will be unable to claim the value of her portion of the land as an asset. This could have serious consequences in case of abandonment or divorce.

Some divorced women are deprived of the right to be allocated forestland or the benefit generated from forestland

Divorced women face specific issues related to village membership depending on whether they choose to return to their birth village or get remarried. In some villages, if a married-in woman divorces within five years of marriage, her married-in village will neither regard her as a member nor allocate her forestland rights. Usually her birth village will accept her as a village member if she returns her registered residence there but not always. Some villages claim that the divorce was a sham orchestrated so that she could somehow benefit from the birth village's wealth. In these situations, a woman could lose membership in both her ex-husband's village and her birth village upon divorce, thus completely losing the right to contract forestland.

Women's rights to benefit from forestland

Even if they have been allocated forestland rights, some women cannot use or benefit from them in the same way as men

Forestland is allocated to each household of the collective based on the number of family members. Women as daughters or wives may be counted as part of the household. However, this does not necessarily imply that women can benefit from those allocated rights.

If a daughter was counted as a household member and allocated forestland in her birth village, she will likely leave her share behind for her parents and brothers when she marries out. By losing her status as member of her family's household and village, she loses access to the benefits of the land she previously had claim to, including income from forestland trees and byproducts, forestland takings compensation, and subsidies.

Similarly, if a woman is counted as a member of her married-in household when forestland rights are allocated, she must leave her share to her ex-husband and children if she divorces. The analogous situation does not occur for divorced men because it is the woman that typically moves to her husband's home for marriage. Some villages will retain the woman's membership for an additional year after the divorce, but all benefits generated from forestland in that time will go to the ex-husband's household.

Thus, married-out daughters can lose their share of forestland and related benefits in their birth village when getting married, and divorced women will lose their share of forestland and related benefits in their ex-husband's village when they divorce. If these women lack other opportunities to receive new shares of forestland, they may be completely deprived of forestland and their livelihoods.

Documentation of women's rights to forestland

Women's names are not included on forestland certificates

Issuance of forestland certificates to farmers' households is one of the most important aspects of the new round of forestland reforms. These certificates provide official and legal recognition of farming households' 70-year use rights to the forestland allocated to them. However, on the certificate standardized by the State Forestry Bureau, only the name of the head of the household is recorded. There is no space on the certificate for other household members to be included. Although this is ostensibly gender-neutral, men are customarily the head of the household and women are far less likely to have their names included on the certificates.

The primary reason for this exclusion of women in forestland certificates is that policy makers are under the mistaken belief that the interests of a woman's household and the interests of her as an individual are one and the same (Yang & Xi, 2006). In this view, it is not necessary to include women's names on forestland certificates; by titling the household head (it is easier for administrators to only list one person), policy makers think they are adequately representing women's interests and defending their rights. Thus, due to strong cultural norms, women almost never have a formal, legal claim to their forestland.

Women's rights and interests in forestland are often different or even in conflict with those of the male household members, especially in the case of a family breakdown such as the death of a spouse, divorce, or abandonment. When women's names are not on the forestland certificates as the legal and official evidence, women's rights to that land are left to the discretion of the heads of household or village leaders, almost all of whom are men.

More specifically, without their names on the certificates, women are denied the right to use forestland as collateral for credit, which in turn reduces income opportunities. Because women are denied the right to transfer or lease land on behalf of the household, they face the risk that the land they are cultivating will be transferred, leased, or mortgaged by their husbands without their consent, and that they will be completely denied any benefits derived from these transactions. Women lack a legal basis to claim land compensation, which often results in less compensation for rural land takings and sometimes in none at all (Standing Committee of NPC, 2010). It would be unjust to deny women these rights in any case, but the injustice and inefficiency of the situation is further compounded because women are the primary users of forestland.

Despite its critical importance, most women interviewed have accepted that their names are not included on the certificates. Each woman stated that she did not understand the value, relevance, or importance of the forestland certificates and was completely unaware of the possible negative impacts of not having her name recorded. Very often in rural areas, women are not aware of their rights and have limited opportunity to learn about them, meet together with other women, or receive information from local officials.

Women's participation in decision-making processes

Few women participate in the decision-making process at the village level

Although the Organic Law of the Villagers' Committees (2010) requires that female representatives shall account for at least one-third of all members of the villagers' representatives' assembly,[14] women in most of the villages we visited were insufficiently represented in the decision-making process. In about four-fifths of the villages, there were only one or two women representatives out of a total of 20–30. In the other one-fifth of the villages, there were more women representatives, but women still accounted for less than 20% of the total.

The women interviewed did not realize the importance of their participation in the decision-making process. Most of them are accustomed to men acting as the representatives of the household. Nearly 95% of the women interviewed never attended any village meeting, thus marginalizing them in the decision-making process. Their interests are therefore less likely to be considered, and their rights more likely to be infringed.

Women's access to information

Women have insufficient access to information on forestland reforms

According to government officials, the local forestry bureaus have greatly raised awareness among farmers at the village level on the forestland reform. Yet field findings suggest a lack of information is a common issue for all forestland rights holders, and women are in a more vulnerable position than men.

Village committee members, village group leaders, and party members in the village, all of whom are predominantly men, have the most information about forestland reform in the village. Except for the occasional female village committee member, women have little information.

Field findings show that women villagers have an incomplete and unclear understanding about the reform. Most women interviewed were ignorant of the relevant laws and policies; they knew little about plans for reform implementation in their own villages, and they were uncertain about the nature, extent, and duration of the forestland rights. When asked about reform in their villages, most women interviewees stated that they needed to ask their husbands or nearby male villagers for information.

Policy recommendations

The following policy recommendations are intended to help China ensure that the benefits of forestland reforms are shared equally between men and women, and that the reforms conform with both the letter and spirit of existing policies and laws.

Legislate a gender-sensitive definition of collective membership

The Rural Land Contracting Law (2002) provides that only members of a village collective are entitled to allocation of the collectively owned land, including forestland,[15] but it is entirely unclear who is eligible for becoming a member of the collective. Without a legal definition of collective membership it is up to the village collective or majority of existing villagers to decide (usually based on cultural norms) whether to accept as a member a woman who moves into or out of the village as a result of marriage or divorce. Moreover, since the Organic Law of the Villagers' Committees authorizes the village assembly to decide on land-related issues with a majority vote,[16] the failure to legally define collective membership tends to invite abuse of power, because it is in the community's interest to have fewer collective members.

China should legislate and implement a definition of what determines membership in a collective. A gender-sensitive definition would clearly state that married-in women must be counted as members of the collective at the time of the marriage. Membership rights in married women's birth villages might be left to those villages.

The Judicial Committee of the Supreme People's Court of China issued suggestions on defining collective membership to the National People's Council. The Committee stated that the determination of collective membership is an issue related to the fundamental civil rights of rural residents. Therefore, the legislators of the National People's Council should address it. Despite the Judicial Committee's statement, membership determination is still an unsettled issue in Chinese law. Policy-makers, legislators, NGOs, and other stakeholders must strengthen their joint advocacy efforts in order to promote legislative progress towards a clear, gender-sensitive definition of collective membership that protects women's rights.

Develop a review and appeals mechanism to supervise the collective's decisions on land rights

The Organic Law of the Villagers' Committees permits broad self-governance of villages in China.[17] Village committees have authority to make rules on key matters in the village with a majority vote in the villagers' assembly.[18] Under the current reform policy, the collective has the right to allocate forestland to households based on their own definitions of collective membership, which as seen above, often excludes married-in, married-out, and divorced women. Field research suggests that some villages have taken advantage of the autonomy empowered to them by the law to neglect or violate the land rights of women, disadvantaging them. Some scholars point out that subjective village membership rules, which at the local level often have greater force than national laws, can prevent women from receiving the benefits of the forestland they manage (Jiang & Wang, 2003). There is currently no mechanism to ensure the legitimacy of village rules.

The Organic Law clearly states that village assembly decisions cannot conflict with national laws and cannot infringe on villagers' personal rights, as they are currently doing. To enforce this legal provision, there must be a review and appeal mechanism added to the village governance system.

Legally define and document the forestland rights of each member of a household who has been allocated land

Although forestland is allocated to each household based on the number of family members' rights to forestland are legally defined as household rights rather than individual rights.[19] The forestland rights of each family member are not clearly defined by the law. This has a profound impact on women's land rights in a way that it does not for men, because women move between households upon marriage or divorce. The absence of clear rules on individual rights to land within the household creates a barrier to women claiming and partitioning their share of forestland or receiving the value of the land.

Moreover, the government is issuing certificates to each household as evidence of household rights, but these certificates rarely include women's names (wives or daughters). This lack of documentation makes it difficult for women to claim their share of forestland and make compensation claims if the forestland is expropriated.

To effectively reduce the ambiguity and uncertainty associated with women's land rights, it is critical to clearly define women's rights to land within the household by law and provide women with legally recognized evidence of their rights to land by formally documenting women's land rights in the land certificates.

Build awareness among women about the importance of participating in village-level decision making and ensure that their participation is meaningful

Field research has demonstrated that despite the Organic Law's requirement that women comprise at least one-third of the villagers' assembly, in China as in many other parts of the world, cultural norms exclude women from village governance, and men, who make the decisions, do not typically consider women's interests. Consequently, women's forestland rights are violated under the guise of village democracy. One of the most difficult things to do in rural China is to organize groups and discuss rights.

It is therefore important for the local government, village committees, and especially local organizations, such as the All China Women's Federation at the county or township level, to build women's awareness, encourage them to participate equally with men in decision-making processes, and provide them with the skills necessary to do so in a meaningful way. This measure will be critical for ensuring women's voices are heard, women's interests are taken into account, and women's rights, including land rights, are not ignored.

Improve women's access to information that directly impacts their ability to fully realize the benefits of household forestland rights

The research demonstrates that women's low participation in decision-making also results from their lack of access to information. This disadvantages women in realizing their forestland rights.

More targeted and effective measures should be taken to ensure that women have a complete and clear understanding of forestland reforms and relevant laws and policies. Considering the increasing out-migration of male labor, women need information about up-to-date forestry policies, so they are able to receive maximum benefit from their efforts.

Targeted measures to increase women's access to information could include face-to-face training, special informative TV and radio programs for women, setting up agricultural information and consultancy centers by Women's Federations at the township level, regular legal education and consultancy activities at the village level, and delivering information to women through printed media such as posters and brochures.

Conclusion

This research clearly shows that although women play very important roles in the management of forestland in rural China, rural women have not benefited from the forestland tenure reform to the same extent as men, and women's rights to forestland are far from secure under the present legal and policy framework. Such vulnerable forestland rights for rural women can adversely impact women and their families' livelihoods. The risk of completely losing forestland because of a change in marital status may anchor some poor women even deeper in poverty. Meanwhile, given the continuing increase in male urban labor migration and the resultant rise in rural women's status as key agricultural laborers, insecure forestland rights for rural women will inevitably have a negative impact on the sustainable development of the forestry sector in China.

This research deepens the understanding of rural Chinese women's current access to forest resources, the challenges they face reaping the benefits from those resources, and their unique needs. Appropriate, gender-sensitive laws, policies, and supporting systems are needed in China to strengthen rural women's forestland rights, promote the well-being of rural households, and ensure the effectiveness and success of forestland reform across the country. Ultimately, a forestland policy that considers both women and men will be more effective at reaching its goals of reducing poverty and improving the livelihoods of rural Chinese people.

Notes

1   Rural Land Contracting Law, art. 20.
2   Rural Land Contracting Law, arts. 16 and 31.
3   Forest Law, art. 3. Rural Land Contracting Law, art. 23.
4   Forest Law, arts. 15 and 31.
5   Forest Law, art. 32.
6   Organic Law of the Villagers' Committees, arts. 22, 24.
7   Organic Law of the Villagers' Committees, art. 30.
8   Organic Law of the Villagers' Committees, arts. 22, 24.
9   Constitution, art. 5.
10   Law Protecting Women's Rights and Interests, art. 2.
11   Law Protecting Women's Rights and Interests, art. 32.
12   Rural Land Contracting Law, art. 6.
13   Marriage Law, art. 13 and art. 17.
14   Organic Law of the Villagers' Committees, art. 25.
15   Rural Land Contracting Law, art. 5.
16   Organic Law of the Villagers' Committee, art. 24.
17   Article 2 of the Organic Law of the Villagers' Committees states that: "A villagers' committee is a mass organization of self-government at the grassroots level, in which villagers administer their own affairs, educate themselves, and serve their own needs and in which election is conducted, decision adopted, administration maintained, and supervision exercised by democratic means."
18   Article 24 of the Rural Land Contracting Law (RLCL) states that matters involving the interests of the villagers, including land contracting plans, shall be dealt with only upon the villagers' assembly's decision through discussion. A villagers' assembly may also authorize the villagers' representatives' assembly to decide on the above-mentioned matters through discussion. Article 26 of the RLCL states that every decision of the villagers' assembly shall be adopted by a majority vote of those present at the assembly.
19   Rural Land Contracting Law, art. 15.

References

All China Women's Federation (2011) *Executive Report of the 3rd Survey on the Status of Chinese Women*, Collection of Women's Studies, No. 6.
Can, L. (2008) *The Collective Forestry Institutions and Forestry Development in China*, Beijing: Economic Science Press.
Central Committee of CPC and the State Council (1981) *The Resolution on the Protection of the Forest and the Development of Forestry*.
Central Committee of CPC and the State Council (2003) *The Decision to Expedite Forestry Development*.
Central Committee of CPC and the State Council (2008) *The Decision on Promoting the Reform of Collective Forest Tenure Regime*.
'China's Main Reform on Collective Forestland System Has Been Completed', *People's Daily* (13 Jan 2014), Available: http://politics.people.com.cn/n/2014/0113/c70731-24101979.html
Constitution, the, National People's Congress of China (1982).
FAO (2012) *Success Cases and Good Practices in Forest Farmer Cooperative Organizations in China*, Rome.
Forest Law, National People's Congress of China (1998).

Haipeng, Zhang, and Jintao, Xu. (2009) "Collective Forest Tenure Reform: Assessment of Motivation, Characteristics and Performance," *Forest Science*, no.7, pp. 119–126.

"How Can the Farmers Benefit from the Forestland Tenure Reform?" *People's Daily* (17 July 2008), p. 2. Available: http://paper.people.com.cn/rmrb/html/2008-07/17/nw.D110000renmrb_20080717_3-02.htm

Jia, Z. (2011) *Speech on the National Forestry Conference*, [Online], Available: www.china.com.cn/policy/txt/2011-01/25/content_21811337.htm [5 Jan 2011].

Jintao, X., Yan, S., Xuemei, J., and Jie, L. (2008) "Collective Forest Tenure Reform in China: Analysis of Pattern and Performance," *Forestry Economics*, no. 9, pp. 27–38.

Keliang, Z. (2006) "The Rural Land Question in China: Analysis and Recommendations Based on a Seventeen-Province Survey," *New York University Journal of International Law and Politics* vol. 38, no. 4, pp. 761–840.

Land Management Law, National People's Congress of China (1998).

Law Protecting Women's Rights and Interests, National People's Congress of China (2005).

Li, Y., and Yin-Sheng, X. (2006) "Married Women's Rights to Land in China's Traditional Farming Areas," *Journal of Contemporary China*, no. 11.

Lihua, H., and Zushan, W. (2013) "On the Poverty Issues in China's Mountain Areas and Its Sustainable Development," *Reformation & Strategy*, no. 9, pp. 42–69.

Marriage Law, National People's Congress of China (2001).

Ministry of Forestry, (1981) *The Briefing of Securing Farmers' Rights to Forestland and Forest and the Implementation of Forestry Household Responsibility System.*

Organic Law of Villagers' Committees, National People's Congress of China (2010).

Property Law, National People's Congress of China (2007).

Prosterman, R. *et al.* (1998) "Rural Land Reform in China and the 1998 Land Management Law," Rural Development Institute. Available: www.landesa.org/our-research/the-rural-land-question-in-china-analysis-and-recommendations-based-on-a-17-province-survey Accessed May 2012.

Quisumbing, A. R. (1996) "Male–female differences in agricultural productivity: Methodological issues and empirical evidence," *World Development* vol. 24, no. 10, pp. 1579–1595, in Research Group, (2011) *The Literature and Policy Review of the Reform of Collective Forest Land Tenure in China*, Beijing: Economic Science Press.

Rural Land Contracting Law, National People's Congress of China (2002).

Standing Committee of NPC (2010) *Report on the Implementation of the Law on the Protection of Women's Rights and Interests*, Available: www.npc.gov.cn/npc/xinwen/jdgz/bgjy/2010-06/23/content_1578400.htm

State Forestry Bureau (2007) *China Forestry Yearbook*, Beijing: China Forestry Publishing House.

State Forestry Bureau (2009) *The Seventh National Forest Resource Inventory*, Beijing: China Forestry Publishing House.

State Forestry Bureau (2010) *The Seventh National Forest Resources Inventory*, Forest Resources Management, No. 2.

State Forestry Bureau (2012) *The Progress of Forestry in Promoting Sustainable Development*, 4 June, Available: HYPERLINK "http://www.gov.cn/wszb/zhibo515/content_2152402.htm"www.gov.cn/wszb/zhibo515/content_2152402.htm

State Forestry Bureau (2013) 2012 *Monitoring Report of the Collective Forest Tenure Reform*, Beijing: China Forestry Publishing House.

State Statistics Bureau, (2013). *2012 China National Monitoring Report on Migrant Workers*, Money China, No. 7, pp. 78–79.

Xinhua News Agency. (2009) *Central Forestry Working Conference on Promotion of the Collective Forest Tenure Reform*, [Online] Available: www.gov.cn/ldhd/2009-06/23/content_1348513.htm [23 June].

Yin, J., and Xiangqian, W. (2003) "Discussion and Analysis on Law-related Issues of Village Regulations and Civil Rules," *Journal of North China Electric Power University (Social Science)*, no. 1, pp. 55–58.

Zhili, C. (2012) *Rural Women Now The Main Labor Force in Rural China*, [Online], Available: www.chinanews.com/gn/2012/08-28/4140456.shtml [28 Aug].

Zongmin, L., and Bruce, J. (2005) "Gender, Landlessness and Equity in Rural China," in Ho, P. (ed.) *Developmental Dilemmas: Land Reform and Institutional Change in China*, pp. 308–315. London: Routledge.

11 Gendered perspectives on rangeland privatization among the Maasai of Southern Kenya

Caroline S. Archambault

Introduction

The Kenyan pastoral rangelands are undergoing tenure reform, changing from "customary" systems of communal management to the privatization and allocation of individual freehold title. This process has stirred up considerable debate among scholars, policy-makers, and pastoralists, with many warning of impending crises regarding livelihood disruption and advocating a return to the customary collective land-tenure systems. At the academic and policy levels, the voices and perspectives of female pastoralists are remarkably absent from this debate. Yet locally, among the Maasai in Kenya, women hold strong opinions about how privatization impacts their well-being.

It is imperative that women's perspectives and opinions inform debates and discussions about rangeland tenure reform. Not only is this consistent with a development policy committed to inclusion, social equity, and women's rights, but also because, as is clear in the context of Maasailand tenure debates, women's positions broaden our understanding of tenure processes and the widespread impacts of tenure change. Maasai women have different concerns and perspectives on privatization than do men. Thus, as attempts to seek solutions to tenure disruptions on local livelihoods continue in Kenya and elsewhere, women's experiences will increase our understanding of the complex ways tenure can affect development. As this chapter illustrates, in current discussions too much emphasis has been placed on productivity and the potential efficiency outcomes of tenure reform. Women remind us that privatization of rangelands has profound and important social consequences that are key determinants of well-being.

By means of a comparative, ethnographic, and mixed-method approach, this chapter illuminates how women's positions on privatization—and the ways in which they are impacted by this change in tenure—are diverse and importantly shaped by cross-cutting factors such as age, socio-economic status, education, and family circumstance, among others. Family case studies illustrate the complexity and widespread nature of tenure change, and how it affects various facets of social and economic life that importantly interact with women's well-being. Privatization has ushered in new potential income-generating possibilities but many of these are hard for women to realize and benefit from, and some may not be sustainable or reliable in the long term. Privatization has also had profound demographic consequences; on the one hand it has given women opportunities to settle and improve their homes, while on the other it has simultaneously changed the dynamics of residential life, resulting in uncertain consequences on women's workloads and social life. From women's perspectives, privatization has also introduced important and intimate levels of social conflict as land sales and inheritance foster tension between spouses and co-wives, as well as between parents and their children.

Continued exploration into the diversity of women's lives, embedded in particular marital, familial, and communal contexts, will provide important insights into how best to align rangeland tenure reform with the goals of social equity. The three case studies presented here suggest that communities may greatly benefit from pursuing more innovative strategies of tenure reform that allow men and women to reap the benefits of privatization and minimize the negative consequences. The case studies make clear that the widespread practice of subdividing an entire group ranch into individual parcels allocated to each member gives rise to a great deal of inequality in landholdings not only from a productive or ecological point of view, but importantly from a social point of view as well. Communities may be better served by a tenure system that makes provisions for communal rangelands and separate individual holdings that are concentrated around social services, infrastructure, and key resource points. Such models exist in Maasailand but are rare. In addition, women's perspectives also highlight the importance of instituting or reinforcing preexisting legislation that can protect community members from land dispossession and landlessness through sales and can clarify or even codify expectations around inheritance, access, and rights.

A history of land-tenure change and exclusion

The lack of attention paid to women's perspectives on land privatization in the Maasai rangelands is rooted both in a patriarchal social system and a long history of tenure change that has excluded women from official landownership and tenure control. While the Maasai once occupied much of the fertile highlands and grazed their livestock throughout the Rift Valley belt from Northern Kenya to Northern Tanzania, a century of dramatic displacements and dispossessions have largely confined contemporary "Maasailand" to the two southern Kenyan districts of Kajiado and Narok and the northern plains and foothills of Tanzania.

These displacements, which included colonial annexations, conservation acquisitions, and encroachments by neighboring agricultural communities, were often justified through narratives of Maasai mismanagement, which persist today (Galaty, 2002). Such narratives are entrenched in the notion that Maasai are culturally conservative, maintaining an irrational love for cattle that inhibits them from modernizing and commercializing their production. The narratives maintain that the main motivation for Maasai is the accumulation of livestock, which will inevitably lead to a tragedy of the commons (Hardin, 1968). Within such a perspective, rationalizing land tenure was seen as the most promising solution to the "Maasai problem."

In 1968, following numerous colonial experimentations in grazing schemes, the newly independent government introduced "group ranches" (Langat, 1986; Ng'ethe, 1993). Under this form of tenure, a designated group would collectively hold title to a demarcated land. In total, 159 group ranches were established in Kenya. They varied significantly in size and population (Ng'ethe, 1993). Group ranch membership was open to all adult males who customarily resided in the designated territories at the time of initial group ranch registration.[1] Members elected a management committee, which took on responsibility for the day-to-day management of the ranch. Major decisions would be voted on by the entire membership during the mandatory annual general meeting. It is important to note that both women and young people were excluded from becoming members of the group ranch and therefore had no direct ownership or control over land use and property arrangements. Alongside the creation of the group ranches, large-scale individual ranches were also established for a small minority of Maasai elite (Grandin, 1987).

It is widely recognized that Group Ranches were a failure (Galaty, 1994; Halderman, 1989; Kipury, 1989; Mwangi, 2006); they did not succeed in reforming the Maasai pastoral system into the commercialized operation envisioned by the government. Nor did they secure land and facilitate improvements for residents in the community. In response to such shortcomings, government and many residents were eager to dissolve such ranches and instead privatize landholdings at an individual level. In 1983, this was made possible and a massive process of subdivision began, resulting in well over two-thirds of group ranches entering into private individual tenure. Subdivision involved a deciding vote by the registered membership, followed by the subdivision of all non-public utility lands into equally sized parcels to be allocated to each registered member.

There has been a great deal of academic and local civil attention paid to the impacts of privatization on the Maasai rangelands (Kimani and Pickard, 1998; Lesorogol, 2008; Mwangi, 2007; Rutten, 1992). While these studies recognize the potential advantages of private ownership for the Maasai, they largely conclude that such advantages are far outweighed by the problems and disruption that have followed subdivision. There is now widespread concern that the privatization has caused crisis in pastoral livelihoods and there is a strong push to return to customary forms of tenure or to explore other forms of institutional tenure innovation that would support and strengthen pastoralism. As noted above, women's perspectives have been absent from these debates and discussions, yet women have strong and important contributions to make, as their daily experience of the tenure change differs from men's and has had profound implications for their personal well-being. If a main goal in this advocacy is to find solutions that better secure livelihoods for Maasai in a socially equitable way, then women should be part of these conversations.

204 Caroline S. Archambault

Setting

Stretching over 200,000 acres in the southern district of Kajiado, Elangata Wuas is home to approximately 10,500 residents.[2] The group ranch was first established in 1972 and comprised 489 registered male adult members. In 1989 the membership voted to sub-divide and an allocation committee was formed and land surveying begun. Due to widespread allegations of corruption in this process, however, the subdivision of this committee was completely overturned in 1999 and a new committee established one year later. In 2001 a second survey took place and by 2006 members began receiving their title deeds to their allocated parcels of land. Although the process of issuing title deeds has been lengthy due to conflicts of allocation and the rising costs involved in receiving titles, estimates suggest that the process is almost complete with more than two-thirds of the membership having received their titles.

Elangata Wuas is ecologically typical of a semi-arid rangeland. Low altitudes, variable and little rainfall, and poor soils combine to produce an environment with little agricultural potential. Consequently, the community depends largely on livestock husbandry as its primary economic activity, often supplemented by a range of other pursuits. Residents keep cattle, goats, sheep, and a few camels. Although grazing patterns and practices are undergoing transformations as a result of privatization, families that keep relatively large herds still practice a form of transhumant pastoralism, in which during the wet season they graze their animals within the vicinity of a more permanent homestead and during the dry season family members graze their animals at distant pastures.

The community of Elangata Wuas is going through dramatic change beyond the issue of tenure too. As found in other Maasai communities, the rapid expansion of education, improvements in basic infrastructure, and advances in communication technology, have facilitated diversification (Archambault, 2007; Archambault et al., 2014; Homewood et al., 2009), and less than a third of families rely exclusively on pastoralism as the only means of income generation. The commercial center of Mile 46, the town that hosts the weekly market, is growing rapidly with the establishment of new businesses.

Such developments have ushered in rather dramatic changes in gender roles. More economic roles and responsibilities for women have followed on from family diversification, increases in male outmigration, and improvements in female education. According to a survey conducted in Elangata Wuas in 2005, 41% of wives reported having had an income-generating activity in the previous month compared with 62% of their husbands. Women most commonly reported engaging with charcoal production, selling grass and milk, and working or owning a small business in town. Women also appear to be increasingly more engaged in pastoralism, often taking over herding responsibilities from their children, who are at school. Women were also increasingly active in the church, in various women's groups, and even, amongst the younger generation, in community activism through social media. Thus, despite popular narratives that relegate Maasai women to the domestic sphere, women are actively and centrally engaged in the economic, political, familial, and spiritual dimensions of life in Elangata Wuas (Hodgson, 2001). In the words of one male research assistant, "They are growing horns." This provides even more reason to ensure that their perspectives and positions are part of debates about the future of land-tenure reform.

Methods

This study is based on long-term ethnographic engagement in the community of Elangata Wuas between 2003 and the time of writing. Several doctoral and post-doctoral research programs on education, tenure change, marriage, childhood, and migration have incorporated an explicit focus on generational dynamics and gender. This chapter draws on data from a variety of projects and data-collection efforts including two household surveys conducted in 2005 and 2008–09. More specifically, this chapter is part of an ongoing research program investigating the gender dynamics of subdivision. Within this program, a number of different methods have been undertaken, including qualitative interviewing on a variety of subjects, livelihood listing, small business census, and most centrally, in-depth family case studies. Ten families were chosen that represent the community diversity in socio-economic status, family size, marital status, livelihood strategies, and landholdings.

Gendered perspectives on privatization

Although women in Elangata Wuas are not traditionally viewed as landowners, and issues related to land politics are often categorized as "male issues," women have strong opinions on privatization. During the 2008–09 survey, wives were asked in both a categorical and an open-ended question, whether they felt that privatization was good, bad, or whether its outcome was uncertain. Forty-three percent of wives responded that it was good, 55% that it was bad, and only 1% that they were unsure. All wives answered this question and were able to elaborate on their opinions in the open-ended follow-up question of why. Among female respondents, the top reasons why privatization was felt to be good included having control and independence over their land and affairs, having ownership, and being able to settle and build a permanent house. Among those women who responded that privatization was bad, their main concerns were that it had increased disputes, excluded them from natural resources and mobility of livestock, and that the parcels were too small for them to be able to continue with pastoralism.

Women not only had an opinion on privatization but their opinions differed from those of men. Men were more favorable on average to subdivision than women. Sixty-three percent of husbands reported privatization to be good, 35% to be bad, and 2% were unsure. The open-ended response revealed some overlap in perspectives. Men favorable to privatization mentioned control and independence as the top reason for their feelings, but other important issues included the ability to invest and develop land, and being able to use resources for themselves. Comparatively few husbands mentioned, for example, settling and building permanent houses. Among the men who felt privatization was bad, their main rationale was that the parcels were too small for pastoralism, followed by an increase in disputes, and landlessness. This simple question does highlight that there are some important gendered differences in perspectives on privatization. Interestingly, in 35% of the couples interviewed, husbands and wives answered the question differently from each other (i.e. the husband felt privatization to be positive while the wife regarded it negatively, and vice versa).

Responses to this question also make apparent that there is not one single female perspective on the issue. In fact, women are quite evenly divided with a little less than the majority reporting favorably on privatization. A simple logistic regression—shown in Table 11.1—where the dependent variable reflects a positive opinion on land privatization (=1), shows that older women are significantly more likely to favor privatization as are more educated women, while total livestock units—a good indicator of wealth—is not a significant predictor.

That education matters is not surprising, since it is correlated with diversification away from pastoralism. The significant age coefficient likely reflects the fact that many young people are not direct recipients of land titles under privatization. That total livestock units are not significant is somewhat unexpected from a purely economic perspective, since those with large herds have arguably the most to lose under privatization given the allocation of parcels that are fixed in size. The lack of significance of such a key pastoral livelihood indicator is indicative of the diversity of considerations that factor into women's views on privatization. This is also underscored by the low pseudo R-squared: 95% of the variation in opinion responses remains unexplained by these factors. As highlighted below, qualitative case studies indeed demonstrate that women's opinions on privatization are contingent on a complex array of factors and circumstances not easily captured in linear regressions. The case studies of Silapei, Priscillah, and Agnes highlight the variation in circumstances that give rise to a complex assessment of the role of privatization in women's lives.[3]

Table 11.1 Women's opinions on privatization

	In favor of privatization (=1)
Years of education	1.09* (0.05)
Age (years)	1.04** (0.02)
Total livestock units	1.06 (0.15)
Number of observations	131
Pseudo R-squared	0.0524

Notes: Logistic regressions showing odds ratios. ** p-value<5%; * p-value<10%. Sample of women.

Comparative case studies

Silapei, who is approximately in her mid sixties, is a widow of the (late) Lenkayoni. She has eight adult children, none of whom attended school with the exception of two of her sons, who finished primary school. She is a traditional birth attendant and full-time pastoralist. Her husband was allocated 270 acres of land, where her sons now live and keep their animals. She has two cows and ten goats and sheep.

Priscillah is 35 years old and the third wife in a polygamous union. She has four children, the youngest only eight weeks old at the time of writing. Priscillah has completed her primary education. She and her husband are primarily livestock keepers but Priscillah also sells some clothes and sugar at the weekly market. They live some way from the town center on the edge of a hill, where they were allocated 270 acres. They have 15 cows, 50 goats, 30 sheep, and three camels.

Agnes is a Kamba married to a Maasai from Elangata Wuas. She is 38 years old and in a monogamous marriage. She has three children, all of whom attend school. Agnes completed her secondary education and owns a shop in the center of Mile 46. Her husband completed teacher training college and is employed as a teacher. They reside in Mile 46, close to their shop, and have 30 acres of land some distance away. They have ten cows and 30 sheep.

Economic dimensions

Maasai gender ideology constructs a distinct gendered division of labor. Men are seen as the primary livestock owners, and are responsible for grazing, watering, and buying and selling livestock. While women care for the young animals that graze near to the home, their main responsibilities include domestic water and firewood provision, purchasing foodstuffs, cooking, cleaning, and caring for children. In practice, many women take on roles traditionally associated as male. However, this ideology of gendered distinction is nevertheless perceptible in the ways men and women think about the economic opportunities and challenges that will be ushered in by privatization of the land.

With regard to economic considerations, men tend to emphasize the value of landownership and the freedom and control that it permits landowners over their own affairs. And even though most men will warn about the dangers of dispossession that have followed land sales, they will quite commonly mention that privatization will allow them to sell, buy, lease out, or rent land and the land-based natural resources (such as grass and water) related to grazing. Those men who perceive privatization as unfavorable to economic development very much stress the negative impacts that such tenure reform has on pastoralism, such as dramatic reductions in livestock mobility and increased challenges in accessing sufficient grass and water resources to sustain family herds.

Women, on the other hand, will emphasize the new potential income-generating activities that are more in line with their traditional roles and responsibilities. Most women will raise the new possibility of using timber resources on their land to produce and sell charcoal, a lucrative activity. They will also make mention of opportunities for cultivation, even though the environment in Elangata Wuas is challenging for reliable agriculture. Nevertheless, where the potential exists, small farms will most likely be cared for and controlled by women and women will be responsible for the marketing of produce and thus will likely retain some control over any revenue generated through this work. These new sources of revenue would allow them to invest in their priorities, such as school fees for children, food security, and housing improvements.

Those women who emphasize the economic disadvantages of privatization often highlight the precarious nature of these potential income-generating activities. They indicate that one's ability to pursue such opportunities very much depends on the land the family has been allocated and the relationship they have with their husband. They also warn of the short-term gains of such activities at the expense of longer-term sustainability, citing environmental damage caused by, for example, charcoal-burning or selling of other natural resources. Many women are also concerned about their economic and livelihood vulnerability now that their husbands have the power and authority to sell land.

Silapei, the widow in her late sixties, offers an interesting and nuanced perspective. As a widow, it is clear that she has taken on a number of the traditionally male roles that inform her assessment of the potential economic changes brought about by privatization. She explains:

> Privatization is good for Elangata Wuas women because they own the land and can sell firewood, burn charcoal, sell sand to constructors for those who have rivers passing by their land, keep grass to sell to those people who want to buy and for their livestock if they have livestock…Women burn and sell charcoal, using the money they get to pay their children's school fees, buy food for the family and some even build iron sheet houses for the family, some start a business of selling *shukas* [clothes].

Interestingly, while Silapei imagines all sorts of potential new income-generating activities, she admits to not having realized any of these advantages herself. In her experience, pastoralism has become considerably more difficult as she is continuously accused of trespassing on her neighbors' property with her animals. She also complains that timber resources are scarce and so she can no longer make money by building homes for other women as she used to do.

On the other hand, Priscillah has pursued many of these new opportunities and yet still shares a negative perspective on privatizations economic advantages. Priscillah's husband was allocated 270 acres on a hillside, which she complains is extremely unproductive. "You can't live on the hill or build a house or even graze and the law does not allow someone to own a hill but that's where we were given and we can't use it because it is not productive." She was fortunate in that her husband had purchased 55 acres of land, upon which she could burn charcoal, pay school fees, and start a business. But she recognizes that many women will not have such opportunities.

There has not been any expansion of business. You can't get firewood or wood to build market kiosks if you don't have it on your land…Those women with grass on their farms are the ones who burn charcoal but the ones without, can't…If land is subdivided and you end up getting a parcel that has no trees, there is no way you can sustain yourself.

Agnes offers a more positive outlook while also recognizing that much of the opportunities depend on your allocation of land. Her husband's land had many trees; this allowed her to burn charcoal, which not only gave her income but also reduced the presence and nuisance of hyenas. She also mentioned that privatization allowed families to invest in water catchment systems that could drastically reduce women's travel time in search of water. She also highlighted other investments made possible by selling land: "Women have become wiser after subdivision…when their husbands sell land, women get a portion of money…They buy iron sheets to build houses to stay or to rent…They buy their sons motorbikes to operate as [taxis]."

It is clear from the very different situations of these three women that a major factor in being able to reap economic benefits from privatization will largely depend on the quality of your land. Women whose land is bare of any resources (grass, timber, water, etc.) will not be able to take advantage of selling resources and will have a much more difficult time sustaining livestock within the confines of their parcel. These women will now have to buy resources from others, which were previously free. Similarly, obtaining loans on credit based on land depends on having land that is valued and against which a bank or other institution will allow you to borrow. Very little institutional formal lending has occurred in Elangata Wuas. Start-up capital from land sales also depends on the land value. As has happened in most former group ranches, the privatization of Elangata Wuas was done through a blanket approach. The total land, minus the public utility lands, were divided into equal parcels and allocated to individual members. The consequence of this is rather dramatic differences in the quality, economic, and ecological viability of different holdings.

Demographic changes

The demographic implications of privatization are a very gendered concern; often unmentioned when speaking with men, they are of central importance to women. With the exception of the few families resident in town, most residents live scattered across the landscape in the traditional Maasai residential homesteads called *inkang'itie* (singular: *enkang*). The ideal *enkang* is a large patrilocal residential unit in which a father and his wives live together with their sons, the wives of their sons, and their grandchildren. In practice, members come together through agnatic and affinal relations, age-set links, clan affiliations, friendships, and convenience. Living together in the *enkang* allows families to pool labor and provides social and economic security. Livestock are often herded together by children of multiple families. Women resident in an *enkang* often share food and help each other in various productive activities, such as house-building, fetching water and firewood, and taking care of each other's children.

Privatization has ushered in fairly dramatic demographic changes in Elangata Wuas (Archambault *et al.*, 2010). As families are allocated parcels, they will typically relocate and physically claim this land unless, of course, they are already residing on the parcel denoted as theirs. Families that have been given land far away from any social services or roads may decide not to relocate. Since *inkangitie* are traditionally patrilocal and multigenerational, it is not uncommon to have a situation where sons who have been allocated land will leave their father's *enkang* in order to start their own on their own land. This has effectively reduced average *enkang* size. In 2005, well before the completion of privatization, average *enkang* size was 2.75 families per homestead. By 2008–09, however, average size had reduced significantly to 1.93 families per enkang. Interestingly, while *enkang* size has reduced, household sizes have increased; this may be a coping strategy for families to retain the support and labor-pooling characteristic of large *inkangitie*.

Women are almost unanimous in agreeing that privatization gives them the opportunity to settle. Many women complain that traditional mobility, when entire households would move seasonally to follow the rains, was an exhausting lifestyle. As they are traditionally responsible for building, breaking down, and maintaining houses, such mobility was extremely demanding physically. Settling permanently in one place also provides women with the opportunity to improve their houses in order to make them more comfortable and to decrease their workloads. For example, families can now invest in more permanent structures and improved roofing that do not have to be taken down and rebuild periodically or replastered following heavy rains. Those families who can afford it can also build stone houses and install technologies such as solar electricity. This is still the exception rather than the rule and exists only among the very elite in Elangata Wuas, but it nevertheless is something many women aspire to. Similarly, knowing that they will stay permanently in one home, many women have experimented with new housing designs, including building kitchens separate from the bedrooms and thus reducing exposure to indoor air pollution. Some have also invested in building latrines.

Along with such home improvements comes a more general appreciation for the sense of belonging, control, and predictability that comes with settling in a permanent place. Women often mention that they can more easily plan their future when they know they will be living in a particular environment.

Priscillah and Agnes share these sentiments when asked whether settlement brings advantages or disadvantages to women. In Priscillah's view:

> Women are the ones who build *manyattas* [houses] and they suffer when they have to build every now and then … It's good to stay on your land instead of moving from one place to another. It's good to settle somewhere and plan your future. I have been able to plan my future after settling here. I know down the hill there are some trees and I have planned that when drought comes, I will cut some of those trees and burn charcoal and get food for my family.

For Agnes:

> Life of moving around is hard and the [traditional] house leaks a lot making life even more difficult ... After a [traditional] house, I lived in an iron sheet house, then I later constructed a brick house, which is where I'm currently living. I would never want to go back to a [traditional] house ... Herding has become less. You fence your parcel and when livestock move up to the fence, they come back. You can just sit at home and relax or you can do other things like beadwork. Before there was no time for beading. I was busy moving from one place to another which was hard and I didn't like it.

However, opinions differ on changes in homestead and family size. Women consider how changes in residential composition will impact not only their workloads but also their social lives. Silapei, the widow, shares her concerns on both dimensions:

> When you are alone in a homestead, you have no one to help you when in need. The advantage is that there is peace and no gossip in smaller homesteads and households ... Smaller homes have created distance between people. People don't visit each other like before. You don't know how your neighbor is doing.

Priscillah adds a provision that much depends on your labor needs and your livelihood strategy. As someone who is quite invested in pastoralism, living in a big home has obvious advantages for her:

> When [the] subdivision was done, people went to their own parcels. If families were big, they went to their own land. With pastoralism, if you are alone, you will have a problem. If you want to travel, you will have to get someone to look after your livestock while you are gone. During drought, you will also have a problem because you can't fetch water alone at the dam for your animals. You have to get someone to help you. If you are a woman, you will suffer because you will have to pay someone to help you or close your business and concentrate on the animals. But when the family is big, you help each other out ... My family has not changed even after subdivision. I have been living with my co-wife both before and after sub-division. Right now I have just had a baby and am getting some help from other women at home. When I am sick, I get help. With herding, we alternate ... There are no disadvantages for me with a big family, only advantages, especially with the household chores.

Agnes, on the other hand, who is a lot less reliant on pastoralism and who lives in town and owns a shop, finds peace and stability in the small home:

If many people live together, there are a lot of conflicts. Women gossip a lot and there is fighting. It also reduces household duties ... when a home is big, there are a lot of responsibilities ... you are forever cooking and you can't sleep well because there are lots of people around. In small families ... you treat your children well. In big families, there is not enough money because you spend a lot on food and you don't get money for school fees and clothes for your children.

Women will all agree that the location of their parcel is a key determinant in whether the demographic changes resulting from privatization will be in their favor. For those families who are allocated parcels far away from social services (like schools, clinics, churches, markets, and public transport) or from important infrastructure (roads, permanent water points, etc.) relocating and settling is far less attractive. Silapei, for example, who currently resides less than a mile from Mile 46, was allocated land several miles away. She has decided not to relocate but her sons have moved and set up homes on the parcel. In a similar vein, women who have been allocated land away from the areas and neighborhoods they have resided in for a long time may also be reluctant to leave their homes. Moving under such conditions would most likely increase women's workloads and their sense of social isolation. This is a real concern for many women and one that is often neglected in any discussion about tenure reform.

Social conflict

Both men and women recognize increased conflict as one of the major disadvantages of privatization, but each gender seems to focus on different forms of conflict. In general, men tend to raise such issues primarily with regard to neighbors over boundaries and trespassing, or with committee officials in the allocation of parcels. Women, conversely, speak much more frequently about more intimate forms of conflict, such as those, for example, between husbands and wives, co-wives, or parents and children (Archambault, 2014).

Agnes remarks on issues of inheritance, which are naturally of more concern among bigger families who will have to divide the parcel into smaller allocations. "The main disadvantage of privatization is conflict. In a family of many wives, if you have fewer sons, you are squeezed in a small parcel of land..." Conflicts between siblings over inheritance have become a major source of strife in the community and one that preoccupies young people but is rarely raised by parents. Among wives and mothers, the focus tends to be on the tensions generated between co-wives over the inheritance allocations of their sons or the distribution of revenue from land sales. "For polygamous families, a husband can sell the land and share the money with only one wife, creating hatred among the wives." She also raises the tensions that can arise between parents and their children, especially for widows: "For widows who fear their sons, the sons may sell land and don't share the money with the widow ... some sons force the widows to divide the land among them so they can sell their portion of land even when the widow doesn't want to divide it."

She asserts that this has not been her own personal experience but that widows are vulnerable to such situations. Finally, Silapei also raises the issue of tension between spouses: "Some men sell land and buy cows but they don't provide for the family and so it is the wife who sells water and firewood to do so." In one of the other case studies conducted as part of this research program, a wife separated from her husband when he sold a significant portion of land without her consent and did not invest the money for the family's benefit. Divorce and separation may become more common in Elangata Wuas as marital tensions rise over land dealings. Unfortunately for women, this would likely result in severing their access to their husband's land.

Conclusion

This chapter has offered a window into the complex gendered realities of men and women in Elangata Wuas as they attempt to make sense of dramatic tenure changes and the implications these may have on their lives. Women have been neglected from participating in local, academic, and policy debates on rangeland tenure reform. Their voices and perspectives need to be included not only as a matter of right, but because they offer different perspectives, concerns, and priorities than men and thus increase our understanding of tenure change dynamics. This gendered analysis exploring both men and women's opinions on privatization has illuminated how both groups have different ideas about the role of privatization in securing well-being. By and large women in Elangata Wuas are less favorable than men toward this tenure reform. They realize that subdivision has rendered pastoralism more difficult and have apprehensions about their abilities to translate landownership into new reliable and sustainable livelihood options, like cultivation, resource exploitation, or small-business development. Much depends on the quality and productivity of the land allocations granted to them, as it does on the relationship they have with their husbands and on whether women will be in a position to develop and control the revenue from new economic opportunities. Many women feel increased vulnerability at the possibility that husbands or sons sell land without their approval and use the revenue unwisely.

Yet many women look on privatization favorably, as it relates to important demographic and residential dynamics rarely discussed by men. Women find great relief in the possibility of settling and investing in homes. This increases their sense of belonging, gives them more control and sense of "predictability." This allows them to better plan for the future, and can reduce their workload considerably, as well as bring them comforts they could not enjoy in temporary residences. Yet again, the reality is that women can gain such advantages only if they are allocated a parcel in a favorable location, one that is close to social services, to their social networks, and to important infrastructure and resources. Distant parcels with poor access to necessary resources and that are disconnected from the areas where women have long resided, may—if coupled with decreases in homestead size—bring about significant increases in women's workloads as well as social isolation and insecurity. Such social dimensions of inequality in land allocations are neglected as the focus is primarily on the economic and ecological viability of parcels.

Finally, women's perspectives on privatization also raise important dimensions around conflict that are rarely raised in current discussions about the negative implications of privatization. Attention to conflict mostly focuses on the corruption in land-allocation processes and the conflicts that families have with neighbors or other members of the community over boundaries and trespassing. Women raise a much more intimate series of conflicts and tensions that are potentially exacerbated by such reforms. New family tensions arise over inheritance allocations or land sales between spouses, between co-wives, and between parents and children.

The three case studies of Silapei, Priscillah, and Agnes have helped bring out the complexity of women's circumstances and the far-reaching impacts that privatization can have on their well-being. It is only through such detailed, ethnographic, and case-specific examples that we can flesh out the range of ways in which women can be positively or negatively impacted by tenure reform and identify strategies to increase women's security under such dramatic changes. Women are not a unified social category. They differ in a variety of cross-cutting identities, including age, class, socio-economic status, ethnicity, religion, marital status, education, etc. It is only after appreciating this diversity and understanding how such attributes shape, constrain, and facilitate development aspirations that we can more clearly articulate strategies to address equitable development through land-tenure reform.

This analysis suggests that women (and men) will be best served by a more innovative approach to privatization whereby entire group ranches are not divided up and allocated. Inevitably this will lead to gross inequalities in the quality of landholdings on both an economic and social dimension. Other group ranches have experimented with privatizing sections of the ranch and maintaining commons for continued pastoralism. This seems to be a more promising approach, as private holdings can be limited to areas that are close to pre-existing social services, infrastructure, and resource points. Extra care should be taken when surveying and allocating the holdings to ensure that the land is equitably distributed not only economically and ecologically, but also socially. Furthermore, certain legal provisions should be introduced or enforced. For example, provisions for spousal co-ownership would reduce the stress on, and vulnerability of, women, while mandating spousal consent over transactions would help prevent future conflicts. Similarly, inheritance rights should be discussed, more clearly articulated, and enforced in order to set expectations and reduce tensions. The very first step, however, would be to bring women into the discussions, debates, and deliberations locally, nationally, and internationally over the future of land in Elangata Wuas and recognizing that they have an important perspective to share.

Acknowledgements

This research was supported by a Standard Research Grant from the Social Science and Humanities Research Council of Canada obtained by Prof. John G Galaty of McGill University and a VENI Research Grant from the Netherlands Organisation for Scientific Research. I would like to acknowledge my special appreciation to Elizabeth Kyengo, my research assistant and coordinator. My gratitude extends to my other research assistants and to the many members of the Elangata Wuas community who supported this research. I am also grateful to my data analyst, Arvind Eyunni, and to Joost de Laat for the many helpful comments.

Notes

1   Today this effectively means that men of roughly 35 years of age and younger are not members.
2   Population estimates are based on a household survey conducted in 2005 (Archambault, 2007).
3   Pseudonyms have been used to protect the identity of families mentioned in the case studies.

References

Archambault, C.S. (2007) *School is the Song of the Day: Education and Social Change in Maasai Society*, Unpublished Dissertation, Brown University.
—(2014) "Young Perspectives on Pastoral Rangeland Privatization: Intimate Exclusions at the Intersection of Youth Identities," *European Journal of Development Research*, vol. 26, pp. 204–218.
Archambault, C.S., J.J. de Laat, and J.G. Galaty (2010) *Maasai Pastoral Rangeland Privatization, Family Fragmentation, and Vulnerability*, Working Paper, Presented at the Canadian Association of African Studies, November 2010.
Archambault, C.S., S. Matter, S. Kimaren, O. Riamit, and J.G. Galaty. (2014). "Maasai Livelihood Pathways in Kenya: Macro-level Factors in Diversifying Diversification," in Deborah Sick (ed.), *Rural Livelihoods, Regional Economies and Processes of Change*, New York: Routledge, pp. 58–84.
Galaty, J.G (1994) "Ha(L)ving Land in Common: the Subdivision of Maasai Group Ranches in Kenya," *Nomadic Peoples*, no. 34–35, pp. 109–122.
—(2002) "How Visual Figures Speak: Narrative Inventions of 'The Pastoralist' in East Africa," *Visual Anthropology*, vol. 15, no. 3–4, pp. 347–367.
Grandin, B. E. (1987) "East African pastoral land tenure: some reflections from Maasailand," in Raintree, J. B., (ed.), *Land, Trees and Tenure*, Proceedings of an International Workshop on Tenure Issues in Agroforestry, 27–31 May, ICRAF and the Land Tenure Center, Nairobi and Madison, WI.
Halderman, J. M. (1989) *Development and Famine Risk in Kenya Maasailand*. Unpublished Ph.D. dissertation, University of California, Berkeley.
Hardin, G. (1968) "The Tragedy of the Commons," *Science*, vol. 162, no. 3859, pp. 1243–1248.
Hodgson, D. (2001) *Once Intrepid Warriors: Gender, Ethnicity, and the Cultural Politics of Maasai Development*, Bloomington: Indiana University Press.

Homewood, K., P. Kristjanson, and Trench, P. (eds) (2009) *Staying Maasai? Livelihoods, Conservation and Development in East African Rangelands*, New York: Springer.

Kimani, K. and Pickard, J. (1998) "Recent Trends and Implications of Group Ranch Subdivision and Fragmentation in Kajiado District, Kenya," *Geographic Journal*, vol. 164, no. 2, pp. 202–213.

Kipury, N. (1989) *Maasai Women in Transition: Class and Gender in the Transformation of a Pastoral Society.* Unpublished Ph.D. dissertation, Temple University.

Langat, R.K. (1986) 'Commercial Ranches in Kenya," in Hansen, R.M., Wole, B.M. and Child, R. D. (eds) *Range Development and Research in Kenya. Proceedings of a Conference.* Winrock International Institute for Agricultural Development: Morrilton, Arizona

Lesorogol, C.K. (2008) *Contesting the Commons: Privatizing Pastoral Lands in Kenya*, Ann Arbor: University of Michigan Press.

Mwangi, E. (2006) "The Footprints of History: Path Dependence in the Transformation of Property Rights in Kenya's Maasailand," *Journal of International Economics*, vol. 2, no. 2, pp. 157–180.

—(2007) *Socioeconomic Change and Land Use in Africa: The Transformation of Property Rights in Maasailand*, New York: Palgrave Macmillan.

Ng'ethe, J.C. (1993) "Group Ranch Concept and Practice in Kenya with Special Emphasis on Kajiado District," in *Future of Livestock Industries in East and Southern Africa* Proceedings of a Workshop July 1992, International Livestock Centre for Africa.

Rutten, M. M. E. M. (1992) *Selling Wealth to Buy Poverty: The Process of the Individualization of Landownership Among the Maasai Pastoralists of Kajiado District, Kenya, 1890–1900*, Nijmegen Studies in Development and Cultural Change, vol. 10.

Part IV

From conflict to peace

An opportunity for gender reconstruction?

Caroline S. Archambault and Annelies Zoomers

In the last decade, many countries such as Angola, Burundi, Côte d'Ivoire, Haiti, Liberia, South Sudan, Uganda, Zimbabwe, Kosovo, Sri Lanka, Nepal, Colombia, and Guatemala have entered phases of post-conflict reconstruction and resettlement. Today more than 40 countries across the world are in varying degrees of conflict (IISS, 2014). The number of Internally Displaced Persons (IDPs), estimated at 33.3 million in 2013, has reached the highest figure recorded since the Internal Displacement Monitoring Centre's (IDMC) began its monitoring in 1989. Sub-Saharan Africa has registered the highest numbers of IDPs of any other region, with 12.5 million IDPs from 21 countries (IDMC, 2014). Peace-building and post-conflict reconstruction will continue to be a major development priority for the coming decades.

As one of the world's most coveted resources, land is often the root cause of violent conflicts and, therefore, at the center of efforts to build peace: "Land issues played a major role in all but three of the more than thirty intrastate conflicts that occurred between 1990 and 2009" (ELI and UNEP, 2013). Conflict often causes major disruptions to land and livelihoods. The displacement of local populations can dramatically alter access to resources and land use patterns (Joireman *et al.*, 2012). The concentration of displaced populations in certain areas may contribute to environmental degradation. Large areas of land may become abandoned, unproductive, and inaccessible if too close to enemy lines or riddled with explosives. Looting and destruction of physical property may result in the loss of housing, farms, and documentation (such as registries and title deeds). The decline or long-term stagnation of food security in countries affected by war is a clear indication of the impacts on land and livelihoods (FAO, 2002).

Countries coming out of conflict face extreme pressure to quickly spur economic growth, maintain political stability, and keep the peace. While post-conflict reconstruction priorities tend to focus on the resettling of refugees, IDPs, and ex-combatants, as well as the provision of compensation and restitution for lost land, major land reforms are often needed and should be prioritized, including reforming land laws and land policies and re-building land administration systems and institutions for dispute reconciliation (Wily, 2009). Such reforms need to be undertaken simultaneously and expediently.

Post-conflict environments offer particular challenges in achieving such reforms. Administrations and institutions are often weak and chaotic. Authority structures, from local administrators and customary leaders to the state political leaders, often change as a result of conflict, creating uncertainties. Disruptions arising from conflict have exacerbated already complex overlapping rights to land and legal ambiguities. The presence of multiple legal systems (customary, religious, and statutory) may provide important flexibility but can also exacerbate inequalities of access as elites navigate these systems to their advantage. Displaced people might be stimulated by government agencies or donor programmes to "return" but might be seen by local groups as "foreign intruders" or as having illegitimate claims.

On the other hand, these environments may provide opportunities to implement substantial legal reforms that can address long-held inequities. In theory, in reconstructing society, post-conflict countries may be able to create the political and social space for change that will build a nation that is more productive, environmentally responsible, socially equitable, and sustainable. As such, these countries have an important opportunity to address gender inequities that may well have been further entrenched by the experience of conflict.

Men and women experience periods of conflict and post-conflict differently (Cockburn, 2013). Unfortunately violence is common in women's lives in periods outside official conflict. The recent World Bank report on "Voice and Agency" (2014: 54) reports that almost one-third (30%) of women have experienced physical or sexual violence or both by an intimate partner. However, the experience of war brings about new types of violence and intensities. Much has been written on the horrific violence women endure as non-combatants during conflicts (Jacobs *et al.*, 2000; Rehn and Sirleaf, 2002; Peterman *et al.*, 2011; Bastick *et al.*, 2007). These include rape, sexual exploitation, mutilation, and torture, among others. Women's bodies are used and abused as symbols of national, ethnic, and/or religious identities (Handrahan, 2004; Goldstein, 2003; Miranda, 2007; Stern and Nystrand, 2006; Baaz and Stern, 2009).

In a disturbing irony, the post-conflict period may be one of continued insecurity for women (Handrahan, 2004). Women who have been violated by the enemy during conflict (abused, raped, captured, betrothed) may be rejected from society. Women who lost husbands in conflict become widows and may experience marginalization and impoverishment. They may have little access to land and natural resources from which to rebuild their livelihoods. Wives whose husbands return home may face considerable loses in authority and autonomy, which may give rise to violent domestic tension. Unexpectedly, however, women might also gain from conflict and displacement, as they access better social services (like education) and new opportunity structures for civic engagement in their new locales and may benefit from increased earning potential and demanding greater participation in local governance (Arostegui, 2013; Norwegian Refugee Council, 2014).

It is thus imperative that post-conflict resettlement and reconstruction efforts prioritize a gender-equitable reconstruction. Efforts need to be made to develop greater understanding of how power struggles, and the processes of identity formation triggered by conflict, implicate gender and how post-conflict land reforms impact women's security and well-being. Chapters in the last section of this book present case studies on the gendered impacts of post-conflict reconstruction and resettlement efforts in Kosovo, Zimbabwe, and Uganda.

In Kosovo, recently legislated egalitarian rights to property are not being implemented and women continue to be marginalized in property ownership. Weak institutions, and a post-conflict resurgence of nationalism embedded with traditional patterns of social organization, has led many women to renounce their rights of inheritance.

Following violent occupations of white-owned farms in Zimbabwe in 2000, the government implemented the "Fast-Track Land Reform" program, which was aimed at redistributing minority-white-owned farms to disenfranchised blacks. While this offered the opportunity to address profound gender inequalities in land access and ownership, patriarchal practices were replicated in the newly resettled areas.

In Uganda, the recent adoption of the National Land Policy creates tension by both providing men and women with equal rights to land while at the same time officially recognizing customary tenure regimes. Acholi women in Northern Uganda struggle to gain rights to land within a patriarchal customary system and major disruptions brought about by decades of conflict.

References

Arostegui, J. (2013) "Gender, Conflict, and Peace-building: How Conflict Can Catalyse Positive Change for Women," *Gender & Development*, vol. 21, no. 3, pp. 533–549.

Baaz, M. E. & Stern, M. (2009) "Why Do Soldiers Rape? Masculinity, Violence, and Sexuality in the Armed forces in the Congo (DRC)," *International Studies Quarterly*, vol. 53, no. 2, pp. 495–518. doi:10.1111/j.1468-2478.2009.00543.x

Bastick, M., Grimm, K., Kunz, R. (2007) *Sexual Violence in Armed Conflict: Global Overview and Implications for the Security Sector*, Geneva, Switzerland: Geneva Centre for the Democratic Control of Armed Forces.

Cockburn, C. (2013) "War and Security, Women and Gender: An Overview of the Issues," *Gender and Development*, vol. 21, no.3, pp. 433–452.

ELI and UNEP (2013) *Land and Post-Conflict Peacebuilding*, Policy Brief #3.

FAO (2002) Multi Stakeholder Dialogue on Food, Security, Justice and Peace. *Conflict and food insecurity*. World Food Summit (www.fao.org/worldfoodsummit/msd/y6808e.htm) Access Date: June 16, 2014.

Goldstein, J.S. (2003) *War and Gender: How Gender Shapes the War System and Vice Versa*, Cambridge: Cambridge University Press.

Handrahan, L. (2004) "Conflict, Gender, Ethnicity and Post-Conflict Reconstruction," *Security Dialogue*, vol. 35, no. 4, pp. 429–445.

IDMC (2014) *IDPs Worldwide*, [Online], Available: www.internal-displacement.org/global-figures [19 June 2014].

IISS (2014) *Armed Conflict Database*, [Online], Available: https://acd.iiss.org/ [19 June 2014].

Jacobs, S., Jacobson, R. and Marchbank, J. (eds) (2000) *States of Conflict: Gender, Violence, and Resistance*, London: Zed Books.

Joireman, S. F., Sawyer, A. and Wilhoit, J. (2012) "A Different Way Home: Resettlement Patterns in Northern Uganda," *Political Geography*, vol. 31, no. 4, pp. 197–204.

Miranda, A. (2007) "Wartime Sexual Violence: Women's Human Rights and Questions of Masculinity," *Review of International Studies*, vol. 33, pp. 75–90, doi:10.1017/S0260210507007310.

Norwegian Refugee Council (2014) *Life Can Change: Securing Housing, Land and Property Rights for Displaced Women*, Oslo: Norwegian Refugee Council.

Peterman, A., Palermo, T., and Bredenkamp, C. (2011) "Estimates and Determinants of Sexual Violence Against Women in the Democratic Republic of Congo," *American Journal of Public Health*, vol. 101, no. 6, pp. 1060–1067. doi: 10.2105/AJPH.2010.300070.

Rehn, E. and Sirleaf, E. J. (2002) *Women, War, and Peace: The Independent Experts' Assessment on the Impact of Armed Conflict on Women and Women's Role in Peace-Building*, New York: UNIFEM.

Stern, M., and Nystrand, M. (2006) *Gender and Armed Conflict: An Overview*, Stockholm: Sida.

Wily, L. A. (2009) "Tackling Land Tenure in the Emergency to Development Transition in Post-Conflict States: From Restitution to Reform," in Pantuliano, S. (ed.) *Uncharted Territory: Land, Conflict and Humanitarian Action*, Rugby, Warwickshire: Practical Action Publishing Ltd.

World Bank (2014) *Voice and Agency: Empowering Women and Girls for Shared Prosperity*. Washington, D.C.: World Bank.

12 Reproducing patriarchy on resettled lands

A lost opportunity in reconstituting women's land rights in the Fast-Track Land Reform Program in Zimbabwe

Manase Kudzai Chiweshe

Introduction

This chapter examines how women's access to land is mediated by patriarchal systems on resettled land in Zimbabwe. It uses the complexities associated with inheritance of resettled land to highlight how land reform in Zimbabwe constitutes a lost opportunity to reframe women's land rights outside patriarchal norms and values. The Fast-Track Land Reform Program (FTLRP) has mainly privileged men as primary recipients of resettlement land, and the involvement of traditional authorities in the land reform process continues to marginalize women. This chapter focuses on the lack of clarity around the inheritance of land in the newly resettled areas. It uses case studies among A1[1] farmers in Mazowe to highlight how women and children are not adequately protected by land-ownership systems on resettlement land. Following independence in 1980, the Zimbabwean government sought to legally empower women by legislating a number of laws such as the Legal Age of Majority (1982) which meant that women—like men— now enjoyed majority status at 18 years of age. Such gains were, however, not enough as the state has increasingly become patriarchal in nature, as has been shown starkly in such as examples as the now seminal Magaya vs Magaya Supreme Court case in 1999, which once again reduced women to "junior males" without full inheritance rights.[2]

The gendered history of land-tenure change in Zimbabwe

Prior to colonization, Zimbabwe was a collection of different kingdoms and chiefdoms and comprised a variety of ethnic groups, such as the Shangani/Tsonga in the south-east, the Venda in the south, the Tonga in the north, the Kalanga and Ndebele in the south-west, the Karanga in the southern parts of the plateau, the Zezuru and Korekore in the northern and central parts, and finally, the Manyika and Ndau in the east.[3] In 1890 Cecil John Rhodes sent a group known as the "Pioneer Column" to invade Mashonaland, marking the beginning of white-settler occupation of Zimbabwe. The white settlers had wanted to take up gold mining but later turned to agriculture. This led to the widespread dispossession of black people from land, as occurred in the creation of the Gwaai and Shangani reserves after the 1893 invasion of the Ndebele Kingdom. By 1914, 3% of the population controlled 75% of the land, while blacks were restricted to a mere 23% of the worst land in designated reserves (Chitsike, 2003). The Land Apportionment Act of 1930 stated that white people were reserved 50.8% and black people 30% of available land mainly in poor soil areas. White farmers began large-scale commercial farming and livestock production.

Pre-colonial Zimbabwe was dominated by a communal system of landownership in which traditional leaders played an important role in land governance. Spirituality formed the basis of natural resource management; individual ownership was alien and instead traditional chiefs were responsible for land distribution. Land inheritance followed male lines and patriarchal families maintained ownership of land through burying their dead, performing rituals, and attaching spiritual value to the land. Women married into the families could not thus claim ownership in any case. However, Chakona (2011: 57) notes that women possessed access rights to land and there was a socially defined minimum amount of land on which to grow women's crops such as groundnuts. This small amount of land is called *tseu* in Shona and this practice is still prevalent on A1 farms in Mazowe where wives are given a small portion of the 6-hectare plot to plant their own crops. In colonial Zimbabwe, women's relationship to land further deteriorated as the government policies meant increased competition for scarce resources among the black population. Women, however, increasingly became *de facto* household heads as men left to seek paid employment in cities, farms, and mines. Wives were left behind to look after the land and protect male interests in it. Yet patriarchal laws of inheritance were maintained as male heirs were preferred. The colonial government turned women into minors as the law prohibited them from legally owning any property. Customary practices were integrated into colonial laws to further undermine women's access to land; for example, the Land Tenure Act of 1969 further marginalized women as it gave widows and divorcees only very small portions of family land that they were not permitted to transfer (Bhatasara, 2010).

From the mid 1960s, a second war of liberation was waged from two fronts by the Zimbabwe African National Union (ZANU) and the Zimbabwe African People's Union (ZAPU). The protracted struggle led to the Lancaster House Agreement, signed in London in 1979, which ushered in majority rule in Zimbabwe. Zimbabwe attained independence from British rule on 18 April 1980. The Lancaster House Agreement effectively insulated private property rights in land from government interference and, therefore, the exercise of sovereignty. When the new Zimbabwe African National Union–Patriotic Front (ZANU–PF) government led by Robert Mugabe came into power, it made land redistribution a high priority. It set itself a target to acquire 8.3 million hectares from white commercial farmers in order to resettle 162,000 black families during the period 1982–5. This target was not achieved, as the government was able to acquire only about 2.1 million hectares, on which about 60,000 families were resettled. The first phase of land reform was characterized by a lack of title to the land. The settlers were given permits but the land remained essentially in the hands of government. The permit provided right of use but the land could neither be sold nor used as collateral.

About 4,500 white commercial farmers owned roughly 15.5 million hectares (39% of the total land in the country). More than a million black farming households, on the other hand, had access to only about 16 million hectares. Land reform during the first two decades of independence was negligible and hopelessly inadequate as it did not significantly address issues of poverty alleviation and historical land inequities. Phase I of Zimbabwe's Land Reform and Resettlement Programme (LRRP) from 1980 to 1996 is marked by the first ten years of independence during which the Lancaster House Agreement was in effect, and the Economic Structural Adjustment Programme (ESAP) that was launched in October 1990. Both the Lancaster House Agreement and ESAP entailed significant global pressure on the post-colonial state, which meant that land reform in Zimbabwe before 2000 was largely externally driven (Chiweshe, 2011).

After independence there was hope among women—many of whom had participated in the war of liberation—that their rights, including access to land, would be upheld by the new government. This came to naught, however, as patriarchal forms of traditional leadership appeared not to have been undermined during the conflict, but in fact had emerged stronger (Alexander, 1993: 160). Zvobgo *et al.* (1994 cited in Chingarande (2004)) found that 87% of all permit holders in the resettlement areas after independence were married men, most of whom had not co-registered with their wives even though there was a provision in the Rural District Councils Act allowing for this. Gaidzanwa (1991) notes that this left women vulnerable upon divorce or widowhood as many lost their husband's land to male relations. Widows could, however, through a resettlement officer obtain land amounting to half the standard area allocated to males provided that their household was deemed to have enough labor to till the land without the husband. That said, Goebel (2005) notes that certain aspects of the resettlement policies and processes in the 1980s and 1990s created strategic spaces for some women, especially widows, to improve their access to arable land. On the death of a husband, for example, a resettlement widow was able to retain control of her homestead and fields, and to even have the name on the resettlement permit changed from the husband's to her own.

By early 2000 Zimbabwe was facing an unprecedented social and economic crisis. The deteriorating economic situation adversely impacted the pace of land reform. The Zimbabwe Congress of Trade Unions headed up a conglomeration of civil society organizations that challenged the ruling hegemony; further, the formation of the Movement for Democratic Change (MDC) in 1999 was the first real threat to ZANU–PF's political supremacy in Zimbabwe. The government had initiated a constitutional process culminating in a draft revised constitution which, among other things, reinforced the right to compulsory acquisition and qualified the existing market criteria for compensation for acquired land (permitting the state to pay only for improvements on the land). A referendum held in February 2000 led to an overwhelming defeat for government. The rejection of the draft constitution was a precursor to the land occupations later in 2000 and 2001, a period popularly known as *jambanja* (chaos) due to the violent nature of the process, which involved occupation of white-owned farms. The Zimbabwe National Liberation War Veterans Association (ZNLWA) was at the forefront of these occupations together with landless peasants, unemployed youths, and a few farmworkers. When leaders of the War Veterans Association and the ruling party realized by the end of March that white farmers were actively campaigning for the MDC, and encouraging farmworkers to do the same, farm occupations became more violent and were intertwined with the political campaign for the June 2000 parliamentary elections (Moyo, 2001: 318).

Land occupations were allegedly instigated by war veterans as part of ZANU–PF's official campaign strategy for these elections and as a response to the dwindling support for the party as shown by the results of the February 2000 referendum on the state-sponsored constitution (Alexander, 2006; Cousins, 2003; Hammar and Raftopoulos, 2003; Shaw, 2003; Zimbabwe Liberators Platform, 2004). Chaumba *et al.* (2003: 534), in describing the scene in Chiredzi soon after the land occupations, argue that this "ostensibly chaotic space was peopled by an anarchic bunch of self-proclaimed liberation war veterans, disaffected jobless and landless youths, and spirit mediums who appeared to be beyond the restraint of the police, and was even encouraged in their lawlessness by members of the governing ZANU (PF) party." And Masipula Sithole notes that the farm invasions and fast-track land reform involved a "normalizing of the abnormal."[4] Only a state which supported (in principle and strategically) such a policy of widespread violence could stand aside and watch as violent acts were perpetrated across the country. Forty people were killed in the wake of the farm invasions, 34 black Zimbabweans and six white farmers (Mitchell, 2001: 588). The exact number of occupied farms is contested but what is clear is that the occupations were national in character.

Women remained at the periphery of the land issue during 2000 as the land occupations (*jambanja*) at that time involved mostly men because of the perceived violence involved; a few women, were however, present. Women—especially those single, widowed, and divorced—were present in greater number in the land occupations that precipitated the FTLRP (Scoones *et al.*, 2010; Chiweshe, 2011), although their attendance was minimized by having to attend to customary domestic duties (Mutopo, 2011). The roles of women within this space mainly followed domestic roles as defined by Shona customs. Women would provide cooking, washing, and even sexual services to males and yet also be at the forefront of the land occupations. Men, however, tended to dominate institutional and social relations on occupied farms.

The land occupations were replaced by the government-initiated FTLRP in 2002 which sought to normalize the occupations. Fast-track land reform had multiple land-administration systems: old and new, *de jure* and *de facto*, and legal and extra-legal all working in tandem. This led to various contestations and confusion at the local, provincial, and national levels over control of the land-reform process (Matondi, 2008: 26). At the local level, there were committees called District Land Identification Committees (DLIC) which reported to the Provincial Land Identification Committee. The DLICs were chaired by District Administrators and made up of district-level government agencies and central state agriculture related ministries together with the army, police, war veterans, and traditional chiefs (Matondi, 2008: 26). These committees usurped the power of local councilors who, under the Rural District Council Act (1988), were the rightful land managers. The government commission headed by Charles Utete (2003) concedes that many new institutions at national, provincial, and district levels were hastily established to ensure that the process was fast-tracked, but this led to duplication of duties as well as conflicts over control of the process. The institutional problems were augmented by certain persons who, although lacking official authority, proceeded to allocate land mainly in districts near the main towns and cities (Utete, 2003: 31).

Even though the FTLRP did not have gender dimensions in its design, since it was a relocation program many felt that it held the potential to empower women with land control since these lands would not be governed under customary patrilineal systems. In practice, however, the patrilineal systems were reproduced on resettled lands and thus women did not benefit from increased control. It became business as usual. In Zimbabwe overall, few women accessed land in their own right under the fast-track system, the Utete Report (2003) claims that only 18% of beneficiaries were women (A1 women received 18%, A2 only 12%). This marginalization of women is disturbing in Zimbabwe given that they constitute more than 52% of the total population (National Gender Policy of Zimbabwe, 2004). The problem is that the debates on land reform had almost totally ignored gender, as Kesby (1999: 38) notes: "Unfortunately, debates about imminent land tenure reform are constructed around issues of race and economic efficiency, leaving those related to gender as a largely unanalyzed set of assumptions." At the same time, the resettlement program opened up a sanctuary for a class of women who had found it difficult to survive and possess land in their own right within the communal areas. Chaumba *et al.* (2003: 10) note that it is quite common for widows and divorcees to be accused of witchcraft and causing the death of husbands (particularly in AIDS cases), and they are sometimes even chased away by their in-laws.

A program such as that undertaken in Zimbabwe offered a chance to reconstitute gender patterns in land possession and access. This is because the land is provided by the state in such a way that there is no connection to patriarchal ancestors or lineage. Patriarchal cultural practices have, however, been replicated in the newly resettled areas. Hellum and Derman (2004: 1800) note that: "[FTLRP] never intended to respond to women's needs for secure tenure, access to support services or right to dispose fruit of their work. It was designed and implemented solely as an instrument to serve President Mugabe's desire to stay in power." Women's issues were thus secondary to the needs or functions of land reform. As such, gender or women's issues remained at the periphery with only the Women and Land Lobby Group speaking with any conviction on women's need for land. Such a situation has shown that land reform was not conducted with gender in mind and consequently the program is rightfully subject to serious criticism in terms of being "highly masculinized" (Bhatasara, 2010: 1) and for not challenging the entrenched existence of patriarchy in Zimbabwe.

Land, tradition, and culture are used as important bases in the construction and reinforcement of masculine domination. Hence, as Goebel (2005: 153) argues, the tenuousness of women's relationship to resettlement land must be understood through the lens of culture and ritual, particularly through the ways in which tradition "is deployed in the resettlement context ... [where] ... aspects of traditional culture such as family ancestor appeasement and bringing home the dead (*kurova guva*) are commonly practiced." These practices enact and express a cosmology that understands the environs as populated by and under the care of ancestral spirits. The practices also reinforce patrilineal control of land and hence distance women from the possibility of controlling land in their own right. Space for women in the newly resettled areas is thus limited and their influence is minimal in terms of decision-making. As Hellum and Derman (2004: 1796) point out: "There is a reason to believe that the ... strengthening of customary authorities in adjudication of family disputes and land allocation that has taken place through fast-track means a severe setback for women."

Fast-track land reform programs

The Constitutional Amendment Number 16 of 2000 led to mass land expropriation based on compulsory land acquisition in Zimbabwe. This initiated the Fast-Track Land Reform Program, which sought to speed up the identification for compulsory acquisition of no fewer than 5 million hectares of land for resettlement; to accelerate the planning and demarcation of acquired land and settler emplacement on this land; and to provide limited basic infrastructure and farmer support services. Officially, access to land was effected through the application process, with forms being submitted by applicants to the Ministry of Lands. Successful applicants were then invited to the survey and demarcation exercise on farms which was carried out by extension officers from the Department of Agricultural Technical and Extension Services. For some applicants who had participated in the land occupations, it was only a matter of regularizing their land possession; other occupiers, though, were resettled on farms that they had not originally occupied. In 2009, 10,816,886 hectares of land had been acquired for the resettlement of 162,161 families with 145,775 settled under A1 status and 16,386 under A2 status (Ministry of Lands and Rural Resettlement, 2009). The former 5,000 or so white farm owners were reduced in number to 400. Chakona (2011) notes that A2 farms are commercially focused holdings owned by either one resettled farmer as a complete unit or areas that have been subdivided into smaller commercially viable units among a number of A2 farmers. When applying for A2 farms, individuals had to prove their ability to finance operations by attaching bank statements or showing access to collateral for credit. A1 farms were geared towards the "decongestion" of communal areas and aimed at offering wider social access to land for subsistence. They are mainly divided into a large number of arable units (often around 6 hectares per household) along with a homestead and common grazing land.

In principle A2 farmers were to be offered 99-year leases with an option to purchase the land (Zikhali, 2008) but only a few have had access to such leases which still do not offer the option to transfer or liquidate the land. Most A2 farmers are thus in possession of permits known as "offer letters," as are the A1 farmers who have been offered limited land-use rights. Communal areas are governed by the Communal Lands Act, which states that all communal land is vested in the State President who has powers to permit its occupation and utilization in accordance with the Act. People inhabiting the land have only usufructuary rights, which may be lost at any given time without compensation. Section 24(4) of the Rural District Councils Act states that each settlement permit shall bear the names of all spouses. It also notes that unmarried women who are heads of households can have permits in their names, as can widows and girls or child-headed households. This is progress but in most cases such information is not known at the grassroots level; most people see land as a male possession and thus it is registered in the husband's name only.

In terms of land governance structures, under FTLRP all land issues pertaining to A1 farmers are handled by the District Lands Committee (DLC). In the Mazowe area, the committee is made up of the district administrator, Mazowe Rural District Council, representatives of key line ministries such as resettlement and agriculture, as well as the police, army, party officials (ZANU–PF), agricultural extension department and traditional chiefs. The various committee members tend to work in isolation, however, and do not collaborate on land administration. For example, chiefs are resentful of the DLC since they consider themselves— and indeed are recognized by law—as the custodians of the land, yet in reality are powerless to make any decision relating to it. This has led to situations where chiefs have acted alone to demarcate farms and give them to new beneficiaries without the committee's knowledge. A2 conflicts are dealt with by the Provincial Lands Committee (PLC), which is chaired by the provincial governor and is composed of provincial-level government leadership, district administrators, war veterans, police, Central Intelligence Organization and the ZANU–PF. The PLC can make decisions at provincial level which can be enforced at district level. Land-governance structures remain male-dominated and only a few women are involved in decision-making positions. Women are mostly disadvantaged by decisions which are based on patriarchal norms on landownership, including the belief that widows or daughters cannot inherit land as they can be married and the land will be lost by the extended family forever. The DLCs are ad hoc state creations that lack any statutory legal backing. Given that there were no legal statutes guiding their members' decision-making process, they had to rely on their own judgment and some central government guidelines. As a result, the committees were accused of being corrupt, unaccountable, unfair, and discriminatory (Matondi and Dekker, 2010).

Mazowe setting

At independence in 1980, Mazowe was prime agricultural land about 60 kilometers from Harare, Zimbabwe's capital city. It was owned and occupied mostly by white farmers, as only a handful of few black farmers were in a position to buy farms. Prior to 2000, only a very small amount of land had been redistributed, as the white farmers were reluctant to give up such prime land. Mazowe district is located in the Mashonaland Central province of Zimbabwe. The district has a total surface area of 453,892 hectares and a population of 205,693 people. The district lies in Natural Region II and III.[5] The high altitude areas closer to Harare generally receive higher and more reliable levels of rainfall (750–1000mm per annum) compared to low-altitude areas. The district has a long history of high yields of both food and industrial crops. Agriculture remains the mainstay of local livelihoods and the principal crops include maize, soya beans, and tobacco. Horticulture has, however, decreased since land reform. Animal-rearing also plays an important role and there are many dairy farms in the region, including President Mugabe's. Other major livelihood activities in the district include remittances especially from family members out of the country. Other activities are illegal but still attract many young people, such as panning for gold.

The high productivity levels achieved historically by white farmers meant that the district was targeted by many land-seekers under the FTLRP. The Mazowe area had arguably the highest applications for land—11,081 in 2004—due to its favorable climatic conditions, which support all forms of agricultural activities. Its proximity to Harare was another important factor, especially for senior government officials and politicians who were able to work in the city during the week and then escape to their farms at weekends. By 2005 there had been 5,000 beneficiaries of both the A1 and A2 schemes on 338 farms. While the cases noted in this chapter from Mazowe cannot be generalized across the country, they bear witness to an emerging pattern for how gender and inheritance intersect in areas without secure tenure. Numerous whole farms were taken over by government elites, although the exact number is a matter of conjecture. Forty indigenous (black)-owned farms as well as land owned by different institutions and international organizations were not affected by resettlement. Mazowe is divided into 29 wards, of which 1–13 are found in Chiweshe communal areas and 14–29 in the newly resettled areas.

Methods

This chapter is based on data collected during doctoral fieldwork and a research program carried out by the Centre for Rural Development focusing on land and livelihoods post-fast-track land reform in Zimbabwe. The fieldwork was conducted between 2007 and 2009 in Mazowe district with follow-up interviews in 2012.

The use of interviews and focus group discussions was important in highlighting the various experiences of farmers on fast-track farms with gendered dimensions of land administration. In total, eight focus group discussions were conducted, each with an average of sixteen participants. The participants in the five group discussions were a mixture of male and female plot holders, farmworkers, and spouses. Ten in-depth interviews were conducted with purposely sampled respondents who were selected from people involved in inheritance cases in the district. The Lands Officer was instrumental in sampling since he kept a list of all cases being heard by the District Lands Committee. The interviews and group discussions were conducted in the local language (Shona), recorded, and then transcribed and translated into English. The study also utilized key informant interviews with committee members of various institutions, traditional chiefs, councilors, council officers, and workers from various government ministries such as Lands, Agriculture, Education, Gender and Health.

Complexities of inheritance

The issue of inheritance elicits very emotional debates in patrilineal societies such as Zimbabwe. These are more intense in the newly resettled areas where the state is not sure of what tenure to provide the new beneficiaries. Offer letters given to A1 farmers and permits awarded to A2 farmers provide these successful applicants with only limited rights, which means that—for example, in the case of divorce—it is impossible for a couple to sell the land and share the proceeds. The land remains owned by the state, and thus inheritance issues associated with this land are complex and require a fully delineated policy that protects women and children. The cases outlined below represent a cross-section of some of land-inheritance experiences within the newly resettled areas. They are a microcosm of what is prevailing across the country; there is uncertainty over tenurial rights and the lack of a clear land policy has led to many women losing assess to assets and indeed their livelihoods. What is evident from the examples is that the customary systems of inheritance that originated in pre-colonial societies and which have been practiced over the years continue to dominate the newly resettled areas.

Case 1: *polygamous household*

There are no readily available statistics on the prevalence of polygamy in Mazowe or Zimbabwe in general. The practice is, however, fairly common within Mazowe. Polygamy adds an additional layer of complexity when it comes to the inheritance of land in newly resettled areas. This is because it is impossible to dispose of the land and share the proceeds as would happen in an officially recognized marital union. Bereaved spouses may compete to have their name registered on the offer letter since it is difficult to have more than one name listed thereon. According to the Lands Officer:

There is no policy on how to deal with polygamous situations when it comes to who takes over land when the husband dies. The District Lands Committee deals with such cases on their own merits.

At Bellavista Farm in Mazowe, a bitter fight over control of the land followed the death of a man with two wives. Both spouses tried to register their names with the District Lands Committee. The traditional leader at the farm noted that:

> This case was difficult for me as the headman. Both women had equal claims to the land yet we could not find a way to settle them together on the farm. The first idea was to help them come up with a sharing agreement, but they were not willing to work together.

The DLC suggesting giving the younger wife a plot elsewhere in the district. While this is an interesting way to deal with such conflicts, eventually there will not be any spare land to use as a solution in this way. Under customary law when a man with multiple wives dies, the eldest son is expected to inherit the estate but crucially, according to traditional practice, he must look after the whole family. The *Magaya* v. *Magaya* case referred to above shows how male inheritance is promoted under customary law. Under the 1997 Administration of Estates Act, in polygamous marriages, each wife keeps the home she was living in at the time of the husband's death, as well as the contents of that household. The remaining property is then divided between the wives, with the senior wife receiving the largest share, and all the children sharing two-thirds of whatever is left. This arrangement is difficult to implement in newly settled areas, however, since—as noted above—the land essentially belongs to the government. In such cases it is left to the discretion of the male-dominated DLCs to make a decision. Both the legal and customary systems thus offer very little protection to women living on newly resettled areas.

Another interesting dimension is the presence of split households and "small houses" on farms in Mazowe. Munyuki-Hungwe (2008) highlights that some men maintain girlfriends on the farms, while their wives stay in the city. These men visit these "small houses" at the weekend and return to their wives midweek. The women occupying these properties are not legally or culturally recognized wives and thus when the men die, do not have any claims to the land—even in the communal areas that use customary tenure systems. Under customary law, these women are not recognized at all in the event of the man dying. Relatives of the man or his wife can reclaim the property and remove the woman from the land. One male respondent in such a situation argued that:

> My wife does not like this farming business so I have another woman living and working on the farm. We are not married formally or traditionally, but my relatives know her and I know some of her people. I cannot marry a second wife for various personal reasons but I will keep her on the farm. She lacks for nothing and I am with her almost every weekend. My wife does not

know for sure that I have another "wife" at the farm, but what can I do? Hiring a manager is expensive and managers can be untrustworthy.

When asked what would happen to the women if he were to die, the respondent explained that it would be difficult for her to inherit any of the land since she did not have a marriage certificate or any other formal document to prove their union. In essence this "other" woman has no right whatsoever to the land, even though she has invested time and labor on into it over the years. This does, however, remain a complex issue, as outlined by a council official who a member of the local Lands Committee: "the question is how do you protect women who are essentially concubines? The law and society cannot recognize their rights in any way because our culture and law protects properly recognized and married women." This was further echoed by a woman respondent who notes: "how do you ask for protection for a prostitute who sleeps with another woman's husband?" Finding ways of protecting such women, particularly given the contribution they make to the farms they work on, remains difficult and requires innovative policy-making.

Case 2: mother versus son inheritance conflict

The majority of male plot holders feel that when they die, the land should remain in their families. They thus prefer to leave the land to their eldest sons, thereby avoiding the risk of losing the land should their wives ever remarry. Daughters are also not preferred heirs because once they marry, the land could be lost to their husband's family. At Kia Ora Farm, there was wrangling over land between a mother and son after the death of the father. The son managed to remove the mother from the farm, but she was left stranded and had to move back to her relatives' rural home. The son was himself later removed by another politically connected male farmer because he had not sought to change the name on the offer letter, which was still in his dead father's name. The DLC then resolved to give the son another plot. The mother was left landless and she had little recourse as the committee failed to hear her case. The lands officer indicated that the case for the mother was somehow not heard by the committee mainly because it kept being postponed until it was forgotten altogether. One female worker at the farm stated that: "women always get a raw deal when it comes to land. How can a son leave his own mother landless and nothing happen to him? It is not right." The son was a preferred heir as according to custom, the land would remain within the husband's "clan" or wider family. The committee in this way was adhering to patriarchal custom, which protects the eldest son's right to inherit property. Yet the 1997 Administration of Estates Act made the surviving spouse and children the primary beneficiaries of the deceased's estate, precisely to stop the abuses discussed above.

Zimbabwean law states that when a person dies, the family of the deceased should acquire a death certificate as a proof of death from the office of the registrar. To acquire this death certificate, the deceased's national identity card and a police/medical report are required. The DLC requires these items in order to change the name on the land permit, and women who fail to obtain them will be unable to register their name on the offer letter. Acquiring the documents is not straightforward, however, and women interviewed complained about the problems they faced with accessing their husbands' death certificates. Often they do not know how to go about it, and transport and accessibility costs compound the problem. When husbands die, they are expected to mourn for a period and this provides opportunity for other people to get their hands on the death certificate, which is also required for claiming benefits for husbands who used to work, such as unpaid salaries and pensions. A female respondent highlighted that: "getting the death certificate can be problematic, especially for women living in remote areas. Most only get to know about the death certificate when their husbands die." What is clear is how stated laws are disregarded in favor of customary norms which are disadvantageous to women.

Case 3: *divorce*

Divorce is another serious issue for both men and women when it comes to landownership in the newly resettled areas. In this case, it is impossible to share the land especially for A1 farmers who have only 6 hectares. Divorced women do not usually know they have rights to the land. On A1 farms there is a new wave of traditional leaders who are in many ways trying to impose the customs typical in communal areas. Such customs include—as happened in one case—allowing a man to remove from the land a wife he caught committing adultery. In Mazowe there are many anecdotal reports of women who were divorced and forced to leave the land with their husbands. A few married women in Mazowe managed to use various networks to access land and register it in their own names. Most women engaged in land reform, however, need to bring their husband's identity cards to apply and register for land. To understand how patriarchy protects male access to land, we can look to the example of a case in which the DLC was sympathetic to a husband who had been evicted by his spouse. At the Rivers Farm, a man divorced his wife, leaving her with four small children. The offer letter was in the name of the wife, who evicted him. In this case the committee agreed to allocate the man an A1 plot. What is interesting is that to date, the committee has never offered alternative land to a woman who has been evicted following divorce.

Matondi (2008) highlights that the majority of people questioned in a survey felt that in case of a divorce, the land should be kept by the plot-holder who, in most cases, is male. The law generally recognizes the equal sharing of property between divorcing spouses. Fast-track farms, however, offer a complex scenario in this regard. Under customary law, following a divorce, the wife usually leaves the husband's land because it belongs to his clan. In resettlement areas, however, the land belongs to the state. It cannot be shared or sold, and so in case of divorce it is difficult to protect the rights of women even when they are jointly registered on the lease or offer letter. Women I came across during my research argued that in relation to divorces, sharing would be the most appropriate way to deal with land, regardless of whose name was registered on the offer letter or lease. They noted a few cases of women who had divorced and lost everything even though they had worked with their former husbands for over seven years on the land. Divorced women often do not have sufficient access to the information they need to fight their corner; there are, however, a number of organizations in Zimbabwe offering free legal services to fight for compensation in divorce settings. The majority of women interviewed during this research are traditionally married and thus feel that without a formally registered union, they cannot claim land. Informal marriages are called "unregistered customary law unions" and arise in a situation where a man pays *lobola* for his wife. Under law, such unions are given limited recognition because it is not registered, but—crucially for women—they are recognized as a marriage for the purposes of inheritance.

Male participants, on the other land, believed that land belonged to the husband. One participant went on to add that: "women cannot claim or own land when they are married. This is not the city, where people have lost respect for our customs and traditions. In rural areas, the land belongs to the father and thus in case of divorce women should just leave the land." This view highlights one of the major problems facing women on fast-track farms. The men in various land-management institutions tend to revert to traditional customs to justify male dominance in landownership. Sithole (2002) argues that the traditional approach practiced in the communal areas has also been adopted in villagized resettlements where divorced women are sent back to her natal home where their fathers or brothers are expected to support them materially, including giving them land. Shona culture is based on a gendered construction of property ownership where valuable assets including land belong to the husband and the wife owns property in the kitchen (Chenaux-Repond, 1993).

Case 4: children with deceased parents (orphans)

There are cases where the land authorities have had to intervene in inheritance issues in order to protect rights of children. Children under 18 years of age are usually put under the care of relatives in the event that both parents die. What usually happens is that relatives of the father take over the property and children lose their claim to property. One such example occurred at Three Sisters Farm, where the deceased father's brother, who was supposed to be responsible for his nieces and nephews, was failing to look after their interests. The District Lands Committee resolved to transfer the plot to the name of the deceased's eldest child. In patriarchal societies, when both parents die children are left under the guidance of the father's brother. The brother takes over the property which he is supposed to use to care for the children but in some instances this does not happen. In the above case, some relatives wisely flagged up the situation to the DLC but in many instances such cases go unreported. Land should be left in the name of the children, who are supposed to have a guardian until they come of age. According to one elderly respondent, the prevailing cultural system did not allow for social orphans, meaning that when biological parents die, children were given another social father. In Shona, this is called "*musarapavana*" (one who is left with the children). He further notes: "the idea behind the practice was to ensure children were protected and taken care of. Nowadays, people are more interested in the property of the deceased and not the children. If the parents are poor, no one wants to be '*musarapavana*' because there is nothing to benefit from; that is why we see the emergence of so many child-headed households." In resettlement areas, this system means that the "*musarapavana*" will be in charge of the land and in some cases, as noted above, may actually attempt to take over the land. Young children without any knowledge about death certificates or land committees are therefore unable to defend their right to land.

Conclusion

The chapter highlights how women's property rights are experienced and practiced in inheritance cases on fast-track farms in Zimbabwe. The tenurial system in the resettlement areas in Zimbabwe does not adequately protect vulnerable groups especially women and children. Experiences in Mazowe show that in many cases women lose land to male relatives and the institutional structures responsible for land management tend to entrench male landownership. Women's access to land is mediated mainly through their patriarchal relations, and this makes it likely that they will lose land in inheritance cases. Examples drawn from Mazowe suggest that there is a need for a tenure system that protects women and children in patriarchal societies. Access to land without effective ownership is not enough. Women and men in newly resettled areas largely lack the legal literacy required to understand how various forms of marriage interrelate with the diverse baskets of rights entailed in the tenure system in place following the Fast-Track Land Reform Program. This chapter concludes that while land reform in Zimbabwe had the potential to reconstitute women's land rights, patriarchal norms of landownership have in fact been transplanted to fast-track farms.

Notes

1   Under the A1 Model, each household is allocated 6 hectares of arable land. Common land such as grazing land, woodlots, and water points are shared by the resettlement group. The A2 Model ranges from small-scale plots of about 15 hectares to large-scale areas of over 200 hectares.
2   Venia Magaya went to the Supreme Court to contest the decision of a lower court to make her younger half brother rightful heir after the death of her father. She lost her house but the court held that with regard to intestate succession, the custom of male preference for heirship, even when there is senior female offspring, must be applied (adopted from www1.umn.edu/humanrts/iwraw/ww12-3-99.html accessed 8 April 2014).
3   See www.zim.gov.zw/index.php/zimbabwe-in-brief/history-of-zimbabwe (accessed 14 March 2010) for more information on the history of Zimbabwe

4   Violence, arson, destruction of property, and general lawlessness became accepted as everyday occurrences. See Masipula Sithole, "Public Eye," *Financial Gazette*, 28 March 2001.
5   Zimbabwe is divided into five agro-ecological regions based on the rainfall regime, soil quality, and vegetation among other factors. The quality of the land resource declines from Natural Region (NR) I through to NR V.

References

Alexander, J. (1993) "Things fall apart. The centre can hold: Processes of post-war political change in Zimbabwe's rural areas," in Laurids S. Lauriden, (ed.) *Bringing Institutions Back in the Role of Institutions in Civil Society, State and Economy*, IDS Occasional Paper No. 8, Roskilde University, pp. 131–161.

Alexander, J. (2006) *The Unsettled Land: State Making and Politics of Land in Zimbabwe 1893–2003*, Harare: Weaver Press.

Bhatasara, S. (2010) *Land Reform and Diminishing Spaces for Women in Zimbabwe: A Gender Analysis of the Socio-economic and Political Consequences of the Fast Track Land Reform Programme*, MSc thesis, Maastricht Graduate School of Governance, Netherlands.

Chakona, L. (2011) *Fast Track Land Reform Programme and Women in Goromonzi District, Zimbabwe*, MA thesis, Rhodes University, SA.

Chaumba, J., Scoones, I. and Woolmer, W. (2003) "From *Jambanja* to Planning: The Reassertion of Technocracy in Land Reform in South-Eastern Zimbabwe?" *Journal of Modern African Studies*, vol. 41, no. 4, pp. 533–554.

Chenaux-Repond, M. (1993) *Gender Biased Land-Use Rights in Model A Resettlement Schemes of Mashonaland, Zimbabwe*, Harare: Rubecon Zimbabwe.

Chingarande, S.D. (2004) *Women and Access to Land in the Context of the Fast Track Land Reform Programme*, Policy Brief Prepared for The African Institute for Agrarian Studies (AIAS), www.zpt.co.zw/docs/women.pdf (accessed 23 June 2008).

Chiweshe M. (2011) *Farm Level Institutions in Emergent Communities in Post-fast track Zimbabwe: Case of Mazowe District*, PhD thesis, Rhodes University, SA.

Cousins, B. (2003) "The Zimbabwe Crisis in Its Wider Context: The Politics of Land, Democracy and Development in Southern Africa," in Hammar, A., Raftopoulos, B. and Jensen, S. (eds) *Zimbabwe's Unfinished Business: Rethinking Land, State and Nation in the Context of Crisis*. Harare: Weaver Press.

Derman, B., and Hellum, A. (2007) "Livelihood Rights Perspective on Water Reform: Reflections on Rural Zimbabwe," *Land Use Policy Review*, vol. 24, pp. 664–673.

Gaidzanwa, R.B. (1991) *Promised Land: Towards a Land Policy for Zimbabwe*, MA thesis, Institute of Social Studies, The Hague.

Goebel, A. (2005) "Zimbabwe: A Policy Review Perspective on Water Reform: Reflect," *Gender, Place and Culture*, vol. 12, no. 2, p. 145.

Hammar, A. and Raftopoulos, B. (2003) "Introduction," in Hammar, A., Raftopoulos, B. and Jensen, S. (eds) *Zimbabwe's Unfinished Business: Rethinking Land, State and Nation in the Context of Crisis*. Harare: Weaver Press.

Hellum, A. and Derman, B. (2004) "Land reform and Human Rights in Contemporary Zimbabwe: Balancing Individual and Social Justice through an Integrated Human Rights Framework," *World Development*, vol. 32 no. 10, pp. 1785–1805.

Kesby, M. (1999) "Locating and Dislocating Gender in Rural Zimbabwe: The Making of Space and the Texturing of Bodies," *Gender, Place and Culture*, vol. 6, no. 1, pp. 27–47

Matondi, P.B and Dekker, M. (2010) *Land Rights and Tenure Security in Zimbabwe: The Case of Zimbabwe and Programme*, Land Academy, Netherlands.

Matondi, P.B. (2008) *The Question of Tenure and Land Rights in Newly Areas in Mazowe*, Land and Livelihoods Programme Working Paper, Centre for Rural Development.

Ministry of Lands and Rural Resettlement. (2009) *Land Policy Review and Land Audit: Options and Strategy*, A Synthesis of the Ministry of Lands and Rural Resettlement Planning Retreat held Caribbea Bay Hotel, Kariba, 11th–13th June.

Mitchell, T.W. (2001) "The Land Crisis in Zimbabwe: Getting Beyond the Myopic Focus upon Black & White," *Indiana University International and Comparative Law Review*, https://media.law.wisc.edu/m/mywzj/thomas_mitchell.zimbabwe_article.pdf (accessed 4 August 2010).

Moyo, S. (2001) "The Land Occupation Movement and Democratisation in Zimbabwe: Contradictions of Neo-liberalism," *Journal of International Studies*, vol. 30, no. 2, pp. 311–330.

Munyuki-Hungwe, M.N. (2008) *Challenges in Constructing Social Space in Newly Resettled Areas in Mazowe: Empirical Evidence from Mazowe*, Land and Livelihoods Programme Working Paper, Centre for Rural Development.

Mutopo, P. (2011) "Women's Struggles to Access and Control Land and Livelihoods after Fast Track Land Reform in Mwenezi District, Zimbabwe," *Journal of Peasant Studies*, vol. 38, no. 5, pp. 1021–46.

Scoones I., Marongwe N., Mavedzenge B., Mahenene J., Murimbarimba F., and Sukume C. (2010) *Zimbabweukume Cand Sukumeyths and Realities*, London: James Currey.

Selby, A. (2006) *Commercial Farmers and the State: Interest Group Politics and Land Reform in Zimbabwe*, DPhil thesis, Oxford University: Oxford.

Shaw, W. H. (2003) "They Stole our Land: Debating the Expropriation of White Farms in Zimbabwe," *Journal of Modern African Studies*, vol. 41, no. 1, pp. 75-89

Sithole, E. (2002) *A Gender Analysis of Agrarian Laws in Zimbabwe: A Report*, Harare: Women and Land in Zimbabwe.

Utete, C. M.B. (2003) *Report of the Presidential Land Review Committee on the Implementation of the Fast Track Land Reform Programme, 2000–2002*, Harare: Government of Zimbabwe.

Zikhali, P, (2008) *Land Reform, Trust and Natural Resources Management in Africa*, PhD thesis No. 178. Gothenburg, University of Gothenburg.

Zimbabwe Liberators Platform. (2004) "What Happened to Our Dream?" in D. Harold-Barry (ed.) *Zimbabwe the Past Is the Future*, Harare: Weaver Press.

13 Resigning their rights?

Impediments to women's property ownership in Kosovo

Sandra F. Joireman

Introduction[1]

Kosovo is one of the newest countries in the world. It achieved independence in 2008 and emerged from international supervision in 2012. As a new country, it has faced the challenge of establishing the appropriate foundations for a flourishing economy through the creation and enforcement of property rights. With the incentive of potential European Union membership in the future, Kosovo has shown significant progress in developing laws that are EU compliant. However, the enforcement of these laws often falls short. One of the areas in which there is an identifiable gap between law and practice is in the area of women's property rights.

Property rights are a particularly important microfoundation for economic growth and a vibrant economy, all the more so in post-conflict settings where violence and population displacement have interrupted normal economic activity. In Kosovo there is a dual challenge with regard to property rights as political violence occurred in the midst of a transition from communist rule, leaving a legacy of uncertain property issues that have taken the better part of the past decade to sort through, and some of which remain unresolved (Smit, 2012). Key among these highly charged political issues are: the restoration of property to the Serbian minority population who lived in Kosovo prior to the war; privatization of formerly socially owned properties; legalizing the many illegally constructed buildings in Pristina; and the resolution of disputes over large government properties whose ownership is contested between Serbia and Kosovo, such as the Trepça mine. These are legally complex issues, some involving human rights concerns, in which the solutions are not always obvious nor the mechanisms in place for implementation. Women's property ownership in Kosovo is not as legally complex, nor is the enforcement process unclear. The steps to achieving women's property rights are unambiguous. Yet there is little compliance with the law regarding women's property rights and without the enforcement of these rights there are significant barriers to women's economic activity. If women are unable to own property in their own names, it is difficult for them to start businesses, invest in property, or to use their homes as a source of capital. In Kosovo, where there are limited formal employment opportunities, impediments to women's property ownership makes the creation of self-employment more difficult. Women's engagement in the economy is a key component of economic growth and legal recognition of their property rights is a first step towards this goal (Hallward-Driemeier and Hasan, 2013; Joireman, 2011).

This chapter addresses the challenges of establishing clear property rights for women in Kosovo. It proceeds in three parts. The first section addresses women's property rights in Kosovo from a comparative perspective, examining the situation of women in Kosovo vis-à-vis women in other former Yugoslav republics. The second part examines why there is a gap between the egalitarian property law and unequal enforcement practices in Kosovo. The third part discusses opportunities to shift from *de jure* articulation of egalitarian property rights to the *de facto* enforcement of them. The majority of the people who suffer from the lack of enforcement of property law are women because of a resurgence in traditional patterns of social organization that accompanied the conflict with Serbia and the poor functioning of the courts. Yet men are also affected by the lack of enforcement of existing property law and this will be explicitly addressed in the analysis.

Research for this chapter was conducted over four months in 2012 and 2013 when I was living in Kosovo and conducting research on property rights. Although some secondary sources are used, most of the data for this chapter comes from 48 interviews I conducted in Kosovo during that time. Interviews on the issues of property rights and legal processes were conducted in Pristina and four different municipalities in Kosovo: Ferizaj/Uroševac, Klinë/Klina, Gračanica/Graçanicë, and Rahovec/Orahovac. The semi-structured interviews were with legal professionals, government officials at the state and municipal levels, academics, and people working with nongovernmental and intergovernmental organizations.

Kosovo and the Western Balkans

Kosovo's independence was the last severing of territory from what used to be the state of Yugoslavia. However, unlike some of the countries that left the former Yugoslavia early (Slovenia) or peacefully (Montenegro), Kosovo's independence was the result of violence and has been contested. Factions in Kosovo began agitating for greater autonomy as early as 1981. By 1989 their efforts resulted in a strong backlash from the Serbian-controlled government, which rescinded all of Kosovo's autonomy in the areas of security, justice, defense, and planning. Removing the territory's already limited authority led to further riots and strikes by ethnic Albanians living in Kosovo. The predominantly Serbian police responded to these demonstrations violently. In April 1990, Kosovo's autonomy was officially revoked and it was ruled directly by the rump Yugoslavian state; later that year the Kosovar Assembly was formally dissolved. Between 1990 and 1999 the Albanian population protested against a school curriculum in the Serbian language, the dismissal of Albanians from government jobs, and violations of human rights. By 1998 what had been a peaceful movement for autonomy gave way to organized violence as a war for Kosovo's independence began. NATO became engaged in 1999, bombing Serbia and forcing it to abandon efforts to control Kosovo. This allowed Kosovo to establish *de facto* autonomy. While the institutions of the state were being created, Kosovo was administered by the United Nations via the United Nations Interim Administration Mission in Kosovo (UNMIK). In 2008 Kosovo declared independence, much to the opposition of the Serbian state which still does not formally recognize it. Kosovo's population is 92% ethnic Albanian; the remainder of the population is composed of Serbs, Roma, Ashkali, Egyptian, and Bosniaks.

Beginning in 2012, talks between Serbia and Kosovo regarding their economic and political interactions commenced. The talks, brokered by Catherine Ashton, the High Representative of the European Union for Foreign Affairs and Security Policy, were a result of pressure from the EU regarding the normalization of Kosovo's status as a condition for considering Serbia as a candidate state for EU accession. In April 2013, Kosovo and Serbia signed an agreement on the normalization of relations, which was an implicit recognition of the sovereignty of the state of Kosovo.

Kosovo shares a political history with its neighbors Serbia, Montenegro, and the Former Yugoslav Republic of Macedonia (hereafter Macedonia FYR), all of which were under the control of the Ottoman Empire and subsequently Yugoslav states. Kosovo also shares an anticipated political future with its neighbors. All of the Western Balkan states, including Albania, can apply for EU membership. EU membership is desirable for these countries due to the increased opportunities for economic engagement and freedom of movement for their citizens. Economically, Kosovo is the poorest country in Europe with unemployment at 35%, a GDP per capita around $3,500, and 35% of the population in poverty (Kosovo Agency of Statistics, 2013). Two-thirds of the population resides in rural areas and agriculture is the main source of employment.

Women's property rights in the former Yugoslavia

In the former Yugoslavia, equal property rights for women were established in the post-World War II era when laws on the equal inheritance of male and female children were put in place. Women were additionally afforded co-ownership of marital property. Although there had been some efforts towards increased women's rights in Yugoslavia before World War II, it was not until 1946 that gender equality was explicitly recorded in the Constitution of the Socialist Federal Republic of Yugoslavia. This victory in women's rights was due largely to the role women played in the antifascist resistance effort (Bonfiglioli, 2012). Women "questioned patriarchal laws that excluded women from land inheritance" and "voice[d] their concerns regarding women's limited legal property rights" (Daskalova, 2008: 190). At this point in time, private property was not as important because of the socialist state and the limited property rights to capital it supported. Unfortunately, we have no statistics from this period for the area that is now Kosovo regarding women's property ownership.

When the Yugoslav state began to crumble in the early 1990s, the new countries that were formed began the transition from socialism to capitalism.

Cohen and Lampe (2011: 194) note that "women were the biggest 'transition losers' throughout the region, suffering from a severely deteriorating economic climate and the loss of the previously substantial welfare measures provided by the various Communist regimes." That said, the successor states by and large maintained egalitarian legislation regarding property for women. This is true both with regard to inheritance law and marital property arrangements. Yet, despite a shared history of egalitarian property law with its former Yugoslavian neighbors, Kosovo has lower rates of business and property ownership for women than other former Yugoslav states. Women's economic engagement is also lower than Kosovo's near neighbors with different political histories, as shown in Table 13.1.

Outside of the business sector, rates of property ownership for Kosovar women are lower than those of their counterparts in other Yugoslav successor states. In Serbia, women own 37% of total real property (houses and land); in some areas, the proportion is as high as 50% (Muhamet Brajshori et al., 2012), whereas in Kosovo the percentage of property owned by women is only 8% (USAID, 2013: 7). It is interesting to note that in the Albanian majority area of Serbia, the Presevo Valley, property ownership for women is also low at 13% (Brajshori et al., 2012).

None of these inequalities can be explained by law, which under the current regimes in both Serbia and Kosovo is egalitarian. There is a puzzle here: how is it that Kosovo is so different from its neighbor states with which it has a shared history? The gap between law and practice in the Kosovar case is significant and in need of explanation.

Table 13.1 Economic engagement of women in the Balkans

	Percent of firms with female ownership, 2009	Percentage of firms with female top manager, 2009	Human Development Index	Gender Inequality Index
Kosovo	10.9	0.3	unavailable	unavailable
Macedonia FYR	36.4	19.1	78	23
Montenegro	26.0	24.5	54	unavailable
Serbia	28.8	15.9	59	unavailable
Bosnia and Herzegovina	32.8	13.5	74	unavailable
Bulgaria	33.9	25.8	55	40
Romania	47.9	24.7	50	55
Hungary	42.4	13.8	38	39
Albania	unavailable	unavailable	70	41

Egalitarian law regarding property rights and inheritance

From the beginning of the legislative project to create an independent political identity and laws for Kosovo, the possibility of future EU membership has influenced the process in both direct and indirect ways. Directly, different European countries have provided advisers and consultants in a variety of areas. During the period of UNMIK administration, there were EU experts present in the assembly committees of the Provisional Institutions of Self-Government (PISG). There was also considerable EU involvement in 'Pillar 4' issues of reconstruction and development, such as privatization, banking, and economic development. When independence was declared in 2008, the European Union launched EULEX, the European Rule of Law Initiative, which focuses efforts on assisting Kosovo in its integration into Europe.

In addition to this direct influence, there has also been an indirect or subtle role played by the future of a Kosovar accession process to the European Union: "On a practical level, all the experience of the last 15 years indicates that it is more efficient to move in the European direction from the beginning, than to have to revise laws and restructure institutions later" (Ben-Gera *et al.*, 2005: 6). Even if it is not specifically on the agenda at any given point in time, EU membership is in the minds of government and policy-makers in Kosovo.

Andrea Spehar has studied the role of the EU in creating legislation regarding gender equality in both Croatia and Macedonia. She observes that "the EU gender strategy in Croatia and Macedonia has shown serious limits. Among these—and perhaps the most fundamental—is the strong contrast between stated goals and their actual implementation" (Spehar, 2012: 363). Indeed, there appears to be a trend in the Western Balkans of countries adopting gender equal laws in order to be in compliance with the EU and then struggling greatly with their implementation (Ler Sofronic *et al.*, 2006; Metani and Omari, 2006; Šmid, 2006). Poor compliance with gender equality standards in the Western Balkans has been recognized by the EU (Committee on Women's Rights and Gender Equality, 2013). Currently, Kosovo is following suit, with egalitarian law in place but poor implementation.

There are three important laws protecting women's property rights in Kosovo, all of which were passed by the Assembly in 2004 while Kosovo was under the supervision of UNMIK: the Law on Gender Equality; the Inheritance Law; and the Family Law. Laws created during the UNMIK administration are modern, egalitarian, and intentionally consistent with European Union requirements. As noted above, Kosovo's aspiration to eventually be a part of the European Union has been a factor in legal development since its declaration of independence.

The Law on Gender Equality sets overarching goals for society. Some sections are aspirational, to be sure, but women's property rights are clearly protected. Section 12.1 reads "The economical [*sic*], financial, employment and social welfare legislation and the macroeconomic, micro-economic, financial and privatization programs including the right of heritage and property, loans and natural resources shall enable the equal and full participation of both females and males" (Provisional Institutions of Self-Government, 2004b). While this is the general rubric of economic equality for women, specific protections are enumerated, including the joint ownership of property acquired during marriage.

The Family Law is consistent with the Law on Gender Equality in protecting the rights of women to consent to marriage, establishing joint ownership of property acquired during the marriage, and the division of property after divorce (Provisional Institutions of Self-Government, 2004a). The last law that is pertinent to women's property ownership in Kosovo is the Inheritance Law. It too is egalitarian, naming spouses and children as constituent members of the first 'rank' of inheritors when a person dies intestate. The estate must be divided equally between them. However, a spouse does not have a claim to any family property bequeathed to the dead spouse by his or her parents or family; that property goes to the children alone or to the siblings of the deceased (Provisional Institutions of Self-Government, 2004c).

The critical aspect of the inheritance law that has the greatest impact on women's property issues is the right to renouncement in Section 130.1. The law states that "The heir may renounce the inheritance by a statement made to the court, until the inheritance proceedings are completed" (Provisional Institutions of Self-Government, 2004c). Although the provision for the renunciation of inheritance rights is a standard part of most inheritance or probate law, it is rarely used; if it is invoked, it is usually for very specific reasons. For example, a person might renounce an inheritance if they felt that a particular plot of land or immovable property would cost them more in terms of taxation and upkeep than it was actually worth. In Kosovo, renunciation of inheritance rights is frequently invoked, but not for reasons of taxation or because of the onerous burden of particular properties. Instead, it is most frequently used by female inheritors to 'refuse' or 'resign' their inheritance rights so as to allow patrilineal secession of family resources and to increase the percentage of resources left to their brothers or sons. It is the use and interpretation of this legal guarantee that has become problematic in the Kosovar case.

Enforcement of property and inheritance law

As we have seen law regarding equality of property rights exists in Kosovo, yet so too do social norms that subvert the law. In this section, the issue of why renunciation of inheritance occurs will be addressed. The facile explanation is cultural norms. Yet there is clearly more at play than culture alone, as many women assert a desire to inherit property. I will below examine how cultural practices became embedded within a resurgent nationalism in the context of Kosovo's struggle for independence and worked to exclude women from inheritance. However, this is only part of the story. As important as culture and nationalism are in the exclusion of women from inheritance, is the court system that facilitates the exclusion of female heirs, and indeed some male heirs, from their share of family property.

Part of the reason for the disparity in property rights is that Albanian tradition, including a written customary law, provides for both patrilineal inheritance and patrilocal residence. In Albanian customary law, which has been codified in written form since 1933, inheritance follows the male line, with property going to a man's children and natal family after his death, rather than to his widow.[2] Traditionally, it is only the male children who inherit family property. Houses and land are held in the name of the oldest male relative. Such is the power of the traditional culture that often immovable property is retained in the name of a male relative long-since dead. Few fear the loss or expropriation of family land that has been held for generations and it is not viewed as worth the trouble to transfer the title of the property when someone dies.[3] It is traditional practice for extended families to live together in a large family home, with each of the brothers getting a floor, or a portion of the house for themselves and their family. Of course, in metropolitan areas these traditional patterns of living are less likely to occur. Yet, even in cities and larger towns, one can find rows of semi-detached houses, each one owned by a different brother, or extended families living together in multi-family dwellings. In Kosovo, as elsewhere, modernity and tradition coexist.

One reason women refuse inheritance rights is that, from a traditional perspective, it is an embarrassment for women to bring property into their marriages. It implies that a woman's husband cannot adequately provide for his wife. A woman claiming inheritance rights would also bring shame to her natal family as it appears that she does not sufficiently value her family, and in particular her brothers, who will lose a portion of their inheritance if it goes to their sister(s). Sisters and brothers are supposed to support one another, with brothers providing social and political support to their sisters and the sisters deferring their property rights to their brothers. The Albanian customary legal code, the *Kanun*, states that: "In the event of the inheritor being female, then a man must be sought up to the 12th remove so that this property is not left to a woman" (Fox, 1989). Leaving property to women means transferring it outside of the lineage.

'Shame' and 'embarrassment' are terms frequently used by women when they describe keeping or inheriting family property (Brajshori *et al.*, 2012; 1107 2012; 1112 2012). In a film created by the European Rule of Law Mission to Kosovo to educate women about their inheritance rights and aptly named *Asking for Inheritance – Asking for Trouble*, one of the characters states, "I would shame my family if I demanded my equal share of property" (European Union Rule of Law Mission, 2011). When this film was shown in Kosovo as part of a women's educational program on property rights, some of those attending became angry with the organizer of the workshop and accused her of trying to create problems in their families (11713 2013).

There is a deeper question as to where these cultural norms come from and why they are so persistent in Kosovo. There are strong differentiated cultural gender norms among the Albanian population of Kosovo, which—as noted above—is approximately 90% of the overall population. One interpretation is that the 'refusal' of inheritance is a performance of nationalist identity and articulation of cultural norms.[4] These cultural norms have been transformed since the era when Kosovo was a part of the former Yugoslavia and have been intertwined with the nationalism that led to Kosovo's independence. When Yugoslavia began to disintegrate in the early 1990s, Kosovo was left as part of Serbia and Montenegro. This compounded problems already in place for the largely Albanian population in Kosovo, which had been progressively excluded from government jobs and educational opportunities since the early 1980s. Albanians responded to social and economic exclusion by establishing parallel systems for education and healthcare. During this era, there was a resurgence of traditionalism that was manifest in a number of different ways, one of which was the greater reliance on the extended family and the strengthening of patriarchal structures within the home and society. As state control over Kosovo weakened and the war began, there were few available mechanisms of societal control and organization. This led to an increased reliance on Albanian customary law to address conflicts (Mustafa and Young, 2008). This resurgence of cultural organizational norms included traditional gender roles. Writing just following the war, at the height of Albanian nationalism in Kosovo, Julie Mertus (1999: 174) noted, "Although a handful of Albanian women's groups now exist in Kosovo, those who have publically attempted to reexamine and redefine women's gender roles in Kosovar society have risked being harshly criticized by their own community as undermining the Albanian national struggle."

With the retraditionalization that occurred in the 1990s in opposition to the Serbian state, relying on family and traditional institutions was a political statement as well as an economic necessity because of the limited opportunities for Albanians to work outside of agriculture or the alternative health and educational institutions they had established. Now, with the independence of Kosovo, the resurgence of cultural traditions to regulate both family and economic life is no longer necessary, but still present.

Supplementing the cultural explanation

In this description of the reasons why women refuse their inheritance, the narrative is one of overlapping familial and national allegiances. Women are choosing to reject property in a performance of Albanian identity. If this is the case, and culture is the sole reason why women have such low levels of property ownership, then public opinion surveys of women should also demonstrate a resounding refusal to inherit property. In the best of all worlds, public opinion survey data would be widely available for this issue, but it is not. However, there has been one large survey of 1,050 women dispersed across the country. In this survey women were asked about their preferences for property inheritance among their own children and for themselves. Vuniqi and Halimi found that 75% of surveyed women think that both male and female children should inherit equally (Vuniqi and Halimi, 2011: 36). If it is indeed the case that women believe that inheritance should be for both boys and girls, then the explanation cannot be simply an issue of choice influenced by cultural norms.

When the same survey asked women if the law supported equal inheritance rights for male and female children (which it does), 41% believed that law did not apply to inheritance issues. Instead, they believed inheritance issues were governed by tradition alone (Vuniqi and Halimi, 2011: 19). These survey results are echoed in the work of NORMA, the women lawyers' association of Kosovo. Some of the work that NORMA does is directed at creating awareness of the law so that women are cognizant of the fact that they do have rights to property. This may make them less likely to resign or refuse their rights when the time comes.

If women are not actually choosing to refuse property and inheritance rights (despite the large numbers of them that do so), there are at least two other factors that may be at play: the coercion of family members; and a process of legal exclusion in the courts preventing women from claiming their property rights. Families can encourage women to assign their property rights to their brothers or other male relatives. There is ample anecdotal evidence of this, and that even young girls are encouraged to refuse their inheritance rights before the court. While we might not be surprised that families are acting in the *perceived* interest of the whole family unit rather than the individual, what is surprising and unlawful is that local courts will affirm what are obviously coerced refusals of rights, such as those coming from minor children (11713 2013). These anecdotal reports suggest that there may be problems in the way the court processes inheritance cases and women's property rights in general. Women are skeptical of the gender sensitivity of judicial institutions when dealing with cases pertaining to property and inheritance (Vuniqi and Halimi, 2011: 48). An investigation into the processes that courts are using suggests that some of this skepticism is justified.

Implementation of law

Legally there are a number of issues in the application of the Inheritance Law that create problems for women claiming their property rights. These issues fall into several categories: knowledge, process, and implementation.

With regards to knowledge, as noted in the survey, it is clear that women do not always know that they are legally entitled to inherit from their parents, and even from their spouses. The fact that female inheritance is unusual makes it possible for ignorance of the law to be perpetuated among those who would have no occasion to actually read the law or seek information.

The second category of legal impediments to women's inheritance of property has to do with the process followed by the courts. Few people make wills in Kosovo, and intestate inheritance cases follow the 2004 Inheritance Law. The first step in the inheritance process is the issuance of a death certificate. Thereafter, any heir of the deceased may renounce their inheritance. Agreements made among family members as to the disposition of property are recognized by the court as they facilitate the rapid distribution of the property and minimize the role that the courts must take in dividing resources. While it is by law optional for families to develop these agreements in the case of intestate heirs, in practice, judges presiding over inheritance cases ask the family to come up with a 'prior agreement' that the judge can use in distributing the estate (1207 2012). The creation of prior agreements leaves ample opportunity for women to renounce their inheritance rights by choice or to be pressured by family members into doing so. It is common for prior agreements to list only male heirs. According to the 2004 Law on Gender Equality in Kosovo, Section 16.13, "Inheritors, females and males can obtain and can renounce his/her share, after the registration of their inherited property" (Provisional Institutions of Self-Government, 2004b). In practice, renunciation of rights is occurring *before* the registration of the inherited property which makes it much easier to ignore the property rights of female heir (1207 2012).

The third category of legal impediment in Kosovo is implementation. Even if female heirs are recognized legally, having a court decision implemented in opposition to the desires of the family members presents an additional challenge, as does a need for legal knowledge. These problems of court process are exacerbated by some unusual problems that exist in Kosovo because of its post-conflict situation. Clearly, ascertaining who the legal heirs ought to be would go a long way towards rectifying issues of women's inheritance and property rights. An investigation into who the legal heirs should be would show whether sisters or daughters had been excluded in a prior agreement. This could take place through a check of the civil birth registers held by the municipalities. Unfortunately, these civil registers are not completely accurate. When the war in Kosovo occurred in 1999, Serbian authorities removed the civil and property registers from Kosovo to Serbia, and the original documents remain there. In 2012, as talks began between Kosovo and Serbia, some steps towards the normalization of relations began. One of these was a project to bring copies of the civil registry documents to Kosovo and that same year a process of the verification of the copies of the civil registry records began. A similar process is anticipated for the cadastral records which were also removed at the time of the conflict.

The use of prior agreements, coupled with the lack of checks for legal heirs to property, allows the exclusion of women from inheriting property, even though they are legally able to do so. What is particularly interesting is that this process of facilitating intestate inheritance cases is also being used to exclude *male* heirs from a share of the family property (EULEX Interviews, 2012). One of the additional effects of the conflict in Kosovo is that families were dispersed across Europe in the wake of violence. Some returned when the conflict ended and others did not. The poor economy in Kosovo has also led to an outmigration of young workers for better jobs in nearby countries. As a result of both factors, it is not uncommon for the heirs of a person who has died intestate to be out of the country. This has led to a number of incidents in which prior agreements written by families have excluded certain heirs, male as well as female. There are an increasing number of complaints being brought to the human rights office at the European Rule of Law Mission in Kosovo (EULEX) regarding complaints from male heirs excluded in the inheritance process because judges have not consulted the municipal registers (EULEX Interviews, 2012). In these cases, the mechanism via which male heirs are excluded from their inheritance is the same process via which women 'refuse' or renounce their inheritance. The family comes to the Municipal Court with a prior agreement regarding how the family will divide the assets. The Municipal Courts then simply approve the family agreement without investigation into whether there might be other legal heirs.

The judiciary's lack of enthusiasm for the enforcement of inheritance law is not entirely surprising. While the law is perfectly egalitarian and aligned with EU norms, not everyone in Kosovo supports the goal of future EU membership or is concerned about international legal standards. Indeed, international involvement in Kosovo, both through the EU and UNMIK, has not been popular with all sectors of the population. After 2008 in particular, political opinion in some circles has opposed any sort of external intervention. There is a 'high degree of hostility' towards the EU and its involvement in national politics (Papadimitriou and Petrov, 2013) despite the fact that many in government are working hard towards the goal of EU compliance and accession. One political party, Vetëvendosje, argues that the UNMIK period was undemocratic and they reject further infringement of Kosovo's sovereignty by external actors, no matter what their intention (Vetëvendosje, 2010). While their perspective represents an extreme, the end of UNMIK sovereignty led to a desire among some Kosovars for complete independence from outside intervention, even that which is intended to help them towards European integration. So significant is this opposition that EULEX launched a public relations campaign in 2013 with the slogan "We have to fix our own house, a friend that comes to help us, we should help him to help us" (EULEX, 2013).

The role played by the UN was critical to early legal development in Kosovo and it is unthinkable that laws would have been passed while the country was under the UN administration that would not have been egalitarian with regard to women or consistent with the most robust understandings of human rights. In the post-UNMIK period, the direct and indirect influence of the European Union should have a positive impact on the enforcement of women's property laws in Kosovo. However, creating property legislation, difficult though it may be, is substantially different from the local processes of enforcing property law in legally pluralistic settings (Joireman, 2011; Sikor and Lund, 2009). This is particularly visible in the case of Kosovo where international engagement has had such an impact on the legislative process and early state formation. There are no losers from the creation of egalitarian property laws—indeed political elites may be rewarded for the creation of laws which meet international norms—but there are many losers from the enforcement of egalitarian property laws. When we turn our focus from the creation of law to its enforcement, our attention must move from the national political arena of each country to the locality and to the exercise of authority within communities and through the judiciary.

The period of direct intervention by the UN in the country left a positive as well as a negative legacy. The positive legacy is apparent in the excellent laws regarding property and gender equality. The negative legacy is perhaps less clear: UN supervision of the country was not regarded by all to be a good thing and the laws implemented under UNMIK are by necessity enforced by judges and bureaucrats who may feel ambivalent about them: that they were imposed by outsiders; that the new laws are a threat to the patriarchal Albanian culture; or that they are simply not an accurate reflection of what citizens of Kosovo would choose for themselves. The imposition of laws from above is one additional reason for the large gap between written law and enforced law in Kosovo.

Conclusion

This is a particularly interesting time in terms of property issues and their enforcement in Kosovo. All citizens, male and female, are affected by the enforcement of property law. Enforcement has been a salient political issue in the past and has the potential to become an even more significant political issue in the near future with the repatriation of the property records from Serbia. Attention to property rights issues is much-needed in Kosovo. After the war, buying and selling of property occurred without proper documentation, the property of displaced people was usurped, illegal construction became common, and the complexities of privatization in a post-socialist setting were compounded by population displacement. The lack of enforcement of women's property rights is just one of the multiple and important property issues that needs to be addressed in Kosovo. In some regards it is easy to resolve compared to the other property issues Kosovo faces. It is not legally complex to grant women their inheritance rights, nor is there uncertainty with regard to the precise nature of the implementation of the law. Moreover, addressing the problems in the legal system that allow for women's inheritance rights to be easily circumvented will benefit the whole population, male and female. This is a strategic moment in Kosovar history in which the state can choose to devote resources and effort to the enforcement of their property laws or to continue with arbitrary processes that do not align with legal codes. One path would set Kosovo firmly on the path towards European integration and economic development; the other will ensure continued economic stagnation.

Notes

1   The author is grateful to colleagues at the American University of Kosovo for their assistance in field research. Thanks also to Lindita Bicaj, Marjan Dema, William Donovan, Terry Slykwa, and Kerilee van Schooten for help with the research and to Brian and BLynn Bowen for their hospitality in Kosovo. An early version of the chapter was read by Leah Anderson, Gresa Caka, Christine Folch, Winnie Fung, Larycia Hawkins, Amy Reynolds, and Rachel Vanderhill. Caroline Archambault also offered helpful editorial comments in the revision of this chapter for the book. The Fulbright Foundation funded the fieldwork conducted in Kosovo. All flaws remain my own.
2   The *Kanun* was not codified until a Franciscan priest, Shtjefën Gjeçov, began to write it down in 1913. The priest was murdered for his pro-Albanian political views before finishing the work and other monks completed the codification in 1933 and published it with Gjeçov noted as the author (Fox, 1989).

3   Indeed, there is a problem in Kosovo of record-keeping with regard to the property cadaster.
4   I thank Nita Luci for this insight.

References

1107. 2012. Interview. Pristina, Kosovo, November 7.
1112. 2012. Interview. Pristina, Kosovo, November 12.
1207. 2012. Interview. Legal Professional. Pristina, Kosovo, December 7, 2012.
11713. 2013. Interview. Kosovo, January 17.
Ben-Gera, M., Tommasi, D., Freibert, A., Jean, S., Loeffler, E., and Reka, B. (2005) "Assessment of Administrative Capacity in Kosovo," United Nations Development Programme.
Bonfiglioli, C. (2012). "Becoming Citizens: The politics of women's emancipation in socialist Yugoslavia" (October 24, 2012). Citizenship in Southeastern Europe 2012 [cited February 8, 2013]. Available: www.citsee.eu/citsee-story/becoming-citizens-politics-women%E2%80%99s-emancipation-socialist-yugoslavia
Brajshori, M., Tokyay, M., and Jovanovic, I. (2012) "Women struggle to have equal access to property," *Southeast European Times*, December, p. 1.
Cohen, L.J., and Lampe, J.R. (2011) *Embracing Democracy in the Western Balkans: From Postconflict Struggles toward European Integration*. Washington, D.C.: Woodrow Wilson Center Press.
Committee on Women's Rights and Gender Equality (2013) "Report on women's rights in the Balkan accession countries." Brussels.
Daskalova, K. (2008) "Balkans," in Smith, B.G. (ed.) *The Oxford Encyclopedia of Women in World History*. New York: Oxford University Press.
EULEX Interviews 2012. Interview. Pristina, Kosovo, December 22.
EULEX (2013) *EULEX new communication campaign*, [Online], Available: www.eulex-kosovo.eu/en/poc/campaignew.php [23 Feb 2013]
European Union Rule of Law Mission (2011) *"Time for Kosovo women to inherit property!"*
Fox, L. (1989) *Kanuni I Lekë Dukagjini = The Code of Lekë Dukagjini*. Translated by L. Fox. New York: Gjonlekaj Publishing Company.
Hallward-Driemeier, M., and Hasan, T. (2013) *Empowering Women: Legal Rights and Opportunities in Africa*. Washington, D.C.: International Bank for Reconstruction and Development.
Joireman, S.F. (2011) *Where There is No Government: Enforcing Property Rights in Common Law Africa*. New York: Oxford University Press.
Kosovo Agency of Statistics (2013) *Republic of Kosovo*. Office of the Prime Minister 2013 [12 Aug. 2013].
Ler Sofronic., Nada, Branka, I., and Lukic, R. (2006) "On the Road to the EU: Monitoring Equal Opportunities for Women and Men in Bosnia and Herzegovina." O. N. W. s. Program (ed.): Open Society Institute.
Mertus, J. (1999) "Women in Kosovo: Contested Terrains," in Ramet, S.P. (ed.) *Gender Politics in the Western Balkans: Women and Society in Yugoslavia and the Yugoslav Successor States*. University Park, Pennsylvania: University of Pennsylvania Press.
Metani, Artur, and Omari, S. (2006) "On the Road to the EU: Monitoring Equal Opportunities for Women and Men in Albania." New York: Open Society Institute.

Mustafa, Mentor, and Young, Antonia. 2008. "Feud narratives: contemporary deployments of kanun in Shala Valley, northern Albania." *Anthropological Notebooks* 14 (2):87–107.

Papadimitriou, Dimitris, and Petrov, P. (2013) "State-building without Recognition: A critical perspective of the European Union's strategy in Kosovo (1999–2010)," in Elbasani, A. (ed.) *European Integration and Transformation in the Western Balkans*. New York: Routledge.

Provisional Institutions of Self-Government (2004a) *Family Law of Kosovo*, in A. o. Kosovo (ed.) (2004/32). Pristina, Kosovo: United Nations Interim Administration Mission in Kosovo.

—— (2004b) *The Law on Gender Equality in Kosovo*, in A. o. t. R. o. Kosovo (ed.) (2004/2). Pristina, Kosovo: United Nations Interim Administration Mission in Kosovo.

—— (2004c) *Law on Inheritance in Kosovo*, in A. o. Kosovo (ed.) (2004/26). Pristina, Kosovo: United Nations Interim Administration Mission in Kosovo.

Sikor, Thomas, and Lund, C. (eds.) (2009) *The Politics of Possession: Property, Authority and Access to Natural Resources*. Malden, MA: Wiley-Blackwell.

Šmid, J. M. (2006) "On the Road to the EU: Monitoring Equal Opportunities for Women and Men in Croatia." New York: Open Society Institute.

Smit, A. (2012) *The Property Rights of Refugees and Internally Displaced Persons*. New York: Routledge.

Spehar, A. (2012) "This Far, But No Further?: Benefits and Limitations of EU Gender Equality Policy Making in the Western Balkans," *East European Politics & Societies*, vol. 26, no. 2, pp. 362–379.

USAID (2013) *Kosovo: Property Rights and Resource Governance*. Available: http://usaidlandtenure.net/sites/default/files/country-profiles/full-reports/USAID_Land_Tenure_Kosovo_Profile.pdf [18 Jan 2013].

Vetëvendosje (2010) "Movement's Manifesto," published on the party's website: Vetevendosje.

Vuniqi, L. and Halimi, S. (2011) "Women's Property Inheritance Rights in Kosovo." Pristina, Kosovo: Kosovar for Gender Studies Center.

14 Strengthening women's land rights while recognizing customary tenure in Northern Uganda

Leslie Hannay and Elisa Scalise

Introduction

Across sub-Saharan Africa, there is a growing consensus that securing land rights for women is important for reducing poverty, ensuring household food security and the sustainable use of natural assets, and advancing equality between women and men (FAO, 2013; Giovarelli *et al.*, 2013; AUC, 2010). Although most agree that the pervasive issue of women's insecure land rights within customary tenure systems is a major barrier to achieving equality and economic development in the region (UN-Women, 2013; FAO, 2011), debate surrounding how to strengthen women's land rights within customary systems continues.

Land rights are a critical asset for Acholi women in rural Northern Uganda, a predominantly agrarian region where as much as 80% of land is governed by customary tenure (USAID, 2010). In the Acholi customary tenure system, men have rights to land by birth while a woman's rights to land depend on relationships to a male clan member. Decades of conflict and the resulting displacement of over 1.8 million people have disrupted many of these relationships, leaving women's livelihood options especially vulnerable. At the same time, while women have rights to land under the formal law, weak formal institutions in the region offer few opportunities for women to be aware of, or be able to enforce, those rights. In effect, women in Northern Uganda may have rights to land that are recognized by law but are not culturally legitimate.

On the national stage, the recently adopted Ugandan National Land Policy attempts to address the many land rights-related obstacles to social equity, economic growth, and poverty reduction in Uganda. Among its many laudable provisions are the formal recognition of customary land tenure on an equal basis with statutory land tenure, and equal rights to land for women and men. These two provisions create a legal tension because in many customary land tenure systems, like that of the Acholi, women's and men's land rights are not equal. Thus, to answer the call of the policy, there is a need for proven strategies which can strengthen the land rights of women without delegitimizing the customary land tenure system.

This chapter will present a case study of an innovative approach to strengthen Acholi women's land-tenure security in a way that is culturally *and* legally legitimate. It will do this by introducing and applying a conceptual framework ("the Framework," below) for women's land-tenure security. It will then describe a project that used that framework to examine the dimensions of women's land-tenure security within the Acholi land-tenure system, and describe results of a project that strengthened women's land tenure in ten communities. The chapter ends by providing options for policy-makers and development practitioners.

"Framing" women's land rights

A brief discussion of what is meant by "secure land rights" may help to demonstrate the distinct analytical viewpoint that the Framework provides. As a general matter, secure land rights are rights that are clearly defined, enforceable, legitimate, and durable (i.e., lasting at least long enough for the right-holder to see a return on any investment made in the land) (Hanstad et al., 2007; Deininger, 2003). Although these elements hold true for both men and women, if one considers the elements without specific reference to women's experience, it is possible (and even likely) that the analysis will overlook critical issues that arise for women, but which are not issues for men. For example, a man who is born into a patrilocal, patrilineal customary group may automatically gain a lifetime right to use and control (and in some cases, rent out, sell, or trade) land from his clan or family land. By contrast, his sister may gain a temporary right to use land, but she will likely lose this right if she marries or bears children (Adoko et al., 2011). Under the rules of such a system, her rights are vulnerable to changes in relationships in a way that her brother's rights are not (Giovarelli, 2007; Doss et al., 2011).

The Framework provides a guide for formulating questions that expose such differences. These questions help to illuminate women's insecure land rights in a particular customary setting, providing a nuanced analysis of the particular drivers, conditions, and participants in creating—or remedying—women's tenure insecurity. By breaking down the issue of insecurity under custom into specific, measurable elements, the Framework serves as a starting point for analyzing land-tenure issues in a way that ensures that women's experiences, needs, and rights with respect to land are considered.

Women's Land Rights Framework

A woman's access and control over land can improve if: (i) she gains access to more land; (ii) she gains access to land of higher quality or in a better location; (iii) she gains additional rights over a plot of land to which she already had access; or (iv) her land rights become more secure.

A woman's land rights are secure if: (i) they are legitimate; (ii) they are unaffected by changes in her social status; (iii) they are granted for an extended period of time; (iv) they are enforceable; and (v) her ability to exercise them does not require an additional layer of approval that applies only to women.

First, the degree to which a woman's land rights are legitimate, and therefore secure, depends on who recognizes these rights. That is, whether her land rights are recognized by law, by custom, by her family, her clan, and her community. Second, a woman's land rights are secure if they are not vulnerable to changes in her family structure such as the death of her father or husband, or her husband taking a second wife; or, to changes in her clan or community, such as changes in the leadership that granted her those rights. Third, for rights that are granted for a fixed period of time, the longer the period the more secure her rights are. Fourth, for her rights to be secure, a woman must be able to enforce them. She will be able to do so if she is aware of where to present her claim, if she can easily get to that forum, if she has the ability and the means to present her claim, if her case will be heard, if the overall process will not take a very long period of time, and if a decision in her favor will be implemented. Lastly, a woman's land rights are more secure if they can be exercised without being subject to conditions that men are not asked to fulfill, such as obtaining the approval and permission of her husband, father, or other male relative.

These elements of land tenure security are often interlinked: the factors that make women's land rights insecure may share common bases in gendered cultural norms that are promoted or influenced by the same actors or institutions. That being so, the particulars of how these norms impact women's rights are critically important to understanding and addressing women's land-tenure insecurity. The value of the Framework is that it facilitates the analysis of these elements individually, so that the root causes and leverage points can be understood, and this provides a clear basis for designing policies and direct interventions. In most cases, each of the elements will come into play to some extent, although the degree of importance and specific manner in which each element impacts women's tenure situation will vary.

The first step in applying the Framework is to assess women's situation in the context of the local tenure system. This means talking to women, to men, to local leaders, and to public officials, reviewing laws and secondary materials that describe the land-tenure system and women's rights within them, and understanding the broader social, political, and cultural context. The elements of tenure security serve as the basis for developing measurable indicators and a questionnaire. This assessment in turn provides the basis for project design and evaluation, highlighting the most important issues to be addressed, and providing a clear mechanism for prioritizing project activities. Finally, the Framework provides a clear way to assess the effectiveness of a project's attempts to improve women's land-tenure security.

Applying the Framework

Social and political background: conflict in Northern Uganda

The conflict in Northern Uganda had its roots in inter-ethnic competition for military and political power reaching back to the colonial era, in which economic and political divisions were established between the North and South, as well as within the North among the Acholi, Langi, and West Nile traditional areas.

Since 1986, there have been frequent uprisings by more than 20 militant groups, overwhelmingly focused in the North. The most prominent of these groups is the Lord's Resistance Army (LRA), led by Joseph Kony, which has become notorious for abductions, the conscription of child soldiers, and campaigns of terror in Northern Uganda. The conflict between the LRA and the national army, the Ugandan People's Defence Forces (UPDF), resulted in large-scale killings, mutilations, abductions, and massive displacement of Ugandans, primarily by the LRA but also by the UPDF. Beginning in 1996, the government forcibly relocated the people of northern Uganda to "protected villages," internally displaced persons' (IDP) camps to which UPDF military detachments were assigned. In total, an estimated 2 million people, or 90% of the total population of the region, were displaced during the conflict.[1] After a ceasefire was negotiated (but never signed) between 2006 and 2008, the government began to close IDP camps, and by January 2012, the majority of IDPs had been relocated.[2]

The conflict of Northern Uganda had profound effects on Acholi social dynamics, especially on women's property rights. In Northern Uganda, women's rights to land rely on a relationship with a male relative (father, husband, brother). Many women and girls lost husbands, brothers, and other male relatives in the war through death, abandonment, or disappearance, thereby severing the links to land rights which would have been provided them within the customary tenure system. Additionally, poverty associated with the conflict meant that certain practices which reify a woman's entry into her husband's clan, and on which rights to clan land for women are founded, such as the payment of bride price, were no longer affordable, and many men and women lived together without being married. This had the effect of excluding those women and their children from the usual customary protections because they were not considered part of the clan.

Women and girls who were abducted by LRA soldiers and forced to "marry" are doubly impacted. In many cases they escaped from their soldier "husbands" but were then rejected by their families for their association with the rebel soldiers. Social stigma attached to this abduction is a critical factor inhibiting girls from being able to return to their natal families, and further exacerbates women's insecure tenure. The prejudice is even more pronounced if they have children because they are regarded as having lost their "purity," so they cannot fetch a bride price for the family. In addition, they have no access to clan land because they have been forced from their own clan but have not been accepted by the clan of the child's father, which is the custom.

Land in Northern Uganda

Land is a fundamentally important resource in Uganda, and is the basis of income, sustenance, and identity for the majority of Ugandans. Agriculture dominates the country's economy, accounting for 80% of export earnings and an estimated 80% of employment nationwide (FAO, 2008). Approximately 85% of Uganda's 36 million people reside in rural areas (World Bank, 2013), the majority of whom are involved in subsistence agriculture (UBOS, 2012). Nationwide, 90% of all rural women work in agriculture, compared to only 53% of rural men (FAO, 2000), and women contribute 56% of crop labor nationwide (O'Sullivan *et al.* 2014). In spite of their central role in Uganda's economy, women face disadvantages in access to and completion of education, employment, and access to and use of agricultural inputs, including land.

Legal history of customary tenure in Uganda

Uganda's tenure system comprises multiple tenure regimes dating back to colonial occupation, with pre-independence British law, Ugandan civil law, and customary law all combining to make up Uganda's pluralistic legal structure. Customary law figures prominently in the day-to-day function of family law and land rights, with wide-ranging impacts on women (Kapur, 2011).

During the pre-colonial period, all land was held under customary tenure, meaning that land was governed according to the rules of the 140 major ethnic groups (UN-Habitat, 2007). Under colonial rule, reforms were implemented to regularize and develop colonial land administration. The British colonial administration introduced four tenure systems (*mailo*, freehold, leasehold, and customary) that reflected colonial arrangements with leaders of some but not all ethnic groups (UN-Habitat, 2007). These reforms exacerbated tensions, in part because they gave some traditional rulers absolute control over land, making them landlords; this was a level of authority that they had not previously enjoyed.[3] The Public Lands Act of 1962 also gave the government the right to alienate land, further undermining customary tenure security (UN-Habitat, 2007).

The post-independence land tenure situation has also seen many changes. The government of Milton Obote passed the Public Lands Act 1969, which provided some protection for customary tenure systems. After a brief period of state ownership during the rule of Idi Amin, the 1995 Constitution gave Ugandans the right to own land, including customary land (Mwebaza, 1999; Namati, 2013). The Constitution declared that all land belonged to the citizens of Uganda, vested according to the four recognized tenure types noted above. This was the first time that customary tenure holders' rights were set on an equal legal footing with those for other tenure types (*ibid*; see also UN-Habitat, 2007).[4]

Customary tenure is the most common form of land tenure in Uganda (USAID, 2010), and is estimated to cover 80% of the total land area of the country. The Constitution recognizes customary tenure, which the Land Act defines as land that is governed by the customs, rules, and regulations of the community. The rules governing land vary among Uganda's 56 customary groups, though similar characteristics can be found among many of the contemporary tenure regimes today. This section provides a brief introduction to customary tenure under the formal law, and a discussion of the resulting framework for women's property rights within the Acholi customary system of Northern Uganda. There is often significant variation in how customary rules are conceived and applied even within the same customary group. This overview does not aim to provide a definitive analysis of

Acholi custom, but outlines key issues for women's land rights within the Acholi framework.

The Land Act 1998 provides extensive protections for customary rights, and creates a framework for the regularization of customary tenure. Though customary rights are considered valid whether customary owners have a title or not, the Land Act provides that any person, family, or community holding customary land may acquire a Certificate of Customary Ownership (CCO) (section 4(1)) or freehold title for that land (section 10(1)). Such certificates confer the right to lease, mortgage, transfer, bequeath, and sell customary land, subject to the rules and conditions contained in the certificate (Uganda Land Act, 1998). Thus, customary tenure is defined in such a way to leave open the possibility of individualized property.

In 2013 the Government of Uganda adopted the National Land Policy, which seeks to reform land tenure in the country. The goal of the policy is "to ensure efficient, equitable and optimal utilization and management of Uganda's land resources for poverty reduction, wealth creation and overall socio-economic development." In this policy there is explicit treatment of customary land tenure and the principle that it should be recognized, resourced, and treated equally with other forms of tenure in the country (Rugadya and Scalise, 2013).

Formal legal framework for women's land rights

The Constitution (1995) sets out broad principles for both women and children; these include equal rights for women, no discrimination based on custom, and special protection for women and orphans. It provides for the right of every person to own property; guarantees women equal rights with men; provides special protection for mothers and women because of previous historical discrimination against women; and expressly prohibits any customary laws, traditions, or customs that discriminate against women.

The Land Act contains some protections for women's land rights. Section 28 requires the safeguarding of the rights of women, minors, and the disabled in decisions that relate to *customary* land. Section 40 contains a limited consent requirement from spouses and children before final transfer of rights to the land (e.g. sale, exchange, mortgage, lease, or *inter vivos* gift). For spouses, this consent is required only for land on which the family resides and any plots attached to the residence that is used for sustenance by the consenting spouse. It is not required for plots that may be far from the residence. For children, consent is only required for the transfer of residential land.

The consent provisions are of only limited usefulness in terms of protecting women and children's rights to land. For one matter the law covers only spouses who are legally married. Many rural women may consider themselves married yet have not legalized the union, meaning their consent is not technically required. In practice, many women in Uganda are not legally married, even under the broad provisions of the Customary Marriage Act, because it requires that the marriage be "registered," which involves an administrative process that is not feasible for the rural poor or the young. As a result, those "informally" married wives must share in the dependent relatives' 9% of an intestate person's estate (see below), since a "dependent relative" is defined as wife or husband, among others, who are dependent on the deceased.

In addition, few women know the law and the obligation that their consent be obtained before a transaction in land and thus the transactions take place without their approval. Moreover, even if a woman is aware of the obligation for her consent to a transaction, her ability to enforce the consent is limited because she would have to speak out against her husband or father, through whom her access to land was granted in the first place. Finally, "consent" is not a right held by the person who must give consent, but rather an obligation on the person making the transaction in land to seek consent, leaving the decision to obtain consent to the male who already holds power in the relationship.

The succession laws recognize a woman's right to inherit from her husband and father. The Succession Act and the Succession (Amendment) Decree, No. 22 of 1972 provides that if a man dies intestate, all of his property (except his residential holding) is distributed to his lineal descendants (75%), "wives" (15%), dependent relatives (9%), and the customary heir (1%) (Sec. 28(1)(a)). If the deceased has no lineal descendants, the wives' share rises to 50% and the dependent relatives' to 49%. If there are no lineal descendants, but either a wife or dependent relatives, the wife/dependent relatives receive 99%.

In some respects, the succession laws are progressive in that they do not distinguish between daughters and sons among the lineal descendants and dependent relative categories. Yet, directly and indirectly, women's inheritance rights in the succession laws are not equal with those of men. For instance, the law has a stated male bias in certain circumstances; a "legal heir" is defined as a living relative nearest in degree to the intestate deceased, with a preference for males over females and elders over youth. In addition, by deferring to customs, the succession law has an indirect bias in favor of males in the selection of the "customary heir." The law defines the customary heir as the person recognized by the *rights and customs* of the tribe or community of the deceased as being the customary heir. The *rights and customs* of all Ugandan tribes would only choose a male as customary heir, thus, although the laws seem ostensibly gender-neutral, in practice they are not. Moreover, by using the term "wife" in the list of those who can benefit from intestate succession, rather than "spouse," the laws presuppose that a woman will not own property which she can leave to a husband who succeeds her.

In addition, only certain women benefit from the succession law. Although the law permits wives to inherit from their husbands, as noted above, the law's definition of a "wife" limits its application to those who are legally married according to the laws in Uganda.

An unsuccessful attempt was made for legislative redress for the gender imbalance by permitting co-ownership of property between spouses. This would have meant that all property acquired during the marriage would have been jointly owned by the spouses. However, opposition to such a law was so great that the prevailing view among scholars and practitioners is that a spousal co-ownership provision is a lost cause in Uganda.

The Acholi customary framework for women's rights to land

Under the customary tenure system of the Acholi, both the men and women have use rights to clan land broadly speaking. They can cultivate the land and produce crops for their livelihood. However, the right to dispose land by both women and men is subject to the decision of the clan or community. Use rights, ownership, control, and transfers are all subject to the superior right of the family, group, clan, or community. The transfer of land at death is done according to the customary laws of inheritance, which are patrilineal. A parcel may be considered "owned" by a family but the community or clan exercises control over all dispositions of the parcel.

Under customary tenure, all land is traditionally regarded as clan land, and falls into three categories: arable land; communal clan land; and unallocated or unused land. Arable land is apportioned, or "individualized" by the clan to a household head, normally at the time of marriage. A male is always the head of the household. The household head is given responsibility for managing and protecting the land, while other members of the family—wife and children— have the right to use and access the land with the consent of the household head. Clan elders oversee the family clan land and ensure that family heads manage the land well, protecting the rights of all users of the land and the interests of future generations of the clan. Traditionally, transactions in land are not permitted without sanction of the clan; today, however, the clan is simply informed of a pending transaction and, in the event of a sale, has the right of first refusal.

Authority over communal clan land is vested in the clan as an institution. Communal land is used as communal hunting grounds, but also includes forest and grazing areas. Also, in times of need, parts of this communal clan land might be used to supplement individualized land.

Unallocated land is land that the head of the household has kept for his own personal use. When the household head dies, the land is managed by the customary heir, who is appointed by the clan. The heir is in all cases a son, most often the eldest son who showed signs of responsibility. The heir is installed in a cultural ceremony by the clan. The heir is responsible for the management of this unallocated land. Unused land cannot be sold or inherited. If there are no male children born to the household head, the land is used by the relative with the next claim to it, most often the brothers of the household head.

Land is regarded as men's property. As noted above, it is usually bequeathed to a male heir, and he has the right to decide the use of the land. Also, because husbands pay bride price, women are regarded as part of the man's acquired property and cannot inherit land ("property cannot own property"). In the unlikely case that a female inherits from her father, it is only use rights that are inherited; such use lasts only for as long as the woman remains unmarried and it cannot devolve to her heirs. Generally, women do not have the right to sell land unless they buy that land in their own names, which is very rare.

Unmarried women

An unmarried woman who lives with her natal family can use her family's land, most commonly to assist with the cultivation of subsistence food products. Her right to use this land lasts as long as she remains unmarried. The expectation is that a woman will marry at some point; if she does not, the head of the family will allocate some family land to her for her use.

However, being unmarried is not a truly viable livelihood option for a girl. Because an unmarried woman is always regarded as being in "transition" (on the way to being married), her continued presence on the individual family land can cause disputes with her brothers, who would otherwise be allocated the land she is using. The longer she stays unmarried, the more pressure from her brothers to leave.

In addition, certain factors may mean that an unmarried woman will never be allocated land. In circumstances of IDP return, where the perceived commercial value of land is high and a woman has lost her parents to conflict, or is a former abductee for whom marriage is now a remote prospect, it is unlikely that she will be allocated land by her brothers at all. Indeed, she may not even seek land from her family simply to avoid the conflict and stress that so doing may cause.

Unmarried woman with children

If a woman has a child outside of marriage (customary or otherwise), she may normally use land allocated to her by her natal family to care for her child. Under normal circumstances, if the clan of the child's father is known, it will be expected to pay a "penalty" to the woman's family in place of the bride price. Alternatively, the child's father will be expected to marry the woman and pay the bride price.

But unlike a single, childless child, an unmarried woman with a child is regarded as more of a burden because she is less likely to marry. Moreover, if her child is a boy he is not considered part of his mother's clan and he is thus not allocated land by her family, which cuts him off from future livelihood options. If the child is a girl, she may be regarded as more valuable to the family because of her potential to fetch a bride price.

To make matters worse, if the child of the unmarried girl has been fathered by a rebel soldier she may face serious opposition to any support from her natal family. If she has escaped her abductor/father of the child, no bride price has been paid and little chance of remarriage since she had been "married" to the enemy. In other circumstances she would go to the clan of the child's father, since it may allocate land to the child, but in such cases the clan may be unknown or unsupportive.

Married women

Under normal circumstances, at the time of her marriage a married woman is given land by her new husband's clan to use. Her clan has received bride price for her, and she is expected not to return to her natal family or they will have to repay the sum received.

Widowed/abandoned girl/divorced women

A widow normally becomes the head of the household on the death of her husband. She then has the responsibility of managing the land and allocating it to male children when they become adults and get married. Clan elders appoint an "inheritor" who is required to support her and protect her and the land from trespassers and for whom she is expected to be a wife. This is sometimes referred to as "bride inheritance" or "levirate." She can choose to not accept the choice of inheritor and select one from the clan herself. If she does not choose one from the clan, she must return to her natal family and seek land from them. If she does select an inheritor from the clan, that inheritor does not gain rights to the land allocated to her children through her deceased husband.

An abandoned or divorced girl may return to her family and be allocated land to use. However, she is regarded as being in transition and is regarded as a burden to the family. In the case of divorce, it is expected that the bride price will be returned to the family of her husband's clan, which her natal family may be reluctant to do. If she returns with children, these children are regarded as members of her husband's clan and are not allocated land by her natal family.

The most recent stage of the ongoing land reforms came with the adoption of Uganda's National Land Policy in 2013 (Uganda MLHUD, 2002). The policy expressly acknowledges the failure of Uganda's formal law to overcome discriminatory practices concerning women's land and inheritance, particularly in section 4.9, titled "Land Rights of Women and Children" (ibid). In that section, the policy calls on the Ugandan government to overhaul the existing statutory regime to confront discrimination in land and inheritance. These needed changes are still underway, though the timeline for implementation remains unclear.

Improving women's land rights within a customary tenure regime

Through action research, Landesa and local partners developed and piloted a scalable, replicable model to strengthen women's tenure security within customary land-tenure systems. The model works with women and their communities using the women's land rights framework to identify and understand barriers to women's rights to land and to help women devise strategies for overcoming these barriers. The project was implemented in Pader and Agago Districts, Northern Uganda, in close collaboration with a local implementing partner. The model and its implementation were informed by assessments of the participant women's needs and aspirations as well as by active monitoring and adaptive management.

Project activities

As described above, land rights for the Acholi are strongly linked to the community. A woman's right to land depends on her status in the family, on the customary institutions and processes that determine rights to land in her community, on leaders' and communities' perceptions about women's rights to land, and on women's awareness of and ability to realize their rights as members of a community. With this in mind, the intervention sought to engage with women at three different levels to empower women to strengthen their land tenure security: in groups, individually, and with their communities, in particular local and cultural leaders.

Activities included weekly meetings, during which women discussed barriers, strategies, and action steps for addressing identified needs and pursuing individual and shared aspirations for land-tenure security. The group meetings were also an opportunity to provide training and capacity-building to the women. In order to target knowledge and awareness gaps identified through the baseline assessment activities, women were trained on women's land rights under customary and formal laws; customary rules and institutions; property rights of married and unmarried women under customary law; conflict-resolution options under formal and customary systems; public speaking; and drama. In addition to group meetings, community-based facilitators met with individual women, with women and their families, with cultural leaders individually and in groups, and with other key stakeholders to discuss women's land rights-related aspirations and challenges, as well as strategies to address those challenges.

Using the Framework to evaluate the project

As with the planning and design of implementation activities, the Framework provided the analytical foundation for evaluating the project. The objective of evaluation activities was to assess whether there were measurable changes in women's land tenure security as a result of the pilot implementation. The Framework provided a mechanism for breaking down the larger questions of "insecure tenure" into discrete, measurable elements that could then be quantitatively and qualitatively evaluated and assessed them for women with different social statuses (married women, single women, cohabiting women, divorced women, and widows).

Summary of project results[5]

Twelve months after the project started, the interim assessment revealed marked improvements among pilot participants with regard to all indicators of security, with particularly strong improvements in the legitimacy, vulnerability, and enforceability of women's land rights. After giving a brief overview of the results across all categories, we will focus on the results around legitimacy and highlight the ways in which the program may have contributed to improved recognition of land rights for women in the community.

Twelve months into the project, almost a third of the participating women (32.5%) reported accessing more land than at the beginning of the project. On average, they reported using 3.0 more acres than at baseline, with the highest increase reported among widows.

Improvements to women's sense of legitimacy were indicated by an increase of 20% in women who reported that their land rights were recognized by their families and their communities. The largest improvements were seen in their husbands' and their husbands' families' recognition of their rights to the household land. High levels of recognition of women's rights to land were seen regardless of whether they were married, cohabiting, separated, or widows.

In a related manner, the proportion of women who perceived their land rights as vulnerable decreased markedly for every single scenario considered: (i) their fathers died; (ii) their husbands divorced or abandoned them; (iii) their husbands married another wife; (iv) their husbands died; (v) they moved to another place; (vi) the leadership in their communities changed; (vii) their clan leaders changed; or (vii) the leaders of their husbands' clans changed. The improvement was most notable—as high as 50 or 60%—regarding vulnerability following their husbands' death or upon relocation.

During the life of this project, significant improvements were also observed in the enforceability of land rights for women: at endline, all the women involved in the project said they know where they should take a land-rights-related dispute—a 15% increase since the project's inception—and the proportion of women who felt they could easily access those institutions had gone up by 57%.

The impact of the project on the duration of rights was more difficult to analyze and assess. Significant numbers of women were leasing and borrowing land for terms that (on average) lasted longer than a year. However, less than a third of the agreements (29.9%) were recorded in writing.

Finally, at the end of the project, women were still less likely than men to have influence on family decisions about land, although the proportion of women who reported being able to effectively influence their households' decisions on whether to sell or rent land, to use it as collateral, or to whom it will be bequeathed, increased. The improvements range between 16% and 29% depending on the decision and are the largest for decisions about renting land. Women's ability to influence land-related decisions has improved regardless of their marital status, but women who are cohabiting and those who are divorced appeared to have experienced the largest gains.

Legitimacy

Focusing on one dimension of secure land rights for women, legitimacy, will help elucidate the project's approach in practical terms. The legitimacy of a woman's land rights depends on whether she knows about her rights to land and who recognizes these rights—the law, local customs, her family, her clan, or her community. The project envisaged that the legitimacy of women's land rights would improve if there was an increase in the recognition of these rights by any of above-named agents in their communities. It asked women whether their partners, their partners' families, their partners' clans, their children, their birth families, their communities, and the leaders of their communities recognized their right to land.

Activities to address legitimacy of women's land rights included the following:

- *Stakeholder meetings.* The project organized networking meetings and courtesy visits to a range of stakeholders and powerful interests in the communities (elders, local and cultural leaders, District Land Board, etc.). In these visits, staff introduced the project, asked for stakeholder input, and gathered their perceptions on issues related to women's rights to land. Discussions included in-depth conversations on how marriage, inheritance, and land disputes were handled in Acholi culture and how the customary system and statutory law affect Acholi women.
- *Women's group meetings.* Women engaged in training and education sessions which helped them to better understand their formal and statutory rights to land. The group meetings also helped raise women's confidence by allowing them to openly discuss land rights violations and encouraging them to initiate consultations at family level.
- *Community-based facilitators.* Trained community-based facilitators taught pilot participants about their rights to land and facilitated women's group meetings. In addition, the community-based facilitators conducted home visits and sensitized other family members to women's land rights.
- *Drama performances and community-wide discussions.* Each women's group performed a drama in their own parish on the theme of women's rights to land. The drama was followed by a community-wide discussion of issues.
- *Recognizing the Acholi clan structure and working within that system.* Land conflicts in Acholi land are mostly mediated by clan leaders. The project engaged clan leaders, thus making its agenda more acceptable to the community as a whole.

After these activities were completed, the proportion of women who responded affirmatively to the question of recognition was at least 23% higher than those who did in the baseline. The greatest increase in recognition of women's rights to land was found in their partners and their partners' families.

Conclusions and policy recommendations

Although women face significant challenges in realizing their land rights in Northern Uganda, the customary tenure setting also offers a unique opportunity to strengthen these rights. Customary land-tenure systems are adaptive in nature.

In the context of changing land arrangements across Acholiland, this adaptability provides an opportunity to help improve land-tenure security for Acholi women through direct engagement with communities and customary institutions.

This opportunity for change also exists at the national level. The new National Land Policy counts among its objectives the aim of strengthening customary land-tenure systems, while at the same time seeking to address the problem of traditions, customs, and practices that discriminate against women's land rights. The example of the Acholi people shows these twin objectives as potentially at odds with one another: strengthening the land tenure of the Acholi as a whole will not necessarily strengthen Acholi women's land-tenure security. Thus, for the competing objectives of Uganda's National Land Policy to succeed, policy-makers must move beyond an either/or approach—either strengthening customary tenure or strengthening tenure for women—and towards identifying concrete mechanisms for achieving both in practice.

Efforts to secure customary land rights at the household or community level often overlook the rights of women in those households. Even when planners make some effort to understand women's rights, they often employ a process that inquires about women's rights as an afterthought. Often, this reflection touches on only one dimension of women's rights to land, such as inheritance rights or how women fare in land-related disputes. These efforts are worthwhile, but very often relegate issues related to protecting or supporting women's land rights to the status of supplemental or secondary components of larger projects.

The model presented in this chapter seeks to improve development practice by inquiring about the nature and scope of rights that women have to land under custom. In essence, the Framework asks: In the context of tenure systems that give power over land to men, how can projects and policies strengthen the security of women's rights to land, and what indicators will show whether such movement is occurring? The Framework provides a method for answering these questions and can be applied to women all over the world and in every land-tenure regime.

The intent of the model is to support a holistic and context-specific approach to women's land rights interventions. The Framework should be combined with a stakeholder analysis and some understanding of the local context to provide a basis for determining who to include in baseline data gathering, what kinds of institutions should be informed of and participate directly in the project, and who should be targeted as indirect participants of the project. An understanding of the local context is needed to ensure that the content of the rights at play and some notion of the structure and function of the relevant tenure systems can inform the use of the model. Finally, the analysis of results from the assessment activities and the development and prioritization of effective and locally appropriate solutions to the issues identified requires working with a local partner who understands in detail the conditions, contexts, and other integral factors that will contribute to or impede the success of the project.

This experience has shown that even though there are general principles that can serve as a basis for strengthening women's land rights, achieving significant and lasting change requires a context-specific and nuanced model that *starts with women*. Strengthening land-tenure security for women in Uganda can be achieved broadly by using this model to design land-sector research, programming, advocacy, and policy implementation so as to ensure better results by placing the needs, obligations, preferences, experiences, and actions of women at the foundation of the intervention, rather than relegating them to an afterthought.

Notes

1   UNHCR (n.d.) A Time Between: Moving on from Internal Displacement in Uganda, accessed at www.unhcr.org/4baa0fd86.html. By 2005, approximately 1,100,000 people were living in camps in the Acholi region alone. See IDMC. Map: Total number of IDPs in northern Uganda. www.internal-displacement.org/sub-saharan-africa/uganda/2009/total-number-of-idps-in-northern-uganda.
2   More than 95% of IDP camp dwellers had left as of 2012, the year UNHCR officially closed its Gulu office, thus ending its assistance in the Northern region. www.unhcr.org/4f06e2a79.html
3   Though *mailo* land was allocated to a small number of elites initially, over time this land was subdivided through sale, donation, and inheritance, with the result that several thousand individuals held land under *mailo* tenure. The Land Act 1998 treats *mailo* almost identically to freehold tenure, except that *mailo* tenants cannot use their rights to the detriment of customary tenants, or bona fide or lawful occupants on that land (UN-Habitat 2007).
4   The Constitution also made several changes to the land administration system, setting up District Land Boards and reinstating the Uganda Land Commission as distinct and mutually autonomous bodies. The Constitution also provided for the creation by Parliament of land tribunals and reaffirmed the state's authority to pass laws regulating land use.
5   The results presented in this report are based on responses collected during the endline assessment. There are two important caveats that should be considered while reading these results. First, the results have not been argued against a control group. Although the project tried to have a control group, it emerged that the area selected could not be effectively controlled for comparable initiatives and undertakings by similar organizations. Therefore, attribution hinges strongly on the testimony of the pilot participants. Second, this report presents perceptions of pilot participants. In this regard, it is important to understand that the baseline in some cases may have presented a hypothetical standpoint which may have been much more positive than the real situation that transpired as the project unfolded.

References

Adoko, J., Akin, J., & Knight, R. (2011) *Understanding and Strengthening Women's Land Rights Under Customary Tenure in Uganda*, LEMU (Land and Equity Movement in Uganda), and International Development Law Organization (IDLO).

African Union Commission (AUC), (2010) *Framework and Guidelines on Land Policy in Africa*, AUC-ECA-AfDB Consortium: Addis Ababa, Ethiopia, Available: http://www.uneca.org/sites/default/files/publications/fg_on_land_policy_eng.pdf [14 Nov 2014].

Atkinson, R. and Hopwood, J. (2013) *Land Conflict Monitoring and Mapping Tool for the Acholi Sub-region, Final Report – March 2013*, Human Rights Focus, Available: www.lcmt.org/pdf/final_report.pdf [14 Nov 2014].

Asiimwe, F. and Crankshaw, O. (2011) "The impact of customary laws on inheritance: A case study of widows in Urban Uganda," *Journal of Law and Conflict Resolution*, vol. 3, no. 1, pp. 7–13, [Jan 2011].

Bennett, V., Faulk, G., Kovina, A., and Eres, T. (2006) "Inheritance Law in Uganda: The Plight of Widows and Children," *Georgetown Journal of Gender and the Law*, vol. 7, p. 451.

Burke, C. and Egaru, E. (2011) *Identification of Good Practices in Land Conflict Resolution in Acholi*, United Nations Peacebuilding Programme, Uganda.

Doss, C. (2013) "Intrahousehold Bargaining and Resource Allocation in Developing Countries," *World Bank Research Observer*, vol. 28, no. 1, pp. 52–78.

Doss, C., Truong, M. Nabanoga, G., and Namaalwa, J. (2011). *Women, marriage, and asset inheritance in Uganda*. Chronic Poverty Research Centre working paper no. 184.

FAO. (2000) *IFAD's Gender Strengthening Programme for East and Southern Africa: Uganda Field Diagnostic Study (Draft)*, Rome: FAO.

FAO, (2007) *Good governance in Land Tenure and Administration*, Land Tenure Studies 9, Rome: FAO.

FAO. (2008) *Gender in Agriculture Sourcebook*. Available: http://www.fao.org/docrep/011/aj288e/aj288e00.HTM [13 Nov 2014].

FAO. (2011) *The State of Food and Agriculture 2010–2011: Women in Agriculture: Closing the gender gap for development*, Rome: FAO.

FAO. (2013) *Governing Land for Women and Men: A technical guide to support the achievement of responsible gender-equitable governance of land tenure*, Rome: FAO.

Giovarelli, R. (2007) "Gender and land tenure reform," in Prosterman, R., Mitchell, R., & Hanstad, T. (eds), *One Billion Rising: Law, Land and the Alleviation of Global Poverty*, Leiden: Leiden University Press.

Giovarelli, R., Wamalwa, B., and Hannay, L. (2013) *Land Tenure, Property Rights, and Gender: Challenges and Opportunities for Strengthening Women's Land Tenure and Property Rights*, Property Rights and Resource Governance Briefing Paper #7, Washington, DC: USAID.

Kapur, A. (2011) *"Catch-22": The Role of Development Institutions in Promoting Gender Equality in Land Law – Lessons Learned in Post-Conflict Pluralist Africa*, 17 Buff. Hum. Rts. L. Rev. 75.

Mwebaza, R. (1999) *How to Integrate Statutory and Customary Tenure? The Uganda Case*, paper presented at the DFID workshop on Land Rights and Sustainable Development in sub-Saharan Africa at Sunningdale Park Conference Centre, Berkshire, UK February 16–19, 1999. International Institute for Environment and Development.

Namati, (2013) *Protecting Community Lands and Resources: Evidence from Liberia, Mozambique and Uganda*.

O'Sullivan, M.; Rao, A.; Banerjee, R.; Gulati, K.; Vinez, M. 2014. *Levelling the field: improving opportunities for women farmers in Africa*. Vol. 1 of *Levelling the field: improving opportunities for women farmers in Africa*. Washington DC: World Bank Group. Available: http://documents.worldbank.org/curated/en/2014/01/19243625/levelling-field-improving-opportunities-women-farmers-africa [18 Nov 2014].

Republic of Uganda (1972) *Succession (Amendment) Decree 22/72*.

Republic of Uganda. Land Act (1998) (*c.227*), Act 16/1998.

Republic of Uganda Uganda Ministry of Lands, Housing and Urban Development, National Land Policy, Draft 4 (May 2010).

Rugadya (2003) *Current Status and Challenges in the Land Reform Process in Uganda: An NGO Perspective*, Uganda Land Alliance: Kampala.

Rugadya, M., Obaikol, E., and Kamusiime, H. (2004) *Gender and the Land Reform Process in Uganda: Assessing Gains and Losses for Women in Uganda*. Associates for Development: Kampala.

Rugadya, M. and Scalise, E. (2013) *Developing a National Land Policy in Uganda: A Learning Process*. Seattle: Landesa. Available: www.landesa.org/wp-content/uploads/National-Land-Policy-in-Uganda_A-Learning-Process_-FINAL.pdf

Scalise, E. (2012) "Indigenous Women's Land Rights: Case Studies from Africa," in *State of the World's Minorities and Indigenous Peoples 2012*, London: Minority Rights Group International, Available: www.minorityrights.org/11374/state-of-the-worlds-minorities/state-of-the-worlds-minorities-and-indigenous-peoples-2012.html

Tripp, A. (2004) "Women's Movements, Customary Law, and Land Rights in Africa: The Case of Uganda," *African Studies Quarterly* 7, no. 4, Available: http://web.africa.ufl.edu/asq/v7/v7i4a1.htm

USAID. (2010). *Uganda Land Tenure and Property Rights Profile*. Washington DC: USAID. Available: http://usaidlandtenure.net/uganda [20 Nov 2014].

Uganda Bureau of Statistics (UBOS) and ICF International Inc. (2012) *Uganda Demographic and Health Survey 2011*. Kampala, Uganda: UBOS and Calverton, Maryland: ICF International Inc.

UN-Habitat (2007) *A Guide to Property Law in Uganda*, United Nations Human Settlements Programme: Nairobi.

United Nations (2011) *Uganda Humanitarian Profile*, New York: Office for the Coordination of Humanitarian Affairs (OCHA), p. 1.

United Nations Entity for Gender Equality and the Empowerment of Women (UNWOMEN) (2013) *Realizing Women's Rights to Land and other Productive Resources*. HR/PUB/13/04, available at: www.refworld.org/docid/5289e2126.html.

USAID. (2010) *Uganda Land Tenure and Property Rights Profile*. Washington DC: USAID. Available: http://usaidlandtenure.net/uganda [20 Nov 2014].

Women's Land Link Africa (2010) *The Impact of National Land Policy and Land Reform on Women in Uganda*, 27 October 2010.

World Bank. (2014) World Bank Indicators. Data webpage. Available: http://data.worldbank.org/indicator [18 Nov 2014].

Index

Page numbers in **bold** refer to figures, those in *italic* refer to tables.

old age *see* age
orphans' inheritance, 233–234
ownership of land *see also*
    formalisation of customary tenure:
    gender inequities, 3–5; indigenous
    peoples' conceptions, 75–76; joint
    ownership, 21; 'secure land rights',
    definition, 252

Papua New Guinea, 35; Community
    Mine Continuation Agreement of
    2007 (2007 CMCA): awareness of
    women's deal, 44–45, CMCA
    usage, 40, family bank accounts,
    success, 46–47, implementation,
    44, local development gains, 48,
    negotiation, 40–41, scholarship
    programme, success, 47, women's
    empowerment gains, 48, women's
    engagement in negotiations,
    41–44, women's fund, impacts,
    44–46, women's under-
    representation, continuance, 47;
    Community Mine Continuation
    Agreement renegotiation 2012:
    negotiation process, 48–49,
    women's engagement, 49, women's
    fund, 49, women's progress
    summarised, 51–52, women's
    success, 49–50; gender inequities,
    38; mining: memoranda of
    agreement (MoAs), 38, socio-
    economic impacts, 36–38, Ok Tedi
    Mine: author's analytical approach,
    36, development trust, 38–39, local
    community relations, 38–39,
    location map, **37**, reasons for
    studying, 35; Sustainable
    Development Programme
    (PNGSDP), administration, 39–40
patriarchy *see* men
peace and reconstruction *see* post-
    conflict reforms
plantation farming, 28–29
polygamous inheritance, 229–231

population growth as land reform
    driver, 2
post-conflict reforms *see also* Kosovo;
    Uganda; Zimbabwe: case studies,
    219; challenges, 218; drivers for
    reform, 3; gender-sensitivity, need
    for, 218–219; gendered
    experiences, 218; land as focus,
    217; opportunities, 218; post-
    conflict reconstruction worldwide,
    217; prioritisation of land reform,
    217; reinforcement of male control,
    7; women's insecurity continued,
    218
primary decision-makers, women as
    see West Bengal (India)
private/public distinction, hardening,
    164
privatisation of communal lands *see*
    also China; Kenya; Mexico;
    Morocco: case studies, 149–150;
    collective holdings, 148–149;
    gendered analysis, 149; reasons for,
    147–148; reinforcement of male
    control, 7; social impacts, 24–25

rangeland privatisation *see* Kenya
redistribution of land *see* Zimbabwe
registration of rights: forestland
    reforms *see* China; indigenous land
    claims *see* Argentina; joint land
    certificates *see* Madagascar; joint
    titling *see* West Bengal (India)
renunciation of inheritance *see*
    Kosovo
resettled lands *see* Zimbabwe
residential tourism *see* Costa Rica
resistance to oppression, land as
    symbol, 156–157
review procedure for land rights
    decisions, 195–196
rights to land *see also* formalisation of
    customary tenure; ownership of
    land; registration of rights: elite
    capture, problem of, 82;